THE
CHINA
MIRAGE

ALSO BY JAMES BRADLEY

Flags of Our Fathers
Flyboys
The Imperial Cruise

THE
CHINA
MIRAGE

THE HIDDEN HISTORY
OF AMERICAN DISASTER
IN ASIA

JAMES BRADLEY

LITTLE, BROWN AND COMPANY
New York   Boston   London

Little, Brown and Company
Hachette Book Group
1290 Avenue of the Americas, New York, NY 10104
littlebrown.com

First Edition: April 2015

Little, Brown and Company is a division of Hachette Book Group, Inc. The Little, Brown name and logo are trademarks of Hachette Book Group, Inc.

The publisher is not responsible for websites (or their content) that are not owned by the publisher.

Copyright acknowledgments appear on page 373.

The Hachette Speakers Bureau provides a wide range of authors for speaking events. To find out more, go to hachettespeakersbureau.com or call (866) 376-6591.

Maps by Jeffrey Ward
Photo research and editing by Elizabeth Seramur and Laura Wyss, Wyssphoto Inc.

ISBN 978-0-316-19667-3 (hc) / 978-0-316-41067-0 (large print) /
   978-0-316-33617-8 (int'l ed)
LCCN 2015933034

10 9 8 7 6 5 4 3 2 1

RRD-C

Printed in the United States of America

I dedicate The China Mirage *to my mother,*
Elizabeth Van Gorp Bradley, whose joy for books
inspired me to read and write them.

CONTENTS

There must not and cannot be any conflict, estrangement or misunderstanding between the Chinese people and America.
—Mao Zedong[1]

THE
CHINA
MIRAGE

INTRODUCTION

The future policy of Japan towards Asiatic countries should be similar to that of the United States towards their neighbors....A "Japanese Monroe Doctrine" in Asia will remove the temptation to European encroachment, and Japan will be recognized as the leader of the Asiatic nations.
— *President Theodore Roosevelt*[1]

The people of China well over a century have been, in thought and in objective, closer to us Americans than almost any other peoples in the world—the same great ideals. China, in the last—less than half a century has become one of the great democracies of the world.
— *President Franklin Delano Roosevelt*[2]

Two American presidents from the first half of the twentieth century blazed the path into Asia still followed by the United States today. These two presidents were cousins, and, although they lived a generation apart, both followed similar paths to power: from New York State legislator to assistant secretary of the Navy to New York governor and, finally, to president of the United States.

Both Presidents Roosevelt conducted their Asian diplomacy in similar style, personally taking the reins to deal directly and secretly with Asian affairs, often circumventing their own State Departments. Neither Roosevelt traveled to Asia or knew many Asians, but both were

Presidents Theodore and Franklin Delano Roosevelt (Courtesy of the Library of Congress)

supremely confident that they had special insights. The parallels are not exact. Theodore was enamored of Japan and allowed himself to be taken in by a propaganda campaign directed from Tokyo and led by a Harvard-educated Japanese friend. In contrast, Franklin favored China and was influenced by his own Harvard-educated Chinese friend.

Theodore Roosevelt was awarded the Nobel Peace Prize for bringing the combatants in the Russo-Japanese War to the peace table. Almost unknown in the United States, though, are the president's backdoor negotiations with Emperor Meiji of Japan over the fate of an independent country, the empire of Korea. During these secret talks, brokered by Meiji's Harvard-educated envoy, Roosevelt agreed to stand aside and allow Japan to subjugate Korea as a colony, becoming the first world leader to sanction Japan's expansion onto the Asian continent.

Sumner Welles, Franklin Delano Roosevelt's friend and the assistant secretary of state, observed, "No one close to the President could have failed to recognize the deep feeling of friendship for China that he had inherited from his mother's side of his family."[3] After a meeting to discuss China policy with FDR, one administration official recalled,

"We might as well have saved our breath. Roosevelt put an end to the discussion by looking up and recalling that his ancestors used to trade with China."[4]

Indeed they had. Franklin Delano Roosevelt's grandfather Warren Delano was one of the first Americans to travel to what was seen by Americans as "Old China," where he made a dynastic fortune in the illegal opium trade. As a U.S. consul, Delano oversaw the first American military incursion into China. It was from his Delano line that Roosevelt inherited his love of the sea, his princely fortune, and his confidence that he knew how to handle China. Roosevelt later observed, "What vitality I have is not inherited from Roosevelts...mine, such as it is, comes from the Delanos."[5]

Dealing drugs was only part of Warren Delano's mission. Much as his European ancestors had carved "New England" territory from Indian lands on America's Atlantic coast, he helped carve "New

Warren Delano, Hong Kong, 1860 (CPA Media /
Pictures from History)

China" enclaves—westernized and Christianized areas—like Hong Kong on China's Pacific coast. Delano, like many Americans, believed that this was only the beginning, that just as they were sweeping across North America, someday Christian and American values would change China.

Like most Americans, the Roosevelts had only a meager understanding of Asia. Waves of immigration had brought people from all over the world to the United States, but after the Transcontinental Railroad was completed, the Chinese Exclusion Act of 1882 made it illegal for a Chinese person to enter the country. True, some westernized Chinese were exempted and allowed in as students, businessmen, and diplomats, but they were few and far between. Almost no Chinese could be found in the halls of the White House or the offices of Wall Street.

Likewise, very few Americans had ever traveled to China. Yes, some American missionaries, businessmen, and diplomats made it across the Pacific, but they clung mostly to the westernized New China settlements on the coast. These Americans wrote home about a cultural and spiritual blossoming of the Chinese under their care, decades of hopeful hogwash foisted on unknowing readers. Both Presidents Roosevelt were thus constantly well informed about New China, that place that was always going to be.

This book examines the American perception of Asia and the gap between that perception and reality. The wide gulf of the Pacific Ocean has prevented Americans and Chinese from knowing each other. Generations of accumulated misunderstanding between these two continental giants has so far led to three major Asian wars that have left millions dead and has distorted U.S. domestic politics and foreign policy.

My father, John Bradley, was one of the six men photographed raising the American flag on the island of Iwo Jima during World War II. When I was forty-six years old I published *Flags of Our Fathers,* a book about my dad's experiences. Now I am sixty years old and I continue to honor the young men who fought in that horrible war, but I increasingly doubt my father's elders, the men in power who allowed Americans to be sucked into a world war at a time when the U.S. military was preparing for war in Europe and was not ready to fight in distant Asia.

Japan surprised the United States at Pearl Harbor on December 7, 1941. On December 8, the U.S. Congress declared war against Japan, but not well remembered is what Americans on that day thought they were fighting *for*. One of the millions who served in America's Asian war was John F. Kennedy, who later recalled,

> It was clearly enunciated that the independence of China... was the fundamental object of our Far Eastern policy...that this and other statements of our policies on the Far East led directly to the attack on Pearl Harbor is well known. And it might be said that we almost knowingly entered into combat with Japan to preserve the independence of China.[6]

For generations, American hearts had been warmed by the missionary dream of a New China peopled by Americanized Christians. Then, beginning slowly in the early 1930s, a foreign-funded China Lobby sprouted in the United States and gained powerful adherents in the U.S. government, in the media, and in pulpits across the country. By 1941, nearly a decade of China Lobby propaganda had been pumped into American churches, homes, and heads, convincing the vast majority of Americans that a Christianized and Americanized New China would blossom as their best friend in Asia if the United States drove the Japanese military out of China.

The China Lobby's premise was that the Japanese military would be forced to withdraw from China if the United States embargoed Japan's oil. President Franklin Delano Roosevelt thought the opposite. Japan—with little domestic production—had only two major sources of oil: California and the Dutch East Indies (today's Indonesia). Roosevelt had a "Europe first" policy in case of war: the United States would defeat Hitler, and then, if necessary, confront the Japanese. Since the United States was supplying over 80 percent of Japan's oil,

FDR thought that if he cut off the California pump, the Japanese military would thrust south toward the Dutch East Indies, and the United States would be drawn into an unwanted Asian war.

Many administration officials were outraged by what they considered to be Roosevelt's appeasement of Japan. They—like the majority of Americans—had swallowed the China Lobby line that an oil embargo would force Japan out of China and that there would be no danger of the United States getting involved militarily. And with the Japanese no longer a threat, the great Chiang Kai-shek would ascend to undiluted command—and a Christian and democratic China would follow. (British prime minister Winston Churchill called the New China dream the "Great American illusion.")

This is the story of how a few of these officials surreptitiously outmaneuvered and undermined the president of the United States and thrust America into an unwanted Asian war. My father and millions of others fought in a conflict that didn't have to happen, a war that Franklin Delano Roosevelt was trying to avoid, one that could have been prevented or delayed if some overconfident administration officials had heeded their president instead of the China Lobby.

Today, seventy years after World War II, many imagine America went to war against Hitler to save England. History books and a recent television series on the Roosevelts recall the fierce tussle between American isolationists and internationalists in the lead-up to World War II, showing a fiery Charles Lindbergh and other public figures debating what the United States should do across the Atlantic. These stories feature a bold FDR reaching out to Winston Churchill via secret private emissaries like Harry Hopkins, Averell Harriman, and Wild Bill Donovan.

Little noted is that the debate about America's helping Britain was never decided. The U.S. did not enter World War II to defend Britain or oppose Hitler. On December 8, 1941, the United States declared war on Japan and only Japan. Three long days passed, and the United States did not declare war on Germany to defend England. It was only when Adolf Hitler rashly declared war on the U.S. that Americans went to war in Europe.

World War II burst upon America from Asia. Charles Lindbergh's Atlantic focus is better remembered, but it was the China Lobby's arguments about peoples across the Pacific that changed American history.

When Mao Zedong rose to power in 1949, the U.S. government and media portrayed him as an angry, anti-American Soviet pawn, going so far as to paint Mao as not a "real Chinese," an idea believable because Americans had for decades been propagandized by the China Lobby that authentic Chinese yearned to be Christianized and Americanized. The American public did not realize that five years earlier, Mao had repeatedly extended his hand in friendship, enthusiastically describing to his State Department interlocutors a symbiotic relationship combining U.S. industrial know-how with China's limitless workforce. Mao—who had never flown in an airplane—reached out to President Roosevelt in 1945, saying he was eager to fly to the United States to discuss his vision, a historic opportunity that New China–believing Americans tragically nipped in the bud.

When the U.S.-spurned Mao turned to the USSR, Americans imagined they had lost China, and the United States replanted its New China dream on the island of Taiwan. Senator Joseph McCarthy asked, "Who lost China?" and launched a witch hunt—supported by the China Lobby—that drove the State Department specialists who had dealt with Mao out of the government. Having made itself blind on Asia, Washington then stumbled into the Korean and Vietnam Wars.

The who-lost-China hysteria helped topple the administration of President Harry Truman, distorted U.S. domestic politics, and haunted Dwight Eisenhower, John Kennedy, Lyndon Johnson, and Richard Nixon as these presidents tried not to lose again in Asia.

The China Lobby also warped U.S. foreign policy. From 1949 to 1979, the world's most powerful country refused to have official state-to-state relations with the world's most populous country. But consider your smartphone, which was probably manufactured in China, and you can see that Mao's vision of the relationship—not America's New China dream—is the one that triumphed. Like World

War II in the Pacific, the destructive thirty years of estrangement between Mao's China and the United States did not have to happen.

The Roosevelts' actions in Asia are relatively unknown to Americans, even though the results are clear.

Go to New York City's Chinatown and you'll see the only two statues that Chinese Americans have erected there: one for the revered Confucius and the other for the Chinese government official who asked Warren Delano to stop smuggling opium into China.

Stroll through Seoul, South Korea, and you will come across a memorial honoring an American civilian, the only such statue in downtown Seoul. In 1905, the emperor of Korea had felt the Japanese military's hands tightening around his country's neck. He dispatched an American friend from Seoul to Washington to plead with President Theodore Roosevelt for Korea's continued independence. Roosevelt refused to help. Korea then fell under Japan's control for forty years. Today Koreans honor the American who begged Theodore Roosevelt for Korea's freedom.

Go to South Asia today, look up at the Pakistani sky, and you might see an American drone. The American president controls this lethal program within the executive branch; it's a private air force that's operated with little congressional oversight. Franklin Delano Roosevelt created this secret executive air force one year *before* Pearl Harbor in an attempt to keep the New China dream alive.

Today the United States is the world's largest developed country and China is the largest developing country. Like two huge balloons in a closed room, they will inevitably bump up against each other. The reactions will depend on each side's understanding of and empathy for the other. This is a book about the American disaster in Asia as a result of a mirage in the American mind. The stakes in understanding these past missteps are enormous and, to me, personal. My father was severely wounded in 1945, and in 1968 my brother almost died, both fighting in Asian wars that didn't have to happen. I don't want my son in boot camp like his grandfather and uncle simply because of more misunderstandings between the Pacific's two great powers.

Today, the United States and China—while cooperating to build wealth—are once again massively uninformed about each other. There was a time when everyone in the United States knew that Mao Zedong and Zhou Enlai were China's top leaders and everyone in China recognized President Nixon and Henry Kissinger. A measure of the current relationship is that almost no Americans can name the top two Chinese leaders today and ninety-year-old Henry Kissinger remains China's most recognizable American friend.

With only a narrow, rickety bridge of fellowship crossing the Pacific, misunderstandings are flourishing and both countries employ heated rhetoric. On the American side, generations of missionary dreams about New China created an assumption in the United States about a reality that never existed in Asia. The China mirage took hold in the nineteenth century, affected U.S. foreign policy and domestic politics in the twentieth century, and continues to misguide America. Perhaps the cautionary tale revealed in this book will motivate people in both countries to strengthen that bridge across the Pacific before it's too late. Again.

Chapter 1

OLD CHINA, NEW CHINA

China can never be reformed from within. The manifold needs of China...
will be met permanently, completely, only by Christian civilization.
—Reverend Arthur Henderson Smith[1]

The written histories of Franklin Delano Roosevelt and his Delano ancestors chronicle their childhoods, schooling, marriages, careers, children, deaths, and legacies. Curiously, the source of Franklin Delano Roosevelt's dynastic wealth is little commented upon by the chroniclers. As the esteemed Roosevelt historian Geoffrey Ward wrote, "The full story of Warren Delano's career in the China trade has not been written."[2]

Warren Delano was a blueblood. His forebears had left Europe and arrived in Plymouth, Massachusetts, just two ships after the *Mayflower* brought the first colonists to New England. The Delanos were among the earliest settlers of the area of southern Massachusetts — New Bedford, Buzzards Bay, and Fairhaven — that produced so many of America's original whalers and sea merchants.

Warren's father — also named Warren — made a substantial income ferrying corn, salt, and potatoes to New Orleans, England, and the

Canary Islands. The first Warren helped found a Fairhaven church—the Washington Street Christian meeting place on Walnut Street—and his former residence is today the Delano Homestead Bed-and-Breakfast. Warren Junior graduated from Fairhaven Academy—a local trade school—in 1842, and he apprenticed with the Boston importer Hathaway and Company and then with one of New York's premier importers, Goodhue and Company.

Great Britain had decided many years earlier that the Chinese frontier was much more lucrative than America's. By sailing halfway around the world, Delano could participate in the single largest commodity trade of the nineteenth century: smuggling opium into China. Such an enterprise promised him a quick killing and world-class wealth before the age of thirty. Delano grabbed his big chance.

For centuries, China was the richest country on earth, and its people thought it natural that outsiders would come to China to learn from their superior culture. The Chinese saw these visitors as barbarians—more specifically, as *fan kuei,* "foreign devils": second-class vassals, pitiful in their desperation for Chinese knowledge and goods.

In the late seventeenth century, the English began to import enormous quantities of Chinese tea to satisfy and stimulate its new factory-worker class. British silver flowed in increasingly alarming amounts from London's vaults to the Middle Kingdom, but the money went only one way; the Chinese wanted few English products. The constant importation of Chinese tea to the West caused a gargantuan drain of silver from Europe to Asia. China was a rich country in the 1700s, its population tripling over the course of the century from about one hundred million to over three hundred million.

The imbalance in trade quickly decimated the coffers of many European nations, hitting Britain particularly hard. Deeply concerned, London hit upon a corrective that took advantage of England's colonial holding of India, its naval might, and its disdain for the Chinese. The Brits' dependence on tea made them subject to the Chinese, but they saw a way to reverse the situation, and the flow of silver.

*   *   *

In the Confucian value system, merchants—consumed by thoughts of profit—were near the bottom of the social scale. Those concerned with the people's welfare—the mandarins who studied the classics and served the emperor—were at the top of the heap. "Barbarian" merchants could access China's market only by making clear they knew their place in the pecking order and following the tribute system. This required foreign missions to travel to Beijing to pay tribute to the emperor and acknowledge their inferiority by kowtowing—kneeling in front of the Son of Heaven (as he was known) and touching their foreheads to the floor. After the foreign devils acknowledged China's superiority and offered valuable tribute, the Son of Heaven benevolently allowed them to purchase the riches of the Middle Kingdom.

Over millennia, barbarians had traveled to China from Korea, Japan, Mongolia, Vietnam, Malaysia, Laos, Cambodia, and many other countries. In the Middle Ages, Europeans ventured in their tiny ships out into the world's oceans, and a new type of foreign devil arrived in China: the sea barbarians, funny-looking, long-nosed cow-eaters in tight trousers and high hats.

In the course of becoming a world power, Great Britain grew accustomed to imposing its trade terms on people around the globe. But China's restrictive tribute system was slow, cumbersome, and devoid of any respect for the British. In 1793, King George III of England sent emissaries to Beijing with impertinent demands. Among these was the unthinkable call for the emperor to cede a piece of land—an island or a coastal strip—where England could establish a permanent trading post.

King George also insulted the Son of Heaven by suggesting peer-to-peer diplomatic relations. The English did not comprehend that the Son of Heaven could never comply with this. China had no foreign affairs office because it shunned official relationships with barbarian countries. Instead, the emperor managed trading relations with foreign devils through his Barbarian Management Bureau, whose mandarins forwarded this response from the Son of Heaven to the English sovereign:

> Our Celestial Empire possesses all things in prolific abundance and lacks no product within its borders. There is therefore no need to import the manufactures of outside barbarians in exchange for our own produce. But as the tea, silk, and porcelain which the Celestial Empire produces are absolute necessities to European nations and to yourselves, we have permitted, as a signal mark of favor, that foreign hongs [private businessmen who paid the government for the right to trade with barbarians] should be established at Canton, so that your wants might be supplied and your country thus participate in our beneficence.[3]

The Barbarian Management Bureau's mandarins designed the Canton system above all to protect ordinary Chinese from infection by the low character and animal nature of foreign devils like Warren Delano. To begin with, the port of Canton, in China's hot and humid south, was about as far away as possible from the Son of Heaven's home in Beijing. The system required the sea barbarians to live and work in whitewashed warehouses located *outside* Canton's city wall.[4] When the roughly four-month trading season was over, the foreign-devil traders had to leave Canton immediately.

If sea barbarians wanted to trade with the Middle Kingdom, they could humble themselves and submit to the Canton system. But the English—and, later, the Americans—were not used to humbling themselves. Quite the contrary.

Like grapes and ginseng, the product that would make Warren Delano a wealthy man grows best in certain parts of the world. The prime opium-producing area was a vast swath stretching five hundred miles across the Bengal region of India. Arab merchants dominated the India-to-China opium trade for hundreds of years, until Portuguese sailors took it over in the sixteenth century. The Portuguese also brought tobacco from their Brazilian colony, and the Chinese especially enjoyed smoking tobacco mixed with opium. Sensing the potential harm to his people, the emperor outlawed the sale and use of opium.

Opium was big business for the British, one of the critical economic engines of the era. Britain controlled India and oversaw one million Indian opium farmers. By 1850, the drug accounted for a staggering 15 to 20 percent of the British Empire's revenue, and the India-to-China opium business became, in the words of Frederic Wakeman, a leading historian of the period, the "world's most valuable single commodity trade of the nineteenth century."[5] Notes Carl Trocki, author of *Opium, Empire and the Global Economy,* "The entire commercial infrastructure of European trade in Asia was built around opium."[6]

The Chinese emperor had outlawed opium, so some back in England judged that this illegal business had to be immoral. To evade criticism, the British government employed the ruse of selling the opium in Calcutta to a private Crown-chartered enterprise—the East India Company—and pretended that London wasn't involved with what happened next. East India Company ships sailed the contraband up the Chinese coast and, with the protection of British naval might and expertise, used both offshore islands and anchored ships to stash the drugs. Chinese criminals would row out to the offshore drug warehouses to get the English opium. Massive bribery of local officials made the trade possible.

The British were breaking Chinese law and pushing back against the restrictive Canton system. Exploiting coves and islands along China's rocky coast, the sea barbarians opened more areas for their illegal trade, while partnerships with local gangsters allowed further circumvention. One English merchant reflected on his work in Asia:

> No doubt your anticipations of future evil have a certain foundation.... But it is my business to make a fortune with the least possible loss of time.... In two or three years at farthest, I hope to realize a fortune and get away and what can it matter to me, if all Shanghai disappear afterwards, in fire or flood? You must

not expect men in my situation to condemn themselves to years of prolonged exile in an unhealthy climate for the benefit of posterity. We are moneymaking, practical men. Our business is to make money, as much and as fast as we can.[7]

The India-to-China opium trade was exclusively the domain of the East India Company; no private English merchants were allowed in. The British Parliament forbade America's colonial merchants to trade directly with China, forcing them to buy tea from British sources and thus generating substantial tax revenue for London. (The Boston Tea Party in 1773 was a protest by American colonists against this British tax on a Chinese product.) In 1784, with the ink barely dry on the Treaty of Paris, which ended the American Revolutionary War, Robert Morris — a wealthy Philadelphian known as "the financier of the Revolution" — dispatched a ship called the *Empress of China* to Canton. Morris had done his research well and sent off an attractive cargo of ginseng (which grew wild on the shores of the Hudson River), a valuable herb esteemed by the Chinese, along with a variety of other wares. The goods sold quickly in Canton, and with the proceeds, the American sailors bought Chinese tea, which they sold profitably back in the United States. Morris's venture — the first successful American round-trip trade voyage to China — turned a whopping profit of 35 percent, which spurred more American interest in the China trade.

A number of East Coast merchants then pooled their resources to send ginseng, South Pacific sealskins, and Hawaiian sandalwood to Canton. But the American sea merchants encountered the same problem as their British counterparts had: before long, the new nation had its own trade imbalance, thanks to its appetite for Chinese tea. American merchants sourced a supply of opium in Turkey, and because private British merchants weren't allowed to carry it, the Americans had a virtual monopoly on the Turkey-to-China opium trade. Soon these East Coast families — led by the Perkins clan of Boston — were raking in fortunes. One American opium merchant estimated that the Turkey-to-Canton opium trade turned profits of 37.5 percent.

Samuel Russell of Middletown, Connecticut, established Russell and Company, which quickly became America's biggest smuggler of Turkish opium into China.

Russell put out the word that he would train ambitious young men and that they could score what China traders called a "competence," a profit of $100,000, by the time they were thirty years old. (This was the equivalent of a young person today amassing millions of dollars within six years of graduating from college.) A fortune of that size in the capital-poor United States would assure its owner a comfortable life of financial independence and social leadership.

Warren Delano's breeding and education made him one of the lucky few who caught the eye of Samuel Russell. Delano, twenty-four years old, sailed out of New Bedford, Massachusetts, in 1833. He met Russell for the first time in Macao, a small Portuguese enclave on China's coast where American sea barbarians lived while awaiting the

Samuel Russell (CPA Media / Pictures From History)

fall-to-winter trading season during which China would allow them entrance into the Middle Kingdom.

Delano began studying the many items Russell and Company imported to the United States, including tea; he learned its many shades and how to buy, store, and ship it. Silk, chinaware, and other items had to be accounted for in the ledger books, and there was a steady flow of mail to tend to. It was an intense apprenticeship, and Delano was learning from the founder, an ideal position.

Then came the exciting day when Delano sailed to China for the first time, going north from Macao to the Pearl River Delta, where the Russell and Company warehouse was situated on the riverbank outside Canton's walls.

The Russell and Company warehouse — a compact three-story building housing about a dozen partners — would become Delano's home, but it also functioned as a place of business and recreation, a storeroom, and even a church. The lower floor held the merchandise, kitchen, and servants' quarters. The upper floors held the offices, dining room, and traders' personal quarters.

As a barbarian within the Canton system, Delano was ordered to stay put. Under no circumstances was he to enter Canton or any other city in China. Delano could not travel to the real China, walk through a Chinese village, or see a rural rice paddy. And that's just how the Chinese wanted it.

Delano was governed by the Canton system's rules. Barbarian traders like him never dealt directly with an official of the Chinese government; the odious business of interacting with foreign devils was assigned to the hong merchants. The rules decreed that one of the worst crimes a Chinese person could commit was teaching the Chinese language to a barbarian. As a result, Delano learned a pidgin or business lingua franca that was neither English nor Chinese. He could not carry a gun. He could not gather with others in a group larger than ten. He could not row a boat on the river, and for exercise, he could stroll along only a small strip of land. Once a year, he and other barbarian traders were allowed a walk in the gardens on the oppo-

The Son of Heaven restricted the sea barbarian traders to a tiny spit of land outside Canton's borders. (CPA Media / Pictures From History)

site shore, but only under the watchful eyes of government-appointed minders. The Russell and Company warehouse had Chinese servants to cook and clean, but these were provided by their hong overseer, who used them as spies.

What little of Chinese life Warren was able to glimpse he found downright weird. At the dinner table his Chinese hosts placed Warren at their left as the honored guest and kept their hats on. The food was served in bowls, the wine was warm, and the Chinese ate with sticks instead of knives and forks. Chinese read from up to down and from right to left. Their last names came first and their compasses pointed south. Chinese friends greeted each other by closing their hands and letting them hang limply by their sides. Porters with Warren's luggage walked ahead of him; Chinese shoes were broad in front and narrow at the heel; the men wore gowns and the women trousers.

The hong merchant assigned to deal with Russell and Company was named Howqua. He was the emperor's official minder of Russell's men, and he would trade with Delano and oversee his warehouse. It is believed that through his dealings with Americans and other barbarians, Howqua became one of the richest men in the world.[8]

John Perkins Cushing — also a Russell and Company partner — had preceded Delano and initiated the close American relationship with Howqua. The two men had established an offshore base — an anchored, floating warehouse — where Russell and Company ships would offload their opium contraband before continuing up the Pearl River Delta to Canton with their legal cargo.

In the dark of night, "scrambling crabs" — long, sleek, heavily armed crafts propelled by as many as sixty oarsmen — rowed out to Russell and Company's floating warehouse and exchanged silver for opium. The entire transaction happened very quickly and enabled Howqua's and Cushing's hands to stay clean. The dirty work — the illegal landing of the drug on Chinese soil, the bribing of officials to look the other way, the wholesaling to opium dens and retailing to street addicts — was performed by Chinese criminal gangs.

In similar fashion, a procession of American sea merchants made their fortunes smuggling opium. They were aware of its poisonous effects on the Chinese people, but few of them ever mentioned the drug in the thousands of pages of letters and documents they sent back to America. Robert Bennet Forbes — a Russell and Company contemporary of Delano's — defended his involvement with opium by noting that some of America's best families were involved, "those to whom I have always been accustomed to look up as exponents of all that was honorable in trade — the Perkins, the Peabodys, the Russells and the Lows."[9]

On a macroeconomic level, the sea barbarians had turned the tables, as Chinese silver now flowed to Europe. But to the Chinese, the opium trade was an unmixed evil, corrupting its officials, demoralizing its people (including, most vexingly, its soldiery), draining its wealth, raising the cost of living, and undermining the Son of Heaven's authority.

Most alarming to the mandarins in Beijing was the potential erosion of what they believed to be the Mandate of Heaven. Peace and prosperity meant that Heaven favored the current ruler; if chaos appeared, it was a sign that Heaven was displeased with the emperor and that the Mandate was in play.

In the West, the divine right of kings granted legitimacy to royal families from generation to generation, guaranteeing that the lowborn would not revolt, for revolution was a sin. In contrast, the Mandate of Heaven gave the Chinese people the right of rebellion. A successful revolt against a sitting emperor was interpreted as evidence that Heaven wanted the Mandate to pass to the next ruler. One of the key indicators that Heaven was displeased was an emperor's inability to discipline barbarians.

In their cramped and restricted situation, Delano and his fellows fantasized about having Christianized and westernized enclaves where they could conduct themselves as they wished, under their own rules. The American missionaries who were just beginning to arrive via merchant ships shared these desires and had additional demands. The Barbarian Management Bureau had earlier threatened American churchmen with beheading if they were caught spreading the evil religion of Christianity. By 1838—with their country's military might supporting them—missionaries insisted on the right not only to preach but also to build schools, hospitals, churches, and cemeteries on Chinese soil, to learn the Chinese language, and in general to be left alone in their quest to change pagans into Americanized and Christianized New Chinese.

In 1839, when Warren Delano was thirty years old and the number-two partner in Russell and Company, the tension between East and West exploded around him. For the previous two years, the governor of Hunan Province—Lin Zexu—had suppressed the sale and use of opium in Hunan. The Son of Heaven now transferred Lin to Canton as an imperial commissioner to stamp out the opium trade there.

Commissioner Lin demanded that Delano and the other foreign devils come clean and hand over their opium stocks.[10] When the sea barbarians coyly replied they had no opium, he tightened the screws by surrounding their warehouses with troops and withdrawing their Chinese servants. Suddenly, Delano found himself cooking his own meals in the Russell and Company kitchen.

To break out of their hopeless situation, the traders eventually forfeited their valuable opium. (Only the biggest English smugglers turned over more than Delano.) Then, in view of cheering Chinese, Commissioner Lin had three enormous trenches dug. Day after day, workers shoveled the seized opium into the water-filled gullies, mixed it with salt and lime, and flushed the mixture out into the ocean.

A month later, in July 1839, Commissioner Lin addressed a letter to Queen Victoria, then just twenty years old, only two years on the British throne:

We have heard that in your own country opium is prohibited... this is a strong proof that you know full well how hurtful it is to mankind. Since then you do not permit it to injure your own country, you ought not to have the injurious drug transferred to another country.... Of the products which China exports to your foreign countries, there is not one which is not beneficial to mankind.... Has China (we should like to ask) ever yet sent forth a noxious article from its soil?... [If] foreigners came from another country, and brought opium into England, and seduced the people of your country to smoke it, would not you, the sovereign of the said country, look upon such a procedure with anger, and in your just indignation endeavor to get rid of it?...

Let your highness immediately, upon the receipt of this communication, inform us promptly of the state of matters, and of the measure you are pursuing utterly to put a stop to the opium evil. Please let your reply be speedy...

P.S. We annex an abstract of the new law, now about to be put in force. "Any foreigner or foreigners bringing opium to the Central Land, with design to sell the same, the principals shall most assuredly be decapitated, and the accessories strangled; and all property (found on board the same ship) shall be confiscated. The space of a year and a half is granted, within the which, if anyone bringing opium by mistake, shall voluntarily step forward and deliver it up, he shall be absolved from all consequences of his crime."[11]

As Timothy Brook and Bob Wakabayashi write in their masterly book *Opium Regimes,* "The British Empire could not survive were it deprived of its most important source of capital, the substance that could turn any other commodity into silver."[12] Queen Victoria speedily dispatched her navy in November 1839 to bombard China's coast, shocking the government mandarins who had built the Great Wall to keep northern intruders out, never imagining their kingdom would be humbled by sea barbarians who had gained entry through distant Canton. Thus began the First Opium War, which lasted until 1842.

Back in America, Delano's congressional representative John Quincy Adams told the country that opium smuggling was "a mere incident to the dispute; but no more a cause of the war than the throwing overboard of the tea in Boston harbor was the cause of the North American revolution. The cause of the war is the pretension on the part of the Chinese, that in all their intercourse with other nations, political or otherwise, their superiority must be acknowledged, and manifested in humiliating forms."[13]

The First Opium War was a boom time for Delano. English traders were forced to observe the British blockade of China, yet valuable cargoes from other sources continued to arrive. Responding to (and encouraging) demand, Delano rented or purchased every ship he could, then charged high transport fees. Delano's accomplishments were recognized in the midst of the war when, on January 1, 1840, the thirty-one-year-old was named the senior partner of Russell and Company.

Russell and Company senior partners often served as U.S. consuls to Canton, an honorific but empty title, because the Chinese would still not countenance state-to-state relations with barbarians. Appointed

U.S. consul in 1841, Delano cheered the British bombing of China and welcomed the first U.S. warship, commanded by Commodore Lawrence Kearny, dispatched to China to protect American interests.

The Chinese had no effective way to defend themselves against the superior arms and technology of a modern industrialized military. Ravaged on land and sea, China reluctantly capitulated and signed the Treaty of Nanking, the first of what many Chinese still consider the odious "unequal treaties" by which the West would chip away at old China's sovereignty. China was forced to pay Britain an indemnity of millions and abolish the Canton system. Most alarming, the Treaty of Nanking required China to cede the island of Hong Kong to Britain and to open five ports to trade. In these New Chinas (called treaty ports), foreigners enjoyed extraterritoriality — freedom from Chinese laws and the right to try their own transgressors. Now, just like the first European incursions onto the American continent in the 1600s, white Christians had created an archipelago of trading hubs where Western ways could root and flourish.

With the Canton system destroyed, the drug trade exploded. Soon the British governor of Hong Kong wrote his London masters, "Almost every person...not connected with government is employed in the opium trade."[14]

By early 1843, Delano had spent a momentous decade in the China trade. He had achieved his financial competence and risen to become the head partner of the biggest American firm dealing with China. He had witnessed the destruction of the hated Canton system, the humiliation of the Chinese government, and the creation of New Chinas. Over those ten years, he had seen Westerners transform themselves from huddled supplicants into victors who dictated terms. Delano decided to return to Massachusetts for a short vacation. Commodore Kearny gave him a copy of the Treaty of Nanking to take triumphantly back to the United States for American officials to study as a model for a comparable U.S.-China treaty.[15]

Delano's Chinese partner in crime, Howqua, gave him an elaborate

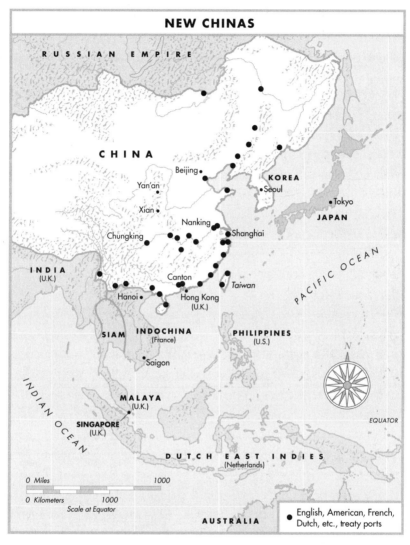

NEW CHINAS

RUSSIAN EMPIRE

CHINA

Beijing

Yan'an

KOREA

Seoul

Xian

Tokyo

Nanking

JAPAN

Chungking

Shanghai

INDIA
(U.K.)

Canton

Taiwan

PACIFIC OCEAN

Hanoi

Hong Kong
(U.K.)

SIAM INDOCHINA
(France)

PHILIPPINES
(U.S.)

N

Saigon

INDIAN OCEAN

MALAYA
(U.K.)

SINGAPORE
(U.K.)

EQUATOR

DUTCH EAST INDIES
(Netherlands)

0 Miles   1000

0 Kilometers   1000
Scale at Equator

AUSTRALIA

● English, American, French,
Dutch, etc., treaty ports

In the nineteenth century, the West forced China to grant it special rights in treaty ports, Christian outposts where foreign devils could live by their own rules.

send-off feast, which a witness reported as "about 15 courses — bird's nest soup — shark fins — pigeons eggs — quail &c — sturgeon's lip, etc. We were 13 hours getting thro' with it. It is many years since Howqua has given a Chinese dinner at his own house and perhaps never before did he give to a friend the like of this."[16]

*　　*　　*

Upon his return to Massachusetts, Delano was viewed as a wealthy young man who had made his fortune in China by dealing in tea, silks, and porcelain. Though considered one of a handful of American experts on China, Delano had never explored the country or its culture. The nation that Delano described to his listeners was a mirage; that China could not be internally reformed, and the pitiful, drug-addicted, backward pagan mess of a place was lucky to have Americans on its coast to civilize it via American values and beliefs.

On July 3, 1844, a meeting that would have been inconceivable just a few years earlier took place between American and Chinese government officials. At a table in the Temple of Kun Yam in Macao, Caleb Cushing, a Massachusetts contemporary of Delano's, sat across from a Chinese official and signed a U.S.-China agreement modeled on the Nanking treaty. For half a century, relations between the United States and China had been strictly commercial. Now, after his country had been pummeled by the combined might of a number of Western navies, a Chinese official had greeted a representative of the United States to negotiate the U.S.-China diplomatic and economic relationship. The Treaty of Wangxia allowed five New Chinas, districts where, extraterritoriality established, Americans would rule supreme. They could buy land and erect homes and businesses in these protected pockets without Chinese interference.

As a show of goodwill, Caleb Cushing noted in the treaty that the Chinese had been just in declaring the opium trade illegal. This was a meaningless concession because Americans in their New Chinas could not be tried by Chinese courts, only by U.S. consuls. The consul at the time was Paul Sieman Forbes; he had succeeded Warren Delano in that position, as well as in the position of senior partner in Russell and Company. Therefore, the man who was head of the U.S. consular court was also the man overseeing the biggest American opium-smuggling operation.

Every American who came to China after the Treaty of Wangxia could consider himself a member of a superior civilization—a co-conqueror of the world's oldest empire. Americans named Delano, Russell, Cushing,

Perkins, Forbes, Low, and Green, among others, had helped transform coastal China into a quasi-colony of the sea barbarians.

Warren Delano returned to the China trade, leaving the United States at the end of 1843 with his new wife, eighteen-year-old Catherine Lyman, whom he had met through John Murray Forbes, another man made wealthy by smuggling opium. For three years, the couple lived in Macao in a grand mansion called Arrowdale. When they returned to the United States in 1846, they assumed their place in the ranks of East Coast society. They purchased a sumptuous town house at 39 Lafayette Square in New York City, where their neighbors included Washington Irving and John Jacob Astor.

Opium merchants like Delano provided the seed corn for the economic revolution in America. Delano invested his new fortune in a host of ventures: New York waterfront property, railroads, copper mines in Tennessee and Maryland, and coal mines in Pennsylvania, where a town was named Delano in his honor. The Perkins family, who had pioneered the transport of Turkish opium to China, built Boston's Athenaeum, the Massachusetts General Hospital, and the Perkins Institution for the Blind. America's first railroad — the Quincy Granite Railway — was built to carry stone from Perkins's quarries to the site of the Bunker Hill Monument.

Opium money funded any number of significant institutions in the eastern United States. John Perkins Cushing's profitable relationship with Howqua helped finance the construction of America's first great textile manufacturing city, Lowell, Massachusetts.

America's great East Coast universities owe a great deal to opium profits. Much of the land upon which Yale University stands was provided by Russell family money. A Russell family trust still covers the budget of Yale's Skull and Bones Society, and Russell funds built the famously secretive club's headquarters. Columbia University's most recognizable building is the Low Memorial Library, honoring Abiel Abbot Low, who worked in China with Warren Delano in the 1830s. John Cleve Green was Delano's immediate predecessor as a senior partner in Russell and Company, and he was Princeton University's single largest donor, financing three buildings. (Green also founded America's oldest orthopedic hospital—Manhattan's Hospital for Special Surgery—from his opium fortune.)

Among the railways financed with opium money were the Boston and Lowell (Perkins), the Michigan Central (Forbes), the Chicago, Burlington, and Quincy (Forbes), and the Chesapeake and Ohio (Low), among others.

The influence of these opium fortunes seeped into virtually every aspect of American life. That influence was cultural: the transcendentalist Ralph Waldo Emerson married John Murray Forbes's daughter, and his father-in-law's fortune helped provide Emerson with the cushion to become a professional thinker. It was found in technology: Forbes's son watched over his father's investment in the Bell Telephone Company as its first president, and Abiel Abbot Low provided start-up money for the first transatlantic cable. And it was ideological: Joseph Coolidge's heirs founded the Council on Foreign Relations. Several companies that would play major roles in American history were also the product of drug profits, among them the United Fruit Company, started by the Coolidge family. Scratch the history of an institution or a person with the name Forbes attached to it, and there's a good chance you'll see that opium is involved. Secretary of State John Forbes Kerry's great-grandfather was Francis Blackwell Forbes, who got rich selling opium in China.

In 1852 Warren Delano and his growing family moved to their dream house, a brown-and-buff mansion on six acres overlooking the Hudson River. Delano named the home Algonac and furnished it with Chinese décor. In the parlor hung a portrait of Howqua. Now in his forties, Delano regaled guests and associates with colorful stories of trading tea and silk in China, but he rarely mentioned opium. This was in line with custom: American drug dealing was downplayed in polite East Coast society, the finger pointed mostly at Britain.

Delano lived luxuriously until stocks crashed and banks collapsed in the financial panic of 1857, and his investments soured one by one.

Delano was suddenly faced with a grim financial future. Forty-eight years old and slowly going broke, he thought long and hard about how to reconstitute his fortune. He still had sterling contacts with leading businessmen across the United States. He had been an investor in railroads, property, copper, and coal mines. He was healthy, and, despite the crash, the American economy still offered plenty of opportunity. But with a growing family (his seventh child was born in 1857) and an expensive manor lifestyle to support, he wanted to make a lot of money quickly. So Delano returned to the most profitable business in the world.

It wasn't an easy decision. Opium smuggling was a young man's game. Delano had been twenty-four years old when he'd first sailed to China; now he was twice that. The trip to Hong Kong was an arduous four-month-long voyage and he risked contracting malaria or life-threatening dysentery in hot and humid South China. But after fourteen years of playing by the rules in the U.S. economy, he was confronting a reduced standard of living. It was time, he concluded, to go back to the game with no rules.

It took almost two years for Russell and Company to repost Delano to Hong Kong. By then, at fifty years old, he had eight children, and his wife, Catherine, was pregnant with a ninth. Delano gave an empty stamp book to five-year-old Sara and promised the tearful girl that he would send her letters and stamps. In 1859, Delano sailed to the British colony of Hong Kong, where he became once again the senior official in the biggest American firm in New China and proceeded to rebuild his fortune.

The tables had most certainly turned since the days when he'd apprenticed to Samuel Russell. The Barbarian Management Bureau mandarins had naively assumed that the sea barbarians would be satisfied with Hong Kong and the five treaty ports granted in 1843. But now that the inch had been given, the mile was insisted upon. The British, French, and American foreign devils wanted China to rescind its prohibition and legalize opium, exempt internal trade by foreigners from duties, adopt English as the official language of all future treaties, and allow official state-to-state relations. The foreign devils were demanding the right to poison three hundred million people with their opium while continuing to stay beyond the reach of the emperor's jurisdiction. Just as shocking to the Chinese, the barbarians demanded that foreign-devil ambassadors be allowed to reside in Beijing near the Son of Heaven.

When the Barbarian Management Bureau refused these demands, the British, French, and American navies retaliated with the Second Opium War, this time ravaging not only coastal cities and forts but also the country's interior; they invaded Beijing, chased the emperor out of town, and, in an orgy of fine-art and jewelry looting, destroyed the Versailles of China, the old Summer Palace.

Overwhelmed again, China bent. A new, even more unequal treaty gave the United States and other nations the right to station their diplomats in Beijing; in addition, it pried open ten more New China treaty ports to foreign trade and allowed foreign vessels—commercial and military—to navigate freely on the Yangtze River, thus giving the foreign devils access to the deepest heart of the Middle Kingdom. Crucially for the Americans, the agreement also provided religious liberty for Chinese Christians and ordered the Chinese government to stop using the word *barbarian* in reference to Westerners. Finally, the Barbarian Management Bureau was abolished and replaced by a foreign ministry forced into relations with barbarian countries.

When Franklin Delano Roosevelt was a young boy, his mother's favorite stories from her own childhood revolved around an adventure in a faraway land. Sara Delano Roosevelt told her son how her mother, Catherine, had packed up Algonac and, on June 25, 1862, sailed out of New York Harbor on a fully crewed ship with nine children, two maids, an upright piano, crates of clothes and books, and a hold stuffed with caged pigs, ducks, geese, and chickens. Over four months of sometimes stormy nights and many becalmed days, Sara's mother passed the time by reading aloud to her children from Nathaniel Hawthorne novels and old issues of *Vanity Fair*. On September 21, 1892, the Delano family was in the Indian Ocean, and they celebrated Sara's eighth birthday with a dinner of roast goose, boiled ham, corn, peas, tomatoes, rice, and cake.

On the morning of October 31, 1862, the Delanos' ship sailed into the Hong Kong harbor. "Papa!" little Sara squealed as Delano came into view, standing at the tiller of a Russell and Company launch rowed by a dozen white-uniformed Chinese. Delano came aboard, embraced his family, and held baby Cassie — born after he left Algonac — for the first time. Little Sara hugged her father's leg.

A procession of sedan chairs took the Delano family up through Hong Kong's steeply inclined streets to their Rose Hill mansion. This large procession of American barbarians proudly asserting their place in New China naturally caught the attention of passing Chinese pedestrians, a few of whom shouted words that young Sara had of course never heard: *Fan kuei*. Both of Sara's parents knew what *fan kuei* meant, but there is no record that they explained it to their eight-year-old daughter. Catherine later wrote in her diary about the Chinese taunts: "I feel very oddly to be again a *Fanqui*."[17]

Rose Hill, Hong Kong. Franklin Delano Roosevelt's grandfather and mother lived on this Russell & Company estate. (CPA Media / Pictures From History)

The stories young Franklin heard from his mother of the two years she spent in Hong Kong were mostly about her experiences within the confines of the Rose Hill estate. Those two years were pleasant but monotonous. Sara mingled with the same small group of people and ventured out only for American-style pursuits, like a day at the racetrack or to ride her horse (and then only if she was escorted by her father or an adult male Russell and Company employee). She never learned the Chinese language. Other than Delano's Chinese servants, little Sara had almost no contact with the locals. She could later tell Franklin stories about peacocks on the property and recall in detail Thanksgiving dinners, but Sara passed on no insights about the real China. How could she?

It's likely that Sara Delano's single foray into a Chinese person's home was on a family visit to a hong merchant's fabulous Canton mansion in February of 1863 when she was nine years old. This would be the equivalent of a foreigner in America dining at the Astor mansion and nowhere else. Sara wrote that before this adventure, "Papa told us children to pretend that we liked Chinese food though it was very strange to us." After five months in their New China sanctuary, the Delano children had apparently not eaten any Chinese food and certainly did not know how to use chopsticks.

Sara and the family marveled at the merchant's opulent mansion as they strolled through rooms furnished with polished ebony and gleaming marble, priceless carved ivory panels and stained-glass windows. When they sat down to dinner, Sara noted in relief that "as it was a very rich and luxurious house, there were knives, forks, and spoons for the strangers."[18]

Sometime later, one of Sara's older sisters — Annie — fell in love with and became engaged to a junior Russell and Company partner, William Howell Forbes. In 1864 Warren Delano had Forbes accompany Sara, Annie, Warren III, and Philippe from Hong Kong to the United States via Saigon, Singapore, Aden, Suez, Cairo, Alexandria, Marseilles, Paris, London, and then across the Atlantic to New York. Delano, Catherine, and the rest of the family returned to the United States in 1866.

*   *   *

Delano had done it. He was back at Algonac surrounded by opulent Chinese furnishings, once again a rich man who told colorful stories about the primitive Middle Kingdom and how America could help make a shiny New China while, with clever sleight of hand, avoiding speaking the name of the commodity that had made it all possible.

Chapter 2

WIN THE LEADERS;
WIN CHINA

The Chinese make good Christians not because they get converted from anything to anything but because the extreme good sense, as expressed in the Golden rule which is the basis of Christianity, the product of another old race, is natural to the Chinese.
—Pearl Buck[1]

Stories told by returning East Coast sea merchants about the heathen Chinese inflamed the hearts of Protestant churchmen. While saving their parishioners' souls remained the ministers' primary aim, a small number went off to China as missionaries and quickly began to mail overwrought reports back home. From American church pulpits there soon came shocking tales of pagan, idolatrous, drug-addicted Chinese with strange business practices who spoke at best a childish, fractured English; of a corrupt, collapsing nation across the Pacific with no right to view itself as superior to any nation; of a backward people who could use a stiff dose of American Puritanism.

The stories that passed from church leaders to millions in the pews were a mirage, the perceptions of a tiny number of American sea

Lady Columbia with a Chinese infant. In the nineteenth century, Americans imagined they were guardians of China's future. (Courtesy Everett Collection)

barbarians and missionaries in their New China havens who had little actual knowledge of the Chinese and their country.

The most widely read manual for American churchmen going off to China was Arthur Henderson Smith's *Chinese Characteristics,* in which the former missionary declared, "There is classical authority for the dictum 'rotten wood cannot be carved.' It must be wholly cut away, and new material grafted upon the old stock. China can never be reformed from within."[2] Continued Smith, "In order to reform China, the springs of character must be reached and purified...it is a truth... that 'there is no alchemy by which to get golden conduct from leaden instincts.'...She needs a new life in every individual soul, in the family and in society. The manifold needs of China... will be met permanently, completely, only by Christian civilization."[3]

A missionary report concluded that the duty of American churchmen to China "is not simply introducing new ideas into the country but modifying its industrial, social and political life and institutions."[4] The American modification of China was vastly ambitious and would be profitable. Wrote Charles Denby, U.S. minister to China, "Missionaries are the pioneers of trade and commerce. Civilization, learning, instruction breed new wants which commerce supplies."[5]

Admiral Alfred Mahan, nineteenth-century America's greatest naval strategist, warned that someday China's power might equal her geographic size, so Americans should expose the Middle Kingdom to Christian values in order that "time shall have been secured for [the Chinese] to absorb the ideals which in ourselves are the result of centuries of Christian increment."[6]

American missionaries styled themselves "representatives of Christendom, in the providence of God brought face to face with China, the representative of paganism."[7] Indeed, with more pagans than any other country, this last great heathen empire seemed to have been preserved intact by God for thousands of years precisely so that its inhabitants might benefit from American conversion. One missionary remembered, "China was the goal, the lodestar, the great magnet that drew us all in those days."[8]

Like the sea merchants, American missionaries spent little time learning about the actual inhabitants of China, focusing instead on a future New China, where the Chinese would pray to Jesus in whitewashed churches and debate Jeffersonian principles in town-hall meetings. Denby wrote the secretary of state, "The educated Chinaman, who speaks English, becomes a new man; he commences to think."[9]

The challenge was immense. The missionary strategy for this New China might today be called trickle-down Christianity: Win the leaders and we win China.[10] Another missionary concluded that they should focus on the next Chinese generation: "Children of today will become the rulers and leaders of tomorrow, and they must be nurtured and raised with the greatest care."[11] And the need was urgent because, as one veteran missionary noted, "A million a month in China are dying without God!"[12]

Reverend Absalom Sydenstricker and Reverend Henry W. Luce were two devout East Coast Presbyterians who answered this missionary call. While he trained at Union Theological Seminary in New York City, young Luce wrote, "God willing...I purpose to go to the foreign field and witness for Him as best I may in the utter most parts of the earth."[13] As an American missionary diplomatically put it later, "In general, missionaries lacked the education for a country where the culture was as old as that of China."[14] Nathaniel Peffer—a *New York Tribune* correspondent who lived in China for twenty-five years—observed,

> There was fundamentally something unhealthy and incongru-
> ous in the whole missionary idea. If the endeavor had been
> confined to primitive savages something could have been said
> for it. But to go out to a race of high culture and long tradition,
> with philosophical, ethical, and religious systems antedating
> Christianity, and to go avowedly to save its people from dam-
> nation as dwellers in heathen darkness—in that there was
> something not only spiritually limited but almost grotesque.[15]

Reverend Sydenstricker's daughter Pearl remembered watching her father deliver his sermon countless times, listening to him preach to the Chinese about sin, guilt, and atonement, Western concepts nonexistent in Confucian thought. She wrote of his Chinese audience: "They did not know what he meant by sins, or who this man was who wanted to save them, or why he did. They stared, half listening, dropping to sleep."[16] Pearl also remembered that when her father left their mission, he always carried a big stick to beat back the dogs sicced on him and to defend himself against enraged mobs chasing him out of town.

The Chinese could not understand why they should embrace an exclusive white God and His white Son. The idea that the American way was superior to that of the Chinese because it was based on Christianity was insulting to an ancient people who now found themselves condescended to by young missionaries from a new country. The Chinese were also confused by the various American sects — Methodist, Lutheran, Congregationalist, and so on — that seemed to be competing against one another for the same God.

What was clear to the Chinese was that the missionaries were friends with the opium smugglers, Christians all. The simplest Chinese peasant understood it was American military might that had foisted both American-supplied opium and American missionaries on the Middle Kingdom.

As the missionary intruders saw it, they and their families were but tiny white Christian islands in an endless sea of yellow pagans. It was desperate work, ill-conceived and all but impossible. After ten years in China, Reverend Sydenstricker admitted that he had made only ten converts.

Despite such paltry success, the missionaries, in the warmth of their homes, surrounded by family, eating with knives and forks and protected by thick, high walls that kept the Chinese rabble out, continued to study the scriptures and dream of an Americanized New China. Their children — "mish kids" — grew up in this otherworld where they absorbed an idealized portrait of their home country. Pearl described the America she learned about as a "dream world, fantastically beautiful, inhabited by a people...entirely good, a land indeed from which all blessings flowed."[17] As Henry R. Luce admitted later in life, "I probably gained a too romantic, too idealistic view of America....I had no experience of evil in terms of Americans."[18] Thus two mirages: one of an infallible United States, the other of a China that, with some effort and internal allies, might be brought to mirror the flawless United States of America.

Churchgoers back in the United States listened attentively as letters from their hometown missionaries, who had answered the call to save the greatest number of pagans in the world, were read from the pulpit. One China-based missionary wrote home, "How can we save [China] from her own weaknesses? How can we touch her heart to her own dreadful wickedness and weakness?...These are the thoughts that burn in us by day and night."[19] Parishioners responded to the mission-aries' hopeful dreams by digging deep into their Sunday-best pockets and purses and sending a river of nickels and dimes flowing across the Pacific Ocean in support of the New China mirage.

The reality in China was that almost none of the Three Hundred Million became Christians. Twenty years after his arrival, Sydenstricker admitted, "We are by no means overtaking these millions with the Gospel. They are increasing on us."[20]

The year of Franklin Delano Roosevelt's birth—1882—was a water-shed year for U.S.-China relations. At America's inception, the concept of illegal immigration did not exist; all foreigners had been welcome to its shores. That changed with the Chinese Exclusion Act of 1882. For the first time, the U.S. erected a gate with the specific goal of excluding nonwhites from the country.

In the early nineteenth century, merchants and missionaries had created the impression that Chinese men and women were laughably inefficient, lazy drug addicts who would be better off in a Christian-ized and Americanized New China. But when Chinese immigrants sailed to California to mine gold, they mined more efficiently, saved more of their earnings, and drank and caroused less than their white counterparts. George Hearst, a mining magnate and later a U.S. sena-tor from California, observed Chinese miners for ten years in four different states, and he worried: "They can do more work than our people and live on less...they could drive our laborers to the wall."[21]

During the building of the Transcontinental Railroad, white immigrants from Europe tried to bore through the hard granite of the Sierra Nevada Mountains and failed. Yet the Chinese, generally with smaller physical stature and strength, succeeded in the Sierras, laying the most challenging sections of the railroad. Governor Leland Stanford of California wrote President Andrew Johnson, "Without the Chinese it would have been impossible to complete the western portion of this great National highway."[22]

The California gold rush and the building of the Transcontinental Railroad were one-off affairs, but what happened next galvanized white-male-dominated Big Labor. With the railway complete, the now unemployed Chinese workers fanned out across the West, becoming miners, farmers, and hotel, restaurant, and laundry owners. With a frugal, disciplined lifestyle and diligent work habits, the Chinese frequently produced goods and services of higher quality and at lower prices than their American competitors. White workers who were merely irritated when a fellow Caucasian did better were shocked and outraged when bested by a member of a supposedly lesser race. Senator James Blaine of Maine warned that those "who eat beef and bread and drink beer...will have to drop his knife and fork and take up the chopsticks" if the Chinese were allowed to stay in America.[23]

Pressure from labor unions moved Congress to act. Samuel Gompers, the president of the American Federation of Labor, explained, "Racial differences between American whites and Asiatics would never be overcome. The superior whites had to exclude the inferior Asiatics, by law, or if necessary by force of arms."[24] Unions led by the Knights of Labor raised the call: "The Chinese must go!"

"The Chinese Must Go!" The cleansing of the Chinese from America's West created a vacuum in U.S.-Chinese affairs, as few Americans would ever encounter a Chinese person again. (Courtesy Everett Collection)

Senator George Hoar of Massachusetts described the Chinese Exclusion Act as "nothing less than the legalization of racial discrimination."[25] Yet most Americans supported the racist legislation. Twenty-four years old and just out of Harvard, Theodore Roosevelt proclaimed in 1882, "No greater calamity could now befall the United States than to have the Pacific slope fill up with a Mongolian population."[26]

The Chinese Exclusion Act allowed Big Labor vigilantes to take things into their own gun-toting hands. Rock Springs, Wyoming, was a windy and dusty coal-mining town that produced almost 50 percent of the coal that fueled the Transcontinental Railroad. Seven hundred to nine hundred Chinese lived in Rock Springs, along with about three hundred whites. On the morning of September 2, 1885, the town's white miners and others fortified themselves with whiskey and talk of solving their "Chinese problem." They surrounded Rock Springs' Chinatown and began to shoot. Unarmed Chinese were killed in cold blood while others ran in terror. White women who had formerly tutored the Chinese in English now entered those homes in search of loot. The Chinese who fled to the surrounding countryside were ambushed by Knights of Labor gunmen who had been waiting to pick them off.

The first Wyoming state official to arrive in Rock Springs described the scene:

> Not a living Chinaman—man, woman or child—was left in the town, where 700 to 900 had lived the day before, and not a single house, shanty, or structure of any kind, that had ever been inhabited by a Chinaman was left unburned. The smell of burning human flesh was sickening and almost unendurable, and was plainly discernible for more than a mile along the railroad both east and west.[27]

A horrified Governor Francis Warren of Wyoming sent this message to President Grant:

> An armed body of white men at Rock Springs, Wyoming, have attacked Chinese coal miners, working for Union Pacific Rail-

way at that point. Have driven Chinamen out of town into hills. Have burned their houses and are destroying railroad property; some forty houses burned; three men known to be killed, many more believed to be. Mob now preventing some five hundred Chinamen from reaching food or shelter.[28]

Sixteen white miners were charged with riot, arson, murder, and robbery. The man who heard the case—justice of the peace John Ludvigsen—was a dues-paying member of the Knights of Labor. When asked to serve on the jury, one prominent Rock Springs man declined, saying his back was "not bulletproof."[29] There were no convictions.

Many communities followed the Rock Springs example. On September 28, 1885, Mayor Jacob Neisbach of Tacoma, Washington, chaired a meeting of white laborers at the Knights of Labor hall to discuss Tacoma's "Chinese problem." The next day Neisbach led an armed mob of about five hundred to Chinatown, where the men forced the Chinese out of their homes and marched them to a waiting train. The train, bound for Portland, pulled out but stopped eight miles down the track, where a second mob robbed the terrified Chinese and herded them into the wilderness, whipping those who didn't move fast enough.

At dawn on February 7, 1885, the Seattle chief of police led an armed mob to Seattle's Chinatown and then marched the frightened Chinese to a warehouse by the wharf, where they spent an uneasy night. The next day the Chinese were loaded onto a steamer at gunpoint and sent off. "The trouble is over," wrote a local reporter, "and the people have proved their ability to govern themselves. They have done this not as the friends of the Chinese, but as the friends of law."[30]

The cleansing of the Chinese continued across the West. In Santa Cruz, New Mexico, the Chinese were given twenty-four hours to leave. Near Douglas Island, Alaska, one hundred Chinese were herded onto a boat and set adrift in the Pacific. In Grass Creek, Utah, all Chinese were run out of town. The Knights of Labor called a mass meeting in

Butte, Montana, site of extensive copper mines and a flourishing Chinatown, and the assembled throng passed a unanimous resolution calling for the dismissal of all Chinese from their jobs and for their expulsion from the area. At a mining camp near Orofino, Idaho, white miners hung the five Chinese who worked there. The Chinese of Cheyenne, Wyoming, fled after posters warned that if they didn't leave they would be tarred and feathered.

For years after the establishment of the Chinese Exclusion Act and the resulting race cleansing of the Chinese from the West, very few Americans would behold a Chinese person. The Chinese remaining in the country were restricted to their Chinatowns, like the Indians on their reservations, invisible to most Americans. The majority of Americans were now cut off from these people of the world's most populous country and thus unable to form direct relationships with Chinese and take their measure. This left an enormous void of understanding.

Four years after the Chinese Exclusion Act, Americans dedicated the Statue of Liberty, which had these immortal words on its pedestal: " 'Give me your tired, your poor, your huddled masses yearning to breathe free, the wretched refuse of your teeming shore.' "

Poor, huddled, wretched—such terms were mostly unheard-of in Roosevelt family parlors in Manhattan and Hyde Park, New York. Theodore and Franklin Delano Roosevelt were raised in a European manner, studied European history and languages, and steamed across the Atlantic numerous times, so that they were able to form their own opinions about Europeans based on firsthand experience. Theodore and Franklin attended America's best private college—Harvard— which offered no courses in the Chinese language or philosophy, and neither one ever crossed the Pacific to see China for himself. China was not much of a subject during Theodore's childhood. But the Middle Kingdom came alive to Franklin as he listened raptly to the exotic tales about New China told by his mother, grandfather, aunts, and uncles, who in truth had only marginally more direct experience of the Chinese than Americans who had never visited.

In 1877, just five years before she gave birth to Franklin, Sara returned to Hong Kong for a long visit with her sisters Annie and Dora (both had married Russell and Company partners), and she stayed at Rose Hill, where she had lived as a little girl. Years later, when Dora and Annie traveled home from Hong Kong for visits, they entertained young Franklin with pidgin English and stories of weird Chinese ways. As one Roosevelt chronicler wrote, "By the time FDR reached adulthood, Delano memories of the 1862 voyage to Hong Kong and their experiences there during the American Civil War were as real to him as if he had personally sailed...to that distant port of call to take up the life of a 'Foreign Devil' of China-merchant pedigree."[31]

James Roosevelt was fifty-four years old and his wife, Sara Delano, was twenty-eight when their son, Franklin, was born. James, a loving but relatively elderly father, died when Franklin was just eighteen years old. His wife, however, was a vigorous young mother who made her son her mission and dominated Franklin's early years, even home-schooling him. One special day Sara gave her son the beloved stamp collection she had assembled from letters her father had sent her from Asia.

Young Franklin lionized Grandpa Delano and loved to visit him at Algonac, just down the Hudson from Hyde Park. The child would race to the parlor where Warren Delano sat surrounded by Chinese art and furnishings, report his progress in school, and read his school-boy essays as Grandpa nodded his approval. Warren was a gifted storyteller and he fired his grandson's imagination with colorful tales of a faraway people who would be better off if they were more like Americans.

Years later Franklin's son Elliott admitted, "Delano ships sailing out of New Bedford made the family rich...[money] earned from the sale of opium."[32] But none of Warren's stories told at Algonac revealed this fact. When Delano's fellow Russell and Company partner Robert Bennet Forbes asked him to write his reminiscences about the

Franklin Delano Roosevelt (top) with his grandfather Warren Delano in a wheelchair (Courtesy of the Franklin D. Roosevelt Library and Museum, Hyde Park, New York)

old China trade, Warren responded with a short account that never mentioned the main source of his fortune. Geoffrey Ward, the prime chronicler of Franklin Delano Roosevelt's younger days, concluded, "In a family fond of retelling and embellishing even the mildest sort of ancestral adventures, no stories seem to have been handed down concerning Warren Delano's genuinely adventurous career in the opium business."[33] One of his sons remembered how strictly Warren Delano "complied with the admonition not to let his right hand know what his left hand was doing."[34]

Franklin Delano Roosevelt had five uncles, five aunts, two great-uncles, and a few great-aunts—all from his mother's Delano line. Having no brothers or sisters except for a much older half brother from his father's first marriage, Franklin shared his childhood with an ever-widening circle of Delano cousins. As her son grew older, Sara told Franklin that he bore a close physical resemblance to her father, which likely pleased him greatly—and she had no doubts about which side of the family he came down on character-wise. Her son, Sara was fond of saying, was "a Delano, not a Roosevelt at all."[35]

Warren Delano's legacy would be much more than financial. His narrative became the foundation of FDR's understanding of China. Roosevelt would tell his secretary of the treasury Henry Morgenthau, "Please remember that I have a background of a little over a century in Chinese affairs."[36]

Chapter 3

THE JAPANESE MONROE DOCTRINE FOR ASIA

Japan is playing our game.
—President Theodore Roosevelt[1]

T he Mexican-American War from 1846 to 1848 resulted in Mexico's ceding to the United States much of what is now the American West. U.S. Navy planners and their political supporters dreamed of a sea-lane across the Pacific that would connect China to America's newly acquired ports on the West Coast—San Diego, Los Angeles, San Francisco, Portland, and Seattle.

In 1848 the U.S. Navy's chief oceanographer opened a new chapter in American and Japanese history with his testimony before the Naval Affairs Committee in the U.S. House of Representatives. Lieutenant Matthew Maury first focused the congressmen's attention on a huge world globe. Maury bent down, opened a leather satchel, and withdrew a ball of string. He placed one end of the string on San Francisco and ran it to the next landfall, the independent kingdom of Hawaii. Maury wanted to show how the string could eventually get to Shanghai, for the purpose of his testimony was to secure funding for the Navy to penetrate Asia, with China — the richest and most populous country in Asia — the prime target. American coal-fired steamships could make it from San Francisco to Hawaii without re-coaling but not from Hawaii to Shanghai. The U.S. Navy needed an intermediate coaling stop and refreshment station. Maury pointed to a tiny island far out in the Pacific, just six hundred miles south of Tokyo, that could serve this function.

The island was Chichi Jima, a beautiful slab of jade-green hills set in sparkling blue waters. (The U.S. Navy also considered Chichi Jima's neighbor island as a candidate for American expansion, but that island was gray and had rotten-egg sulfur fumes rising from its sands. In English, its name translated to "Sulfur Island." Its Japanese name was Iwo Jima.)

If the U.S. Navy could acquire land on Chichi Jima and build a coaling station/refreshment stop there, then the last leg of America's sea-lane to Asia would be in place, as the distance from Chichi Jima to Shanghai was only fifteen hundred miles.

Japan at that time was a closed country to Americans, but it was at peace with its neighbors, bothering nobody, with no military-industrial complex. Its highly literate population enjoyed what some historians argue was the highest standard of living in the world in terms of education, health care, culture, food, and longevity.

To "open" Japan, Commodore Matthew Perry was chosen to lead the largest U.S. naval squadron in history. The U.S. Navy wanted Japan to serve as what a twentieth-century Japanese prime minister would describe as America's "unsinkable aircraft carrier."[2] Japan would be America's springboard to China.

At the time, Commodore Perry was arguably the most famous and admired naval commander in the world. Perry had mounted the largest amphibious attack in U.S. history on Mexico's Pacific coast. He sailed to Asia with huge modern warships bristling with cannons; his armada could pulverize Japan's wood-and-paper cities in hours. Perry brought along two books (*War in Mexico* and *History of the War in Mexico*) about his previous military exploits as gifts for the Japanese, so they'd get the message about what would happen if they resisted America's "friendship."

As an explanation for Perry's hugely expensive mission, the American public was told, somewhat vaguely, that the U.S. was going to open Japan to Western, Christian, and American civilization. Americans perceived this as a kindly outreach to help the heathen Japanese. How U.S. Navy ships packed with cannons and rifles were going to achieve such a benevolent outcome was neither questioned nor explained.

Commodore Perry's squadron steamed from America's East Coast, went around Cape Town at the bottom of Africa, crossed the Indian Ocean, skirted Singapore, and then sailed up to the western New Chinas on the coast. In Hong Kong and Shanghai, Perry lived in luxury in Russell and Company palaces, surrounded by servants.

Perry left China's coast and headed for Tokyo. Along the way, he stopped off in Okinawa and sailed near Iwo Jima, and on the morning of June 16, 1853, Perry and his sailors rowed ashore at Chichi Jima. On behalf of the U.S. Navy, Perry purchased fifty acres of land from an American living there, fifty-eight-year-old Nathaniel Savory. The price paid was fifty dollars, four cattle, five Shanghai sheep, and six goats. The U.S. Navy now had a key stepping-stone to China. (It would be many years before I realized that my father, U.S. Navy corpsman John Bradley, fought in 1945 among Japanese islands that had been eyed ninety-two years earlier by the U.S. Navy.)

Two weeks later, on Friday, July 8, 1853, Commodore Perry steamed into Tokyo Bay. The Japanese politely but firmly asked him to leave, as his ships' presence there violated Japanese law. Perry demanded a meeting. The Japanese pleaded with him to leave them alone. Perry threatened war, claiming he could muster one hundred British and American warships within a month. The Japanese reluctantly agreed to one meeting.

When the two sides met, Perry grandly presented a custom-made gold box with President Millard Fillmore's letter to the emperor inside. A Japanese official then gave Perry a note: "The letter being received, you will leave here."[3]

Insulted, Perry returned to his armada and threatened to attack Tokyo. Many more threats by the U.S. military caused the Japanese to give in and sign the United States–Japan Treaty of Amity and Commerce on July 29, 1858, an unequal treaty similar to the ones America had forced upon China.

The American challenge startled and alarmed Japanese leaders. This was the era of aggressive ambition by the West. The American military had just chewed off a chunk of Mexico and was in the midst of clearing Native Americans off the fruited plain, the marauding Russian bear had Pacific intentions, and the British, Dutch, and French would soon have a string of colonies from Hong Kong to Morocco.

The Japanese understood that Americans saw Asians as they did Indians and African slaves: a racially inferior people in need of American help. So the men around Emperor Meiji opted for a Leave Asia/ Tilt West foreign policy that presented the Japanese to Americans as more Western than Asian.

The Western powers were powerful because they threw their militaries around. Japanese leaders chanted a new national slogan: *Fukoku kyohei,* or "Rich country, strong military." Japan built a Western-style military-industrial complex, something no other Asian nation would do for generations.

"Japan's new leaders soon concluded that they needed a counterpart to God and Christianity in the West," my former professor John Dower wrote in *Japan in War and Peace.*[4] These founding fathers elevated their boy emperor to a god and dressed Meiji in a Western-style military uniform with medals on his chest.

To appear more Western, Japanese who dealt with foreigners donned Brooks Brothers suits and practiced drinking French cognac from snifters. Japan's leaders sent college-age men abroad to study the West's governmental and military systems.

So successful was the Leave Asia/Tilt West policy that Americans began referring to the Japanese as the Yankees of the Far East. One American marveled that it was as if the U.S. had "unmoored Japan

Emperor Meiji. To deal with the West's threat, he did what no other Asian leader did: he built a modern military-industrial complex. (Mary Evans Picture Library / Everett Collection)

from the coast of Asia, and towed it across the Pacific, to place it along-side of the New World, to have the same course of life and progress."[5]

Japan required large amounts of American oil and steel to build its modern Western-style military-industrial complex. Beginning soon after Commodore Perry opened Japan and, except for 1941 to 1945, continuing until recently, Japan has been America's number-one Asian customer.

Emperor Meiji's most trusted confidant was Prince Hirobumi Ito, the man who helped install Meiji on his throne, wrote Meiji's first consti-tution, served as Meiji's first prime minister, and went on to serve as prime minister three more times.[6] Irrespective of these formal posts, Ito was constantly at Meiji's side. Schooled in London, Ito was a worldly man who was acquainted with several world leaders, among them Theodore Roosevelt. According to Meiji's biographer Donald Keene, "The emperor valued Ito's opinions more than those of anyone else."[7]

In the spring of 1895, the fifty-four-year-old Prince Ito journeyed back to his hometown to proclaim Japan's entrance into the league of the big powers. The little island of Japan had just shocked the world by besting huge continental China in the bitterly fought Sino-Japanese War. Ito insisted that Chinese diplomats come to Japan to negotiate peace terms. On April 17, 1895, as cherry blossoms bloomed outside, Ito sat erect across a huge table from his Chinese counterparts in the grand Shunpanrō Hall and proudly signed his name to the Treaty of Shimonoseki, which forced China to cede lands, including Taiwan,

Prince Hirobumi Ito: Meiji's most important adviser, Japan's first prime minister, Baron Kaneko's influencer, and admirer of Theodore Roosevelt (CPA Media / Pictures From History)

to Japan and pay an expensive indemnity. Japan had come a long way in the forty-two years since the scare of Perry's black ships.

Nine years after the end of Japan's previous war, on the afternoon of Thursday, February 4, 1904, Emperor Meiji held an imperial conference with his royal advisers. The subject: whether Japan should launch a surprise attack on the Russian navy.

The problem for Japan was that the Russians, driven by their own sense of manifest destiny, were expanding eastward. The Trans-Siberian Railway, currently under construction, could significantly alter the regional balance of power. Now Russia was focused on Manchuria, in North China, a vast land the size of Germany and France combined, with virgin forests, lush farmland, and great mineral wealth. Furthermore, the warm-water anchorage at its southernmost port would provide the czar with a naval base to make Russia a Pacific power.

Most alarming to the Japanese was the possibility that Russia would penetrate North China, which would put Korea in play. Kaiser Wilhelm of Germany wrote to his cousin the Russian czar, "It is evident to every unbiased mind that Korea must be and will be Russian."[8] Japan had its own dreams of expansion, and because it was an island nation, its first step onto the Asian mainland had to be at the Korean Peninsula. (At their closest point, Korea and Japan are less than two hundred miles apart.) Russian control of Korea would not only squash Japanese expansionism but threaten Japan's very existence. Prince Ito styled Korea as the "dagger pointed at the heart of Japan."[9]

Ito had tried many times to negotiate with the Russians, but the czar brushed him off, believing that the Japanese were afraid to fight mighty Christian Russia. Fearing the expansion of the Trans-Siberian Railway and the Russian threat to Korea, and outraged by the czar's condescending treatment of Japan's emissaries, the Japanese public howled for war.

Emperor Meiji and Prince Ito believed there was little alternative to a military clash, but they were not optimistic about their chances. Both knew that Japan was much weaker financially and militarily than the Russian bear. To defeat the czar, Japanese forces would have to make

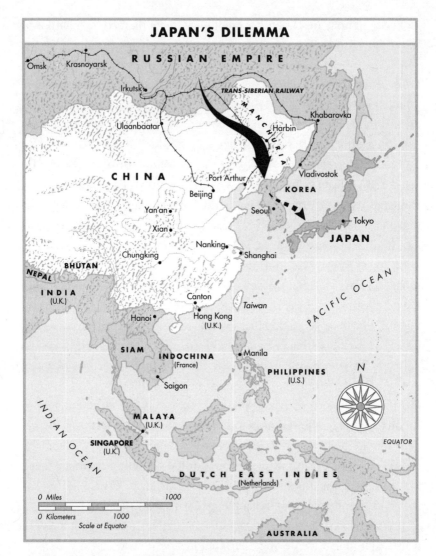

In 1904, Japan worried about its survival. If Russia took Korea, Japan's westward expansion would be blocked and Russia could invade Japan.

an almost impossible march across thousands of miles of territory to St. Petersburg and then contend with the millions of men Russia had to throw into the fight. Meiji and Ito decided that the best thing Japan could do was launch a surprise attack against Russia's navy, fight to a stalemate, and hope for a mediated peace. Looking ahead, they wondered which neutral country could mediate. The European powers were out of the question because Japan was allied with Great Britain while Russia had treaties with Germany and France. The conversation turned to Japan's best chance: the United States and its young president, Theodore Roosevelt.

Emperor Meiji's conference with his advisers broke up just after five o'clock in the afternoon. Prince Ito returned home, having decided that he would dispatch a trusted lieutenant to the United States to present Japan's case in the court of public opinion (a combination of what the Japanese called *koho gaiko,* "public diplomacy," and *gaikoku shinbun soju,* "manipulation of foreign newspapers"). At about five thirty, Ito telephoned Baron Kentaro Kaneko at his home.

Baron Kaneko was quietly celebrating his fifty-first birthday when he received Ito's urgent phone call. The prince had been instrumental in Kaneko's career and had sent him to Harvard to learn American ways. In 1888, Kaneko graduated from Harvard Law School, where he

Baron Kentaro Kaneko. The secret Roosevelt-Kaneko talks lasted nineteen months.
(Courtesy of the Library of Congress)

had studied under Oliver Wendell Holmes. When Ito became Japan's first prime minister, Kaneko served as his secretary and helped Ito write Japan's first constitution. Kaneko had visited the United States twice after his graduation from Harvard and was acquainted with many American leaders.

Kaneko rushed through Tokyo's darkened, wintry streets in a hired car, arriving at Ito's doorstep about six thirty. The prince was pensive as the two men sat at a simple dinner while discussing the news of Japan's forthcoming war and Kaneko's relationship with Theodore Roosevelt.

Baron Kaneko and Theodore Roosevelt shared a warm and strong bond in an era when few but the highborn attained college degrees. They had attended Harvard, America's greatest university, at the same time, but they didn't meet there, as Roosevelt had been an undergraduate when Kaneko attended the law school. They first connected in 1890 at Roosevelt's Washington home, when a mutual Harvard friend provided an introduction. At that point, Kaneko had already been a prime minister's right-hand man and the first president of Japan University. Roosevelt, serving in Washington as a civil service commissioner, would probably have been bewildered by the average Japanese, but Kaneko appeared to be an Americanized Asian, the kind most likely to appeal to Roosevelt's patrician class. He was wellborn (of samurai blood), a titled aristocrat, and a Harvard lawyer.

Kaneko was taken with Teddy, as he later wrote: "From the moment we first met and spoke together, I realized how great a man this was. I could see that he would surely become President in the future."[10] After Kaneko returned to Japan, the two men maintained their friendship by exchanging occasional letters and Christmas cards.

When their dinner dishes had been cleared, Prince Ito issued Baron Kaneko his orders:

> I want you to go immediately to America... whether this war continues for one year, two years or three years, if the outcome (victory or defeat) is not clear a third country will have to come between Japan and Russia as mediator... [and] the only coun-

try we can ask to do this is America. Only President Roosevelt can stand impartially between Russia and Japan and advise them about achieving peace.... You have previously been on intimate terms with Roosevelt, so we want you to go immediately and meet him and tell him this privately, and also do your best to arouse the sympathies of the American people for Japan.[11]

President Roosevelt had hosted Prince Ito at a White House luncheon soon after President McKinley's assassination in 1901.[12] The men had discussed the Russian threat in North China and the czar's attempts to pressure China into granting Russia special privileges there. Roosevelt had never traveled to Asia and knew few Asians. Indeed, at the time, he had never seen the Pacific Ocean. Raymond Esthus notes in *Theodore Roosevelt and the International Rivalries*, "Roosevelt was poorly informed about the Far East...[his] personal diplomatic contacts remained almost completely Europe-oriented."[13] He was far from alone in this orientation.

In 1898, the United States had declared its Open Door policy, which proposed free trade for all countries within China, with no country taking over whole areas and blocking access to other countries. To stateside Americans, the Open Door policy sounded like a high-minded defense of China's territorial integrity against rapacious European imperialists. In reality, the policy was an attempt to keep the playing field level for American business interests. Great Britain had long benefited from trade with China, and now the expanding United States wanted some of the action. Chinese people were not welcome in America, but Americans had no qualms about demanding a red carpet for themselves in China when it came to commerce.

In 1898, a secret U.S. Treasury memorandum identified the Philippines as a key stepping-stone to the Chinese marketplace:

The Philippines [stand] guard at the entrances to trade with the millions of China...the possession of the Philippines by a progressive, commercial power, if the Nicaragua canal project should be completed, would change the course of ocean navigation as it concerns a large percentage of the water-borne traffic of the world.[14]

The Panama Canal had not been built yet, but it would complete the long-sought route that would stream China's riches to ports on America's East Coast. The United States then fomented the Spanish-American War and took over the Philippines, Guam, Hawaii, Cuba, and Puerto Rico to establish an American sea-lane from China.

By the time Theodore Roosevelt became president, in 1901, China was being squeezed between the Anglo-American and Russian empires. Roosevelt realized that the Russian extension of the Trans-Siberian Railway meant that China's riches would flow overland to Europe rather than across the Pacific to the United States. Like the Japanese, Roosevelt grasped that Russian control of the warm-water anchorage at Port Arthur on the China Sea would enable the czar to base part of his navy there and dominate the region. Professor Franklin Giddings of Columbia University warned, "The great question of the twentieth century is whether the Anglo-Saxon or the Slav is to impress his civilization to the world."[15] Passenger guidebooks found on the Trans-Siberian Railway saw that battle as won, proclaiming, "The honor of having planted the flag of Christianity and civilization in Asia is due to Russia."[16]

Theodore Roosevelt had entered Harvard College in 1876, at the age of eighteen. Like all American universities at that time, Harvard considered social and historical questions primarily from their race standpoint. Roosevelt learned about the glorious destiny of the "higher races" and how the Aryan had arisen in the Caucasus to found the white race, migrated to Europe to become the Teuton, and then gone on to the British Isles to morph into the most superior race of all, the Anglo-Saxon.[17]

After Harvard, Roosevelt studied for a year at Columbia University, where his favorite teacher was the renowned professor of political science John Burgess. Burgess taught that because the white Teuton possessed "superior political genius" and "political endowment," Teutonic countries like the United States had the right to submit "un-political nations" to "political subjection." Wrote Burgess, "I do not think that Asia and Africa can ever receive political organization in any other way."[18] Roosevelt echoed Burgess when he later declared that for the teeming millions in Asia, "fitness [for self-government] is not a God-given, natural right, but comes to a race only through the slow growth of centuries."[19]

Theodore Roosevelt had grown up during the peak anti-Chinese years in U.S. history, a period when Americans were ridding their nation of the inferior Chinese. Like many of his fellow citizens, Roosevelt referred to Chinese people as "Chinks" and viewed Chinese men as particularly ludicrous, with their dresses and their hair tied in sissy pigtails, both of which were likely seen as affronts to a masculine man like Teddy Roosevelt.

When Theodore Roosevelt became president, Terence Powderly, the former leader of the Knights of Labor, the group that had led the race war against the Chinese in the 1880s, was head of the U.S. Bureau of Immigration. Early in the Roosevelt administration, Powderly wrote, "American and Chinese civilizations are antagonistic; they cannot live and thrive and both survive on the same soil. One or the other must perish."[20] In 1902, Roosevelt tightened the Chinese Exclusion Act, requiring the very few Chinese who had somehow managed to enter America to carry ID cards or face arrest and deportation.

Analyzing Asia through the prism of race, Roosevelt concluded that China was on the verge of collapse, like an old rotted barn. Yet he had no fondness for the Slavs moving in from the west. Teddy took to calling Nicholas the "preposterous little Tsar"[21] and wrote about the Russians, "No human beings, black, yellow, or white[,] could be quite as untruthful, as insincere, as arrogant—in short, as untrustworthy in every way—as the Russians."[22]

But Roosevelt's opinion of the Japanese was just as Japan had shaped it to be with decades of Yankees of the Far East propaganda in its Leave Asia/Tilt West campaign. Instead of resisting Western incursion, as other Asian countries had done with barbarians, the Japanese feigned cooperation. Instead of criticizing Westerners, Prince Ito told the Yankees what they wanted to hear, that just as the Japanese had earlier in their history adopted and adapted to Chinese ways, now they would Americanize. The new Japanese, in Ito's telling, were a distinct race separate from the Chinese, just as an ocean separated Japan from the Asian mainland. Americans learned that the new Japanese embraced American manners, dress, and technology and welcomed American teachers, missionaries, and governmental advisers to help modernize their economy.

Teddy Roosevelt was convinced that the Japanese were indeed different from other Asians. While he was president, Roosevelt wrote that, unlike the Chinese, the Japanese were "a wonderful and civilized people...entitled to stand on an absolute equality with all the other peoples of the civilized world."[23] In particular, he believed that Japan's

"The Progress of Civilization": American hearts were warmed by the belief that their values were spreading in Asia as the Japanese became the Yankees of the Far East. (Mary Evans Picture Library / Everett Collection)

military success was a key indicator of the worth of their civilization: "All the great masterful races have been fighting races; and the minute that a race loses the hard fighting virtues, then...it has lost its proud right to stand as the equal of the best."[24] After observing the Japanese army fighting alongside the allies in the Chinese Boxer Rebellion of 1900, Roosevelt gushed to a friend, "What extraordinary soldiers those little Japs are."[25] Roosevelt likened the Japanese to the Teutons of two thousand years earlier who had risen in Europe and become civilized, just as the Japanese were doing now in Asia.

Roosevelt divided the world into what he called civilized and uncivilized nations. The civilized were mostly white industrialized nations, the citizens of which used the natural resources of the uncivilized nonwhites, who in turn purchased the industrial products of the civilized. To Roosevelt, it was the duty of the civilized to police the uncivilized, as Britain did in Africa and India.

In 1821 President James Monroe had announced to the European powers that they must not meddle in South America. Now Teddy upped the ante with his Roosevelt corollary to the Monroe Doctrine, declaring to Congress that the U.S. had "international police" power in the Caribbean, Central America, and South America, as well as in China, to enforce the Open Door policy.[26]

Looking toward Asia, Roosevelt saw Japan as an America-admiring civilized power that could guide uncivilized China. Roosevelt appreciated Japan as a counterweight to the czar's ambitions; Japan's fierce army could, he felt, stymie the Russian advance. He also believed that Japan — so accepting of wise Yankee ways — would help the United States Americanize the rest of Asia.

There was another big piece of the Asian puzzle: the ancient empire of Korea. To Roosevelt, Korea was an insignificant player, an "utterly impotent" country with a nonmartial people who could not defend themselves from either the Russians or the Japanese.[27] He saw the small empire wedged between China and Japan as a chip to be played to encourage the Japanese to oppose the Russians in North Asia. Roosevelt's opinions were at odds with what Americans understood to be their government's policy. In 1882, the United States and thirty-year-old Emperor Gojong of Korea[28] had signed a treaty. The very first article declared that there "shall be perpetual peace and friendship" between Korea and the United States. The U.S. promised to exert its "good offices" to help Gojong if Korea's independence was ever threatened.[29]

To Emperor Gojong, the good-offices clause was much more than a legal phrase. Koreans felt that the agreement meant that Elder Brother Roosevelt had a moral commitment to Korea. Said the emperor, "We have the promise of America; she will be our friend whatever happens."[30] He had no idea that back in 1900, Vice President Roosevelt had secretly written: "I should like to see Japan have Korea. She [Japan] will be a check upon Russia."[31]

On February 6, 1904, Roosevelt learned that Japan had broken off relations with Russia. Roosevelt wrote privately, "The sympathies of the United States are entirely on Japan's side, but we will maintain the strictest neutrality."[32] On February 8, 1904 — with no declaration of war — the Japanese navy attacked Russian ships in Korean ports. The Russians denounced the infamous sneak attack as a violation of international law. Roosevelt wrote, "I was thoroughly well pleased with the Japanese victory, for Japan is playing our game."[33]

Kaneko steamed into San Francisco Bay on March 11, 1904, his fifth journey to the United States. He told the reporters that America "sowed the first seed of Western civilization in our land, and from that seed has developed...a nation which is to-day doing what...[the] great powers long hesitated over — making a defiant stand against the Russian empire."[34] In Chicago and New York, he explained that Japan was fighting Russia to uphold Anglo-Saxon values.

When Kaneko reached Washington on March 26, 1904, Roosevelt set aside all other matters to give the baron his full attention. As Raymond Esthus wrote in *Theodore Roosevelt and Japan,* Roosevelt "took the Baron into his confidence completely."[35] Roosevelt maintained publicly that the U.S. was neutral, but he blurted out to Kaneko in their first meeting, "I have wholehearted sympathy for Japan...I have been waiting for an opportunity to tell you the real state of my mind....I am firmly convinced that Japan will win both on land and at sea."[36]

Over the next nineteen months, Kaneko was almost constantly in the president's presence or on his mind. When the baron was in town, Roosevelt hosted him in the White House from morning until midnight, in his office, over the dining table, and upstairs in his personal quarters. When Japan scored a battle victory, Roosevelt was quick to dash off a congratulatory "Banzai!" telegram. When one of the baron's many articles hit the press, Kaneko would receive a complimentary handwritten note on presidential stationery. Roosevelt welcomed the baron into his family. He introduced Kaneko to his children and instructed them to read the books Kaneko recommended; entrusted his wife, Edith, to Kaneko's care for a cruise down the Potomac; even hosted the baron at Sagamore, the "Summer White House," located in Oyster Bay, Long Island. For a year and a half, Prince Ito and Emperor Meiji would be privy to the president's innermost thoughts about the future of Asia, since Kaneko was quickly telegraphing Roosevelt's views to Tokyo in code.

Roosevelt swallowed Japan's Leave Asia/Tilt West pose, telling Kaneko that the Japanese were racially closer to Americans than to Russians, praising Japan for adopting a constitutional government, and agreeing that Japan's destiny was to be the great civilizer of Asia.[37] Roosevelt even suggested using the network of Harvard Clubs as a conduit for Japan's propaganda: "All members of the Harvard Club throughout the country are sure to have sympathy for Japan."[38]

Four days after Kaneko arrived in Washington, Roosevelt sat his family down for a White House luncheon in the baron's honor. Lunch with an Asian was quite a novelty for the Roosevelts, and now suddenly at the First Family's table was a Japanese baron from Roosevelt's alma mater who spoke excellent English.

"Edith, do you hear that?" Teddy called across the table at one point. Kaneko had just said that he'd believed that Roosevelt would be president from the moment they'd met, ten years earlier. "Here is a man who has kept a friendly eye on me from away off in Japan," Roosevelt exclaimed.[39] His ego stroked, Roosevelt said to Kaneko, "My love and respect for Japan is second to none." Roosevelt also sought some information: "I have not yet been able to understand the mentality of the Japanese people. If there are some books which I should read regarding the Japanese character...please tell me their titles."[40]

Kaneko asked if the president had read Inazo Nitobe's *Bushido: The Soul of Japan*. Neither Teddy nor Edith had heard of it, though Roosevelt was a voracious reader. Kaneko now had the opportunity to influence the president, who had just admitted that he was less than informed about things Japanese. Kaneko explained that the word *Bushido* referred to the samurai's code of honor, which was similar to the European tradition of chivalry. Kaneko promised to give the president a copy of the English version the next day.

A long private meeting with Theodore Roosevelt and a family luncheon in the White House within five days of the baron's arrival were highly visible seals of Teddy's approval, and soon Washington's elite vied to meet the president's Asian friend. Kaneko's Harvard mentor Supreme Court justice Oliver Wendell Holmes—one of the most respected men in Roosevelt's Washington—hosted an introductory luncheon. The main topic discussed was Japan's following of American-style legal norms, but the conversation was almost secondary to the fascination of Holmes and his guests with a Harvardized Asian. Between private events and lobbying, the baron spoke at George Washington University. Within a fortnight, the Japanese legation had become the hottest ticket in town; congressmen and senators stood in line to shake hands with the Japanese baron who spoke English with a Boston accent.

Then it was on to New York, where Kaneko passed muster with Wall Street's barons at a gathering on April 14 at the prestigious University Club, just off Fifth Avenue. For many of New York's powerful financiers, this was their first opportunity to converse with a Japanese person. Once again, Kaneko presented the mirage: America had westernized Japan, the Japanese were grateful, and now they would push back the Russians and help Christianize and Americanize the rest of Asia. Once again, he was successful; within forty days, Wall Street banks had sold millions of dollars of Japanese bonds. Roosevelt wrote Kaneko, "The extent of our sympathy for Japan can be seen in the foreign bonds...they have been subscribed five times over, which can only be because of the passionate sympathy of Americans for Japan."[41]

After conquering Washington and New York, the baron moved on to Boston for a speech at Harvard's historic Sanders Theater. An overflow crowd of several hundred people stood outside in heavy rain that night to hear the Japanese nobleman's speech.

Kaneko's presentation was a masterstroke of public diplomacy. In a long and impassioned plea to the American public, Kaneko explained, "Japan simply seeks in the present war to maintain the peace of Asia and conserve the influence of the Anglo-American civilization in the East."[42]

The Harvard Club of Japan reprinted six thousand copies of Kaneko's speech and distributed them to Harvard Clubs across the land as well as to President Roosevelt, his cabinet, Congress, state governors and legislators, newspaper publishers, and libraries. Under the impressive Harvard logo was Kaneko's claim: "Japan is really acting as the pioneer of Anglo-American civilization in the East. It is for this which we are fighting, and only this which is the meaning of the war."[43]

Prince Ito was thrilled with the extraordinary access he had to Roosevelt's thinking. Again and again, Roosevelt welcomed Kaneko into the White House for breakfasts, lunches, dinners, early-morning chats, afternoon meetings, and late-night ruminations. Perhaps only Edith and his children were at Teddy's side more frequently than Kaneko during this period.

Roosevelt's inner circle was well aware of the president's love affair with the Japanese. At one of the White House luncheons with Edith, Roosevelt gushed to Kaneko about the book *Bushido:*

> I gained a clear understanding for the first time of the Japanese moral character, and right away I ordered 30 copies from the bookstore to be sent to my friends and acquaintances. I also gave a copy to each of my five children and told them that they should read this book daily.[44]

Among those who benefited from Roosevelt's newfound Asian expertise were the members of his cabinet, to whom the president lectured from *Bushido.* Roosevelt hired a judo coach to compete against an American wrestling coach and then ordered a group of military officers to come to the White House to observe the East versus West match. (The judo expert triumphed.) Roosevelt peppered his secretary of state with memos explaining why the U.S. should favor Japan: "The Japs have played our game because they have played the game of civilized mankind."[45]

On March 17, 1905, Theodore and Edith Roosevelt awoke early, left the White House, and took a morning train to New York City. The First Couple paraded with thousands up Fifth Avenue in celebration of St. Patrick's Day. Soon after three o'clock, Teddy and Edith exited the procession, walked east along Seventy-Sixth Street for half a block, and then entered a private home. They were there for an important family wedding. Teddy was to give away the bride; his niece Eleanor Roosevelt was marrying his fifth cousin Franklin Delano Roosevelt.

The four Roosevelts had last seen each other two weeks earlier at Teddy's March 4 inauguration ceremony, where he'd made the ringing appeal "All I ask is a square deal for every man." Twenty-year-old Eleanor was more famous than twenty-three-year-old Franklin; she was the president's "orphan" niece, as the *New York Times* called her, the daughter of Teddy's deceased brother, Elliott.

At three thirty sharp, Teddy's daughter Alice, dressed in a white veil and holding a bouquet of pink roses, led the wedding procession down the wide flight of stairs from the third to the second floor. Behind the six bridesmaids came the president with Eleanor on his arm. The *New York Times* noted that Eleanor wore a pearl collar and a diamond bowknot. Theodore Roosevelt gave Eleanor Roosevelt to Franklin Roosevelt. The Reverend Endicott Peabody, founder and head of the Groton School—Franklin's prep-school alma mater—performed the ceremony.

A majority of the wedding guests had something in common: their families had made their fortunes in the China opium trade. Eleanor's jewelry and Franklin's money came not from the Roosevelts but from the Delano line. Reverend Peabody was wealthy because his grandfather Joseph Peabody had made a fortune dealing drugs in New China. Paul Forbes, descendant of the man who had replaced Warren as consul in Canton and who had hosted Commodore Perry, was in attendance. A. A. Low was there, a descendant of Warren Delano's opium friend, the man who had provided the ship in which the Delano family sailed to Hong Kong. The bloodlines of many of the guests intertwined, owing to numerous marriages among the Cushings, Cabots, and other families, all clans with roots in the most profitable commodity trade of the nineteenth century.

Back in Washington after the wedding, Roosevelt informed Kaneko that he was about to leave for a monthlong bear hunt in Colorado's snowy Rocky Mountains. The baron noted that Russia's symbol was the bear and joked that he hoped Roosevelt would kill one. Roosevelt promised he would bag a bear for Meiji.

In March of 1905, when wave after wave of Japanese soldiers ran directly into Russian bullets during Japan's victory at the Battle of Mukden, Roosevelt wrote, "The Japanese are the most dashing fighters in the world!"[46] For the first time in modern history, an Asian country was besting a white Western Christian country. Roosevelt wrote Kaneko on White House stationery, "Judging by the state of affairs, all is going well and your army is advancing at full speed and power. Banzai!!"[47] When the baron later arrived at the White House for a celebration of the Mukden victory, Roosevelt's "face shone with joy over the unprecedented victory."[48] After his chat with Kaneko, Roosevelt told Secretary of War William Howard Taft, "I heartily agree with the Japanese terms of peace, insofar as they include Japan having the control of Korea."[49]

Roosevelt wrote to Kaneko after the Japanese navy defeated its Russian counterpart in the largest sea battle in world history, the Battle of Tsushima, "This is the greatest phenomenon the world has ever seen... I grew so excited that I myself became almost like a Japanese, and I could not attend to official duties."[50]

Though Japan appeared to be powerful—winning every battle against the Russians—the war was bleeding the tiny nation of men and money, while Russia had comparably inexhaustible resources. Prince Ito knew that Roosevelt had earlier told Baron Kaneko he was willing to mediate a settlement between the two countries while favoring the Japanese. Ito now gave the green light to begin the negotiations.

On May 31, Roosevelt received a telegram from Prince Ito requesting that the president invite Russia and Japan to open direct negotiations. Ito and Teddy agreed to keep Teddy's close communications with Tokyo a secret, as Roosevelt wrote to Senator Henry Cabot Lodge:

> I have of course concealed from everyone—literally everyone—
> the fact that I acted in the first place on Japan's suggestion....
> Remember that you are to let no one know that in this matter
> of the peace negotiations I have acted at the request of Japan
> and that each step has been taken with Japan's foreknowledge,
> and not merely with her approval but with her expressed
> desire.[51]

Roosevelt saw no need for China to participate in a peace conference that would give away Chinese territory. As Howard Beale observed in *Theodore Roosevelt and the Rise of America to World Power,* "Blinded by his concept of the Chinese as a backward people, he utterly failed to comprehend or take into account the rise of an independent and assertive China to a role of major importance in the twentieth century."[52]

Roosevelt discussed the peace negotiations with Baron Kaneko, knowing that Prince Ito would be apprised of the supposedly secret details. Kaneko was astonished that the president revealed so many confidential matters to him, but Roosevelt explained that he was able to speak to Kaneko without reservation as he was a fellow Harvard alumnus.

On July 2, Roosevelt announced that Russia and Japan would negotiate a treaty in Portsmouth, New Hampshire.

On the afternoon of Friday, July 7, 1905, Baron Kaneko strolled out of Manhattan's Hotel Leonori, went to the train station, and boarded the 4:50 train bound for Oyster Bay, on his way to spend the night at Sagamore Hill, Roosevelt's Long Island mansion. "Coming to see us here [in the White House,] you don't get an accurate idea of what our family life really is," Teddy had told Kaneko at one point. He had invited Kaneko to Oyster Bay, saying, "Then you will know more about us."[53]

Kaneko disembarked at the Oyster Bay station and waited for the president's train, which arrived soon after. Kaneko wrote that when the two men encountered each other on the train platform, Roosevelt welcomed him "with a face beaming all over with joy."[54]

Roosevelt's wood-and-stone home made a favorable impression on the descendant of samurai: "Compared with vacation houses of American politicians and wealthy men of property, the structure and decoration are very plain, and this is admirable in a president who advocates the 'simple life.' "[55]

At about eleven o'clock, Roosevelt and Kaneko withdrew to the president's study, where they talked about the peace negotiations. At around midnight, the two men grew tired. Kaneko recalled the tender manner in which Roosevelt made sure he was settled for the night:

> The President...lit two candles, one of which he gave me, while he carried the other himself, and showed me to my

bedroom upstairs. Thinking that the bed cover was too thin and that I would be cold in the night — he explained that a cold northeast wind usually came from the bay after midnight — he went downstairs and returned with a blanket on his shoulder.[56]

After breakfast the next day, Roosevelt led Kaneko out onto the porch where they could talk alone. Now the president readied himself for a momentous suggestion that Roosevelt knew Kaneko would relay to Emperor Meiji. It was an idea that would lead to a future day of infamy.

Kaneko later recalled what Roosevelt told him:

Japan is the only nation in Asia that understands the principles and methods of Western civilization. She has proved that she can assimilate Western civilization, yet not break up her own heritage. All the Asiatic nations are now faced with the urgent necessity of adjusting themselves to the present age. Japan should be their natural leader in that process, and their protector during the transition stage, much as the United States assumed the leadership of the American continent many years ago, and by means of the Monroe Doctrine, preserved the Latin American nations from European interference, while they were maturing their independence. If President Monroe had never enunciated the doctrine, which bears his name, the growth of the independent South America republics would have been interfered with by influences foreign to this continent. The future policy of Japan towards Asiatic countries should be similar to that of the United States towards their neighbors on the American continent. A "Japanese Monroe Doctrine" in Asia will remove the temptation to European encroachment, and Japan will be recognized as the leader of the Asiatic nations, and her power will form the shield behind which they can reorganize their national systems.... I will support [Japan] with all my power, either during my Presidency or after its expiration.[57]

*   *   *

Roosevelt dispatched his number-two man to Tokyo to seal the deal. Three weeks after Baron Kaneko's sleepover at Sagamore Hill, Secretary of War Taft arrived in Tokyo on a secret mission: to make Roosevelt's vision of a Japanese Monroe Doctrine official.[58]

Early on the morning of Thursday, July 27, Taft and Prime Minister Taro Katsura met secretly with no one else but an interpreter, who took no notes. (Taft later summarized the discussion in a secret memorandum to Roosevelt.) The order of topics and the content of the conversation were modeled on previous talks between President Roosevelt and Baron Kaneko.

Secretary Taft and Prime Minister Katsura first discussed race, agreeing that the yellow men of Japan posed no threat to the West. As an up-front quid pro quo, Katsura assured Taft that "Japan does not harbor any aggressive designs whatever on the Philippines." Katsura said that peace would come to North Asia only with an understanding between Japan, the U.S., and the UK. He realized that the U.S. Senate would not approve of what he was discussing but, as Taft noted, "in view of our common interests [Kaneko] could not see why some good understanding or an alliance in practice, if not in name, should not be made between these three nations insofar as respects the affairs in the Far East."[59]

Taft told him that the United States was "fully in accord with the policy of Japan and Great Britain in the maintenance of peace in the Far East" and that "whatever occasion arose, appropriate action of the Government of the United States, in conjunction with Japan and Great Britain...could be counted on by them quite as confidently as if the United States were under treaty obligation."[60] Taft's commitment to support Japan's expansion into Korea—"as if the United States were under treaty obligation"—would remain secret for almost two decades.[61]

Upon reading Taft's summary of the meeting, Teddy secretly cabled his secretary of war: "Your conversation with Count Katsura absolutely correct in every respect. Wish you would state to Katsura that I confirm every word you have said."[62] The *New York Times* soon published an interview with Prime Minister Katsura in which he said,

The introduction of all the blessings of modern civilization into the East Asiatic countries—that is our Far Eastern policy and behind it there is no more selfish motive than a simple desire for our own commercial and educational betterment. China and Korea are both atrociously misgoverned. They are in the hands of a lot of corrupt officials whose ignorance and narrow-mindedness are a constant menace to political tranquility in the Far East. These conditions we will endeavor to correct at the earliest possible date—by persuasion and education, if possible; by force, if necessary, and in this, as in all things, we expect to act in exact concurrence with the ideas and desires of England and the United States.[63]

In Seoul, Emperor Gojong had no idea that President Roosevelt, rather than standing up for Korean freedom as he was obliged to do by treaty, had instead approved Korea's death warrant. A court official in Seoul had assured a Western reporter, "We have the promise of America. She will be our friend whatever happens."[64]

In early September, the Russians and the Japanese signed the Portsmouth Peace Treaty, which, among other things, gave Prince Ito what he sought: control of Korea. After the treaty was announced, Roosevelt forwarded to friends highly selective accounts of his dealings with European heads of state Czar Nicholas and Kaiser Wilhelm. Based on these retellings, Roosevelt was awarded the Nobel Peace Prize.[65] Teddy kept mum about his extensive dealings with Emperor Meiji, thus cutting this critical U.S.-Japan story from American history.

Roosevelt threw a farewell party for Kaneko at Sagamore Hill on September 10, 1905, the seventh and last time the president hosted the baron at the Summer White House. After a family lunch, Roosevelt led Kaneko to his study and asked for advice on a presidential letter to Emperor Meiji. Then the two men walked to the living room, where Teddy had spread three large bearskins on the floor. Pointing to the largest, Roosevelt said, "This is the bearskin which I promised before.

*Emperor Gojong of Korea: "We feel that America is to us as an elder
brother," Gojong said. (CPA Media / Pictures From History)*

[Please] present it to the Emperor, and tell him that it is a souvenir
from me to commemorate the Russo-Japanese War."[66]

Kaneko thanked Roosevelt and promised to give the presidential
bearskin to Meiji. Then he brought up their earlier chat on the porch,
when Roosevelt had suggested a Japanese Monroe Doctrine for Asia.
Kaneko asked the president to go public with the idea.[67] Roosevelt
hedged: "I have no objection to your making this suggestion privately
to the leaders of your country's government, but I would like you to
delay making a public announcement for the time being. The reason is
that I would like to announce it publicly to the world myself after my
term of office has expired."[68]

Kaneko later wrote that at that point Edith strolled into the room, and the moment between the two men vanished. The three friends walked out onto the expansive lawn for their final good-bye.

Mission accomplished, Baron Kaneko returned to Japan. In several royal audiences attended by Prince Ito, Kaneko regaled Emperor Meiji with stories of his "public diplomacy" with President Roosevelt and the American media and people.

With Roosevelt's green light, Korea was now within Meiji's grasp, a goal he had pursued through two wars. To reward Prince Ito, Meiji asked him to be Japan's first civilian ruler of Korea. Ito would travel to Korea to inform the Korean emperor that his country now belonged to Japan.

Emperor Gojong knew the Japanese noose around his country's neck was tightening, and he reached out to Elder Brother Theodore Roosevelt by sending an American emissary, Homer Hulbert, to Washington. Hulbert was a Cornell graduate who had gone to Korea in 1886 as an educational missionary, and he and Emperor Gojong had become close.

Emperor Gojong asked Hulbert to appeal to President Roosevelt and ask him to use America's bully pulpit to forestall Japan's takeover of Korea. Hulbert later wrote,

> The appeal of the Emperor to the President of the United States cited the fact that Korea has heretofore received many tokens of good-will from the American government and people, that the American representatives have been sympathetic and helpful, and that American teachers of all kinds have done valuable work...he asked the President to bring to bear upon this question the same breadth of view and the same sympathy which had characterized his distinguished career in other fields; and if, after a careful investigation, the facts above enumerated and others that would come to light should seem to warrant him in so doing, he should use his friendly offices to prevent the disaster to Korea which seemed imminent. It will be noted that the Emperor asked that the President's action be based upon a careful examination of all the facts, and not upon mere hearsay.[69]

Homer Hulbert. Emperor Gojong dispatched Hulbert to Washington to plead for Korea's independence with President Theodore Roosevelt. (No credit given, part of the Public Domain)

Japanese detectives trailed Hulbert when he traveled to the U.S., and he later wrote, "The Japanese surmised what was being done. A Japanese spy on board the steamer at Yokohama discovered the exact hour when the message would arrive in Washington, and from that very hour events were hurried to their culmination in the Korean capital."[70]

When Hulbert reached Washington, both President Roosevelt and Secretary of State Elihu Root refused to see him. They were waiting for Japan's other shoe to drop in Seoul. As Hulbert later recalled,

> At the moment when Japan was just crouching to spring at the throat of Korea, the emperor of Korea called upon President Roosevelt to keep America's treaty with him—a treaty which held in its first clause the promise that if Korea were endangered by any third party this government would use its good

offices to effect an amicable arrangement. Roosevelt refused to read, or even to receive the written message sent to him from the emperor of a friendly power with which we were supposedly on friendly relations. That written message was taken to the state department, but the secretary of state refused to receive it for 48 hours. Meanwhile Japan at the point of the sword had forced her "protectorate" upon Korea.[71]

On November 15, 1905, Prince Ito shocked the Korean emperor by telling him that Japan would now control Korea and that Gojong would report to Ito. Emperor Gojong resisted, hoping that some force like Elder Brother Theodore Roosevelt would stay Japan's hand. Ito threatened Gojong, telling the Korean monarch that he had to agree to Japan's terms because Emperor Meiji had already approved the use of the Japanese military to overthrow Gojong if he refused. Defiant, Gojong told Ito to go try his luck with the Korean cabinet ministers.

Prince Ito ordered Gojong's cabinet to meet with him in the Japanese legation building in two days, on November 17, 1905. After hearing Ito's shocking demands, the Korean officials patriotically insisted that they would not forfeit their country. In response, Ito ordered the Japanese military police out of their barracks and onto the streets. (Japanese troops had occupied Korea since the outbreak of the Russo-Japanese War.) According to a Korean account, Japanese "machine guns were everywhere in the streets, and even field guns were brought out to command the strategic points of the city. They made feint attacks, occupied gates, put their guns into position, and did everything short of actual violence to prove to the Koreans that they were prepared to enforce their demands."[72]

That evening Prince Ito barged into Emperor Gojong's palace and demanded an audience. The Korean leader refused to see him. Ito forced his way into Gojong's presence and insisted the emperor summon his prime minister. Ito then shoved a Japanese-drafted agreement in front of the prime minister and ordered him to sign. The prime minister started crying. "Try to imagine what is in my heart!" he pleaded with Ito.[73] The prime minister, along with Emperor Gojong, the minister of finance, and the justice minister, refused to sign. But the next day, Ito was able to get the signatures of six lesser Korean cabinet members, the ministers of education, the army, the interior, foreign affairs, agriculture, and commerce and industry. Witnesses recalled Japanese soldiers with drawn bayonets threatening the men and the cries of the Koreans who signed. As Homer Hulbert later wrote, "At the point of the sword, Korea was forced to acquiesce 'voluntarily' in the virtual destruction of her independence once for all."[74]

The Japan-Korea Protectorate Treaty began: "The government of Japan, through the Department of Foreign Affairs at Tokyo, will hereafter have control and direction of the external relations and affairs at Korea, and diplomatic and consular representatives of Japan will have the charge of the subjects and interests of Korea in foreign countries."[75]

Korean newspapers courageously published editorials denouncing the treaty. Protesters filled some streets, and shops and schools closed. Japanese firing squads soon quieted things down.

A week after Japan took control of Korea, Secretary of State Elihu Root finally faced Homer Hulbert. As Hulbert remembered,

> President Roosevelt had hurriedly acknowledged that seizure without a word of warning to the Korean government nor a word to the Korean legation in Washington, and had cabled to our legation to get out of Korea. The State Department then offered to see the written message from Korea, and the writer has in his possession a note from the secretary of state saying that the message is "too late." It was there 48 hours before President Roosevelt took action and he knew its contents, for one of his secretaries at the White House told me so with his own lips.
>
> When that written message was handed to the secretary of state he leaned over the table and said to the envoy of the emperor: "Do you want us to get into trouble with Japan?" This

he said as Roosevelt's secretary of state, and it shows the cow-
ardly state of mind to which the administration was reduced by
the distant possibility of a clash with Japan. We did not dare to
assert our treaty rights nor live up to our treaty obligations.[76]

After his friend Prince Ito forced Korea's hand, Roosevelt finally
got around to addressing Emperor Gojong's plea, and he penned this
finely reasoned response to Secretary of State Root:

> I have carefully read through the letter of the Korean Emperor
> handed to you by Mr. Hulbert, an American long resident in
> Korea, to whose hand this letter had been entrusted. I under-
> stand from you that the Korean representatives here, so far as
> you know, are unacquainted with the existence of such a letter
> and that Mr. Hulbert understands that it is the wish of the
> Emperor that the existence of the letter should be kept secret
> and nothing said to anyone about it, and particularly not to the
> Japanese. Of course, these facts render it impossible for us to
> treat the letter as an official communication, for there is no way
> in which we could officially act without violating what Mr.
> Hulbert says is the Emperor's wish. Moreover, since the letter
> was written we have been officially notified that the Korean
> Government has made the very arrangement with Japan which
> in the letter the Emperor says he does not desire to make. All
> things considered I do not see that any practical action on the
> letter is open to us.[77]

Korea found few advocates. John Ford, the secretary of the American Asiatic Association, a major trade group, defended Japan's takeover of Korea because "the true peril of Asia and of the world is the
Muscovite, and not the yellow peril." (The American Asiatic Association's annual dinner the next year featured this toast: "The United
States and Japan—Guardian of the Portal and the Defender of the
Open Door."[78]) So it went.

On November 28, 1905, President Roosevelt turned over the U.S.
legation building in Seoul to Japan. Roosevelt later wrote a British offi-

cial that the closing of the U.S. legation was a signal that he, along with England, supported Japan's control of Korea. A State Department official in Seoul wrote in his diary that his fellow Americans fled Seoul "like the stampede of rats from a sinking ship."[79]

Emperor Meiji appointed Prince Ito to the colonial post of resident-general of Korea, the new boss of Emperor Gojong and Korea, a job that came with a custom-made uniform on which Ito proudly displayed a chestful of shiny medals.

Roosevelt later claimed he had not betrayed the U.S.-Korea treaty: "The treaty rested on the false assumption that Korea could govern herself well."[80] In his autobiography, Roosevelt wrote, "[Korea was] utterly impotent either for self-government or self-defense."[81] Homer

Resident General Hirobumi Ito (Korea's new Japanese dictator) and the Korean crown prince (Courtesy of the Library of Congress)

Hulbert concluded, "It was our duty to protest against Japan's encroachment in Korea...Roosevelt failed to protest the rapacity of Japan in 1905."[82]

Theodore Roosevelt was the first world leader to endorse Japan's military advancement onto the Asian continent. Roosevelt's Japanese Monroe Doctrine for Asia assumed the Japanese would push back the Russians, respect the Anglo-American Open Door policy, help Christianize and Americanize China, and maintain the Anglo-Americans' naval channel. But an American businessman who watched his fellow countrymen abandon Korea observed, "The Japs have got what they have been planning for these many moons and it is clear that Roosevelt played into their hands when he posed as the great peacemaker of the 20th century."[83]

A few years later, an American missionary visited Resident-General Ito in his headquarters nestled on the slope of Mount Namsan, overlooking the city of Seoul. Ito was dressed formally in his resplendent uniform and seated behind an enormous polished desk. On the walls of his cavernous command post, Ito had hung only two pictures. One was a portrait of Meiji. The other, slightly lower than the emperor's, was a photo of President Theodore Roosevelt. The missionary asked why Ito had so honored the American president. Ito responded, with a smile, "President Roosevelt is a man I admire for he is an honest man. He always means just what he says. He is frank and straightforward and never leaves you in doubt. He gives every man a square deal."[84]

Chapter 4

THE NOBLE CHINESE PEASANT

When the Christian prayer first came to China the humblest farmer instantly understood it, so like it was to his: "Our father who are in heaven"... China has embarked upon a vast reformation—inspired by the Christian gospel.... In their great crisis they found the man they needed... the greatest soldier in Asia, the greatest statesman in Asia, America's friend: Chiang Kai-shek.
—Henry Luce[1]

Days after Secretary Taft and Prime Minister Katsura agreed on Japan's Monroe Doctrine for Asia, another secret meeting occurred blocks away in hot and humid downtown Tokyo. The participants were Chinese revolutionaries in pursuit of the Mandate of Heaven to rule. (After Japan bested China in the 1894–1895 Sino-Japanese War, a number of Chinese intellectuals and nationalists traveled to Japan to study its seemingly successful westernizing ways.)

Dr. Sun Yat-sen was a revolutionary firebrand from Canton, the southern Chinese city that had endured so much at the hands of the sea barbarians. Sun had studied in Hawaii and Hong Kong and had been

Sun Yat-sen. Sun's "Three Principles of the People" were Nationalism, Democracy, and People's Livelihood. (Courtesy of the Library of Congress)

baptized a Christian by a Congregationalist missionary. Sun, a charismatic dreamer, had led two failed uprisings by the summer of 1905, and Manchu officials sought his head.

Sun's goal for China was what he called the Three Principles of the People: Nationalism, Democracy, and People's Livelihood. *Nationalism* meant the reassertion of the ethnic Han population over Chinese affairs. In 1638, the Manchu—the ethnic majority in Manchuria—had taken Beijing from the Han and had ruled since then as the Qing dynasty. Sun's nationalistic calls to kick out the interloping Manchu and the Western foreign devils resonated with the broader Han majority. *Democracy* promised eventual rule by the people after an interval of political tutelage. Sun believed that China's masses were not yet ready for democracy and needed a training period during which he would teach them, and then, at some undefined future date, Sun would

Charlie Soong (CPA Media / Pictures From History)

transition China to full democracy. *People's Livelihood* was that happy time that would result from following Sun's principles.

Sun's continual headache, apart from simply staying alive, was raising money to support his revolution, which was the subject of this gathering on Sunday, July 30, 1905. As talk turned to fund-raising, eyes turned to Charlie Soong, the richest man in the room.

Charlie Soong was a wealthy Shanghai publisher and mill owner and one of Sun's key moneymen. He had been born Han Jiaozhun on Hainan island, south of Canton. At about the age of fifteen, Charlie had made his way to the United States as a laborer. The West Coast of the U.S. was aflame at that time with the "Chinese must go!" pogroms. Soong wisely chose the East Coast, where few Americans had ever seen a Chinese person.

Southern Methodists in North Carolina took Soong under their wing, introducing him to the word of God and baptizing him in 1880.

Charlie Soong, Duke University, 1881: "The only Chinese Christian in North Carolina." (CPA Media / Pictures From History)

No longer a poor, faceless Chinese laborer, Charlie became a hot topic of discussion in Southern Methodist parlors. A Chinese person in North Carolina was a rarity—indeed, Soong was the first and only Chinese Christian in the state at that time.[2] Southern Methodists realized that they could mold this young Chinese man and then return him to his homeland to help build a Southern Methodist New China.

Church leaders reached out to thirty-six-year-old Julian Carr of Durham, North Carolina, to assist in that effort. Carr was one of America's outsized characters, a devout Southern Methodist and a partner in the manufacturing company that produced the Bull Durham brand of tobacco, which he had helped make famous with creative and attractive advertising across America and around the world.

In April of 1881, Carr met eighteen-year-old Charlie Soong at the Durham train station. They rode in Carr's horse-drawn carriage to Somerset Villa, one of the South's grand homes. Soong was suddenly living in a mansion and learning from one of America's leading Southern Methodists—who also happened to be a marketing genius—about Jesus, business, and life.

Carr gave Soong a beautiful leather-bound Bible. Durham was a religious town, and Soong observed that every family in Durham had not just one but often a number of Bibles. Indeed, Charlie saw people walking to church on Sundays clutching their personal Bibles like jewels. Furthermore, every classroom in Durham displayed Bibles, as did doctors' waiting rooms and restaurants. Charlie was amazed; everywhere he turned, it seemed, he saw a Bible.

In church, Charlie heard Southern Methodist missionaries' letters read from the pulpit, describing a New China in the process of being Christianized and Americanized. After the letters were read, Soong saw the plate passed for the missions in China and watched in amazement as pew after pew of parishioners put nickels, dimes, quarters, and dollars into collection plates. The ushers then heaped the take from the collection plates into one glittering pile, every cent bound for China.

Trinity College—later renamed Duke University—was North Carolina's finest Southern Methodist institution of higher learning. Julian Carr was one of the school's biggest benefactors, and though Charlie lacked academic qualifications, Trinity accepted Soong into its theology department, where he would study Christianity.

While Trinity carried plenty of prestige as a local institution, the premier Southern Methodist college in the United States was Vanderbilt University, in Nashville, Tennessee. Bishop Holland McTyeire, who had helped found Vanderbilt, learned of Soong's progress at Trinity and successfully recruited North Carolina's only Chinese Christian. Vanderbilt awarded Charlie a degree in theology in 1885.

Charlie Soong offered hope for a Southern Methodist New China. Soong was an object of fascination not for who he was (a Chinese) but for what he had become (an Americanized Chinese Christian). Perhaps this young man would help the Southern Methodists win China.

Charlie Soong returned home to China in 1886, assigned to preach to Shanghai's pagans. He quickly realized what American missionaries had missed: very few of his countrymen wished to be either Christianized or Americanized. As a Chinese who had lived in the United States, Soong understood the difference between the reality in China and America's New China mirage. Soong had been duly impressed by all the funds flowing to China from the pews of American churches, and he made a practical and, some might say, cynical calculation: while in reality, few Chinese would submit to being Christianized, there was a lot of money to be earned from American Christians who believed that mirage.

American missionaries were spending a small fortune to print Bibles in the United States and ship those heavy piles of paper across the Pacific. Charlie approached the American Bible Society and secured permission to print much cheaper Bibles in Shanghai. He founded the company that would make him a wealthy man, the Sino-American Press. Soong was soon China's biggest publisher of Christian books, selling Bibles by the box to Americans chasing the dream.

Charlie Soong and Sun Yat-sen met for the first time at the Shanghai Methodist church in 1894. Charlie and Sun—a rare pair of English-speaking Chinese Christians—were delighted to learn how much they had in common. They were about the same age, came from the same area—southern China, near Canton—and spoke similar dialects, and both had studied American ways and craved change in China. The men soon became best friends and revolutionary partners. Sun supplied the ideas, and Charlie risked his own life by secretly printing them. And with his own personal fortune and contacts with wealthy Americans, Soong became one of Sun's behind-the-scenes financiers.

Soong needed to go to the U.S. to raise funds, but Chinese who entered the United States during Theodore Roosevelt's administration risked detention. To avoid being held in a Bureau of Immigration pen, in 1905, Soong purchased a Portuguese passport in Macao and came through U.S. customs at San Francisco as a Portuguese citizen. Charlie raised money from patrons in San Francisco, New York, and other cities, but the largest contributor to Sun's cause lived in Durham, North Carolina.

Julian Carr—now sixty years old—again rode in his horse-drawn carriage to the Durham train station to welcome Charlie Soong, now forty-two years old. The two friends had done a lot of business together over the past nineteen years, as Carr had helped Charlie diversify his Bible empire and move into wheat and cotton milling. Back in Somerset Villa again, Soong told Carr the exciting news: the American New China dream was about to come true.

Carr gathered friends to hear Soong make his case, and at Durham's Old Club, a group of North Carolinians witnessed what no other Americans had ever seen: a nattily dressed, Vanderbilt-educated, North Carolina–baptized Southern Methodist Chinese man describing, in Southern-accented English, the coming of a Christianized New China. To his devout listeners, Charlie was the China mirage made flesh, a living, breathing incarnation of the missionary dream.

Soong told his audience that Dr. Sun would become China's George Washington and that Sun's Three Principles of the People were modeled after Abraham Lincoln's "of the people, by the people, for the people." His sales pitch was believable only because Carr and his friends knew so little. If a revolutionary had come from Germany or England seeking support, the Old Club men could have evaluated his assertions critically, having the benefit of a wealth of prior cultural experiences in Europe. But China to them was a great blank canvas, now skillfully colored in by Soong.

Soong was especially convincing as he explained Sun's platform of Nationalism, Democracy, and People's Livelihood. The gathered men were hearing Sun's concepts translated from Chinese into English by a Vanderbilt University theology major smart enough to filter and slant. What Charlie termed *nationalism* meant to most Chinese an intense hatred of all foreigners, *especially* white barbarians like the men listening to Soong in Durham. Indeed, it was the Manchu leaders' failure to stop the sea barbarians from slicing New Chinas from Middle Kingdom territory that had convinced most Chinese that the Manchu were losing the Mandate of Heaven. (That was not how Soong explained it to his North Carolina audience.) And while democracy sounded just fine to the Old Club bunch, there was a catch that Charlie did not elaborate on: during the tutelage period, Sun would become a Christian dictator with one-man rule.

Julian Carr and those like him dug deep into their pockets. Charlie returned to Shanghai with over two million U.S. dollars for Dr. Sun's revolutionary cause.

Charlie Soong married well, and by 1897, he had sired three daughters (Ailing, Chingling, and Mayling) and a son (Tse-ven, called T.V.).[3] Raised in a world between two cultures, his children were influenced by their father's Christian faith, his American education and business success, his support for Sun's revolution, and his ability to leverage the China mirage for financial gain. The Soong family lived in a Western-style house in a New China area of Shanghai carved out by the sea barbarians. They were Chinese and connected to the hundreds of millions who sought the expulsion of foreign devils, but they ate with knives and forks and went to Christian schools.

The Soong sisters: Ailing, Chingling, and Mayling. Two of the sisters sided with Chiang Kai-shek; one sided with Mao Zedong. (CPA Media / Pictures From History)

Charlie provided his offspring with American college educations at Harvard, Wellesley, and Georgia's Wesleyan College. While living in the United States, the Soong children saw how little Americans knew about China and realized that these people believed China was destined to be Christianized and Americanized. Like their father, they understood that Americans accepted them not for who they were (Chinese) but for what they had become (Americanized Chinese Christians).

Ailing Soong, Charlie's oldest child, inherited her father's drive. Ailing journeyed to the United States alone at the age of fourteen and graduated from Wesleyan College in Macon, Georgia, in 1911. She then returned to China to serve as Dr. Sun's personal assistant.

The Mandate of Heaven had for years been in play. Sea barbarians on China's coast had humiliated the Manchu dynasty, which then endured the nineteenth century's largest civil war—the Taiping Rebellion—and was further humbled by foreign troops who marched on Beijing during the Boxer Rebellion. The corrupt Empress Dowager Cixi finally died in 1908, at the age of seventy-three, after forty-seven years of rule. At the age of two, Puyi—depicted in popular culture as the Last Emperor—became the new Son of Heaven.

By 1911 the Manchu dynasty was on its last legs, its emperor only five years old. Numerous uprisings—some of which Sun Yat-sen led or participated in—sought to gain the Mandate of Heaven. In the fall of that year, Sun was in the United States raising funds when he learned from press reports that on October 10, 1911, one of his allies had staged a successful military uprising in the city of Wuchang. Sun arrived back in China on December 21, 1911. On December 29, a meeting of representatives from some of China's provinces elected Sun provisional president of what would be proclaimed on January 1, 1912, as the Republic of China. But Sun had competition within the ranks for the Mandate and was unable to dominate the unruly coalition of revolutionaries. Sun lost out in a clash of arms, and China descended into chaos as warlords quickly divided the country among themselves. Suddenly the lives of Sun and Soong were in jeopardy. In 1913 Sun and Charlie Soong packed up their families, boarded a ship in the dark of night, and fled to Japan.

*   *   *

Ailing continued as Sun's personal assistant in Japan, but she soon grew uncomfortable with the unwelcome sexual advances made by her married, older boss. Even as a young woman, Ailing was a shrewd operator, more interested in money than power. In 1914, twenty-six-year-old Ailing extracted herself from the forty-eight-year-old Sun's grasp with no hurt feelings and married H. H. Kung, a Chinese Christian also in Japan who was reputedly China's richest banker and a lineal descendant of Confucius.

At this point, Chingling Soong, Charlie's second daughter, was twenty-one years old and, like her sister, a graduate of Wesleyan College. Chingling took Ailing's place as Sun's secretary.

Sun made advances to the beautiful young Chingling as well. Unlike her older sister, Chingling fell for Sun and/or his ideas. As she later remembered: "I didn't fall in love. It was hero-worship from afar. It was a romantic girl's idea...but a good one. I wanted to help save China and Dr. Sun was the one man who could do it, so I wanted to help him."[4]

When Charlie realized that his married best friend was pursuing his young daughter, he dragged Chingling back to Shanghai and ordered her to forget Sun. Father and daughter quarreled. One night, Chingling escaped through a window, boarded a ship, and returned to Sun's arms in Japan.

Forty-nine-year-old Sun abandoned his wife and married twenty-three-year-old Chingling in Tokyo on October 25, 1915. Chingling recalled, "My father came to Japan and bitterly attacked Dr. Sun. He tried to annul the marriage on grounds that I was underage and lacked my parents' consent. When he failed he broke all relations with Dr. Sun and disowned me!"[5]

Charlie Soong died three years later, in 1918, having had no contact with Sun and Chingling since their marriage. Friends remember Soong lamenting, "I was never so hurt in my life. My own daughter and my best friend."[6] Dr. Sun did not attend his funeral.

Ailing took the reins of the Soong empire upon her father's death. At this point, many factions were competing to unite a fractured China,

*Chingling Soong and Sun Yat-sen. She was twenty-three years old; he was
forty-nine. "I wanted to help save China and Dr. Sun was the one man who
could do it, so I wanted to help him," Chingling said.
(Courtesy Everett Collection)*

one of them the Dr. Sun–founded Nationalist Party, which espoused
his Three Principles of the People. Ailing naturally supported the man
who was her father's former best friend and her sister's husband. Sun's
fortunes — and those of his Nationalist Party — rose, fell, and then
rose again, with Sun sometimes close to grasping power, other times
fleeing into exile once more. All along, the Wesleyan-educated Ailing,
her Yale-educated husband, H. H. Kung, and her Harvard-educated
little brother, T. V. Soong, raised funds for the Nationalist Party. Sun
and the Soongs would have liked American help, but actions by the
United States at this time enraged millions of Chinese, and in the fallout, another white Western country emerged as Sun's chief supporter.

*   *   *

When World War I erupted in Europe, Britain used its New China colony of Weihaiwei to recruit an eventual 140,000 Chinese to serve in the Chinese Labor Corps (CLC) in Britain, working in place of the British men marching off to war. While in Europe, these CLC forces—and millions of relatives back in China following them in press reports—learned that America had declared this Great War to be a "war to end all wars." President Woodrow Wilson entered the Paris peace talks preaching "self-determination" as a salve for a ravaged world.

Wilson accidentally inspired millions of colonized Asians held in the clutches of white Westerners. A young Ho Chi Minh petitioned Wilson and other leaders to help him free Indochina from the grasp of the French, a request that was cast aside. The Chinese warlords who controlled Beijing at that moment sent a delegation representing China's interests to Paris. Inspired by Wilson, the Chinese imagined that the conference would help China evict the Germans—who had lost the war and who were being taken to the cleaners by the victorious Western powers—from the Middle Kingdom. Instead, Wilson and other leaders at the Paris Peace Conference upheld the right of foreign devils to *expand* their New Chinas by granting Japan the former German China area of Shandong, on China's Pacific coast.

When news of the West's—and especially Wilson's—sellout hit, millions of Chinese protesters flooded the streets, among them a youthful Mao Zedong who "attacked Wilson's failure in his first recorded criticism of the United States."[7] To protest the people's treatment, the Chinese delegation to the Paris Peace Conference was the only one that did not sign the treaty officially ending hostilities between the Allied and Central Powers.

As Chinese seethed at America, a new revolutionary player, the Soviet Union, cannily renounced many of the deposed czar's unequal privileges in China (which imperial Russia, along with other Western countries, had gained in the nineteenth century under the unequal treaties but that the new Soviet Union didn't have the power to exploit).

This created a tremendous sense of goodwill between those two nations. Communist Russian agents soon established warm contacts with important Chinese intellectuals and political figures. For over two generations, America had sent thousands of political, cultural, economic, and missionary workers to China. Communist Russia didn't have a single school, church, or even debating society in China. Yet, within little time, the new Soviet Union had made a greater impression on the Chinese than all the Christian missionary influences combined.

Eventually, Moscow agreed to bankroll two small factions within the fractured China and dispatched advisers to found a Chinese Communist Party and help organize Sun's Nationalist Party along Soviet lines. Moscow's advisers told the Nationalists and the Communists to combine forces in a united front. Both parties would receive Soviet aid.

In the Nationalist camp was a rising star, Chiang Kai-shek, a traditional Confucian thinker on the political right. He'd trained as a soldier in Japan, and Sun had appointed him Generalissimo of the Nationalist army. In Chiang's idea of revolution, he would seize military control of the country, and the masses would then obey him as a father figure according to his code: inferior yielded to superior, soldier deferred to general, and the general bowed to Heaven. Chiang bought into the father-son model as long as he was the father: "I believe that unless everyone has absolute trust in one man, we cannot reconstruct the nation and we cannot complete the revolution."[8] About his army, the Generalissimo said, "I look upon the soldiers under me as a father regards his children."[9] Chiang valued loyalty above ability and surrounded himself with yes-men. When someone criticized an incompetent general, Chiang replied, "But where do you find a man who is so obedient?"[10]

Chiang chanted Sun's principles of Nationalism, Democracy, and People's Livelihood, but what interested him most was the tutelage period during which one leader would control China. He ruled out democracy as "absolutely impossible for the entire nation."[11]

While he didn't say it to foreigners' faces, Chiang later wrote a too-candid book in which he attributed almost all of China's ills to the foreign devils and their unequal treaties. Yet Chiang was not on the side of China's peasant majority; instead, he favored the wealthy bankers and landlords who got fat on peasant labor. Indeed, while claiming to be a revolutionary, Chiang was actually a staunch defender of the status quo — with one exception. When Sun appointed him Generalissimo, Chiang exclaimed to his wife, Jennie: "If I control the army, I will have the power to control the country. It is my road to leadership."[12]

On the left, within Sun's Russian-supported politically flexible big tent, was a far different character, the Communist Party's Mao Zedong.[13] Mao grew up in relatively comfortable circumstances in the province of Hunan with a financially successful father and his own bedroom, a rare luxury in rural China. As a boy, Mao read voraciously, developing what would become a lifelong habit. "What I enjoyed were the romances of Old China, and especially stories of rebellions," he later recalled. "I used to read [these outlawed books] in school, covering them up with a [Chinese] Classic when the teacher walked past... I believe that perhaps I was much influenced by such books, read at an impressionable age."[14] Mao also devoured books about the history of Western countries, including the United States. He remembered, "I had first heard of America in an article which told of the American Revolution and contained a sentence like this: 'After eight years of difficult war, Washington won victory and built up his nation.'"[15] Rebellion in search of the Mandate of Heaven — a long and hallowed Chinese tradition — excited the young man.

As a youth, Mao read an 1894 pamphlet written by white Christians entitled "The Dismemberment of China"; it repeated the claim that China could not be reformed from within but would have to be civilized by foreign countries. Years later, he remembered the opening line: "Alas, China will be subjugated." Mao credited the reading of this pamphlet with the beginning of his political consciousness; as he later recalled, "I felt depressed about the future of my country and began to realize that it was the duty of all the people to help save it."[16]

In the early 1920s, the young Mao joined the New Culture movement, which held that traditional Confucian values would not help China advance. Leaders advocated a cultural revolution to regenerate China. Old ways had to be dispensed with, and the consciousness of the people had to be transformed. Until there was a cultural revolution, there was little hope that China would become strong enough to oust the foreign devils.

Mao and the members of the New Culture movement were young men who faced away from China's past and toward its future. Inspired by the success of the Russian Revolution, he and a small group of others founded the Chinese Communist Party in Shanghai in July of 1921. Mao accepted Russian guidance and Marxist language before he fully understood many Western—and especially Marxist—concepts. In *Mao Zedong: A Political and Intellectual Portrait,* Maurice Meisner writes, "It is a striking feature of the origins of the Chinese Communist Party that its founders became politically committed to Communism well before they became intellectually committed to Marxist theory, indeed, in most cases well before they acquired any significant knowledge of Marxism."[17] Marxism addressed itself to modern industrial countries where the urban workers would supposedly rise in revolution, so Mao began by attempting to organize China's urban workers into trade unions. But soon he imagined a revolution the exact opposite of that prescribed by conventional Marxism or Communism.

Most Chinese people lived in small villages; only a small fraction had jobs in the coastal cities. The villages were often little more than a dozen or so mud huts, with no electricity or sewers. Half the people died before the age of thirty. Landlords held sway, owning the vast majority of the land, and the farmers often paid them more than 50 percent of their crops in confiscatory taxes. A British social scientist compared the Chinese farmer to "a man standing permanently up to the neck in water so that even a ripple is sufficient to drown him."[18] Mao imagined a revolution in which the powerless peasants would rise together to become powerful and take land from the landlords. This was the beginning of Maoism.

When Mao revealed his new thinking, his fellow Communist Party members were aghast. Communist dogma held that peasants were low-class, simple-minded conservatives who could not be roused to revolution. Mao begged to differ and submitted an article arguing for a revolution in which the countryside would dominate the cities, but Communist leaders refused to publish his heresy.

Against the majority's criticism, Mao retained his certainty. As early as 1925, Mao was already talking about organizing the peasant masses. In January of 1926 Mao published an astute analysis of rural society, identifying as China's real problem the big landlords who controlled too much land. Mao complained that the revolution had focused too much on city people and not enough on the peasant majority. Almost alone, he predicted that those who rode the wave of peasant revolution would inherit the Mandate of Heaven. Duxiu Chen, the secretary-general of the Chinese Communist Party, expressed the majority view as he rebuked Mao: "The peasants are scattered and their forces are not easy to concentrate"; their "culture is low, their desires in life are simple, and they easily tend toward conservatism... these environmental factors make it difficult for the peasants to participate in the revolutionary movement."[19]

Sun Yat-sen died in 1925, his principles of Nationalism, Democracy, and People's Livelihood an intellectual construct that he had never translated into a real revolution. Many had approved of Sun's rebellious ideas because he called for Chinese nationalism, but Sun was a Western-oriented Christian who had inspired no impassioned nationwide mass movement. His Nationalist Party (along with its Communist adjunct) was a Moscow-funded organization with influence mostly in southeast China. Traditional Chinese society had not changed and the status of the peasantry versus the landlords remained the same.

Sun's United Front had been a big tent masking fundamental differences. Sun's death set off a struggle for succession. Chiang Kai-shek was allied with the urban, Western-oriented moneyed classes and the bankers and landlords who feasted on the status quo. Diametrically opposed was Mao Zedong, who thought that China's future rested with the rural poor. As the English author Philip Short puts it in his excellent study *Mao: A Life,* "Among a nation of 400 million, 90 percent of whom were peasants, land redistribution—taking from the rich and giving to the poor—was the primary vehicle carrying the Communist revolution forward, the fundamental point of divergence between [the Communists] and [the Nationalists]."[20]

Sun's passing also meant a realignment within the Soong family: number-two sister Chingling, although only thirty-three years old, was now the revered widow of the sainted Sun Yat-sen. Chingling appreciated Communist Russia's support for her husband's revolution and was a liberal who believed, like Mao, that a resolution of the peasants' plight was the key to China's future. However, the oldest Soong sister, Ailing, remained the most powerful force within the family. Ailing exuded confidence and strength. An American correspondent observed, "Here was authority, conscious of itself, conscious of power.... I suspected a mind that forgot nothing and forgave little."[21] Another American correspondent with experience in Asia noted that as a "hard-willed creature possessed of demonic energy and great will-to-power, violently able, cunning, and ambitious, she is as powerful a personality as any in China."[22] U.S. State Department cables from China to Washington referred to Ailing as the "most powerful person in China."[23] The FBI later described her as "an evil and clever woman [who] sits in the background and directs the family."[24]

In July of 1926, the Russian-funded Chinese United Front—combining Chiang's Nationalist forces and Mao's Communist followers—launched the Northern Expedition, a military effort involving a hundred thousand troops that was designed to break out of southeastern China, beat back various warlords, conquer central China (with the booming metropolis of Shanghai), and gain control of the vital Yangtze River. In United Front spirit, Generalissimo Chiang Kai-shek led the military assault while Mao Zedong helped spearhead the political effort.

Mao sent his political operatives in advance of Chiang's military forces, creating support for the Nationalist cause among the peasants with promises of land reform. When Chiang's armies arrived, peasant support, as Chiang later recorded, "sprang up with the vigor of storms and cloudbursts."[25] Despite Chiang's forces being outnumbered by his warlord opponents ten to one, the peasants—newly liberated and promised land by Mao—welcomed his armies.

Ailing Soong was alarmed by Mao's peasant uprisings and workers' strikes. Landlords and industrialists were Ailing's friends and business associates. With a deal in mind, Ailing took a Bank of China steamer upriver to the city of Jiujiang, Chiang Kai-shek's temporary headquarters on the Yangtze, and invited him aboard for a heart-to-heart talk. Chiang might have been the Generalissimo, but Ailing took control— she made Chiang come to her, and they negotiated for hours. She proposed an alliance between the powerful Soong empire and the ambitious Chiang. The Generalissimo listened attentively as Ailing described an opportunity for him to leave the United Front, reject the Russians, eliminate Mao's threat, and seize control of a cleansed Nationalist Party.

Ailing made three demands that would later have a dramatic impact on U.S.-China relations. Each demand concerned her family. To assure herself of political control, Ailing told Chiang to appoint her husband, H. H. Kung, as prime minister. For financial control, Ailing told Chiang that her little brother T. V. Soong would serve as Chiang's finance minister. The third condition was both political and personal. Ailing possessed something priceless through her father's support of, and Chingling's being the widow of, Sun Yat-sen: around the Soong family hovered the aura of the fabled Mandate of Heaven. Ailing offered Chiang an unimaginable prize: marriage into the Soong clan and a stake in the Mandate.

Ailing had earlier told younger sister Mayling that she would offer Mayling's hand in marriage to Chiang Kai-shek. Twenty-nine-year-old Mayling was one of Shanghai's most desired bachelorettes, a beautiful, cultured, rich Chinese Southern Methodist. She had spent a decade of her young life living and studying in New Jersey, Georgia, Tennessee, and Massachusetts, learning to speak perfect American-style English. In 1917, when twenty-year-old Mayling graduated from Wellesley College with a major in English literature and minor in philosophy, she had lived half her life in the United States. Mayling later admitted, "The only thing Chinese about me is my face."[26]

Sun Yat-sen's widow, Chingling, was appalled by the idea of Chiang marrying into the Soong family; she regarded the militaristic Generalissimo as a traitor to her late husband's memory. But young Mayling saw no choice but to side with dominant sister Ailing. Little brother T.V. was also less than enamored by the stiff, militaristic Chiang, but he, too, fell in line behind his oldest sister.

Ailing was proposing a Soong-Chiang syndicate with her relatives in the Generalissimo's bedroom, office, and pockets. As a final condition, Ailing demanded that Chiang Kai-shek become a proper Southern Methodist like the Soongs. Chingling later observed, "If Elder Sister had been a man, the Generalissimo would have been dead, and she would have been ruling China."[27]

Ailing dismissed Chiang after making her proposals, saying she would await his answer. Chiang hurried home and told Jennie Chen, his wife of seven years:

> I am desperate. Ailing has struck a very hard bargain, but what she says is true. Her offer is the only way for me to achieve my plans to unite China. I now ask you to help me. I beg you not to say no. After all, true love is measured by the sacrifice one is willing to make.[28]

Chiang pleaded with Jennie to go to America for five years so he could consolidate power with the Soongs. Jennie was dubious, so Chiang lied to her, saying her time overseas would be short and that she could later return.

On March 19, 1927, Chiang wrote separate letters to Ailing and Mayling agreeing to Ailing's bargain. He would exile his wife to the

Ailing Soong called the shots with Generalissimo Chiang Kai-shek. Note that Ailing is leading and Chiang is holding her arm. (Associated Press)

United States, marry Mayling, and appoint Ailing's husband and her brother to top posts. Chiang and Jennie were never divorced. When Jennie arrived in the U.S., Chiang gave an interview in which he disavowed his wife as a minor concubine. Regarding Ailing's demand that he be baptized a Southern Methodist, Chiang proposed a shrewd strategy, arguing that religion shouldn't be taken all at once, like a pill, but rather sipped slowly, like hot, rich soup. Chiang suggested that they put out the story that he was studying the Bible in preparation for a possible conversion. Chingling later observed, "He would have agreed to be a Holy Roller to marry Mayling. He needed her to build a dynasty."[29]

*   *   *

In April of 1927 Chiang moved to oust Sun Yat-sen's Russian advisers, end the United Front, eliminate Mao, and crush the peasant and labor union uprisings. In one of history's bloodiest betrayals, forces loyal to Chiang massacred between twenty thousand and thirty thousand presumed Communists in Shanghai alone. The majority of Chiang's killings took place in the countryside. The Mao-oriented peasant revolutionaries were far greater in number than their urban counterparts, and they were more socially radical — a very direct threat, since the majority of Chiang's army officers were sons of landlords. The Generalissimo's slaughter in the countryside took hundreds of thousands of lives, yet it was little reported in America, as Chiang turned his Soviet-funded and -trained armies against those who had been his Communist allies. Chiang's forces still represented a small percentage of the Chinese population but were regionally strong enough to muscle Mao and his comrades away from China's east coast.

The Soong-Chiang coup was for China both a turning point and a point of no return. Chiang, apparently triumphant, aligned with New China urbanites like the Soongs to impose his Confucian militarism, while the Communists were seemingly decimated, with only a few survivors like Mao hiding in the countryside. Ailing, her obedient husband, H. H. Kung, little brother T.V., and little sister Mayling hoped that after Chiang's "extermination" of the Communists, the Soong-Chiang syndicate would go on to control China from an urban base with foreign support. But Chingling understood Mao's strategy of helping the rural poor majority, and she never forgave her sisters for lending the Soong name to Chiang Kai-shek: "He has set China back years and made the revolution much more costly and terrible than it need have been," she declared. "In the end he will be defeated just the same."[30]

The Soong and Chiang families were officially joined at a public wedding in Shanghai on December 1, 1927. The Soong-Chiang syndicate staged the event, which was tailor-made for the international press.

Over thirteen hundred guests—including the consuls of France, Britain, Japan, and the United States—packed the ballroom of Shanghai's prestigious Majestic Hotel. Cameras ringed the room. The crowd hushed as forty-year-old Chiang Kai-shek, dressed like an American bridegroom in a natty morning coat, striped pants, and wing collar, entered. Thirty-year-old Mayling, resembling a demure American bride in a silver-and-white beaded gown with a lace veil, followed on her brother's arm. As cameras clicked and filmed, Chiang and Mayling met in front of the dais and bowed to a huge portrait of the departed Sun Yat-sen, emphasizing the couple's tie to Sun's Mandate of Heaven. The bride and groom then bowed to each other and to the guests. Their marriage certificate was read, signed, and sealed. (The couple had earlier exchanged vows in a private ceremony in

Mayling Soong and Chiang Kai-shek: Suddenly China had Christian rulers.
(CPA Media / Pictures From History)

the Soong home.) The newlyweds exited to the American song "Oh Promise Me": "Hearing God's message while the organ rolls / Its mighty music to our very souls."

As with the marriage of Sun Yat-sen and Chingling, charges of bigamy surrounded the Chiang-Mayling marriage. Chiang's decision to repudiate Jennie, with Mayling and Ailing's connivance, was seen by many Chinese as reprehensible, and they scorned the couple as hypocrites who used their supposed Christianity as a front. But the Chinese were not the main audience for this spectacle. Soong-Chiang publicists focused the American press on the promise that China's new leader would welcome the Americanization of his nation. Up until that day, photos of weddings in old China that had appeared in American newspapers were studies in strangeness: the men were exotic-looking pagans in man-dresses with greasy pigtails and long, lacquered fingernails. In contrast, the wedding photograph distributed by the Soong-Chiang press machine was all American-style New China, portraying a demure and virginal Southern Methodist bride marrying a hunky aspiring Christian, both dressed for a Park Avenue wedding. The Soong-Chiang money laid out to make this impression was well spent. The *New York Times* featured the wedding as front-page news. American influence was winning the leaders, and perhaps would win China.

Madame Chiang would become a favorite of U.S. newsmen looking for a colorful quote. American readers were delighted to learn that Mayling was teaching China's new leader the English language. His first assignment was the word *darling*.

On October 10, 1928, the Soong-Chiang syndicate declared a national government in China led by Ailing's favorite, Generalissimo Chiang Kai-shek. In certain corners, the applause was loud and prolonged. American missionaries liked Chiang because Ailing, Mayling, and T.V. told New China fables about how the Generalissimo would Christianize and democratize the Middle Kingdom. Ailing, Mayling, and T.V. had spent an accumulated twenty-eight years studying Americans in the United States. Now they used their insights to provide a military dictator with an American-friendly front.

Chiang's government controlled the westernized New Chinas where the American merchants and missionaries lived, places like Shanghai and Nanking. These cities had modernized areas with electricity, running water, and Western-style beds. The Four Hundred Million lived beyond these enclaves, by day bent over their rice fields and at night sleeping with their animals. American-style democracy, Chiang Kai-shek, the United States, the Soviet Union, Communism—these were unknowns to most Chinese, who lived by the eternal rhythms of the sun and the moon. To them, Chiang was just another hopeful warlord.

Parishioners in the United States learned that Chiang studied the Bible an hour each day. One missionary described Chiang as "introspective, patient, tolerant, full of wisdom, ascetic and almost saintly."[31] Another wrote that Chiang's party was "distinctly Christian and therefore [they had to] prevail for China sooner or later."[32]

Ailing Soong was the unseen financial power behind Chiang, using as front men her fabulously wealthy but simple-minded husband and her brainy little brother. H.H. and T.V. would float government securities; Ailing took her insider's cut and channeled some to Chiang. Ailing consistently and brazenly profited from inside information. Chingling later remembered:

> She's very clever, Ailing. She never gambles. She buys and sells only when she gets advance information from confederates in the Ministry of Finance about changes in government fiscal policy. It's a pity she can't do it for the people instead of against them.... It is impossible to amass a fortune here except through criminal dishonesty and misuse of political power backed by military force. Every dollar comes right out of the blood of our poor people, who seldom have enough to eat. One day the people will rise and take it back.[33]

Mayling served Ailing as the primary Soong-Chiang mouthpiece, giving interviews and translating her husband's utterances into English, always massaging his words into what English-speaking listeners wanted to hear. She also wrote letters and magazine articles for publication in the United States and broadcast "news" from China via U.S. radio networks. Mayling, in appearance and speech, was the merchant and missionary dream made flesh; to far-off Americans, it was as if a fresh-faced Wellesley girl were guiding China and providing a running commentary. And after decades of opposition from Chinese leaders, American missionaries found themselves seated in Western-style chairs listening to Chiang and Mayling talk about spreading American culture and religion in China. Naturally flattered by their newfound influence at court, the missionaries eagerly portrayed the Generalissimo and Madame Chiang as champions of democracy.

Since 1919, the U.S. State Department had maintained an arms embargo against China. (In the spirit of the humanitarian Open Door, keeping American arms out of China was meant to help those caught in the country's constant civil wars.) In 1928, when Chiang had supposedly unified China and declared a government, the State Department lifted many aspects of the embargo, but the sale of U.S. warplanes to China continued to be prohibited.

The State Department narrowly defined military warplanes as "(a) all types of aircraft actually fitted with armor, guns, machine guns, gun mounts, bomb dropping or other military devices, and (b) aircraft presumed to be destined for military use, whether actually fitted with armament or not." Britain's Foreign Office was more flexible and conveniently classified aircraft into two categories, "armed and unarmed."[34] This allowed Chiang to buy unarmed British aircraft and arm them later.

The U.S. Army Air Corps flew the world's finest airplanes (made in the U.S.) and thus produced the world's best pilots. Unsurprisingly, there was a global demand for the services of these highly trained American flyboys. However, the State Department considered American pilots who would fly for a foreign nation the lowest of the low — guns for hire, mercenaries — and informed Chiang that if he hired any such mercenaries, the U.S. would issue warrants for their arrest, deport them, and possibly take their passports away.

The State Department didn't want Chiang to use American war-planes, but Chiang quickly found himself being courted by American commercial-aircraft manufacturers. The largest of these was the Curtiss-Wright Corporation of Buffalo, New York. Curtiss-Wright dispatched George Westervelt, a Naval Academy and MIT graduate with a distinguished record as a U.S. Navy captain, to China as their representative, and in April of 1929, after many banquets and probable payoffs, the company received the contract to develop commercial aviation in China. The U.S. State Department readily agreed because the sale involved only civilian aircraft.

Like most foreign-devil imports into China, civilian aviation failed to catch on. The vast majority of the Four Hundred Million couldn't afford airline tickets. Curtiss-Wright found few Chinese passengers for its airplanes.

Yet Chiang's priority had never been passenger service. In 1930, Chiang dispatched high-ranking Chinese air force officers on scouting missions to United States airplane manufacturers like Boeing in Seattle and Curtiss-Wright in Buffalo. Chiang's officers went to Washington and had meetings at the Departments of War, Navy, and Commerce, but they avoided the State Department.

Ailing and Chiang soon noticed that the various parts of the U.S. government did not speak with one voice regarding the Chinese purchase of American warplanes. The Commerce Department in particular encouraged American businessmen to sell aircraft to the Chinese, because its task was to promote the sale of American products to other countries, especially important during the Great Depression. Curtiss-Wright knew that the Generalissimo desired American warplanes and encouraged the Soong-Chiang bunch to set up private companies in the United States to purchase warplanes and then ship them to China, circumventing the State Department's continuing embargo.

American newspapers flashed the headline on October 24, 1930: "Chinese President Becomes Christian."[35] The Generalissimo's baptism was held in the Soong family's Shanghai home, where Ailing and

Mayling watched as the Reverend Z. T. Kuang poured holy water over Chiang's bald pate to make him a Southern Methodist. The Soong-Chiang press machine later released a suitable one-liner from the newly saved: "I feel the need of a God such as Jesus Christ."[36] Chingling's observation didn't make it into the newspapers: "If he is Christian, I am not."[37]

Pulpits across America heralded this remarkable turn of events. China's leaders — Generalissimo Chiang Kai-shek, his wife, Prime Minister H. H. Kung, and finance minister T. V. Soong, among others — were Americanized Christians. Just fifty years earlier, North Carolina's Southern Methodists had Americanized young Charlie Soong. The resulting spiritual chain reaction surely meant that America was winning the leaders, and the New China mirage was coming to fruition. At a time when the Great Depression was shaking Americans' confidence in themselves, many were heartened to see leaders of the world's most populous country adopting Christian and American ways.

Chiang's converting to Southern Methodism had been one of Ailing's conditions. He identified with the New Testament's hero and decided he was nothing less than the Jesus Christ of China: "So long as the task of national salvation is not accomplished, I shall be responsible for the distress and sufferings of the people."[38]

In 1931, Henry Luce, the famous founder of Time Inc., was thirty-four years old. The wealthy and powerful publisher had his own private elevator that whisked him up to his New York office every morning and then back down again in the evening. The elevator operator who shared these rides was instructed never to speak to Mr. Luce, who preferred to close his eyes and silently lean against the back wall of the elevator, communicating with his God.

A cold and gruff man who barked orders to subordinates from behind closed doors as he chain-smoked the cigarettes that would one day kill him, Luce had grown up in a tiny New China as a missionary's son. Henry learned from his father that his Christianity and

Henry Luce. A biographer wrote that "the Christianization of China" was the supreme effort of Luce's life. (Time Life Pictures / Getty Images)

Americanism made him superior to the pagan and impoverished Chinese. And in Reverend Luce's telling, America was a promised land of milk, honey, green lawns, sturdy homes, and the right kind of people.

Young Luce grew up believing that the Chinese needed above all to be Christianized and Americanized and that they should be grateful for their improvement rather than resentful of his father's and others' interference. His father's mission had been to change China, not to understand it. Later, the reverend's son would chisel his father's New China beliefs into the American consciousness.

What young Henry Luce learned about China was his father's American mirage. Henry had little direct contact with Chinese people except for the servants he bossed around. (Luce later said, "My favorite Chinese was our cook, who smoked opium."[39]) Many evenings Henry saw his father bent over his desk writing hopeful fiction about the New China to come. Having little contact with the reality of China, young Henry accepted his father's pronouncements as fact. Reverend Luce's failure to convert the Chinese (a washout in terms of numbers, in line with his fellow missionaries) but success in fund-raising from optimistic Americans was testament to the two coexisting realities, one in China, the other in the American mind.

Fourteen-year-old Henry Luce left China knowing neither its language nor its people. He entered Yale in 1916 and became a serious student and the managing editor of the *Yale Daily News*. After being voted "most brilliant" in his class, Luce studied for a year at Oxford University in England and then worked as a reporter for the *Chicago Daily News* and, in 1921, the *Baltimore News*. In 1922 Luce and a partner raised $86,000 to start a magazine, and on March 3, 1923, they published the first issue of *Time* magazine.

Luce came along in a historical era when news and events entered American homes almost exclusively via newspapers and radio. That initial issue of *Time,* which came out when Luce was all of twenty-five years old, would be the seed of the world's first multimedia news empire.

Luce's genius was his ability to clarify and simplify complex events. He made it *Time*'s goal to summarize the week's news using snappy language and pictures. Luce told stories through the lives of colorful personalities that he thought represented the kind of "right thinking" he wished to promote. As W. A. Swanberg wrote in *Luce and His Empire,* "The fact that this Right Thinking referred to Luce's own thinking attested to the same missionary certainty his father had felt, and placed him vis-à-vis the American reader in the same position as Rev. Henry Luce vis-à-vis the Chinese peasant."[40]

With the massive eventual successes of *Time, Life,* and *Fortune* magazines, as well as the *March of Time* newsreels, the topics Luce chose became important across America. Biographer Swanberg wrote that "the Christianization of China" was the supreme effort of Henry

Luce's life.[41] In *American Images of China,* T. Christopher Jespersen wrote, "Like the Protestant missionaries of his father's generation, Luce believed that if Christianity could be brought to China, democracy would certainly flow and from there, the development of trade would rapidly ensue."[42] Luce was certain that an America–New China partnership would rule the Pacific, just as the Anglo-Americans dominated the Atlantic. One of Luce's most talented writers, Theodore White, observed, "[Luce] loved America; he loved China; with his power and his influence he meant to cement the two together forevermore."[43] Luce proclaimed, "One of the best bets for the future of the things we consider important is this New China."[44]

Henry Luce and *Time* magazine quickly gained a troubling reputation for manufacturing facts and quoting unnamed sources. David Halberstam wrote, "[Luce] was the missionary, the believer, a man whose beliefs and visions and knowledge of Truth contradicted and thus outweighed the facts of his reporters."[45] A former *Time* editor admitted, "The way to tell a successful lie is to include enough truth in it to make it believable — and *Time* is the most successful liar of our times." Another of Luce's men said, "The degree of credence one gives to *Time* is inverse to one's degree of knowledge of the situation being reported on." Author Bertrand Russell wrote, "I consider *Time* to be scurrilous and I know, with respect to my own work, utterly shameless in its willingness to distort."[46]

Luce understood that for visual symbols of New China, he would need, first and foremost, good-looking, English-speaking, Christianized, Americanized, right-thinking Chinese individuals with whom his readers could identify. Presenting the Soong family as representatives of real Chinese was like suggesting that the Rockefellers were typical Americans, but facts didn't matter when it came to promoting Reverend Luce's unfulfilled dream. From the 1930s to the 1970s, Ailing, Mayling, and T. V. Soong hosted Luce at their mansions in Nanking, Shanghai, Chungking, Hong Kong, Taipei, Washington, and New York, and the publisher dutifully took notes as they spun the mirage just as Father Charlie had.

Luce especially appreciated the media value of the beautiful and charming Mayling Soong. The two had lived remarkably parallel lives: they were the same age, had been born as Christians in separate New Chinas within thirty days of each other, and were later sent to America to be appropriately educated. The two shared any number of cultural references: the Lord's Prayer, Bible verses, New York sophistication, Washington power, Shakespeare's sonnets, and the never-to-be-forgotten American mission in Asia.

In Chiang Kai-shek, Henry Luce believed he had found a photogenic, unblemished savior, "the greatest soldier in Asia, the greatest statesman in Asia, America's friend."[47] A prominent *Time* staffer later wrote, "We felt we were on the side of the angels in most cases, with the possible exception of Chiang Kai-shek, whom we regarded as a protégé of Mr. Luce, and who was the only sacred cow we admitted."[48]

Luce was a communications genius who made New China easy for American readers to comprehend: Beijing was China's Boston, Shanghai was New York, Nanking was Washington, Hankow was Chicago, and southern Canton was "the teeming, sultry New Orleans of China."[49] Charlie Soong was "Old Charlie";[50] Sun Yat-sen was "China's George Washington";[51] Ailing was "Mother of Confucius's 76th generation"; Ailing's husband, H. H. Kung, was "China's Sage"; Chingling was the "widow of China's saint"; Mayling was "the Christian Miss Soong"; and the Generalissimo was "Southern Methodist Chiang."[52] Chiang and Mayling would be featured on more *Time* covers than any other people on the planet.

Just months after Southern Methodist Chiang's blessed conversion, a remarkable novel shot to the top of American bestseller lists. This story of a farm family's struggle appeared at an opportune time: 1931 was a disastrous year for American farmers, as the Great Depression further emptied their pockets and bruised their souls. Severe drought and decades of extensive farming without crop rotation had caused soil erosion, and now gigantic dust storms drove farm families off their land. The novel *The Good Earth,* by Pearl Sydenstricker Buck, told a similar story, but it was set in China.[53] As a young girl, Pearl had watched her missionary father, Absalom, churn out fantasies for American consumption about the coming of New China. She had later served as a Presbyterian missionary in China and, like her father, ran from howling mobs chasing her as a foreign devil. Yet she still penned notes back to the U.S. about a future Christianized and Americanized China.

Just as the fictional dispatches of Reverend Sydenstricker and his fellow delusionaries had been a nearly exclusive source of information about China to millions in the U.S., *The Good Earth* was the only book most Americans would ever read about China. At the same time that Walt Disney was creating lovable characters like Mickey Mouse, Buck created the Noble Chinese Peasants, whose major attraction was that they embodied American values.

Buck's views of Chinese city and country life had more in common

Pearl Buck (Courtesy Everett Collection)

with American mythology than Chinese experience; *The Good Earth* was a Jeffersonian tale in which rural life was good, city life was bad. The husband-wife team of Wang Lung and O-Lan worked hard on their farm, loved their children, and cherished their community, but outside forces uprooted them from their good earth, just like what had happened to millions of Dust Bowl Americans. In the city, the Noble Peasants experienced demeaning extremes of wealth and poverty and were forced into debasing labor. Wang and O-Lan eventually rejected the city in favor of the good earth and returned to the soil and their honest farmer values. The happy ending has the admirable Noble Peasants embracing their simple yet fulfilled lives. *Christian Century* magazine observed, "As far as the spiritual content of Wang Lung is concerned, it would not have differed greatly had he toiled on the Nebraska prairie rather than in China."[54]

The Good Earth became a phenomenal blockbuster, the only twentieth-century book to top *Publishers Weekly* bestseller lists two years in a row (1931 and 1932). Millions of Americans had fallen in love with cuddly images of a distant people that U.S. laws protected them from knowing in reality.

Americans had cheered Japan as it gobbled up Korea in Theodore Roosevelt's time, but they had grown wary over the years as they watched Japan's ambitions grow. *Time* magazine reported from Tokyo that leaders there spoke of a "Japanese Monroe Doctrine claiming the right to protect all Asia...and that the originator to be cited for this idea was none other than the late great Theodore Roosevelt."[55] Few Americans knew what to make of this information about their former president. Teddy had died more than a decade earlier and had successfully hidden his involvement in handing Korea over to Japan. Without citing Roosevelt's authorship, the prestigious *Foreign Affairs* magazine noted, "The idea of a Monroe Doctrine for Asia arose in Japan shortly after the Russo-Japanese War" and "the intent of the Japanese Government to claim the rights of a Monroe Doctrine for the Far East is perfectly clear."[56]

Americans who had believed they were providing Open Door moral protection for the Noble Chinese Peasants were shocked and angry when the Japanese military advanced beyond its Korean colony and invaded Manchuria on September 18, 1931. Japanese warplanes and tens of thousands of Emperor Hirohito's troops soon brought one of Asia's richest areas under control.

The world gasped when Japan expanded from its Korean colony into Manchuria, but it was Mao Zedong's embryonic movement in the Jinggang mountains that would eventually conquer China.

The United States had, of course, been encouraging Japanese expansion ever since Commodore Perry opened Japan in 1853. True, in recent years the messages had been mixed; after World War I, the United States, Britain, and France tried to give imperialist expansion a bad name—after all, they had enough colonies and wanted everyone else to stay put. The Western democracies now called imperial conquest "immoral" and even contrived to make it illegal with policies like the Kellogg-Briand Pact, which renounced all war. In the United States, isolationist peace movements had become a major political force, and supporters feared that Japan's military aggression was a contagion that might drag America and other countries into future wars.

By contrast, many in Japan felt constrained by their country's "potted-plant existence" and yearned to broaden its boundaries. Japanese leaders believed that their nation needed to expand just as England and America had. Japan's minister of war observed, "The United States loudly professes to champion righteousness and humanity, but what can you think when you review its policy toward Cuba, Panama, Nicaragua and other Latin American nations?"[57] Japanese foreign minister Yosuke Matsuoka asked, "What country in its expansion has ever failed to be trying to its neighbors? Ask the American Indian or the Mexican how excruciatingly trying the young United States used to be once upon a time."[58]

Why was it fine for the United States to ship American soldiers halfway around the world to keep its hold on the Philippines but not okay for Japan to expand into its sphere? Prince Konoe, later Japan's prime minister, explained that Japan "was perfectly entitled to aggrandize [its] Chinese territory to meet the needs of its own exploding surplus population....It was only natural for China to sacrifice itself for the sake of Japan's social and industrial needs."[59]

At the time of Japan's invasion of North China, Baron Kaneko was a spry seventy-nine-year-old. He penned a magazine article suggesting that if his friend Theodore Roosevelt were alive, he would understand Japan's actions: "Now when Japan's policy in Manchuria is much criticized by foreign Powers, it is a matter of the greatest regret to me and to Japan that Theodore Roosevelt died unexpectedly without having uttered in public speech his views on a 'Japanese Monroe Doctrine' in Asia. This opinion, held by one of the greatest statesmen of our time, would have been of high importance, had Roosevelt lived to announce it himself at the present moment, when Manchuria is once more a burning international question."[60]

Henry Stimson was secretary of state when the Japanese invaded North China. A Harvard Law graduate and Wall Street lawyer, he had been brought into government by Theodore Roosevelt. He would serve every president from Teddy to Harry Truman except Warren Harding. Stimson had been secretary of war under President Taft, fought in World War I during Wilson's administration, mediated in Nicaragua for President Coolidge, and served as governor-general of the Philippines, and in 1931 he was secretary of state under President Hoover. Pulitzer Prize winner Kai Bird wrote that "no man casts a longer shadow over the American Century than Henry Lewis Stimson."[61] Indeed, one of several Stimson biographies is subtitled *The First Wise Man*.[62]

A follower of Theodore Roosevelt, the First Wise Man believed in a hierarchy of peoples. In this hierarchy, American white males groomed in the Ivy League—especially at Harvard, like Roosevelt and Stimson—were the best of the best. Stimson accepted the notion of the white man's burden, that only by the application of American values did lesser nations have any hope of succeeding. Stimson had already experienced firsthand the inadequacies of the lesser races. In 1927 President Calvin Coolidge had appointed him to the biggest bwana job in the American portfolio: governor-general of the Philippines. Stimson felt himself well qualified to provide tutelage to his Filipino inferiors, which he did for two years, until 1929.

Stimson had not uttered a peep during the long years of Japanese mistreatment of Koreans because Korea had been Teddy's gift to Japan. But Roosevelt's Japanese Monroe Doctrine for Asia had envisioned Japan's expansion eventually being blocked by Russia in North

Asia and by the Anglo-American Open Door policy in Manchuria and the rest of China. Roosevelt had been wrong. Now the Japanese had overstepped their promised bounds and challenged America's Open Door.

Roosevelt had detested the Chinese, but by 1930, Stimson and many Americans came to prefer them to the Japanese. After all, the Japanese had defied American strategic expectations, whereas the Noble Chinese Peasants were progressing down the road of Christianity and democracy. On October 9, 1931, Stimson met with President Herbert Hoover and demanded that the United States and the League of Nations jointly condemn Japan's actions on the grounds of a number of international treaties. Hoover based his calculations of America's interests in Asia on hard dollars and cents. The bottom line was that the value of U.S. trade with Japan was many times larger than it was with China. While Americans might shed a tear for Noble Peasants Wang and O-Lan, the Japanese were buying fully half of America's cotton crop, and Japan's military-industrial complex bought large amounts of U.S. oil and steel. Nelson Johnson—the U.S. ambassador to China from 1929 to 1941—wrote that Japanese control of North China would not cause "the loss of a dollar from an American purse."[63]

At this critical point, Henry Luce featured Generalissimo and Madame Chiang on the cover of *Time,* a major media event. At a moment when *The Good Earth* was all the rage and Americans awaited the U.S. reaction to the Japanese incursion into Manchuria, here were brave, smiling, Christian Noble Chinese Peasants standing firm against the Japanese.

Time's October 26, 1931, cover was startling, historic, and well timed. As Stimson searched for a policy Hoover would endorse, Americans held in their hands a picture of Noble Chinese Peasants like those suffering at Japan's cruel hands.

When Stimson was secretary of war under President Taft, from 1911 to 1913, the U.S. Navy developed a contingency plan for war against

On October 26, 1931, Time *magazine's cover featured Chiang Kai-shek and Mayling Soong as "President of China and Wife." (Courtesy Everett Collection)*

Japan. The Navy admirals of that time had in their youth served as officers enforcing the Union's economic embargo against the Confederacy, which was, like Japan, an "island" that could be blockaded. The U.S. Navy and their civilian overseers advocated a nonviolent economic war against Japan, a resource-poor island nation dependent on imports. In this siege plan, the U.S. would establish bases near Japan, choke off vital exports, and, finally, strangle the island chain financially by denying it funds. This U.S. naval plan was based on the theory that it was possible to force Japan to capitulate with no risk to the United States of a prolonged war.

Since Meiji's time, the military had become powerful. Indeed, the army's invasion of Manchuria had surprised many civilian officials in Tokyo. Stimson wrote that the "Japanese Government which we have been dealing with is no longer in control" and that "the situation is in the hands of virtually mad dogs."[64]

The United States was Japan's largest supplier of oil and steel, the profitable blood and muscle around which the Yankees of the Far East had built their Western-style military-industrial complex. Though there would be some economic pain in the U.S., Stimson reasoned that via a stoppage in exports, he could bring Japan's military to its knees. The First Wise Man's logic was that the Japanese mad-dog military, once deprived of U.S. oil and forced to withdraw from China, would be humiliated back home. Stimson theorized that moderates in Tokyo would then retake the government, resurrect democracy, and become peaceful partners with the United States once again.

The First Wise Man had little insight into Japanese thinking, and some worried that an American embargo might cause an indignant Japan to attack the United States. Stimson dismissed such concerns, confidently asserting that the Japanese would never dream of making such a move. There were plenty of things for the First Wise Man to worry about when it came to Japan, but that country's attempting a direct strike against America was certainly not one of them.

Wrote Stimson biographer David Schmitz, "Stimson distrusted mass politics, had concerns about too much democracy, and believed in a greater concentration of power in the executive branch of the government. He was comfortable only with those of his own class and attitudes, and those who accepted authority and followed clear lines of power."[65] Stimson believed in a "strong Executive," meaning that the president of the United States had the right and duty to intervene in the affairs of other countries without consulting Congress. As the First Wise Man said, Congress tended to take "more and more the viewpoint of the locality rather than the viewpoint of the nation. On the other hand the President and his Cabinet by force of their position represent the national viewpoint."[66]

On the afternoon of Sunday, December 6, 1931, Stimson met with President Hoover. He argued that the risk of war had to be weighed "against the terrible disadvantages which Japan's action was doing to the cause of peace in the world at large and the danger that Japan was setting off a possible war with China which might spread to the entire world."[67] From Japan went China, from China went Asia, from Asia went the world; in years to come, other advisers in Stimson's wake would sell a similar domino logic.

Harvey Bundy, Henry Stimson's closest associate at that time, later recalled that Stimson "had been brought up in the Teddy Roosevelt tradition and believed in the exercise of power, and not waiting...he believed in taking the bit in his teeth and going forward." But though Stimson "was on his horse and ready to shoot the Japanese at sunrise," he did not have Hoover's support.[68] The president quashed Stimson's dream of an embargo but came up with a compromise, and on January 7, 1932, Stimson announced America's nonrecognition of Japan's conquests in China.

Stimson's nonrecognition doctrine—like the Open Door policy—was ignored by Japan and the other Western powers, who were busy with their own colonies in Asia. And as Hoover had hoped, American companies continued to supply the Japanese war machine with all the steel and oil it wanted. Generations of missionary letters and the Open Door policy had convinced the American people that the nation's priority was to help China, so there was now a wide gap between the actual U.S. foreign policy in Asia and Americans' perception of it. Sympathy for the Noble Peasants ran higher than ever as Americans clutched copies of *The Good Earth* and read headlines about China's new Christian leaders. The heavily Protestant churchgoing public felt that America had a responsibility to save the Noble Peasants and not lose China to Japan's aggression. But the business interests reaping profits from the Japanese felt no such religious or moral compunction. A Chinese newspaper noted, "The Chinese people thank Mr. Stimson for his pronouncements but they are only words, words, words, and they amount to nothing at all if there is no force to back them. At present there is no force, because America [has] made it very plain that they will not support with force the ideals, which they themselves assert are just and desirable."[69]

Hoover opposed an economic embargo against Japan, but he allowed Stimson to write a public letter to the chairman of the Senate Foreign Relations Committee appealing to the world to join in nonrecognition of Japanese aggression and warning Japan that if it expanded its military, the U.S. Navy and Army would also build up its involvement in Asia. Instead of backing down, Japan responded by announcing the creation of a new country—the former Manchuria was now Manchukuo (Land of the Manchu). Soon, a pro-Japanese government headed by the Last Emperor, Puyi, was installed. The League of Nations agreed with Stimson's nonrecognition policy and condemned Japan for invading Manchuria. Japan thumbed its nose at Stimson, walked out of the League of Nations, and continued to feast on both Korea and Manchuria.

Japan's easy seizure of Manchuria was not entirely due to its military prowess. Generalissimo Chiang sat atop a large Nationalist army, but he retreated from the Japanese menace and focused on his top priority of vanquishing Mao, who had regrouped and was again posing a threat. Chiang had trained with the Japanese military and had decided that Japan's army was too strong to be resisted and that such a conflict would be damaging to his own troops, which he needed for his fight against Mao.

China had erupted in outrage when Japan invaded its north. Tens of thousands of demonstrators took to the streets of Nanking and Shanghai. Mao called for Chiang to have some spine and fight the Japanese. The *China Times* published a song: "Kill the enemy! Kill the enemy! Hurry up and kill the enemy!"[70] But Chiang decided to "cede land for time," hoping that his going passive and allowing the Japanese to have a large piece of territory might satisfy them. As Jonathan Fenby wrote in *Chiang Kai-shek,* "This would be seen as his first great failure to stand up for national interests against the enemy from across the sea, setting a pattern for the following years."[71]

From his early years in the Roosevelt administration and on throughout the 1920s, Henry Stimson was one of the East Coast elite who supported various right-wing dictatorships. By 1930, the U.S. executive branch had "sent gunboats into Latin American ports over 6,000 times, invaded Cuba, Mexico (again), Guatemala, and Honduras; fought protracted guerrilla wars in the Dominican Republic, Nicaragua, and Haiti, annexed Puerto Rico, and taken a piece of Colombia to create both the Panamanian nation and the Panama Canal."[72] America preached democracy in Asia, but by the end of the First Wise Man's term as secretary of state, dictators with U.S. military support ruled fifteen of Latin America's twenty republics. Among these dictators was Nicaragua's brutal autocrat Anastasio Somoza. Stimson and the strongman went way back: Somoza's first step up the ladder was serving as Stimson's interpreter when Stimson refereed Nicaraguan peace talks in the 1920s. Taken with the polite, Philadelphia-schooled Nicaraguan, the First Wise Man had green-lighted the brutal Somoza family dictatorship that would rule into the 1970s. Although Stimson withdrew American Marines from Nicaragua by 1933 (despite the inevitable protests of American businessmen), control remained with a U.S.-supported military dictatorship. In his diary Stimson claimed that intervening south of the border "would put me in absolutely wrong in China, where Japan has done all this monstrous work under the guise of protecting her nationals with a landing force."[73] So said the pot to the kettle.

On January 28, 1932, the Japanese bombed Shanghai, China's best known and most visible city in the West. Stimson was ready to go to war with Japan, although Hoover had repeatedly told his secretary of state that he would not risk war by denying U.S. steel and oil to Japan. Still, the First Wise Man continued to insist that there was no danger in cutting off Japan's supply, because "Japan was afraid of" America's "great size and military strength." Hoover, however, understood Japanese thinking better than the First Wise Man and told Stimson his idea was "folly," that a strict embargo would indeed lead to war with Japan and "that such a war could not be localized or kept in bounds." A defiant Stimson challenged the president to be a strong-willed executive in foreign affairs like Theodore Roosevelt and to "speak softly and carry a big stick!"[74]

Hoover declined to take the advice of his upstart secretary of state. He would fight to defend U.S. territory, but—unlike Theodore Roosevelt—Hoover had no interest in becoming the world's policeman.

Chiang's armies skirmished with Japanese soldiers in the winter and spring of 1932, not in North China where Japan had invaded, but far to the south, in Shanghai. Both sides employed airpower; Japan had a sophisticated carrier-based air wing, while Chiang had a ragtag bunch of battered planes flown by mercenary pilots who were mostly from America but also from Britain, France, Italy, Russia, and Germany. A U.S. Army Air Corps–trained airman named Robert Short became the very first of these pilots to die flying for Chiang Kai-shek in China. Short, a native of Tacoma, Washington, had been sent to China by the Boeing Company to sell airplanes. Once in China, Short crossed the line and became a mercenary. On February 22, 1932, he took off and encountered Japanese planes from the aircraft carrier *Kaga;* they destroyed his plane in midair.

Japan eventually beat back Chiang's ill-trained and badly led troops. Chiang never imagined that his forces alone would be able to defeat Japan in China and expected that he would need foreign support, in line with the ancient Chinese state strategy of *yi-yi-zhi-yi,* which meant playing one barbarian—in this case, Japan—against the other. On May 24, 1932, the U.S. ambassador to China, Nelson Johnson, met with Chiang, who spoke enthusiastically about a future war between America and Japan "in which the United States will figure as the champion and savior of China."[75]

George Westervelt, the Curtiss-Wright airplane salesman, observed some of the bombing of Shanghai from his hotel-room window. Seizing his opportunity, Westervelt wrote finance minister T. V. Soong and told him that if China had possessed a professional air force, Chiang could have prevented the Japanese from landing at Shanghai by bombing their ships in advance. Westervelt further pointed out that if Chiang now got serious and built a major air force, airplanes flown from China could burn down the paper cities of Japan.

Soong was excited about the Curtiss-Wright plan, especially Westervelt's intimation that the U.S. War Department might provide leadership for the Chinese air force and perhaps even foot the bill to stimulate American airplane production. T.V. contacted the U.S. military attaché in Shanghai, Colonel W. S. Drysdale, and asked for his help in securing War Department backing. Drysdale was enthusiastic and wrote a message supporting the plan to the War Department in Washington. In response, General Douglas MacArthur, the Army chief of staff, told Drysdale, "The War Department is not interested in sending an aviation training mission to China."[76]

Most thoughtful military men understood why Chiang would never be able to establish an efficient air force: warplanes required secure airfields, and Chiang's armies were incapable of defending an airfield against the Japanese. So now both the State Department and the War Department impeded Chiang's efforts.

T. V. Soong was not about to give up, however, and he contacted the Commerce Department's trade commissioner in Shanghai, Edward P. Howard. This was 1932, and Howard knew that airplane sales would be a boon to the sagging U.S. economy. Within a week, Howard gave T.V. a plan to build a U.S.-supplied air force, beginning with twelve aircraft and eight instructors to train fifty pilots within one year.

When the State Department in Washington learned what the Commerce Department was up to, it wired Howard in Shanghai to explain that Commerce could help with "civilian aviation," but "in relation to plans for the Chinese Government in connection with 'military air training,' it is the Department's opinion, known to and concurred in by the War Department, [that] it would be inadvisable for this Government or any of its officers to be associated with military training."[77] Commerce's Howard advised T.V. to ignore State and proceeded to present to him a more elaborate training mission with more airplanes and pilots.

Ailing's husband, H. H. Kung, served as both Chiang's prime minister and Standard Oil of New Jersey's main representative in China.

Retired U.S. Army Air Corps colonel John Jouett managed Standard Oil's private airplanes. When he learned through Kung that T.V. was looking for someone to head his Chinese air force, Jouett jumped at the chance.

T.V., working around the State and War Departments and with the help of Curtiss-Wright and the Commerce Department, deposited dollars in American banks in May of 1932 for the purchase of aircraft and spare parts and to pay the salaries and travel expenses of American airmen.

The State Department realized what was happening when Colonel Jouett and his hopeful mercenaries applied for passports. State called in the chief of Commerce's Aeronautics Trade Division and explained that as long as the mission to China was civilian in nature, it would have no objections, but that State's policy was that the United States government was not to become involved with Chinese military aviation. Commerce coyly tried to portray the sales as purely civilian but eventually admitted the truth and explained that "this whole situation had now gone pretty far; that the Department of Commerce had transmitted messages to and from the Chinese government and the interested Americans; that the interested Americans had signed a contract; that the Chinese government had advanced money; and that the interested Americans had made the necessary arrangements to leave for China."[78]

State was now between a rock and a hard place. Chinese purchases of American-made airplanes would mean millions of sorely needed dollars for the United States. Curtiss-Wright and the other airplane manufacturers who would supply T.V. were politically powerful, and they provided high-paying jobs in a high-tech industry. The exchange was already in midstream. State hesitated, then noted its disapproval but did not block the transaction.

T. V. Soong had hit the jackpot, acquiring not only American airplanes but also access to the inner workings of the U.S. Army Air Corps. Colonel Jouett had served as chief of personnel of the Army Air Corps during the 1920s. He had inside information on American training methods and could get to the personnel files of almost all the American pilots, active and retired. Now on T.V.'s payroll, Jouett looked through confidential records and took away copies of Air Corps training manuals, expertise derived from decades of trial and error and many millions of American tax dollars.

In early July, Jouett, nine instructors, a flight surgeon, four mechanics, and a secretary—all U.S. Army Air Corps–trained—arrived in Shanghai. Major Howard of Commerce introduced Colonel Jouett to his new boss, T. V. Soong. T.V. selected Hangzhou—a prosperous city on the Yangtze River about a hundred and ten miles from Shanghai—as the training site. Jouett and his men reached there by the end of July and quickly set up the Central Aviation School. Through a corporation called the Central Aircraft Manufacturing Company—CAMCO—that she founded with Harvard graduate William Pawley, Ailing became Curtiss-Wright's Chinese manufacturer. Having successfully done an end run around the State and War Departments, the Soong-Chiang clan was finally getting a barbarian air force with which to destroy another barbarian.

The Japanese had invaded North China thinking they'd wrap up hostilities in a few months, but soon they were bogged down in China's vastness. They were further surprised to see the United States opposing Japan by building Chiang an American-style air force. On January 16, 1933, the Japanese Foreign Office complained to the U.S. State Department that the U.S. Army Air Corps had lent American mercenaries to Chiang to "take part in the hostilities against Japan."[79] To those who knew Japan, such language was ominous. But among the American leadership, there was almost no one who knew Japan.

The phenomenal success of *The Good Earth* made Pearl Buck an assumed authority on all things Chinese. In a major speech at the University of Virginia, Buck explained why the Noble Peasants were just like Americans:

> The real reason why we do not like Japan as well as China is because the Japanese are emotionally different from ourselves....I believe of course that these emotional likenesses and differences...are due simply to geography. That is, peoples

living, as do the Chinese and ourselves, in broad, rich, abundant land—in continents, really—upon landscapes varying from seacoast and northern cold to high mountains and tropical plains, come to be alike.... The lands of the United States and of China arc extraordinarily alike—the northern plains in China and our western plains, the deserts of north and west, the rich central plains of both countries, the long seacoast, the vast, long rivers the bleakness of the north and the tropics of the south...here are great similarities, inevitably producing, or so I think, similarities in temperament....

In brief, then, our emotions are not so much the result of our ideas or our religion as of the food we eat and the land and the climate in which we live, and because China and the United States are so much alike in these respects, we are very much alike in the way we feel.... The same kind of land, feeding the same kinds of foods, under the same sun and winds, the shores washed by the same seas, will produce the same kind of hearts and minds, however the skins may differ. The skin, the color of the hair and eyes—these are, after all, only a kind of dress given us by our chance parents, and not more important than dress ever is. Inside we have the same heart and lungs, the same organs by means of which we live and feel and are.[80]

In a speech to the American Academy of Political Science, she claimed that China would change only if forced to by outside forces: "[China] is at last knocking at [American] doors...entering eagerly into the colleges and universities, examining critically all that she sees, seizing ideas which she thinks will be useful to her, and returning again to her own land to use her new knowledge in her own fashion."[81]

But the Noble Chinese Peasants were not knocking on American doors—the Soongs were. And soon Charlie Soong's offspring would have someone new to approach: Warren Delano's grandson.

Chapter 5

THE CHINA LOBBY

Chiang Kai-shek and the Madame and their families, the Soong family and the Kungs, were all thieves, every last one of them, the Madame and him included.
—President Harry Truman[1]

On November 8, 1932, Warren Delano's grandson was elected president of the United States. Franklin Delano Roosevelt was fifty-one years old, and his new job came with a salary far below his needs. Roosevelt enjoyed a wealthy man's lifestyle: several homes—one in New York City's tony East Side, another along the banks of the Hudson River, and a third on the coast of Maine—as well as sailing yachts and other luxuries. Roosevelt had five children at the time he was elected—Anna (twenty-seven), James (twenty-six), Elliott (twenty-three), FDR Jr. (nineteen), and the baby, John Aspinwall Roosevelt (just seventeen)—and with all the private schools and vacations, they had cost a bundle to raise.[2]

Yet Roosevelt had never earned much money. For two decades he had held public service jobs with relatively low pay: member of the New York State Senate, assistant secretary of the Navy, and governor of New York. His new title, president of the United States, held immense power and prestige but again had a relatively small salary compared to FDR's large expenditures. Luckily for Franklin and many of the rich people of his era, one of his ancestors had made a fortune in what was politely euphemized as "the China trade."

When Warren Delano died, on January 17, 1898, at the age of eighty-nine, he left each of his children a small fortune; to Sara he bequeathed a staggering $1,338,000. (In comparison, FDR's father had inherited $300,000 from his father.) One million dollars–plus was a substantial amount in 1898, when the average family income was $650 a year.[3] Sara's fortune grew, and during her lifetime she held the purse strings in the family. FDR's mother paid for FDR's town houses and yachts; she paid his electric bills and his children's tuitions. The money that funded the new president's lifestyle came from Warren Delano's made-in-China opium fortune.

Franklin Delano Roosevelt and Sara Delano Roosevelt. Sara paid FDR's bills from her father's China fortune. (Courtesy of the Franklin D. Roosevelt Library and Museum, Hyde Park, New York)

*   *   *

Franklin Roosevelt's besting of Hoover in the 1932 presidential election left Henry Stimson a lame-duck secretary of state. The First Wise Man recorded in his diary that he felt his immediate task was to assist the president-elect with the transition and "make sure that whoever comes in as Secretary of State after me shall have a fair chance to understand the policies we have been working out during this time, and, as far as possible, not do something to reverse them unnecessarily."[4] Hoover, a conservative man bitter over his embarrassing defeat, did not trust the liberal Roosevelt. Hoover had invited the president-elect to endorse some of his policies, but Roosevelt responded that he would keep his powder dry. The chill between the two men intensified.

On December 22, 1932, Stimson answered his phone and heard the voice of Professor Felix Frankfurter. In 1906, when Frankfurter graduated at the top of his Harvard Law School class, U.S. attorney for the Southern District of New York Henry Stimson had hired him as an assistant attorney. When Stimson became secretary of war in 1911, he brought Frankfurter into the War Department as his closest adviser.

FDR met Frankfurter in 1917 in Washington's old State, War, and Navy Building, where they both had offices. Assistant Secretary of the Navy Roosevelt and Chairman Frankfurter of the War Labor Policies Board were the same age (thirty-five) and were both connected to Theodore Roosevelt, FDR by birth and Frankfurter through the trust-busting projects he had done for Teddy under Stimson. Working together on labor issues in the Navy yards, the two men developed a warm first-name-basis relationship. Roosevelt and Frankfurter kept in intimate touch from 1917 until FDR died in 1945, writing each other hundreds of letters and spending innumerable hours on telephone lines.

After serving Stimson, Frankfurter joined the Harvard Law School faculty, where he remained for twenty-three years. For almost a quarter century, Harvard Law students would hear him praise the First Wise Man, his former boss. The impact on America's twentieth century would be profound.

That December, Frankfurter called Stimson from Albany, where he was Governor Roosevelt's guest. Frankfurter explained to Stimson that Roosevelt "feels very badly that all cooperative efforts had been broken off" and that in the middle of a conversation, FDR had suddenly proposed that Henry Stimson be a bridge between the outgoing and incoming administrations. Frankfurter suggested that Stimson extend an olive branch by phoning FDR, who would then invite Stimson for a talk.

Hoover, when informed by Stimson about Frankfurter's overture, was against his secretary of state meeting with FDR. Stimson argued that it made no sense to "deprive the incoming president of the United States of important information about foreign affairs." Nevertheless, Stimson obeyed Hoover, and for a while, there was little contact between the two camps. Frankfurter personally knocked on Secretary Stimson's office door in Washington on December 28, 1932. The First Wise Man listened as Frankfurter pleaded the case for FDR, creating an image of him that Stimson described in his diary as "a more attractive picture than we have been getting from the other side."

When Hoover returned to Washington after his Christmas vacation, Stimson told him that he wanted to meet with the enemy and that he felt it was his responsibility to give the president-elect the national security information he sought. A wounded Hoover maintained that Roosevelt was "a very dangerous and contrary man and that he would never see him alone."[5] Having made his point about how little he trusted the incoming president, Hoover relented the next day and told Stimson that he could meet with FDR.

On January 9, 1933, the president-elect welcomed Secretary of State Stimson to Sara Delano Roosevelt's mansion on the Hudson River. Both men were New Yorkers who had been schooled at Harvard. They spoke for almost six hours and found that they saw eye to eye on most national security matters, such as the need for "stability" in Latin and South America. Stimson was relieved to learn that Roosevelt "fully approved" of his nonrecognition doctrine against the Japanese.[6] A week later, FDR publicly backed a Hoover policy for the first time:

President-Elect Roosevelt made his initial statement on world affairs when he endorsed Stimson's nonrecognition doctrine. When later questioned by two surprised advisers as to why a Democrat had given a Republican policy such visibility, FDR replied, "I have always had the deepest sympathy for the Chinese. How could you expect me not to go along with Stimson on Japan?"[7]

Unknown to Roosevelt, Stimson had recorded his observations after their meeting, recalling that when he briefed FDR on China, Roosevelt showed a "lively interest": "Roosevelt told me that one of his ancestors, I think a grandfather, had held a position there and that his grandmother had gone out to the Far East on a sailing vessel."[8]

Henry Luce's presentation of a united China led by democracy-loving Christians left out informed coverage of Mao Zedong's revolution, which meant that Time Inc. missed what was certainly — in terms of the number of people affected — one of the twentieth century's biggest stories.

After toiling in the cities as a good Communist — following the Marxist line that revolution would originate with urban workers — Mao had returned to his native province of Hunan at the time Chiang had been allying with Ailing Soong. For thirty-two days, in January and February of 1927, Mao interviewed many disgruntled commoners. Mao concluded that he was witnessing the Mandate's future thrust: "Several hundred million peasants will rise like a mighty storm, like a hurricane, a force so swift and violent that no power, however great, will be able to hold it back.... They will sweep all the imperialists, warlords, corrupt officials, local tyrants and evil gentry into their graves."[9]

Mao saw these peasant uprisings as organic events, forces of nature that could not be stopped; China's revolutionaries had to decide whether they would ride the wave.

> Every revolutionary party and every revolutionary comrade
> will be put to the test, to be accepted or rejected as they decide.

There are three alternatives. To march at their head and lead them? To trail behind them, gesticulating and criticizing? Or to stand in their way and oppose them? Every Chinese is free to choose, but events will force you to make the choice quickly.[10]

Mao understood that the key issue in China was the ownership of land—with land, a peasant ate; without it, he starved. Thus Mao sensed that the verdict of the Mandate was in the peasants' hands, and he clearly described the violence that would be required to change China:

A revolution is not a dinner party, or writing an essay, or painting a picture, or doing embroidery; it cannot be so refined, so leisurely and gentle, so temperate, kind, courteous, restrained and magnanimous. A revolution is an insurrection, an act of violence by which one class overthrows another. A rural revolution is a revolution by which the peasantry overthrows the power of the feudal landlord class. Without using the greatest force, the peasants cannot possibly overthrow the deep-rooted authority of the landlords, which has lasted for thousands of years.[11]

Generalissimo Chiang's government had complete control in a few provinces and partial control in some others, which left a vast portion of China under the rule of various warlords. Chiang worked through local elites—warlords and landlords—hated by the Four Hundred Million. To most Chinese, Chiang was merely China's biggest warlord, an aspirant to the Mandate but not China's absolute ruler. *Time* may have proclaimed the Generalissimo leader of the nation, but as the journal *Foreign Affairs* told its few readers, "Chiang is the apex of a loose pyramid of sand, and his peculiar gift is his ability to anticipate the shifting in the immense weight beneath him in time to maintain his own precarious balance."[12]

Unremarked upon by Pearl Buck, Henry Luce, and others was that Chiang admired fascist models of government, with their strong militaries and disciplined societies. German army officers trained Chiang's elite troops from 1934 to 1937. Chiang also created the Blue Shirts—modeled on Hitler's Brown Shirts—who swore loyalty to him. With some ten thousand members, the fascist group established branches throughout Chiang-controlled territory. And Chiang's Special Services was a secret Chinese gestapo headed by the Dai Li, whom some called China's Himmler.

The United States was an established nation with a military, while Chiang's government was but a military masquerading as a nation. Military spending accounted for 70 percent of Chiang's expenditures.[13] John Fairbank pointed out that "[Chiang's] China in its equipment and modern plant was a small show. In industrial production it was smaller than Belgium, in air and sea power negligible, in the gadgets and equipment of American life not as big as a middle western state."[14] Journalist Edgar Snow described the Chinese economy as a Soong-Chiang plaything: "Nobody knows—except Chiang, Kung, and the Soongs—exactly how much treasure China has shipped to England and America, or how much gold and silver reserve there is for China's currency. Because of the family's key financial positions and close relationships with foreign banks and governments...it is doubtful if anyone but a member of the Chiang-Soong-Kung family could draw on China's bullion reserves abroad."[15]

Chiang didn't have as much centralized control as Adolf Hitler, but he certainly oversaw a comparable share of media whitewash. He moved quickly to silence critics, sometimes by brutal means. In early 1932, for instance, Chiang had six young writers critical of him arrested and buried alive. When observers pointed out that Chiang's fascist methods were at odds with the democratic ideals he supposedly harbored, Soong-Chiang propagandists said that conditions in China were difficult and that Chiang was taking his countrymen through Sun Yat-sen's tutelage period in advance of full democracy.

After watching the Generalissimo slaughter five-sixths of his comrades, Mao realized that "political power grows out of the barrel of a gun."[16] After Mao's escape westward, his small area of support was entirely surrounded by Chiang's hostile troops and had no access to a seaport. Mao could not depend on a foreign country to supply him with instructors and arms. Instead, Mao developed what became known as People's War, built on winning the political support of the disenfranchised peasant majority and then drawing the attacking enemy deep into China's interior, where the invaders could be bled dry through a mix of mobile and guerrilla warfare. Mao understood that a tiny band of a few dozen ragtag soldiers (as was typical of his forces) would easily be routed in a head-on confrontation with Chiang's foreign-supported army, so instead, Mao preached a strategy of fighting only those carefully chosen battles that his warriors could win.

Mao began his People's War in a remote area with mountainous and difficult terrain where Chiang's authority was weak. The Jinggang Mountains are now known as the birthplace of the People's Liberation Army and the cradle of the Chinese revolution. It was in this remote area of rural poverty that Mao attracted some of China's later historic giants: Zhou Enlai, Lin Biao, Zhu De, Peng Dehuai, and Chen Yi.

Mao had led about a thousand men to these isolated mountains where roving bandit gangs ruled. His first recruits were these same bandits and derelict beggars, the impoverished homeless — essentially, anyone he could find. Mao was confident that he could teach them a new way for China, and he spread his influence through the surrounding mountains, gaining popular support by transferring land from the rich to the poor. (Some peasants who felt abused by their landlords summarily executed them. Mao essentially offered the landlords these options: they could stay but retain only as much of their land as they were able to till on their own; they could flee; or they could refuse to do either, in which case they'd be arrested and, probably, killed.)

Mao made his People's Army the core of his revolution. Two thousand years earlier, the Confucian philosopher Hsün-tzu had written, "The people are the water and the ruler is the boat: the water can support the boat but it can also sink it."[17] Mao adapted this to "the soldiers are fish and the people the water in which they swim." Because Mao welcomed everyone who would fight, orthodox Communists in both Russia and China were aghast and warned that his armed collective would degenerate into roving bandit gangs. But Mao was in firm control from the start, stating what would become a Maoist maxim: "The Party commands the gun. The gun shall never be allowed to command the Party."[18] Eventually, Mao hoped, he and his peasant followers would have the strength to encircle and capture small cities, then larger ones, until finally the entire country would embrace his movement.

Chinese culture generally looked down on military men. Soldiers were referred to as *ping,* a derogatory term. In contrast, Mao called his recruits *than-shih,* "warriors." In the People's Army, there was upward mobility. Unlike in any other army in Chinese history, the lowliest peasant could, with hard work, advance to the rank of general. For the peasants, such ascension was a staggering innovation; for generation after generation, their lives had been predicated on near absolute restriction to the bottom of the ladder.

Mao's warriors and officers received no regular salaries. Instead, every enlisted man was entitled to a portion of land and some income from it. In the soldier's absence, his family or a party member tilled the land for him.

Historically Chinese leaders treated soldiers as little better than beasts of burden. Mao turned tradition on its head by educating his warriors, teaching them that they were fighting for a future in which they and their families possessed land. The soldiers came to understand that if Chiang's forces beat them, their families' lands would be confiscated for landlords who would browbeat them once again. Mao instructed his soldiers to be defenders of the peasantry from which they were drawn, issuing these rules:

All actions are subject to command.
Do not steal from the people.
Be neither selfish nor unjust.

Replace the door when you leave the house.

Roll up the bedding on which you have slept.

Be courteous.

Be honest in your transactions.

Return what you borrow.

Replace what you break.

Do not bathe in the presence of women.

Do not without authority search the pocketbooks of those you arrest.[19]

For tactics, Mao looked to China's storied past, back to the great Chinese military strategist Sun Tzu, who had written,

All warfare is based upon deception. Hence, when able to attack, we must seem unable; when using our forces, we must seem inactive; when we are near...we must make the enemy believe that we are far away; when far away, we must make him believe we are near....If he is superior in strength, evade him. If your opponent is of choleric temper, seek to irritate him. Pretend to be weak that he may grow arrogant. If he is inactive, give him no rest. Attack him where he is unprepared; appear where you are not expected.[20]

Mao cleverly reworked Sun Tzu's ideas into four slogans consisting of four Chinese characters each, simple enough for his peasant army to sing during their morning exercises:

1. The enemy advances, we retreat!
2. The enemy camps, we harass!
3. The enemy tires, we attack!
4. The enemy retreats, we pursue![21]

Mao later remembered,

These slogans were at first opposed by many experienced military men, who did not agree with the type of tactics advo-

cated. But much experience proved that the tactics were correct. Whenever [we] departed from them, in general, it did not
succeed.[22]

People's War focused as much attention on the retreat as it did on
the attack, a strategy designed to exhaust the enemy. As Mao explained,
"The enemy wants to fight a short war, but we just will not do it. The
enemy has internal conflicts. He just wants to defeat us and then to
return to his own internal battles...we will let him stew, and then,
when his own internal problems become acute, we will smite him a
mighty blow."[23]

Mao was still formally under the control of Communist authorities
hiding out in Shanghai, where party chief Lisan Li ridiculed his ideas:
"All the talk of 'encircling the city with the country'...is sheer nonsense."[24] Unable to understand the new creed of Maoism, the Chinese
Communist Party criticized Mao for his military opportunism.

Mao put his social ideas into play, becoming a Robin Hood who
took land from the rich and gave it to the poor. Mao's policies against
opium use, prostitution, child slavery, and compulsory marriage
improved peasants' lives. Mao pushed mass education, and in some
areas, the populace attained a higher degree of literacy than rural
China had seen in centuries. His movement spread, attracting many
converts, and soon he had established bases in neighboring provinces.
Chinese peasants supported Mao because he gave them land, which
meant that they and their families could live. Mao also lightened taxes
and promised resistance against Chiang and his landlord allies. Soon
Mao held sway over a constituency of five million people.

Alarmed by Mao's growing popularity and power, Chiang had mounted
his grandly named Bandit Extermination Campaign in December of
1930, marching more than a hundred thousand troops into Mao's territory. The majority of Chiang's officers were sons of landlords. Promo-
tions were based on politics rather than ability. Chiang's soldiers were
ill trained and badly supplied, and they behaved in the Chinese tradition of locust armies, surviving by plundering the peasants' homes. A

British writer visiting Chiang's front observed, "If anything is calculated to make the Chinese peasant turn spontaneously to Communism... it is having troops permanently billeted on him."[25]

The Generalissimo, portrayed by Luce and other Americans as beloved by the Chinese people, had to kidnap most of his soldiers. Fearing that their "recruits" would desert, Chiang's commanders marched the shanghaied men, all of them tied together with ropes around their necks, hundreds of miles from their homes. They were stripped naked at night to keep them from running away. Unsurprisingly, many perished. U.S. military attaché Colonel Joseph Stilwell observed Chiang's dragooned "scarecrow" soldiers: many were less than four and a half feet tall, under fourteen years of age, and barefoot. Stilwell wrote in his diary, "The wildest stretch of the imagination could not imagine the rabble in action except running away."[26]

Mao's warriors moved in small groups, luring Chiang's troops deep into their territory, relying on the local peasantry for food, shelter, and intelligence. Then with "sharp attacks," the People's Army battered the vulnerable parts of Chiang's armies. So strong was the Soong-Chiang mirage in the U.S. that few Americans were aware that after two months of fighting, Chiang had withdrawn in defeat. Mao's warriors gathered the German, French, British, and American arms abandoned by Chiang's troops as they retreated.

Chiang launched his second Bandit Extermination Campaign in May of 1931 with two hundred thousand troops, twice as many as before. His strategy was to march on Mao's base area and crush him against an anvil of warlord forces pre-positioned to block escape routes. Chiang moved more methodically this time, reinforcing the areas he occupied before each new advance.

With a main force of only thirty thousand men, Mao, in a series of brilliant maneuvers, attacked five vulnerable segments of Chiang's army in five days. In the very first battle, Mao captured large amounts of valuable ammunition, guns, and equipment that Western countries had sold or given to the Generalissimo. Chiang retreated in June after eight weeks of fighting.

Mao Zedong (CPA Media / Pictures From History)

In some battles, Chiang's forces were ten or twenty times larger than Mao's, and Chiang was much richer in war materials, yet Mao not only clobbered Chiang but also increased his volunteer troops in the process. Mao later said,

> The explanation is that [we] created among all people within their areas a rocklike solidarity, because everyone was ready to fight for his government against the oppressors, because every person was voluntarily and consciously fighting for his own interests and what he believed to be right.... The enemy was infinitely our superior militarily, but politically it was immobilized.[27]

Confused by his defeat and unable to understand Mao's winning ways, Chiang amassed three hundred thousand troops for a "final"

Bandit Extermination Campaign in July of 1931. In October, after three months of frustrating battle, Chiang withdrew in defeat for the third time. The Generalissimo doubled the price on Mao's head from fifty thousand dollars to a hundred thousand. Mao ordered that the flyers announcing the bounty on his head be saved, their blank reverse sides used to ease the paper shortage.

With little outside support, Mao ruled a sizable area with a population of over five million. His warriors fought and won with less foreign help than any other army in modern history. Yet, although Mao had won huge battles in the most populous nation on earth, at this point, almost no information about his ideas and victories had reached the United States. No American missionary or reporter ever ventured out from his or her New China to penetrate Chiang's wall around Mao. No Time Inc. mirage believer witnessed Mao's remarkable rise.

Unable or unwilling to comprehend Maoism, Washington officials found it easy to assume that another white Western country—Communist Russia—was the outside force animating Mao. But while some of Moscow's money had trickled to Mao, Sun Yat-sen and Chiang Kai-shek had both accepted much more from the USSR. Money from barbarians would not be the decisive factor in the movement of the Mandate. The truth was that the world's top Communist at the time—the general secretary of the Central Committee of the Communist Party of the Soviet Union, Joseph Stalin—didn't respect Mao's belief that the revolution would come from the Chinese peasantry. The People's Army was mostly on its own, and it was winning.

Two U.S. State Department officials based in China correctly analyzed Mao during this period. O. Edmund Clubb presented a lengthy report suggesting that the breeding ground for revolution in China was the sorry plight of the Chinese peasants, and if Chiang didn't find a way to alleviate their suffering, he might be swept from power.[28] Consul General Walter Adams observed that Mao's movement was not directed by Joseph Stalin; it was a homegrown, increasingly popular revolutionary movement with a "Chinese character indelibly marked

upon it." Adams wrote to Washington that Chiang's efforts to extermi-
nate Mao's movement would be "an exceptionally difficult matter," as
Mao's guerrilla tactics were besting Chiang.[29] But back in Washington,
at the State Department, the mirage held that Chiang was China and
Mao was Stalin's puppet; Adams's and Clubb's reports noting otherwise were routed to State's Russian section.

It was during his third defeat at Mao's hands that Chiang learned of
Japan's incursion into North China. Although Henry Luce depicted
the valiant Generalissimo as itching to fight Japan, Chiang had no
intention of doing so. Declaring that "the Japanese are a disease of the
skin, the Communists are a disease of the heart," Chiang saw Mao as
the biggest threat to his power, with the Japanese a far second.[30] As
Chiang focused on fighting his fellow Chinese, the Japanese conquered about a fifth of China's territory, taking much of China's railways, large swaths of fertile soil, coal and iron mines and foundries,
textile factories, and the main urban areas and transportation arteries
of eastern China.

Mao criticized Chiang for his "nonresistance to imperialism" and
his "no-war policy" and formally declared war on Japan in February
of 1932, calling for the United Front of all Chinese to fight the Japanese. It was a patriotic declaration but could not be put into effect.
There could be no unity if one general was attacking the other.

Three enormous campaigns involving over six hundred thousand
troops and more than a million civilian casualties were a huge drain on
Chiang's finances. Unlike Mao, Chiang could not rely on his own
people for support, so he sought help from foreigners.

On the evening of May 16, 1933, American radio listeners coast to
coast heard a highly unusual broadcast. From the radio came the voice
of a Chinese man speaking in a clear, easy-to-understand Boston
accent. It was the finance minister of China, Mr. T. V. Soong:

> During the years immediately following the American Revolu-
> tion, your trade with England was at a standstill. As a result,

a severe depression set in. Then suddenly the depression vanished, and your nation embarked on its greatest expansion of the early 1800s. American merchants had discovered the China trade. Some of your most distinguished families were engaged in the China trade. The family of President Roosevelt, in both the Roosevelt and Delano branches, was prominent in the early commerce between the two countries. Millions of dollars changed hands without one word being put down in writing. It .was a superb example of trust and mutual respect....

Do you realize that over half the present Cabinet of our government are graduates of your colleges? I have the honor of being an alumnus of Harvard. In my immediate family, one of my sisters, Mrs. Chiang Kai-shek, went to Wellesley. Two sisters, Mrs. Sun Yat-sen and Mrs. H. H. Kung, whose husband was Minister of Commerce and Labor, attended Wesleyan College in Macon, Georgia.[31]

Fortune magazine followed with a flashy piece about "Money Wizard" Soong, a New Chinese Harvard graduate who "was one of the very few Finance Ministers in the world who...brought in a balanced budget." Luce speculated whether "history will eventually accord to Mr. T. V. Soong a place of more importance than that of Alexander Hamilton." Luce explained that China had "a more unified government today [than] at any time in the past twenty years, and a more enlightened government than it has had for centuries," one that maintained "the essentials of sovereignty over nearly all the seaboard and over the vast majority of the peoples of China." For those few Americans who might have heard rumors of a civil war, Luce explained away the fuss: "Each of the eighteen provinces of China proper have a high degree of autonomy ('states' rights') sometimes amounting to secession."[32]

Unmentioned by Luce was Chiang's bigamous marriage to Mayling, his converting to Christianity for political reasons, Ailing's financial shenanigans, and the fact that Chiang was offering no resistance to

T. V. Soong. Life *magazine called him "Asia's greatest statesman."*
(Thomas D. McAvoy / Getty Images)

the Japanese but had hundreds of thousands of his troops surrounding Mao, who had already bested Chiang three times.

Author Warren Cohen noted in *America's Response to China* that President Franklin Roosevelt's Asia policy constituted "a return to his cousin Theodore's policy of appeasing Japan."[33] With the Great Depression weighing on their shoulders, Americans had mostly turned their attention away from foreign events. J. P. Morgan, Standard Oil, and U.S. Steel continued to make good money selling to the Japanese, and FDR believed, as had President Hoover, that interrupting the flow of American oil and steel to Japan would be a "folly" that could propel the U.S. into a war in Asia. President Theodore Roosevelt had cheered

Wall Street's support of Japan in the Russo-Japanese War. Now President Franklin Roosevelt oversaw the American financing and supplying of Japanese military expansion into China.

Many of FDR's innovative ideas would probably have gotten bogged down in typical bureaucratic infighting if they'd been sent through traditional channels, so Roosevelt constructed a shadow government. This shrouded latticework consisted of new executive agencies and private individuals, and FDR "deliberately organized—or disorganized—his system of command to insure that important decisions were passed on to the top."[34] Wrote historian Arthur Schlesinger:

> His favorite technique was to keep grants of authority incomplete, jurisdictions uncertain, charters overlapping. The result of this competitive theory of administration was often confusion and exasperation on the operating level; but no other method could so reliably insure that in a large bureaucracy filled with ambitious men eager for power the decisions, and the power to make them, would remain with the President.[35]

FDR appointed Cordell Hull, a former U.S. senator from Tennessee, as his secretary of state in order to secure Southern votes in Congress. Hull had a pronounced speech impediment, and associates snickered when he declared his priority to be "twade tweaties" (trade treaties). Deliberate to the extreme, he doled out words painfully slowly. Due to Hull's speech impediment and his Tennessee-molasses style, many wrongly judged Hull a lightweight, but he retained great sway in Congress, where he had served in the House and Senate and where he had won the respect of many powerful men. However, Roosevelt wanted to act as his own secretary of state, and he appointed his Harvard friend Sumner Welles as undersecretary of state. He dealt directly with Welles when he wanted something done.

Roosevelt felt that the State Department was full of conservatives opposed to him and decided he would deal with China through his own trusted lieutenants, people who might or might not have had any relevant experience in Asia. Grandpa Delano had advised his grandson never to let his left hand know what his right was doing. Regarding his China policy from 1933 to 1945, it is clear Roosevelt had heeded his grandfather.

State Department China Hand John Davies — born in China and fluent in Chinese — later wrote that Roosevelt "was essentially ignorant and opinionated about China. He had a concept of China's place in the scheme of things which overrode Chinese realities."[36] FDR believed that China could become a "great country" if the United States treated Chiang Kai-shek as a great ruler. And if all went well, China would become America's best friend in Asia.

T. V. Soong penetrated the Roosevelt administration with the assistance of Felix Frankfurter.

Once president, Roosevelt asked Frankfurter to be his solicitor general, but his friend turned him down. Instead, Frankfurter aided Roosevelt from his professorial perch, dispensing advice and enlisting Harvard's best and brightest to help create the New Deal. It was in his role as FDR's chief recruiter that Frankfurter most influenced America's twentieth century. A brilliant legal scholar, he scanned his classes for the cream of the crop to send on to Roosevelt. One insider wrote that there were "literally hundreds of Frankfurter disciples scattered through the Washington agencies...Frankfurter may not have been the master of all these young men, but...they were undoubtedly his disciples."[37] The press began referring to these bright Harvard men as Frankfurter's "Hotdogs." Some of Frankfurter's Hotdogs, particularly Thomas Corcoran and Dean Acheson, would have an enormous impact on President Roosevelt and American history.

T. V. Soong used Ludwik Rajchman, a Polish intellectual and a Soong-Chiang employee since 1930, as his bridge to Felix Frankfurter. Both European-born, Jewish intellectuals, Frankfurter and Rajchman had met and bonded during one of Rajchman's visits to the United States. Rajchman believed that Western culture flowing through his Soong-Chiang employers would determine China's future, and he admired T. V. Soong as one of the best American-oriented New Chinese. Frankfurter, with no knowledge of China beyond the mirage, easily got on board. FDR was next.

T. V. Soong and Franklin Delano Roosevelt had a lot in common. Both had been born into wealthy upper-class families that had made their fortunes in New Chinas, and both were quick-witted, wisecracking Harvard graduates. However, having lived for years in both countries, T.V. grasped the reality in China and understood how differently Americans like Roosevelt perceived it.

Attempting to connect with Roosevelt, T.V. had made a habit of sending congratulatory notes and gifts of tea to the president. Soong learned that Roosevelt loved sailing and ships and sent a model of a Chinese junk with an accompanying note:

> Knowing your interest in sailing vessels, I am taking the liberty of sending you through our Minister at Washington an accurate model of a Hainan sea-going junk, which has been carefully made according to scale under the supervision of our Customs.[38]

Connection established, Roosevelt did Soong the favor of introducing him to his best male friend, Henry Morgenthau Jr.[39] Thus, on his very first trip to Washington, T.V. met the man who over the next decade would funnel billions of dollars to the Soong-Chiang syndicate with no strings attached and no receipts provided.

FDR once gave Morgenthau an autographed picture of the two of them together and inscribed it, *To Henry. From one of two of a kind. Franklin D. Roosevelt.* They had been gentlemen farmers on the Hudson River when they met in 1915 within the Dutchess County Democratic political machine, and Morgenthau became one of FDR's most loyal political supporters. From 1922 to 1933, he was the publisher of *American Agriculturist,* an independent journal. In 1929, Governor Roosevelt appointed Morgenthau New York State commissioner of conservation. When Roosevelt moved to Washington, he appointed Morgenthau chairman of the Federal Farm Board.

To most of the world, FDR offered a happy smile and a ready laugh.

Henry Morgenthau and Franklin Delano Roosevelt. "To Henry. From one of two of a kind. Franklin D. Roosevelt." (Courtesy of the Franklin D. Roosevelt Library and Museum, Hyde Park, New York)

Morgenthau was one of the very few people with whom FDR could remove the mask. Eleanor Roosevelt later said, "My husband never held political office from the time of his governorship without having Henry Morgenthau in some way in his official family.... There was an underlying deep devotion and trust...Henry was Franklin's conscience."[40] As a sign of Roosevelt's fondness for someone, he would bestow a nickname. FDR called his friend "Henry the Morgue."

Morgenthau knew almost nothing about China and listened to his friend's stories about the country without comment because FDR projected himself as unusually perceptive about the Middle Kingdom.

Another of Soong's important Washington connections was Thomas Corcoran, a Frankfurter Hotdog who would go on to help draft the New Deal legislation and become Roosevelt's unofficial chief of staff.

Thomas Corcoran. Tommy the Cork was once FDR's favorite, and he went on to become Washington's most powerful lobbyist. (© Bettmann/CORBIS)

The *New York Times* summed up the relationship between FDR and his young assistant when it wrote that Corcoran was "an able, brilliant young Harvard man, who thinks closely along the same lines as another Harvard man"[41] in the White House and that Corcoran's style was "a symbol of how Mr. Roosevelt operates."[42]

He was born Thomas Gardiner Corcoran on December 29, 1899, in Pawtucket, Rhode Island, where the Corcoran family was up-and-coming lace-curtain Irish. Tommy was a big man on campus at Brown University, a football star as well as president of the debate club, class vice president, an accomplished pianist and accordionist, a star of stage plays, and valedictorian of his graduating class.

At Harvard, Felix Frankfurter recognized Tommy as one of the best legal minds in the country and recommended him to Supreme Court justice Oliver Wendell Holmes. Frankfurter later told Roosevelt that, of all Justice Holmes's legal clerks, "Tom was the dearest to him."[43]

Frankfurter urged FDR to make Tommy his de facto chief of staff even before that office had been invented: "Very, very rarely do you get in one man such technical equipment, resourcefulness, personal and persuasive style, unstinted character, wide contacts, and rich experience in legal financial and governmental affairs."[44]

Roosevelt and Corcoran were quickly on intimate, almost father-son terms. FDR nicknamed him "Tommy the Cork," and Tommy affectionately called the president "Skipper." What made Tommy invaluable to FDR was his ability to maintain complete confidentiality. Tommy instinctively recognized Roosevelt's secretive, left hand/right hand style and was sensitive to the competing swirl of egos around the Skipper. When reporters asked Tommy for inside poop on FDR's White House, Tommy quipped, "I never have anything to say. Professionally I am deaf, dumb, and blind."[45]

Corcoran, unlike almost everyone else in Washington before or since, took no title and sought no credit. Posing as a middle-level official in the Reconstruction Finance Corporation, he had a standard-size office without even a picture of himself and Skipper. Corcoran observed, "[Justice] Holmes told me, 'Never, never reach for a title, for there will always be others who want it. Instead, aspire to command.'"[46]

For a few years in the 1930s, young Tommy the Cork was the apple of FDR's eye. Corcoran would enter the White House early in the morning through a back door and ascend a private staircase to FDR secretary Missy LeHand's office, which connected to the Oval Office. As he later explained, "That way I avoided crossing paths with any of Roosevelt's old guard and kept the jealousies down to a manageable level."[47] When FDR wanted to hear the morning gossip, Tommy was there to regale the president with the latest news using the theatrical and debate skills he had honed at Brown. When FDR sought sound legal advice, there was Corcoran — as Frankfurter proclaimed, one of the best legal minds in America.

When overworked senators and congressmen, who at that time did not have large professional staffs, needed help drafting legislation, Tommy was ready to assist. (Corcoran teamed with another Hotdog, Ben Cohen, to write much of the Securities Exchange Act, developed to regulate and revive confidence in Wall Street.) Once, after dazzling a group of senators, Tommy received a phone call from Roosevelt, who exclaimed, "By God, you're the first man I've had who could handle himself on the Hill."[48]

Tommy was a jack-of-all-trades; he even wrote some of Roosevelt's best lines, including one in what would become known as his "Rendezvous with Destiny" speech: "To some generations much is given. Of other generations much is expected. This generation has a rendezvous with destiny." And when Roosevelt relaxed in the evening with Missy, there was Corcoran, cracking jokes and playing FDR's favorite ballads—"The Yellow Rose of Texas" and "Father O'Flynn"—on the piano or accordion.

Washington insiders saw Corcoran as one of the most powerful men in the country.[49] Vice President John Nance Garner told a colleague, "If I was going to rob a bank, I'd want to go along with Tommy Corcoran."[50] One in the know said, "The role of chief advisor is undoubtedly held at present by Thomas Corcoran, 'Tommy the Cork.'"[51] FDR's son Elliott went further, writing that Corcoran "had a major hand in most items of New Deal legislation" and "apart from my father, Tom was the single most influential individual in the country."[52]

In his Washington discussions, T.V. painted a picture of a New China whose population admired America and yearned to embrace Jesus and Jefferson. Soong pointed out the value of four hundred million potential new customers for America's goods and assured Morgenthau and the Hotdogs that Chiang was fighting the Japanese and that the bandit Mao was on his last legs. FDR's men, having taken notice of the model Chinese junk on Roosevelt's desk, listened up.

Henry Morgenthau longed to help birth New China, but as chairman of the Farm Board, he was hardly well positioned within the U.S. government to deal with the Middle Kingdom. The best he could offer T.V. was a loan of fifty million dollars' worth of wheat and cotton. Soong assured Morgenthau and FDR that such a large surge of valuable commodities would stimulate China's milling sector, strengthening Chiang in his fight against the Japanese. Roosevelt approved the fifty-million-dollar loan from his best American friend to his best Chinese friend. A frustrated Secretary Hull later wrote in his memoirs that Morgenthau often took "long steps across the line of State Department jurisdiction" and "acted as if he were clothed with authority to project him into the field of foreign affairs."[53]

Soong returned to China a hero, for, like Father Charlie, he had brought home some American treasure. Unremarked upon by the Roosevelt administration, big sister Ailing controlled or was an investor in many of China's largest wheat and cotton mills. Indeed, Father Charlie had—with Julian Carr's help—imported the first American-made milling equipment to Shanghai. Morgenthau's wheat and cotton would flow through Ailing's hands.

Via loans and aid efforts, FDR hoped he could goad Chiang into a policy of "unity *by* resisting"—getting Chiang to unite with Mao to fight the Japanese. Chiang, however, consulting with his Nazi advisers on how to vanquish Mao, remained intent on his policy of "unity *before* resisting." The waste of the first fifty million dollars could have been a warning to someone who understood the simple realities in China. But like the ineffective missionaries before him, Franklin Delano Roosevelt would keep chasing the mirage, failing again and again over the next decade to exercise his will in China.

Later, after Roosevelt's death, many would complain of the undue influence of a well-funded, politically connected China Lobby that distorted U.S.-China relations, had a baleful effect on America's democratic institutions, backed Senator Joseph McCarthy on his who-lost-China rampage, and caused the U.S. to spurn Mao Zedong and support Chiang Kai-shek in an invented New China on the island of Taiwan. The roots of this China Lobby lay in T. V. Soong's successful penetration of Franklin Delano Roosevelt's administration in 1933. At the time, few noticed that FDR was running U.S.-Chinese relations off to the side. Secrecy was key to Roosevelt's technique. FDR once told Morgenthau what Grandpa Delano had taught him at Algonac—"Never let your left hand know what your right is doing"—and Morgenthau had asked, "Which hand am I, Mr. President?"

Roosevelt replied: "My right hand, but I keep my left hand under the table."[54]

*   *   *

Roosevelt's aid not only fattened Nationalist coffers but also boosted T. V. Soong's ego. Upon his return to China, he quarreled with the Generalissimo, arguing that Chiang should use the proceeds of the loan to improve the civilian economy and oppose the Japanese. Chiang did not appreciate the advice. Ailing sidelined little brother T.V. and put forth her husband, H. H. Kung, who brought promises from Italy's Benito Mussolini to fund and build an air force. T.V.'s American mercenary Colonel Jouett had performed well but did not have a foreign government footing the bills, and Kung's Italian offer was too good to turn down. H. H. Kung took over T. V. Soong's portfolio as finance minister. On the outside, it appeared as if a big change had taken place, but it was simply a shuffling of duties between Ailing's little brother and her husband, with the reins still firmly in her hands.

With guidance from both Hitler's and Mussolini's militaries, Chiang began his fourth Bandit Extermination Campaign in April of 1933. The result was the same as it had been for the previous three campaigns: Mao lured the Generalissimo's superior forces into deep positions and then slashed and hammered them. Chiang wrote to his field commander General Chen Cheng that he considered this fourth defeat at Mao's hands his "greatest humiliation." Cheng agreed and responded that in his opinion, fighting Mao was a "lifetime job" and a "life sentence." Chiang then removed the general from command.[55] So many of Chiang's foreign arms flowed into Mao's hands that Mao jokingly referred to Chiang as his supply sergeant.

From Moscow, Joseph Stalin viewed what was going on in China with uncomprehending eyes. Ideological divergence was perhaps the greatest crime against Stalinism, so the Communist leader hatched a plan. As Mao was beating Chiang, a group of urban-oriented Chinese Communists had traveled to Moscow, where Stalin indoctrinated them in proper Marxist thought and then dispatched these Twenty-Eight Bolsheviks, as they were later known, back to China. Their mission was to tilt the Chinese Communist Party away from Mao's rural pipe dreams and back toward a focus on urban workers. The Twenty-Eight Bolsheviks allowed Mao to continue as the chairman of the Soviet Chinese Republic but in name only; in reality, they took control. Philip Short wrote in *Mao: A Life,*

> Six times, in the twelve years since he had become a Communist, he had been pushed aside ... on all previous occasions, however, he had either had powerful friends, who eventually came to his aid, or he had withdrawn for tactical reasons, prefiguring a return in strength later on. This time he had been forced out by a central leadership which was implacably hostile to him.[56]

Meanwhile, Chiang was in his capital of Nanking, huddling with his foreign military advisers, who sold him on the idea of slowly strangling Mao's forces by surrounding them with thousands of cement blockhouses from which relentless machine-gun and artillery fire could be coordinated. For the fifth Bandit Extermination Campaign, Chiang's troops built such blockhouses, moving forward in small steps only when well protected by artillery and airplanes. In turn, the Twenty-Eight Bolsheviks foolishly abandoned Mao's mobile and guerrilla strategies in favor of conventional warfare. As Mao later observed, "It was a serious mistake to meet the vastly superior Nanking forces in positional warfare, at which the Red Army was neither technically nor spiritually at its best."[57]

As Chiang's troops advanced, they killed peasants in their path, an attempt to dry up the wellspring from which Mao's warriors flowed. Chiang's troops left behind a wasteland of torched houses and piles of rotting bodies, with over one million dead.

Realizing that Chiang was too powerful to beat in a head-to-head match, the Twenty-Eight Bolsheviks decided that their followers must flee to the west to save themselves. On October 16, 1934, about ninety thousand troops began what was later called the Long March. It started out as a great disaster, the urban-oriented Twenty-Eight Bolsheviks stumbling through the wholly unfamiliar Chinese countryside. These true Communists had no real military experience and managed in the first month to lose half their army in skirmishes with Chiang. It soon became clear that Stalin's students were in over their heads, overwhelmed by the difficulties of managing a constantly harassed military force that was far from pavements and streetlights. Their suffering was so severe that Chiang boasted that he had exterminated the menace of Communism. The civil war, at long last, seemed over.

Mao had tagged along, but because of his heretic status, he had not been consulted in the planning. It was impossible, however, for the new leadership to ignore the respect that the rank and file had for Mao. Pummeled and out of excuses, in early January 1935 at the town of Zunyi in Guizhou Province, the Twenty-Eight Bolsheviks — much to their disgust — handed over the reins to the man who was against everything Marx had theorized and real Communists like Joseph Stalin practiced.

In a stroke of tactical genius, Mao recast what had been a humiliating retreat into what he called a triumphal march, portraying it as an *advance* to confront the Japanese in China's north, a noble effort, unlike Chiang's policy of Chinese fighting Chinese.

Edgar Snow wrote that the Long March was "the biggest armed propaganda tour in history."[58] The "poor man's army" staged mass meetings and theatrical performances at which appreciative peasants learned that Mao would help them get land, lower their taxes, improve their lives, push back Chiang's armies, and oppose the Japanese invaders. Mao's Robin Hood reputation preceded him and "oppressed peasant associations" petitioned him to come to their villages. In the end, Mao and his troops passed through provinces populated by tens of millions of peasants.

In the spring of 1935 the southern city of Kunming was abuzz about the approach of the poor man's army.[59] The American vice-consul in Kunming was John Service. Service's wife and many foreigners had evacuated to Haiphong, French Indochina, but Service remained in Kunming, as he had unique survival skills: he had been born in 1909 in China (Chengdu, Sichuan Province) to missionary parents who lived in a traditional Chinese compound. Service was an intelligent

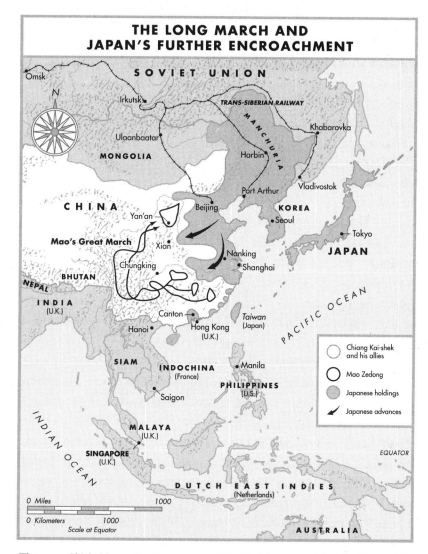

THE LONG MARCH AND JAPAN'S FURTHER ENCROACHMENT

The years 1936–37 saw the Japanese and Mao Zedong expand their holdings while Chiang Kai-shek abandoned his capital of Nanking and moved to Chungking.

and precocious child, bilingual and fascinated by China. By the time he was ten years old, he was taking thirty-mile strolls through the Chinese countryside, chatting his way across various warlords' territories. Service also met other missionaries' children, like John Davies.

At the age of eleven, Service entered the Shanghai American School, joined the Boy Scouts, and took long walks through Shanghai to acquaint himself with the city and its colorful denizens. In 1927, the year that Chiang and Mayling were married, Service entered Oberlin College, in Ohio, where his youthful trekking in China paid off: he became a star long-distance runner, winning the state conference's mile competition three years in a row and serving as Oberlin's track team captain. After graduation, Service heard that his boyhood pal John Davies had become a U.S. diplomat in China and he decided to become one also.

John Service was one of the few Americans in China with the language skills and cultural experience to understand the Chinese peasants' opinions about the poor man's army. They reported that Mao's warriors treated them with respect and paid for food, water, and shelter. Service recalled, "It made a tremendous impression because people were not used to being paid for anything that was provided to soldiers."[60]

Mao led his band for six thousand miles, about twice the width of the American continent, as he spearheaded one of the most remarkable sagas of human courage and endurance in history. Mao was near death more than once, his wife carried shrapnel in her body, and perhaps eighty thousand died. As Mao later remembered, they traveled "across the longest and deepest and most dangerous rivers of China, across some of its highest and most hazardous mountain passes, through the country of fierce aborigines, through the empty grasslands, through cold and through intense heat, through wind and snow and rainstorms, pursued all the way by [Chiang's armies]."[61] Chiang's troops pursued and attacked them from beginning to end; there was about one skirmish a day. The marchers averaged an incredible twenty-four miles daily, a phenomenal pace for a harassed and beleaguered army traveling over some of the most challenging terrain on earth.

Colonel Jouett's mercenary effort in China had received scant notice in the United States but it was front-page news in Japan, where the popular press dramatized the American threat with detailed maps and articles about U.S. planes attacking Japan from bases in China. Members of Japan's parliament charged that the American government was sending "many aviators to China as instructors," which threatened the Japanese homeland.[62]

On April 17, 1934, Japan's Foreign Office issued a statement objecting to the Roosevelt administration's "supplying China with war planes, building aerodromes in China, and detailing military instructors or military advisers to China."[63] The Japanese ambassador to the United States warned Roosevelt in an interview that appeared in the *Washington Star,* "All the new purchases of airplanes are intended by the Chinese to be used eventually against Japan so we cannot tolerate such things...any assistance given to the Chinese which might help them to continue their internal wars or to prepare themselves to fight Japan will have to be stopped."[64] In a front-page declaration in the *New York Times* that continued on inside for six columns, vice minister for foreign affairs Yosuke Matsuoka loudly complained about "the sales of American fighting planes and the training of Chinese aviators by former American military officers."[65]

Colonel Jouett was now vulnerable, his protector T. V. Soong having been pushed aside in favor of H. H. Kung and the Italian government now providing airplanes and pilots. Chiang informed Jouett in July 1934 that when his contract expired, in June 1935, it would not be renewed. Jouett wrote a letter directly to President Roosevelt seeking U.S. government support. Pointing to the Italian domination of Chinese aviation, Jouett asked Roosevelt to write Chiang and finance minister Kung to express his approval of Jouett's work and suggest a continuance of the mission.

Roosevelt referred Jouett's letter to the Department of State for comment. State had never approved of Jouett's mission, as its central policy in Asia was to avoid offending Japan, and it responded huffily to Jouett: "It is felt that action on the part of the Chinese or of the American or of both Governments tending to give the impression that the American Government is inciting the Chinese Government to

military preparedness or is assisting that Government in its own program of preparedness or is attempting to create special bonds between
the military forces of the two countries would have a net effect disad-
vantageous to each and to both countries."[66]

The Chinese contract for Jouett's mission was allowed to expire on
June 1, 1935. Chiang awarded Jouett the Order of the Commander of
the Jade, and Jouett returned to the United States. Few Americans
remained in China as instructors, as Mussolini's Italians were now
predominant.

Mao Zedong and the approximately eight thousand survivors of the
Long March eventually made their way to the town of Yan'an in northern China. Yan'an is in an arid, sun-drenched, dusty region of loess
soil. For millennia, the winds of North China have blown particles of
yellow silt larger than clay but finer than sand. The silt settles finely
and loosely in layers; in some areas, the resulting loess is several hundred feet thick. Loess is easy to dig into, and throughout Chinese history, millions have lived in caves burrowed into the face of loess cliffs,
accommodations that stay warm in winter and cool in summer. Here,
in Yan'an, Mao would establish a safe rear base and mold the men who
would lead China. For miles around, the loess was broken up by deep
eroded gullies that made it difficult for wheeled vehicles to penetrate
the area, and although Chiang's and Japan's planes bombed Yan'an
frequently, the sorties did not disturb even the flower vase on Mao's
deep subterranean desk.

Mao dug his new empire into the sides of Yan'an's hills. Huge caves
housed classrooms, theaters, hospitals, training fields, barracks, homes,
and supply depots. Mao turned Yan'an into an idea factory. He attracted
the young and adventurous, indoctrinated them in his thinking, and
sent them back to their villages to oppose the Japanese and promote
revolution. Mao established a university for military study in a large
natural cave. As the chairman lectured, his commanders squatted on
stone stools and used soft slabs of stone as notepads. (Among the topics inevitably discussed were the merits of the traditional Communist
model of revolution. Mao argued that the Russian and Chinese revolu-

tions would be very different, and he mocked those who studied the Russian model as "cutting the feet to fit the shoes."[67])

Chiang surrounded Mao's Yan'an sanctuary with four hundred thousand soldiers. Cut off from most of the rest of world, Mao once again set out to build a self-sufficient economy. He confiscated land left uncultivated by the landlords in the rugged region where Shaanxi, Gansu, and Ningxia Provinces met and distributed it to the landless. Mao abolished all forms of taxation for the first year to give peasants and small merchants some breathing space, and he later collected a progressive single tax on land.

Mao rebuilt his army, made up of willing recruits from the peasantry to whom he had given land. Mao now had China's only true national fighting force, with volunteers drawn from nearly every province. He didn't have the highly paid generals and fancy equipment that absorbed most of Chiang's army funds, and since everyone from officers down to the rank and file ate and dressed alike and there was very little difference in living quarters, Mao's peasant armies existed on very modest sums.

Mao's warriors had a six-day workweek, arising at five for a day of exercise, meals, military drills, political lectures, writing classes, games, and sports, and then going to bed when taps sounded at nine. Officers and soldiers mingled freely, with little formality. In Mao's army, unlike Chiang's, opium smoking was prohibited, and there were no swarms of prostitutes following the men.

Chiang constantly complained to his foreign helpers that he couldn't fight the Japanese without outside assistance, but Mao preached that the Chinese could do it primarily by themselves. Mao saw the Japanese military as surrounded by hostile Chinese people whom he could inspire and train to offer effective resistance. Japan's supply lines were long, and the Japanese had to guard them and their provisions, forcing them to fight debilitating rearguard battles nearly constantly. Mao told author Edgar Snow,

> China is a very big nation, and it cannot be said to be conquered until every inch of it is under the sword of the invader. If Japan

should succeed in occupying even a large section of China, getting possession of an area with as many as 100 or even 200 million people, we would still be far from defeated.[68]

Western military thought held that the combatant who had the best and most weapons would prevail. Mao taught the opposite: "Weapons are an important factor in war, but not the decisive factor; it is people, not things that are decisive. The contest of strength is not only a contest of military and economic power, but also a contest of human power and morale."[69]

Colonel Joseph Stilwell was the U.S. embassy's military attaché in China in 1936. It was his second tour of duty there and he had traveled the country and was fluent in Chinese. Stilwell understood Chiang's strategy of yi-yi zhi-yi, passively waiting for a barbarian to oust the barbarian Japanese. He visited the Chinese army's front lines, where he had been told Chiang's troops were preparing for aggressive military action against the Japanese. Stilwell wrote, "No evidence of planned defense against further Japanese encroachment. No troop increase or even thought of it. No drilling or maneuvering."[70] Stilwell also observed Mao's warriors, about whom he noted, "Good organization, good tactics. They do not want the cities. Content to rough it in the country. Poorly armed and equipped, yet scare the Government to death."[71]

As Mao slowly but surely solidified his claim to the Mandate, Henry Luce placed Chiang Kai-shek on Time's cover for the fourth time. Under a handsome picture of the Generalissimo looking confident in his Western-style uniform, a white-gloved hand gripping his sword, the caption read: Premier of China. Good roads, good morals, good bombs are his answer to Japan. Readers learned that the "Christian Miss Soong" had convinced "Southern Methodist Chiang" to convert. After becoming a Christian, the Generalissimo "proceeded to conquer all China." Time claimed that Chiang's "brain and will have driven the Chinese people to extraordinary achievements," that Chiang "succeeded in uniting the Chinese people in a way that has not been known for centuries," and that he "was unquestionably the greatest man in the Far East, recognized joyfully as such by Chinese." Chiang had even "rammed some rudiments of Christian conduct and morality" into his soldiers.[72]

About Mao Zedong and his growing movement, Luce made no mention. About Chiang's inactivity against the Japanese invaders, Luce said that Southern Methodist Chiang was simply "turning the Christian other cheek."[73]

Chapter 6

THE FIRST WISE MAN'S
NEW CHINA

---

*The United States has handled Chiang very badly. They have let him get
away with blackmail.*
—Mao Zedong[1]

In the summer of 1934 the Generalissimo and Madame Chiang vacationed with their favorite sycophants—American missionaries—in the cool mountain resort of Kuling on the Yangtze between Nanking and Hankow, high above the Four Hundred Million. Mayling courted these men, who enjoyed sitting with one of the most beautiful women in the world. She spoke to them of "the importance of spreading American culture in China," coyly solicited their opinions, wrote down their best ideas, and complimented and thanked them for helping to create New China.[2] The missionaries in turn continued to write to audiences across the United States about how the Christian Miss Soong and Southern Methodist Chiang were champions of the American way.

The missionaries noted that Chiang didn't have programs to help the peasants the way FDR's New Deal was helping the common man in the United States. Sterling Seagrave wrote, "Mayling was quick to grasp their point. She went to Chiang with an idea, and he agreed with surprising speed. Mayling sat down with the missionaries to work out the details of China's 'New Deal.' She called it the 'New Life Movement.' "[3]

The term *new life* appealed to the American missionaries, with its allusion to the resurrection of Christ combined with the social consciousness of the New Deal. Mayling proclaimed, "Except a man be born again, he cannot see New Life."[4] Millions of Christians in America nodded their heads in agreement. The relatively few of the Four Hundred Million who heard it wondered what she was talking about.

Mayling refashioned Chinese virtues into an American style that the missionaries could translate to the target audience in the United States. Americans saw China as filthy, and Mayling would scrub it clean with theological conviction and public-hygiene campaigns. Americans were heartened to learn that she was asking the Four Hundred Million to wash their hands and faces three times daily, to bathe at least once a week, even to stop smoking. (The Christian Miss Soong stopped smoking in public, though she constantly chain-smoked menthol cigarettes as she sat at her desk writing her New Life dicta.) Laura Tyson Li wrote in *Madame Chiang Kai-shek* that Mayling was New Life's "driving force":

> She and Chiang flew around the country, evangelizing the movement to Chinese and foreign missionaries alike. She formulated much of the movement's propaganda and often wrote the English versions herself. She wrote articles for American publications and gave interviews to foreign journalists extolling the movement's aims and achievements.[5]

Madame Chiang splashed New Life slogans on buildings, and missionaries loved to quote these sayings to the people back home, not realizing that the Chinese victims of Mayling's Americanization paid the words little attention. To counter Mao's success, Mayling claimed, "We are giving the people what the Communists promised but could not perform."[6]

For his part, Chiang saw New Life as a vehicle to further discipline his countrymen. Blue Shirt terror squads beat people up for spitting in the street, for drinking alcohol with their meals in restaurants, for dressing improperly, and for many other infractions. Those who dared to criticize Chiang disappeared and didn't return.

As usual, *Time* magazine explained New Life with an American comparison:

> What Chinese officialdom needed, the Generalissimo and Mme. Chiang had decided, was a big dose of the castor oil of Puritanism. The tablespoon with which they dished this out they called the New Life Movement, and with every ounce of Nanking's authority they dosed all China. Batch after batch of local mayors and magistrates were ordered to Nanking, drilled and exhorted there in the primary decencies—to stop wiping noses on sleeves, to stop taking bribes from litigants. They were warned that he who did not practice the new Puritanism might expect the worst—and this was no empty threat.[7]

While New Life made a lot of positive noise in the United States, it flopped in China. The American ambassador to China, Nelson Johnson, observed, "It is doubtful whether the personalities interested in the movement are sufficiently pure themselves to give the movement much prestige."[8]

It wasn't only the Luce press that constantly pushed the Soong-Chiang party line. American missionaries in China promoted articles supposedly penned by Chiang; in one item, titled "What the Sufferings of Jesus Mean to Me," Chiang (or someone) wrote, "Now I have become a follower of Jesus in his plan for saving the world."[9] Americans learned that Chiang's favorite Christian value was love—"love for the emancipation of the weaker races, and for the welfare of the oppressed people."[10] Certainly some missionaries knew that Chiang was a one-party despot with legions of Blue Shirt thugs terrorizing the populace. They also knew that Chiang's government was still a weak collection of warlord states held together by Ailing and Chiang through financial payoffs. But for reasons of either blind faith or strategic amorality, these men of God overlooked Chiang's shortcomings. The *Missionary Review of the World* wrote, "China has now the most enlightened, patriotic and able rulers in her history."[11]

In the fall of 1936, Chiang received troubling reports about troops allied with him under the command of a warlord, thirty-five-year-old Marshal Xueliang Zhang. Based in the city of Xian in North China, closest to the forces of both Mao and the Japanese, these two hundred thousand troops were now growing resentful because it was their Manchurian territory that Chiang had ceded to the Japanese to buy time. It had been five years, and now they wanted their homeland back.

Mao declared, "The core of our policy is to work with Chiang to resist Japan."[12] On April 9, 1936, Marshal Zhang met with Mao's emissary Zhou Enlai. Zhou argued that Chinese should not be fighting Chinese and that Zhang should unite with Mao to oppose the Japanese in Manchuria. In defiance of Chiang Kai-shek, Zhang heeded Zhou and even agreed to supply Mao with weapons in a joint campaign against Japan.

Chiang—who knew about Zhang's contacts with Mao—warned Zhang not to be taken in by him. Meanwhile, Chiang prepared another Bandit Extermination Campaign—his sixth. On December 4, 1936, he flew to Xian to confront Marshal Zhang. In a tense meeting, Zhang asked Chiang to follow Mao's wish of unifying China by resisting Japan. Chiang countered with his policy of resisting after unity, which meant crushing Mao first.

On Wednesday, December 9, ten thousand students demonstrated in the streets of Xian demanding that Chiang end the civil war and unite with Mao to fight Japan. Police shot and wounded two of the students. At five in the morning on December 12, a two-hundred-man detachment led by Marshal Zhang's personal guard, twenty-eight-year-old Captain Ming Jiu Sun, set out to kidnap Chiang. When Captain Sun captured Chiang, he said, "The [northeast] army demands that you fight Japan as soon as possible, for their homes have been seized by the enemy, and all of China suffers because of their loss." Chiang snorted.

"I am the leader of the Chinese people, I represent the nation. I think that my policy is right, not wrong."[13]

When he learned that Zhang had Chiang in custody, Mao at first wanted Chiang put on trial as a traitor. But many — including Zhou Enlai, Marshal Zhang, and Joseph Stalin, who supported both sides — feared the greater disunity to war-torn China that would result.

The Xian incident was worldwide news, but press reports were mostly speculation, as the central character — Chiang — was incommunicado, and the marshal's lips were sealed. The world wondered, Was Chiang alive or had he been murdered? Who was holding him and why?

Behind the scenes, Zhang asked Chiang to put aside differences with Mao and recommit to a United Front to fight the Japanese. These were humiliating conditions for Chiang. When Zhang proposed a patriotic United Front with Mao, Chiang shouted that Mao was duping Zhang and that the smart strategy was to oppose Mao rather than Japan.

Madame Chiang bravely flew to Xian to confront her husband's captors; T.V. also came along to ease negotiations with payoffs. Chiang grudgingly agreed to halt the civil war. After thirteen days in captivity, Chiang suddenly appeared back in Nanking and announced a new United Front with Mao against the Japanese.

China Hand John Service was now serving in the U.S. embassy in Beijing. By the age of twenty-eight he had already lived in four different provinces, mastered three Chinese dialects, and developed wide contacts with Chinese of all social strata. He was well aware of the ordinary man's desire for Chiang and Mao to unite and oppose Japan. Service later recalled, "I remember seeing Chinese weep when Chiang was released."[14]

The scraps of information leaked about Chiang's time in captivity did not accurately portray the Generalissimo's reluctance to participate in a United Front or reveal that he had caved in to Mao's demands.[15] Simplifying things for her American audience, Pearl Buck wrote, "The differences between Chiang Kai-shek and his followers and the

Communist leaders and their followers were as grave and as irreconcilable as the differences between the black and white races in our own country. But for the sake of the defense of China those differences were put aside."[16]

The Soong-Chiang bunch used their Bibles to project their version of the Xian incident. In a Good Friday sermon, the Generalissimo claimed he had remained strong because of the example of "the forty days and nights Christ passed in the wilderness withstanding temptation."[17] Another story stated that when Mayling appeared at her husband's prison door, Chiang claimed that her arrival had been predicted in a Bible passage he had just read: "Jehovah will now do a new thing, and that is, he will make a woman protect a man."[18] As Chiang explained,

> I have now been a Christian for nearly ten years and during that time I have been a constant reader of the Bible. Never before has this sacred book been so interesting to me as during my two weeks' captivity in Xian....I found myself placed under detention without a single earthly belonging. From my captors I asked for but one thing, a copy of the Bible.... The greatness and love of Christ burst upon me with new inspiration, increasing my strength to struggle against evil, to overcome temptation and to uphold righteousness.... The many virtues of Christ I cannot possibly enumerate....Entreating forgiveness for His enemies, He cried, "Father, forgive them; for they know not what they do." Truly great is the love of Christ.[19]

The Chinese public was elated that Chiang would abandon his commitment to "unity before resisting" in favor of Mao's more popular "unity by resisting." On New Year's Day 1937, a Chinese newspaper editorialized, "From today China will have only the united front, and never again will there be internal hostility."[20] Suddenly Chiang was a national hero, the leading symbol of China's unity. But while Chiang spoke of a second United Front with Mao, in private he prepared for his sixth Bandit Extermination Campaign.

*   *   *

In 1938, Pearl Buck traveled to Stockholm to accept the Nobel Prize in Literature for her depiction of the Noble Chinese Peasants. Just one year before, her most famous book had been brought to celluloid life. Most of the Chinese characters in *The Good Earth* were white actors made up to look Asian, as the Chinese Exclusion Act meant that there were very few Chinese actors in Hollywood. Even the two main characters, Wang Lung and O-Lan, were played by white actors, since Paul Muni, a white actor, had been cast in the leading role of Wang Lung, and movie-industry codes did not allow the portrayal of a sexual relationship between members of different races.

The characters in The Good Earth *movie, Wang and O-Lan, were played by white actors, Paul Muni and Luise Rainer, made up to look Chinese.*
(Courtesy Everett Collection)

The summer of 1937 represented the nadir of Chiang's efforts to make Franklin Delano Roosevelt his barbarian. That July, the Japanese expanded from Manchuria into central China and took Beijing, ancient home of the Son of Heaven. Mao wanted Chiang to fight the Japanese in northern and central China, but in one of the most disastrous decisions in military history, Chiang decided to battle the Japanese in the city of Shanghai, in China's south. Chiang chose Shanghai for its publicity value—there were more Americans there than in any other Chinese metropolis. Chiang's goal was not to beat the Japanese but to attract the sympathy of the Americans so that they would step in and oust them. Ambassador Johnson heard Soong-Chiang syndicate members speak of "the responsibility of America...to preserve the independence and integrity of China."[21]

The fighting in Shanghai was horrendous. The Japanese landed their superior forces, and Chiang threw thousands into the doomed struggle. These battles in and around China's biggest city received the international press attention the Soong-Chiang bunch sought. As Steven Mosher wrote in *China Misperceived,* "The new images of the Chinese provided by Pearl Buck and others could not have come at a better time. When a few years later the Japanese escalated their piecemeal attacks to all-out war, it was not the nameless, faceless masses of China who took up arms against the invaders, but Buck's Noble Chinese Peasants."[22]

Sympathy for the Noble Chinese Peasants grew to a fever pitch when Japan bombed civilians in Shanghai. A photo of Ping Mei, a Chinese baby bombed by the Japanese, caused a sensation and was one of the most reproduced images of the 1930s, creating another sympathetic archetype. Yet Ambassador Johnson wrote that Chiang's attitude was "let us fight to the last drop of coolie blood" and noted that "in the midst of it all the Soong family carries on its intrigues which sometimes disgust me completely."[23]

On September 4, 1937, George Haas, director of research and statistics in the Treasury Department, wrote to Secretary of the Treasury Morgenthau, "It would appear then that the peace of the world is tied up with China's ability to win or to prolong its resistance to Japanese aggression. It is our opinion that a Japanese victory increases greatly the chances of a general world war." Morgenthau wrote to a Chung-

*Ping Mei amid the Japanese-bombed ruins of Shanghai's South Railway Station,
Saturday, August 28, 1937. One of the most famous photos of the 1930s.
(Courtesy Everett Collection)*

king official: "We feel we can [help] you and in the long run we will be
helping ourselves. We feel it very important to the world peace to help
China."[24] Morgenthau wrote to Roosevelt: "What greater force for
peace could there be than the emergence of a united China?"[25]

In a speech that was broadcast to America in September 1937, an
American-educated Soong-Chiang propagandist proclaimed, "The
present situation in the Far East is very much like a case of one's neighbor's house on fire. Unless one helps to extinguish it in time, there is no
telling that it will not spread and endanger one's own house."[26] In a
Chicago speech weeks later, President Roosevelt said, "When an epi-
demic of physical disease starts to spread, the community approves
and joins in a quarantine of the patients in order to protect the health of
the community against the spread of the disease."[27]

Roosevelt's quarantine speech momentarily raised Chiang's hopes
that the United States might enter the conflict. Emboldened, the Generalissimo ordered his troops to make more suicide stands. But like the
Open Door and Stimson's nonrecognition doctrine, FDR's words had

no force behind them. Isolationist-minded Americans refused to become involved in the outside world's conflicts.

Henry Stimson, now a top Wall Street lawyer, was convinced that if Hoover had taken stronger action and embargoed Japan, the Noble Chinese Peasants would not be suffering so. But many Americans feared that embargoing Japan would result in war. The First Wise Man thought otherwise, and in an October 7, 1937, letter to the *New York Times,* he wrote,

> Today the aggression of Japan is being actively assisted by the efforts of men of our own nation.... It is not only being actively assisted, but our assistance is so effective and predominant that without it even today Japanese aggression would in all probability be promptly checked and cease.... China's principal need is not that something should be done by outside nations to help her, but that outside nations should cease helping her enemy. Does the safety of the American nation and the safety of the British Empire require that we go on helping Japan to exterminate by the methods she is daily employing, the gallant Chinese soldiers with which she is confronted—not to speak of the civilian Chinese population that she is engaged in terrorizing? Is the condition of our statesmanship so pitifully inadequate that we cannot devise the simple means of international cooperation, which would stop our participation in this slaughter? I for one do not think so. I believe that it can be done, and done effectively, without serious danger to us.

On December 12, 1937, the USS *Panay* was at anchor in the Yangtze River twenty-seven miles north of Nanking. Suddenly Japanese warplanes strafed the old gunboat, killing two Americans and wounding fifty. Roosevelt wondered how to pay back Japan and asked Morgenthau if it was legal for a president to confiscate Japanese property in the United States. Morgenthau was ready with Stimson's argument that the U.S. could do as it pleased with Japan and not suffer retaliation.

Henry Stimson: the First Wise Man (Courtesy Everett Collection)

Roosevelt liked what he heard from his treasury secretary, and at a December 17 cabinet meeting, the president said he wanted Morgenthau to take further steps. But at the same time, a repentant Tokyo recalled in disgrace the commanding admiral who'd overseen the *Panay* bombing, disciplined eleven naval officers, apologized to the U.S., paid indemnities, and promised there would be no recurrence of the event. Secretary Hull's program of keeping the peace with Japan held, but Roosevelt's call for retaliation had excited Morgenthau, who knew that a policy option placed on the table never really went off it.

*   *   *

The Shanghai fighting, often seen in newsreels before screenings of *The Good Earth,* planted the illusion in American minds that Generalissimo Chiang was a noble leader, but in reality, the Shanghai battle marked the last time Chiang would confront Japan on a massive scale. Chiang's appalling sacrifice of his best troops in an attempt to attract a foreign barbarian ally had availed him nothing. From then on he would resume ceding land for time, continue his search for a barbarian to pit against the Japanese, and return to his main game of exterminating Mao.

On December 8, after promising that he would defend Nanking to the end, Chiang took Mayling and fled the capital city by airplane. The Japanese army then closed in on a defenseless population and carried out the atrocity that would later be called the Rape of Nanking — massacres of soldiers and civilians and mass rapes, with victims numbering in the hundreds of thousands.

Before she left, Mayling penned a note to *Atlantic Monthly* magazine requesting that her subscription be forwarded.

For *Time*'s 1937 Man of the Year, Henry Luce had been considering various candidates, including Franklin Delano Roosevelt, Joseph Stalin, British prime minister Neville Chamberlain, Dale Carnegie — author of the blockbuster *How to Win Friends and Influence People* — and Clark Gable. In the end, he decided to choose a Man and Wife of the Year, a couple who were derided in China over their New Life movement, who had recently endured a mutiny within their ranks, and who had just lost China's east coast to the Japanese.

> He is a salt seller's son, she a Bible salesman's daughter. No woman in the West holds so great a position as Mme. Chiang Kai-shek holds in China. Her rise and that of her husband, the Generalissimo, in less than a generation to moral and material leadership of the ancient Chinese people cover a great page of history....

After losing their largest coastal city—Shanghai—and their capital—Nanking—
Chiang Kai-shek and Mayling Soong fled over the mountains from the Japanese. On
January 3, 1938, Henry Luce made them Time *magazine's first "Man and Wife of*
the Year." (Associated Press)

Today Generalissimo & Mme. Chiang have not conceded
China's defeat, they long ago announced that their program for
as many years as necessary will be to harass, exhaust and eventually ruin Japan by guerrilla warfare. If Generalissimo Chiang
can achieve it, he may emerge Asia's Man of the Century....He
and Mme. Chiang have made themselves Man & Wife of 1937.[28]

In Luce's fantasy world, Mao's popular appeal was fleeting, his military influence purely negative.

China...has had the ablest of leadership. Through 1937 the Chinese have been led—not without glory—by one supreme leader and his remarkable wife. Under this Man & Wife the traditionally disunited Chinese people—millions of whom seldom used the word "China" in the past—have slowly been given national consciousness.... The armies or bandit hordes of Chinese Communists who tried to harass Nanking from the hinterland were turned by Generalissimo Chiang into an excuse for not fighting the Japanese. He used them as a football coach uses a scrub team to train the regular army of New China—the first Chinese War Machine, complete with European artillery, German military advisers, U.S. and Italian warplanes....No fault of Generalissimo Chiang was it that he was forced to use his War Machine at least two years before it was finished. His hand was forced by overzealous Chinese patriots, by canny Japanese who believed that unless they beat China in 1937 they might never do so.[29]

Chiang had just fled over the mountains from his capital of Nanking, but Luce quoted the Generalissimo's optimistic prediction: "Tell America to have complete confidence in us. The tide of battle is turning and victory eventually will be ours!"[30]

Hollington Tong was the Soong-Chiang syndicate's chief propagandist. As a young man, Tong had taught English to Chiang at Longjing High School, near Chiang's hometown of Ningbo. Later Tong studied journalism at the University of Missouri and Columbia University. After returning to China, Tong became managing editor of the *China Press* newspaper, a Soong-Chiang organ. Before long, Tong was in charge of managing the foreign press corps and censoring their dispatches. After the Shanghai and Nanking fighting, Tong was appointed head of the Ministry of Information with a mandate to influence opinion in the United States.

On February 6, 1938, Chiang ordered Tong to send agents to America "to win sympathy from the American public and prompt the U.S.

government to put sanctions in place."[31] Tong moved quickly and submitted a plan to Chiang and Mayling on how to influence American public opinion. Tong recommended three basic steps:

1. Recruit American missionaries, arm them with evidence of Japanese atrocities, and have them return to the U.S. to give testimony and speeches. (Tong emphasized that the American target audience would not know that the paid missionaries were acting as agents for the Soong-Chiang syndicate. Tong wrote that he would "search for international friends who understand the realities and policies of the Chinese war of resistance and have them speak for us, with Chinese never coming to the fore."[32])
2. Hire Frank Price (Mayling's favorite missionary) to lead the missionary campaign.
3. Recruit American newsmen and authors to write favorable articles and books.

To Americans, Frank Price was a devoted Presbyterian missionary in China who had translated and expanded Sun Yat-sen's Three Principles of the People in an English-language book. To Mayling, he was a Soong-Chiang employee.

Frank and his brother Harry Price were, like Pearl Buck and Henry Luce, born in China, the children of missionaries. After receiving college educations in the U.S., the siblings Price had both served as Presbyterian missionaries in China. Now the Price brothers—Frank in China and Harry in New York City—constituted the China Lobby's main Christian public relations pipeline. Few knew they were Mayling's agents, paid by the Soong-Chiang syndicate, and because they were brothers, they could communicate confidentially.

After final instructions from Mayling and Tong, Frank Price left Chungking and set out for New York on a China Lobby mission to convince the American public that the best thing the U.S. could do for peace in Asia was embargo Japan. It would lead, three years later, to the Japanese assault on Pearl Harbor.

*　　*　　*

Frank stayed in Harry's New York apartment, and soon a stream of important people flowed through the premises, including reporters, editors, missionaries, and activists interested in New China. Frank told of shocking Japanese atrocities while Harry made the case that the only way to stop the horror was to choke off U.S. exports to Japan. There was no need to worry that it might lead to more war; little Japan, they explained, would never attack the great big United States.

After two months of talks, a number of people interested in China gathered in Harry's apartment to found the committee that would fulfill Chiang's goal. They included, in addition to Frank and Harry Price, George and Geraldine Fitch; Dr. Edward Hume; Philip Jaffe, editor of *Amerasia* magazine, a small specialty publication; and Earl Leaf, a Soong-Chiang propagandist and financial bagman. The name of the organization—the American Committee for Non-Participation in Japanese Aggression—was quite a mouthful, but it effectively made clear what the China Lobby wanted Americans to do: stop assisting the killing of the Noble Chinese Peasants by selling the Japanese American oil and steel. The committee set up a professional operation in high-rent office space on Fortieth Street between Fifth and Madison Avenues in the center of Manhattan, the communications hub of the country, and employed a missionary-led staff of about twenty workers whose output over the next two years would convince the American public that the United States could embargo Japan without fear of reprisal.

At the beginning, Earl Leaf was executive director of the committee, and Mayling funded the effort through the Chinese ambassador in Washington. However, on June 8, 1938, Congress passed a law requiring American organizations that received money from abroad to register as foreign agents. Leaf was too closely identified with the Chinese, so to create the impression that the committee was an American organization, Leaf turned over the executive directorship to Harry Price. Price gave the committee a respectable missionary face but continued to accept Soong-Chiang funding through American friends of China. The public never knew that the Manhattan missionaries diligently working on East Fortieth Street to save the Noble Peasants were paid

China Lobby agents engaged in what were possibly illegal and treasonous acts.

In June of 1938 an article by the well-known economist Eliot Janeway appeared in *Harper's* magazine. Janeway, a friend of both Stimson and Luce and a good China Lobby man, made the committee's case:

> The Japanese government is engaged in a war in which it would be helpless without necessities — oil, steel, munitions, and various commodities — which it imports from the United States.... We are selling Japan the means of mass production for war.... We are helping her to conquer North China by selling her the vital raw materials she needs for armaments.... The Japanese menace is made possible by American exports....
>
> Oil is notoriously the weakest link in Japan's economy.... Seventy-five per cent of the gasoline Japan used last year, gasoline for tanks and bombers and warships, came from the United States.[33]

When pollsters asked Americans to name the most frightening international event of the past year, Japan's invasion of China beat out Germany's invasion of Austria.[34] That same month, *Reader's Digest* published letters from missionaries describing the Japanese military's atrocious behavior in the Rape of Nanking. *Digest* editors concluded: "The cruelty of the Japanese army in China is one of the blackest pages in history. Barbarian invasions of ancient days furnish no parallel."[35]

In August of 1938, every U.S. senator and representative in Washington received a booklet from the American Committee for Non-Participation in Japanese Aggression. Thousands of influential Americans — governors, pastors, mayors, state representatives, professors, newspaper editors, foreign policy groups, and community clubs like Rotary and Kiwanis — also received the pamphlets. The publication was a masterpiece of simplicity. The back and front covers featured Japanese planes dropping bombs on China, the bombs provocatively labeled *Made in the U.S.A.* The pamphlet's title: "America's Share in Japan's War Guilt."

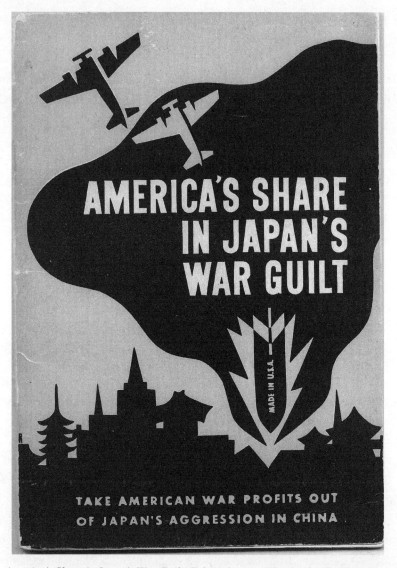

*America's Share in Japan's War Guilt: Take American War Profits Out of Japan's
Aggression in China. The Stimson Committee, August 1938. (American Committee
for Non-Participation in Japanese Aggression, August 1938)*

The pamphlet repeated the mirage that China was "a great nation
whose citizens have traditionally regarded Americans as their best
friends" and promised that all the New China dreams would come true

if Americans only had the moral rectitude and courage to embargo Japan.

> This is definitely a *peace* policy, not a *war* policy. It is a road *from* war, not *to* war. We simply withdraw from our part in Japan's war upon China. We do what we can to hasten the end of hostilities. We act to bring an earlier peace in the Pacific. Whatever other nations may do, our consciences then will be clear....
>
> The issue is clear-cut for those who oppose war and seek peace. Japan could not continue her invasion of China another six months or continue as a potential menace to the security of other nations without aeroplanes, munitions, trucks, scrap iron, oil, steel and other materials from the United States....
>
> If the American people become fully aware of the part they are taking in the deliberate and frightful bombing of helpless civilians in China, the mad attempt to subjugate a great people, and the ambitious expansion of a militaristic power, there is little doubt what they will say or do. Americans will say, "Count us out."[36]

Nowhere in "America's Share in Japan's War Guilt" was there any suggestion that an embargo on Japan would lead to anything other than Japanese retreat — and multiple benefits to the American public.

> A more speedy end to the war; an end to Japanese expansion at the expense of the Chinese and of other peoples; a reduction of the tax burden levied upon the American people for naval armaments; a probable change in the Far Eastern balance of power whereby China would emerge independent and free to cooperate with other powers; a discrediting of the military regime in Japan and the rise of a now repressed liberal element to a new degree of influence; a general discrediting of military aggression in this day as a means to nationalistic expansion; an earlier beginning of reconstruction in China and Japan; and an

earlier restoration of peaceful trade and international security in the Pacific area.[37]

Instead, the pamphlet reassured Americans,

It is not likely that Japan's militarist leaders would be so rash as to attempt reprisals against the United States. They recognize that, if they cannot readily win a war against China in their own backyard, they cannot dream of wandering afield, when economically exhausted, in order to engage in conflict the strongest power in the world. War with the United States at this time would mean a certain end to their dream of becoming a great world power.

There is no historical support for the supposition that an American embargo on war materials to Japan would lead to war. An embargo by Russia and an effective stoppage of war supplies from France to Japan have not done so.

It is reasonable, moreover, to believe that a policy of non-cooperation now would involve far less risk of war than a continuation of the support, which we are rendering to Japan.[38]

In late 1938 the interests of the China Lobby and Henry Stimson merged. Harry Price approached the First Wise Man about his joining the committee and becoming its marquee name. Stimson agreed and was made honorary chairman. This was a fantastic coup for Mayling; now the First Wise Man, perhaps the most powerful and articulate American voice opposing Japan, was fronting the China Lobby. On January 19, 1939, the *New York Times* ran an article headlined "Group to Ask Curb on Aid to Japan; Stimson Heads Committee That Will Fight American Sales of Iron, Steel and Oil."

Stimson's name was on the committee's masthead, along with the names of others from the cream of American society. Members included the former heads of Harvard University, the Union Theological Seminary, the Church Peace Union, the World Alliance for International Friendship, the Federal Council of Churches of Christ in America, the Associated Boards for Christian Colleges in China, and the Christian Medical Council for Overseas Work. Stimson's honorary vice chairmen were the former top admiral of America's Pacific Fleet and a former president of the U.S. Chamber of Commerce.

The Stimson Committee pumped out press releases and slickly designed pamphlets to inject the China Lobby line into editorials and sermons across the country. The Manhattan missionaries disseminated the message through the mouths and pens of individual supporters. Prominent and prestigious citizens — professors, government officials, bankers, judges, and others — provided what appeared to be their personal opinions in the traditional outlets: local newspapers, magazines, radio interviews, Rotary Club speeches, and church sermons. As Donald Friedman, author of *The Road from Isolation,* wrote, "It became a principle of operation that whenever possible members should continue to work through their customary channels, using the medium of the national office only when needed. This decentralization was stressed partly in order to preserve and foster a kind of spontaneity that would have a deeper effect upon the government and upon the public at large than if an obviously organized series of releases were given out solely by an agency whose function was to promote the embargo."[39]

The American Committee for Non-Participation in Japanese Aggression poured out thousands of copies of pamphlets, leaflets, flyers, memos, and direct mailings. One mailing targeted over one hundred thousand Protestant ministers. The committee provided newspapers with a steady stream of "factual" stories and editorials by Stimson. Radio listeners heard Stimson and other committee members challenge the morality of American sales of oil and steel to Japan. Friedman observed, "In terms of the range of its publicity and information efforts, [the committee] was certainly the most active nongovernment organization dealing with the Far Eastern situation, and perhaps, with America's role in international affairs in general."[40]

The Stimson Committee affiliated with local committees in "Boston, Baltimore, Richmond, Durham, Pittsburgh, Cleveland, Toledo, Chicago, Kansas City, Minneapolis, Denver, Seattle, Portland, San Francisco, Los Angeles," and other cities. Hundreds of small towns had ties to the committee through "church groups, business associations, civic and professional clubs, labor unions, women's organizations," and other groups.[41]

With notes cribbed from Stimson Committee propaganda, American commentators with no experience in Asia or with Asians were suddenly experts on Asian affairs. The committee proudly reprinted the *New York Post*'s assurance that there would be no trouble with Japan after an American embargo: "Military experts in Europe and the United States have declared that Japan would have to withdraw her troops from China if American imports to Japan were stopped."[42] Among many other publications, *Atlantic Monthly* repeated the widespread assumption that the United States "had" China in some way and fretted about its possible loss:

> It would be the most disastrous defeat in the history of America's participation in world affairs if, just as we are coming within reach of the evolutionary, non-revolutionary liberation of China foreseen by John Hay and guarded as an article of faith in our Far Eastern policy ever since, we should bring it to abortion by lending our money, our industry, and our political influence to the uses of Japan.[43]

Protesters demonstrated in front of Japanese consulates, Boston hosted a conference on the boycott of Japanese goods, and religious leaders sent resolutions to President Roosevelt calling for a "policy of nonparticipation in aggression."

This China Lobby propaganda juggernaut had a profound and immediate impact on how the majority of Americans viewed the conflict across the Pacific. Chiang's directive to his China Lobby had been for them "to win sympathy from the American public," and with the Stimson Committee, he achieved his goal. By February 1940 an incredible 75 percent of Americans supported the First Wise Man's plan to embargo Japan.

The China Lobby, with assistance from Henry Stimson, had made an American embargo against Japan politically viable for President

Roosevelt. The second half of Chiang's directive was to "prompt the U.S. government to put sanctions in place." Now the First Wise Man would see if FDR would wave a Theodore Roosevelt–like big stick.

Secretary of the Treasury Henry Morgenthau swallowed Stimson's version of the China Lobby argument hook, line, and sinker, and he wanted FDR to embargo Japan's oil. Roosevelt didn't buy it. FDR reasoned that Japan had only two gas pumps available: California and the Dutch East Indies (today's Indonesia). As early as 1938, the Department of State had opined: "Any attempt by the United States, Great Britain and the Netherlands to cut off from Japan exports of oil would be met by Japan's forcibly taking over the Netherlands East Indies."[44] Joseph Grew, a lifelong friend of Roosevelt's and now his ambassador in Tokyo, wrote that economic sanctions would not work "unless the United States is prepared to resort to the ultimate measure of force."[45] In early June of 1940, State again warned that an oil embargo would "impel Japan toward moving into the Dutch East Indies...therefore... no restrictions should be placed at this time on exportation of petroleum products to Japan."[46]

FDR agreed. California was supplying the vast majority of Japan's oil, and he was confident that if he cut off that supply, Japan would be forced to go south. Getting there would require massive Japanese military operations, and because the path lay through several European colonies, it would inevitably involve Britain, France, and the Netherlands (and quite possibly America) in an unwanted Pacific war.

In his right hand/left hand manner, Roosevelt went around the State Department to get more information about what was going on in China, working through private emissaries like his friend William Bullitt, who met with Chiang. Bullitt reported secretly to FDR, "Chiang Kai-shek's will to fight and the courage of the Chinese people remain unbroken; but there will be just no money to buy anything."[47]

Money. It seemed there was agreement on the need for it, if not on how it would be used. Chiang wanted money so he could fight Mao;

FDR believed that Chiang needed money to fight Japan. Soon a Treasury Department proposal to give Chiang twenty-five million dollars—"a highly publicized loan"—circulated throughout the Roosevelt administration. Hull thundered *no* from the State Department, judging that giving any funds to the incompetent and passive Chiang would be throwing good money after bad. Morgenthau thought differently:

> We are talking about the future of the Pacific for the next 100 years. Here's the fate of the Pacific at stake. Do we want to do something? Do we want to show these people our friendship and do we want to do it in a substantial way? Personally, I am very keen to do it.[48]

Morgenthau wanted to give Chiang the proposed sum, which would be repaid by ten years of tung oil exports to the United States. (Tung oil was used widely in the paint industry.) Hull continued to oppose the loan, and in mid-October Morgenthau sent an emotional plea to Roosevelt:

> I am taking the liberty of pleading China's cause so earnestly because you have three times told me to proceed with the proposals for assistance to China. All my efforts have proved of no avail against Secretary Hull's adamant policy of doing nothing which could possibly be objected to by an aggressor nation. I need not tell you I respect Secretary Hull's integrity and sincerity of belief that his course is the right one, but the issues at stake go beyond any one of us and do not permit me to remain silent. It is the future peace and present honor of the United States that are in question. It is the future of democracy, the future of civilization that is at stake.[49]

More sober was an internal State Department memo:

> To adopt a course of assistance to China now, after Japan has almost completed its positional warfare, would be of no decisive aid to China and would be a profitless irritant to Japan, unless the United States is prepared to give really substantial

and long-continued assistance to China. And if that decision be made, it should be made with realization that that course may lead to armed conflict with Japan.[50]

Morgenthau told his Chinese counterparts that the U.S.-China relationship should now be based on "business, not diplomacy." As a way to work around the State Department, he suggested that the Chinese form "an American corporation and deposit your money in this corporation to be used for the purchase of supplies in the United States." Morgenthau added, "I don't want to get in diplomatic channels. The State Department, if they heard me talk like this, would be very excited."[51]

The Soong-Chiang syndicate founded the Universal Trading Corporation and based it in New York's Rockefeller Center. Roosevelt suggested several officials currently serving in his administration for the UTC's board of directors and its staff. Thus, this China Lobby front company, located in midtown Manhattan, was run by the president's men. While Morgenthau and FDR discussed the UTC a number of times, nobody informed Secretary Hull.

In October of 1938 Morgenthau wrote a note to Ailing's husband, H. H. Kung: "We here are watching with the deepest interest and sympathy the unfolding events in the Pacific. It is indeed reassuring that the Chinese nation is actuated by ideals which we are proud to think have so much in common with those of the United States."[52] But still no loan. The State Department continued to make the case that the United States had no vital interests in China, that Japan was America's biggest customer in Asia, and that Japan would eventually exhaust itself militarily in China's vastness.

On Friday, November 25, 1938, Secretary Hull left Washington for a conference in Lima, Peru. While Hull was aboard ship, far out to sea, FDR and Undersecretary of State Sumner Welles met and approved the twenty-five-million-dollar loan that Morgenthau had been pushing to help save New China.

Morgenthau would later tell friends of the coup he'd carried out while Hull was at sea. Roosevelt never directly informed his secretary of state about this change in China policy; Hull learned that Morgenthau had done an end run around him four days after FDR had given his approval.

Roosevelt's assumptions about China would now guide United States policy. Like Theodore Roosevelt's Japanese Monroe Doctrine for Asia, FDR's plans regarding New China were a secret from the American public, undebated and unannounced.

For American consumption, the Soongs and Chiang assured FDR and Morgenthau that China would use the U.S. aid to fight Japan. But a dispatch from a Soong-Chiang representative in Washington to Ailing's husband in Chungking illustrated the Chinese perspective:

> The $25 million is only the beginning...further large sums can be expected. This is a political loan. America has definitely thrown in her lot and cannot withdraw. We will have two years [of a] sympathetic Washington administration, possibly six. Our political outlook is now brighter.[53]

Chapter 7

WASHINGTON WARRIORS

*China's principal need is not that something should be done by outside
nations to help her, but that outside nations should cease helping her enemy.*
—*Henry Stimson*[1]

In 1940, war raged around the globe as Adolf Hitler and Emperor
Hirohito rained bombs on London, Chungking, and Yan'an. Millions
of Europeans and Asians had already been killed in the fighting, but
many Americans — stung by World War I — wanted no part of foreign
wars and would not allow their government to once again send troops
to fight overseas.

The American debate regarding events in Europe was multilayered.
America was then mostly a mixture of European immigrants with loy-
alties to the old countries. No significant organization advocated that
the U.S. join in the fighting. (The Committee to Defend America by
Aiding the Allies argued that material support of Britain was the best
way to keep the United States *out* of the conflict.) There were few
Asians in the United States to contribute to government deliberations
or counteract the China Lobby line. While American opinion was
divided over policy toward Europe, it was relatively united about policy in far-off Asia.

Japanese propaganda skills had fallen into disuse since the days when Prince Ito dispatched Baron Kaneko to canoodle with Teddy. There were few Ivy League–educated Japanese who spoke American English, and the Japanese diplomats in Washington seemed stiff and formal. Many fewer missionaries had toiled in Japan than in China, and Tokyo spent much less than the Soong-Chiang syndicate did on public relations in the United States.

In contrast, sympathy for the Noble Chinese Peasants reached into nearly every American home, including the president's. Sara Delano Roosevelt was the honorary chairwoman of both the China Aid Council and the American Committee for Chinese War Orphans. Eleanor Roosevelt became honorary chairwoman of Pearl Buck's China Emergency Relief Committee.

In January of 1940, Henry Stimson wrote a letter to the editor of the *New York Times* in which he asked Americans to "discriminate between right and wrong" and take a "first step toward an affirmative foreign policy."

> Both the press and the Gallup polls overwhelmingly show that there is no international question on which our people are more thoroughly united than as to the Japanese aggression against China.... More than four-fifths of those who have expressed their opinion in a recent Gallup poll are in favor of stopping the evil with an embargo.
>
> The very last thing which the Japanese Government desires is a war with the United States.... [Japanese] leaders desire strongly to subjugate China, but they also clearly recognize that a head-on quarrel with us would be fatal to that project....
>
> [The Japanese army]...has succeeded in obtaining domination over the civil authorities of Japan.... It is highly desirable in the interests of the United States that the Japanese military organization should become discredited in the eyes of the Japanese people....
>
> The course of action easiest and most practicable for the United States would be to discontinue the assistance which

some of our people are now rendering to the efforts of the Japanese to destroy the independent sovereignty of China.[2]

In April 1940, the Stimson Committee blanketed the country with thousands of professionally produced copies of a slick booklet with the provocative title "Shall America Stop Arming Japan?" Like all of the committee's publications, this one argued that an embargo against Japan would "leave China free to achieve her own independence, which she doubtless can and will do against an unaided Japan. No outcome could contribute more to the peace and well-being of all Pacific nations."[3]

The risk of a military conflict was perceived to be so slight that the brochure never spoke of what the United States would do if an embargo incited the Japanese military to retaliate. Instead, a fund-raising letter for the committee proclaimed, "We have laid out a program which, if it can be put through, will probably take America out of this war."[4] Dr. Walter Judd, a China missionary and Stimson Committee member, testified before the Senate Committee on Foreign Relations that embargo legislation against Japan "will have minimum cost and almost no risk to ourselves."[5] The chairman of the Stimson Committee wrote, "No person with real experience in the Far East during the last 10 years has any fear that an embargo would lead to war."[6]

Henry Luce's New China came to life in American movie theaters with the *March of Time* newsreel entitled "China Fights Back!" It opened with a dramatic crisis: scenes of Japanese killing Noble Chinese Peasants as the narrator explained that Chungking was "the most intensively bombed spot in the world." Then the narrator identified the hero: "Symbol of the New China and Chinese determination is lean, hard-bitten fifty-two-year-old Chiang Kai-shek, undisputed ruler and idol of China's four hundred million."

The China shown in the film would have bewildered the Four Hundred Million: American-style row houses and libraries, mothers pushing children in prams on neat sidewalks, knitting sessions on American-style porches, factory smokestacks, department stores, "coolies...learning the ways of the modern machine," Chinese kids frolicking in chlorinated swimming pools.

The shots of uniformed, orderly soldiers would also have been a surprise to the Chinese, so different were they from Chiang's diseased, straw-sandaled real-life locust troops. American viewers learned that Chiang's army was "lacking only modern armaments to turn them into a military machine of the first rate [and] China awaits weapons from America, which alone will allow her to take the offensive and drive out the invading Japanese." The narrator closed with words sure to have warmed the Time Inc. chairman's heart: "To help the Chinese is to help ourselves. They are fighting the battle of freedom and of free peoples on what is literally our western front.... The responsibility which China has borne alone in the Far East is one free men everywhere must accept. The responsibility of upholding freedom as an ideal." The finale featured Chinese schoolchildren in Western clothes sitting at American-style school desks and copying from the blackboard:

A = America
B = Britain
C = China
D = Democracy[7]

In the spring of 1940, the Stimson Committee distributed a pamphlet entitled "Local Labor Unions Protesting Aid to Japan." It was an eighty-nine-page list of almost two thousand labor unions that supported an embargo against Japan to help the Noble Chinese Peasants. As Donald Friedman noted, "The fact that many millions of men subject to military service were willing to advocate that the United States take measures to stop American economic aid to Japan indicates that they, like many Americans, did not yet link the issue of an embargo with the possibility of America becoming involved in war with Japan. These union members reflected a striking and almost universal American naiveté concerning the effect of an embargo upon Japan."[8]

The spring 1940 German blitzkrieg on Norway, Denmark, Belgium, the Netherlands, and France changed how Washington viewed U.S.

interests in Asia. Suddenly the European colonizers — Britain, France, and the Netherlands — had homeland crises to tend to, and the U.S. was the only Pacific power left to confront Japan. The shocking fall of France altered Roosevelt's calculations about a country later called Vietnam.

If Japan expanded into Southeast Asia via French Indochina, American assembly lines might grind to a halt. (If Japan conquered all of China, American industry could continue to hum, for China had no resources — other than tung oil — that the U.S. couldn't get somewhere else.) Manufacturers from Buffalo to San Diego depended on Southeast Asian products — rubber, tin, tungsten, and much more — that they could not source easily elsewhere. The Dutch East Indies alone supplied more than half of fifteen important commodities used in U.S. industry. As author Jonathan Marshall noted in *To Have and Have Not,* "Cut off from their Southeast Asian supply lines, whole industries would be unable to begin even the first stage of production and would face agonizing readjustments or total ruin."[9]

French Indochina was also strategically important to Roosevelt because its long coastline and excellent harbors could be used by the Japanese navy to block Western navies' access to much of Southeast Asia. And if the Japanese took Indochina, they might be able to topple other countries in the area like dominoes.

Suddenly Roosevelt comprehended a hugely heightened role for China. Before, his aid to Chiang was intended — he'd imagined — to help push Japan out of China. China was now the front line in a continental theater of war, the all-important domino that must continue to stand, as Roosevelt assumed that Japan's toppling of China would result in the loss of all of Southeast Asia and possibly even more. As he told his son Elliott:

If China goes under, how many divisions of Japanese troops do you think will be freed — to do what? Take Australia, take India — and it's as ripe as a plum for the picking. Move straight on to the Middle East... a giant pincer movement by the Japanese and Nazis, meeting somewhere in the Near East, cutting

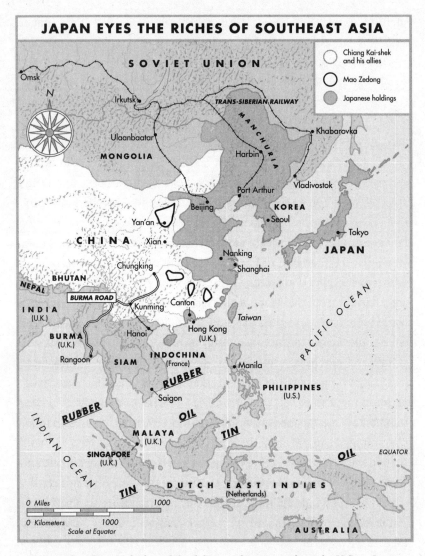

JAPAN EYES THE RICHES OF SOUTHEAST ASIA

As President Roosevelt slowed the delivery of resources from the U.S. to Japan, Tokyo turned to its only other source in Southeast Asia.

the Russians off completely, slicing off Egypt, slashing all communication lines through the Mediterranean?[10]

As Marshall wrote, FDR now agreed with the "fundamental proposition that the United States could not afford to lose the raw material wealth and the sea lanes of Southeast Asia" even if it meant war.[11] But when FDR changed his view, he apparently did not inform his military that the U.S. might be forced to fight for Southeast Asia. Instead, FDR played his cards close to his chest, telling the military to ignore the area and continue planning for action only in Europe. Jonathan Utley observed, "Roosevelt was at his worst when he had to coordinate conflicting views of foreign policy.... Now Roosevelt found himself with a foreign policy that endorsed the vital importance of Southeast Asia and a military strategy that ignored the same region, and he did nothing to bring the two into balance. Issuing conflicting orders, telling different people different things, Roosevelt permitted the nation to move along in two mutually exclusive directions."[12]

Instead of cutting Japan's oil and starting a war, FDR sent strong signals to Tokyo warning against further expansion into Southeast Asia. One such signal was FDR's order to move the U.S. Pacific Fleet from California to Pearl Harbor. Admiral James Richardson, commander of the fleet, argued that the shift to Pearl Harbor would enrage Tokyo. FDR coldly told Richardson, "Despite what you believe, I know that the presence of the fleet in the Hawaiian area has had, and is now having, a restraining influence on the actions of Japan."[13]

Roosevelt's intended message got lost in translation. Japanese admiral Isoroku Yamamoto told a colleague, "The fact that the United States has brought a great fleet to Hawaii to show us that it's within striking distance of Japan means, conversely, that *we're* within striking distance too. In trying to intimidate us, America has put itself in a vulnerable position. If you ask me, they're just that bit too confident."[14]

Roosevelt froze German and Italian assets in the U.S., but he took no action against Japan. With Washington fixated on Hitler's rampage, the Stimson Committee cleverly shifted the argument; Japan should be embargoed not in order to help China but so the U.S. could husband its resources at home. Hull agreed to this defensive domestic measure.

The fruit of the China Lobby's work through the Stimson Committee was the National Defense Act, signed into law on July 2, 1940. The legislation gave Roosevelt executive control over the export of valuable resources. Though it was passed as a domestic measure, many—including Henry Stimson—saw its potential for use against Japan. Roosevelt had no intention of cutting Japan's oil, but the First Wise Man had succeeded in placing the power to do so in the hands of the executive branch.

On June 20, 1940, President Roosevelt surprised many when he named two prominent Republicans to lead the U.S. military. It was a smart election-year move on FDR's part, made on the eve of the Republican National Convention. Henry Stimson would become secretary of war and Frank Knox would be secretary of the Navy. Both Stimson and Knox were Theodore Roosevelt Republicans. Knox had fought as one of Roosevelt's Rough Riders in Cuba, and Teddy had first tapped the now-seventy-three-year-old Stimson for greatness.

By 1940 Franklin Roosevelt had had more than a decade of experience managing massive bureaucracies. While there would be disagreements within his big tent, he was confident that he had the finesse to work his will through the labyrinth of agencies, committees, and paperwork sultans. Even though he had just appointed two gung-ho Republicans with beliefs and styles at odds with his, FDR was confident that he could maintain control. But suddenly he had a cabinet in which Secretary Morgenthau had three strong allies on the New China front: Stimson, Knox, and secretary of the interior Harold Ickes. The rest of the bureaucracy mirrored the changes in the cabinet: more pro–New China, anti-Japanese Americans streamed into Washington every day. As Washington geared up for the expected war in Europe, new government agencies were sprouting and attracting bright men. These new public servants came from across a nation in which the majority believed the China Lobby line that the U.S. could stop the flow of oil to Japan and suffer no repercussions. Soon there were many hands other than FDR's and Hull's near the spigot. One of Frankfurter's Hotdogs, Dean Acheson, coined a name for these men who supported Stimson's hard-line stance: Washington Warriors.

The First Wise Man was a canny bureaucratic player who had studied up close the ways of Presidents Theodore Roosevelt, William Howard Taft, Woodrow Wilson, Calvin Coolidge, Herbert Hoover, and, now, Franklin Delano Roosevelt. For those in FDR's administration who might not have gotten the word, Stimson created study groups in eight different agencies to promulgate the China Lobby fable that the U.S. could choke Japan with no consequences.

The National Defense Act altered who influenced U.S. foreign policy. President Roosevelt created the National Defense Advisory Commission (NDAC) to advise him on which war-related supplies the U.S. should husband. To head the NDAC's seven divisions, FDR appointed some of the best corporate, finance, and union leaders in the nation. The new men who staffed the NDAC knew little about Roosevelt's foreign policy and focused on the country's domestic needs. Only a few top officials knew that Roosevelt was postponing action in Asia by appeasing Japan in order to first confront Hitler.

In June of 1940, T. V. Soong did something that almost no other Chinese person at the time was able to do: he, along with his wife, entered the United States without being arrested. While a British, French, or Peruvian couple could freely enter the U.S., the Chinese Exclusion Act was still in full force. A mirage about distant and cuddly Noble Chinese Peasants was all the rage, but Americans still wouldn't risk a Chinese person living next door.

T. V. Soong had come to Washington to lobby Roosevelt, Frankfurter's Hotdogs, and Stimson's Washington Warriors. Joseph Stalin had been a generous barbarian for the past three years, providing Chiang with hundreds of millions of dollars of credit at low interest rates. With his goal of having Chiang occupy the attention of Japan's military to protect the Soviet Union, Stalin had also provided a huge amount of military aid, including thousands of planes, pilots, military advisers, tanks, and rifles. Now, with Adolf Hitler threatening Russia's European flank, Stalin curtailed his generosity.

Ailing, T.V., Mayling, and Chiang had seen that FDR would not act to defend China, but through their China Lobby contacts, they learned that the Roosevelt administration now valued China as a strategic barrier protecting U.S. access to the riches of Southeast Asia. On the shopping list oldest sister Ailing had given little brother T.V. were requests for U.S. loans with no strings attached and a secret U.S.-funded mercenary air force.

While Stalin had been forking over large amounts of aid, FDR gave only sporadic morsels. Now Ailing wanted a big chunk from FDR with no conditions. In 1905 Charlie Soong had brought home two million dollars in private funds from American hands. In the next two months, his son T.V. would seek over a hundred million dollars from his Harvard friend in the Oval Office.

Before T.V. descended on Washington, Soong-Chiang press people arranged for Henry Luce's *Life* magazine to interview him in his extraordinary Hong Kong residence. T.V.'s home had both Chinese and Western furnishings—to these American journalists "an expression of... T.V.'s political philosophy, molded, even more than his father, by the influence of two hemispheres." In one corner of T.V.'s living room, the *Life* team came upon a triple-tiered shrine. On a table stood "a large, new American radio, complete with short-wave dial." Hanging on the wall above the American radio was "a photograph of the President of the U.S." inscribed " 'To my friend T. V. Soong, Franklin D. Roosevelt.' " Above the Roosevelt photo was an "extremely modernistic terra-cotta head of the Virgin Mary."[15]

In his *Life* interview, T.V. adroitly framed the argument he would use to pry money and airplanes from Washington: "As the wars in Europe and in Asia drag on, it becomes more evident every day that they are parts of one great struggle—the struggle of democracy against totalitarian aggression. In this struggle China fights on the side of democracies." *Life* noted, without evidence, that T.V.'s "American admirers... call him Asia's greatest statesman."[16]

Secretary Hull—perhaps sensing the disruptive influence of the China Lobby before it had a name—opposed T.V.'s trip to Washington. An internal State Department memo warned, "It is not advisable that T. V. Soong be invited or be permitted to come to this country to discuss the matter with the Secretary of the Treasury or any other high official or officials."[17] State worried that T.V.'s direct dealings with Roosevelt would jeopardize the U.S. government's "legitimate diplomatic procedures."[18] Nevertheless, Roosevelt met with Soong in the Oval Office many times with neither witnesses nor note takers. One of Roosevelt's close associates later observed, "At the White House, the making of FDR's China policy was almost as great a secret as the atom bomb."[19]

John Davies, the State Department China Hand who had been born in China, spoke Chinese fluently, and understood the gap between the reality in China and the mirage in Washington, wrote, "Roosevelt's approach to China was rooted not so much in what existed as what should be. Like so many Americans before him, he thought less in terms of the actuality than of the potential of five hundred million Chinese. China was to be treated as a great power so that it would become a great power, a grateful friend eventually helping the United States to keep order and peace in the Far East."[20]

Someone like T.V. was a rarity in the Roosevelt White House; very few Asians walked those halls, and suddenly here was a tall, handsome, impeccably tailored graduate of Harvard and Columbia who joked that his Boston-accented English was better than his Chinese. Contrary to the images of bucktoothed Asians with halting English and awkward body language that had already become a staple of American popular media, T.V., *Life* wrote, was "easy for Washington officials to get along with"; the article noted that he was "unusually tall and stocky for a Chinese...his eyes, behind horn-rimmed glasses, looked clear and confident...he did not bow and scrape, like Chinese politicians...throughout months of long-drawn-out meetings and complicated negotiations in Washington, Soong sometimes even managed to create the illusion that he was really not a foreigner at all."[21]

In his campaign for money and airplanes, T.V. presented the situation and participants in a multiplicity of ways, depending on the moment and on his audience: China as supplicant; Noble Peasants desiring to make an American-like New China; Chiang's regime's Christian nature; noble soldiers fighting in Shanghai; helpless victims

of the evil Japanese; and a bulwark against a row of collapsing dominoes. John Davies recalled how China Lobby messaging had penetrated American culture:

> Somehow a legend gained currency that the Chinese had fought
> with persistent valor and that, if only weapons were placed in
> their hands, they would push the Japanese back into the sea. On
> top of this was an American sense of shame that, rather than
> helping the gallant victims of aggression, we had provided the
> Japanese the wherewithal to mangle the Chinese.[22]

T.V. realized that FDR was sensitive to the domestic political fallout
of losing China, and he warned Roosevelt that without aid from the
outside, Chiang might make terms with Japan, side with Russia, or be
defeated by Mao (whom T.V. portrayed as a puppet of Stalin). The
dreaded threat of losing China worked. Over a sandwich lunch at
FDR's Oval Office desk, the older Harvard alumnus promised the
younger that the U.S. would give Chiang another twenty-five-million-
dollar loan.

After receiving Roosevelt's assurances, T.V. and his wife moved out
of the Shoreham Hotel where they'd been staying since their arrival
and into a tony Woodley Road mansion from which T.V. networked
into the heart of the Roosevelt administration. The mansion was home
to poker games, eight-course Chinese banquets (T.V.'s favorite food
was American steak but Henry Morgenthau's was Peking duck), casual
sandwich luncheons, outdoor Sunday barbecues, and numerous parties
at which Washington's power brokers, opinion makers, and munitions
salesmen mingled. The finest whiskies accompanied talk of New
China; pop music wafted through the rooms. Guests who moved to
T.V.'s den, with its fine inlaid wood and impressive library of books in
English, would notice a Bible on his desk. Charlie Soong's son would
eventually shake from the U.S. almost three times as much as America
would spend on the atomic bomb.

Felix Frankfurter had recruited the Hotdogs and was a fan of both
Henry Stimson and T. V. Soong. Many of the Hotdogs would soon be

on the China Lobby's payroll. One of them, former Harvard professor Lauchlin Currie, was serving as the very first economic adviser to an American president. On and off the Bank of China payroll even as he worked for FDR, Currie was a fortunate catch for T.V. — close to the president and almost totally ignorant about the reality in China.

Jesse Jones was also enormously important to Soong. Jones was chairman of the Reconstruction Finance Corporation, one of the agencies the president would use to funnel money to Chiang. When T.V. played poker with the powerful Texan, he made sure he lost.

Warren Lee Pierson was president of the Export-Import Bank of the United States. Pierson, like Morgenthau, Stimson, and Knox, enjoyed card games with T. V. Soong, oblivious to the larger hand being played.

Joe Alsop was a powerful syndicated newspaper columnist and a distant Roosevelt relative; at the time, Washington was essentially a small town, and a blood connection to FDR meant a lot. Alsop was soon cashing T.V.'s checks for filling the role of "adviser," a remarkable breach of journalistic ethics and a coup for the China Lobby.

All of these men and many more would work hard to support the Soong-Chiang version of reality and, in so doing, would help bring about disaster in Asia for the United States.

In July of 1940 Japan pressured Britain to close the Burma Road — China's backdoor supply route from the port of Rangoon — and withdraw British troops from the International Settlement in Shanghai. An American admiral fretted that Japan's full control of Shanghai would close "the last open chink in the 'open' door in China."[23]

The U.S. Marine Corps commandant in Shanghai announced that his Marines would patrol the British sector of the International Settlement. When the Japanese threatened to confront the Marines, Hull kept them out of the British sector and avoided a hostile encounter. The Washington Warriors shrieked about Hull's lack of a big-stick policy. But Hull's policy was to avoid a war in the Pacific.

On the evening of July 18, 1940, Henry Morgenthau, Henry Stimson, and Frank Knox dined with British ambassador Lord Lothian. Stimson needled Lothian about Britain's buckling under Japanese pressure to close the Burma Road. The British ambassador countered by bringing up FDR's continuing sales of oil to Japan. As voices rose in argument, Lord Lothian outlined an Anglo-American plan to bring Japan to its knees. First, Roosevelt would stop U.S. exports of oil to Japan. From its Singapore base, the British navy would help the Dutch destroy the Dutch East Indies oil fields, rendering them useless to the Japanese. The British and Americans would then purchase the world's remaining petroleum. The supply thus claimed, the British would bomb Germany's synthetic fuel plants. *Voilà!* Japan, and perhaps Germany, would be brought to heel.[24]

None of the three cabinet members—present were Morgenthau, Stimson, and Knox, representing the Treasury, War, and Navy Departments—questioned these aggressive moves. Morgenthau later confided to his diary that Lothian's idea left him with his "breath…taken away."[25] There was no one at the table to ask an elementary question: Would Dutch colonists in far-off Asia really blow up those oil wells when Adolf Hitler occupied their country and held their relatives hostage?

Morgenthau presented Lothian's plan to FDR in the Oval Office the next morning, July 19. The last time Morgenthau had tried to slip something by the State Department, he waited until Hull was on a ship bound for South America. This time Hull was again out of the country, at a conference in Havana.

After Morgenthau outlined the idea to Roosevelt, the two men were joined by Stimson, Knox, and Undersecretary Sumner Welles, who would represent the State Department. Roosevelt presented Lothian's idea without mentioning Morgenthau's involvement. Stimson and Knox, of course, loved it. Welles was prepared to accept a limited aviation-gasoline embargo for domestic stockpiles but not this outrageous plan, which he thought would result in war with Japan. The debate dragged on for two hours.

Roosevelt seemed intrigued by the idea of economic warfare, though he neither approved nor vetoed Morgenthau's scheme. To directly oppose powerful cabinet members while he prepared for his third presidential campaign was not his style and would not have been politically wise. Welles stated his fierce objections, and the meeting ended inconclusively.

Though FDR had seemingly agreed with Welles, Morgenthau was not finished. On Monday, July 22, Stimson informed Morgenthau that Japan was buying up all the aviation gasoline it could find in California. Morgenthau asked Stimson to forward this information to FDR, who had left for Hyde Park.

Roosevelt apparently figured he could not tell the public that continued oil sales to Japan were his attempt to forestall a Japanese invasion of European colonies in Southeast Asia. But Roosevelt was facing an election; he announced that he would embargo Japan's aviation gasoline. It seemed that Roosevelt was following what the China Lobby had convinced Americans was the correct policy: choking off Japan's oil supply to stop American participation in Japanese aggression. But the fine print told a different story: The president intended to embargo only those aviation fuels with octane numbers of 87 and over. Setting the octane-number level at 87 was important because Japanese aircraft could run on 86-octane gasoline. (The more powerful American aircraft burned 100-octane gasoline, so the embargo would assure ample supplies at home.) Japan was still able to buy aviation fuel; in fact, it could buy more than before—which is exactly what it did. Roosevelt was playing an increasingly subtle and risky right hand/left hand game with Japan and the American people.

As Welles's draft of the aviation-fuel embargo wended its way through the bureaucracy, Morgenthau quietly asked a low-ranking Warrior to substitute the words *petroleum products* for *aviation fuel*. The secretly changed draft now stated that Roosevelt would cut off *all* oil sales to Japan. This altered legislation went to Hyde Park for FDR's signature. Unaware of his friend's scheming, Roosevelt signed it late on Thursday. The document then left Hyde Park and returned to Washington so the State Department could countersign it and affix the official seal.

Sumner Welles reread the entire document, spotted the Morgenthau wording, and rewrote it so Japan could get all the below-87-octane gasoline it wanted. Bureaucratic routine and FDR's ally at State had thwarted Morgenthau. At a press conference on Friday morning, July 26, Roosevelt said the U.S. was merely husbanding supplies and that rumors of an oil embargo against Japan were incorrect.

Roosevelt had a cabinet meeting scheduled after the press conference, so by the time Morgenthau, Stimson, Knox, and Ickes met, they knew that Roosevelt would continue to appease the Japanese military with all the oil it wished to purchase. Roosevelt held firm in front of his cabinet, telling them that the United States would "not...shut off oil from Japan...and thereby force her into a military expedition against the Dutch East Indies."[26] As scholar Irvine Anderson wrote, "Nowhere in the available documentation is there evidence that Roosevelt seriously considered anything other than a check on excessive exports of high-octane aviation gasoline to Japan in the summer of 1940."[27]

Japan had invaded China in 1937 with the expectation that the fighting would last three months. It had been three years. The Japanese military, looking for excuses, pointed to a key supply route still open to Chiang: the French railroad from Haiphong, Indochina, to Kunming, China. Cut Chiang's ocean link, and the war would be over, Japanese generals argued. Since France was in the hands of Germany, Japan's ally, Japan asked the Vichy regime for "permission" to occupy northern Indochina. France "agreed."

At the September 25 cabinet meeting, the secretaries of treasury, war, Navy, and interior pummeled Hull in front of the president. They argued that the secretary of state's policy of appeasement was not stopping Japan's southern advance, so why was Hull continuing it? Morgenthau, Stimson, Knox, and Ickes were exasperated as Hull haltingly defended his position. In his deliberate Tennessee manner he said he would finally approve the twenty-five-million-dollar loan that Roosevelt had promised T. V. Soong in July. He also approved a scrap-iron embargo that amounted to only a slap on the Japanese wrist, as Hull would still allow Japan to buy most of the steel and oil it desired. Fumed Morgenthau, "My own opinion is that the time to put the pressure on Japan was before she went into Indochina and not after and I think it's too late and I think the Japanese and the rest of the dictators are just going to laugh at us. The time to have done it was months ago and then maybe Japan would have stopped, looked and listened."[28]

Seeking friends in a hostile world, Japan's foreign minister met with Adolf Hitler in Berlin and signed the Tripartite Pact uniting Japan, Italy, and Germany. The Tripartite Pact held that if an Allied nation attacked an Axis country, the other two Axis countries would enter the war against the Allies. The Japanese saw the Tripartite Pact as a way to dissuade the United States from attacking, but just as Roosevelt's signals had not been understood in Tokyo, Japan's intended message wasn't grasped in Washington. By seeming to threaten the U.S. with a two-ocean war, Japan transformed itself in the American mind from a regional threat to a potential global extension of Hitler's agenda.

In the next two cabinet meetings — September 27 and October 4 — Hull continued to serve as a punching bag for Secretaries Stimson, Morgenthau, Knox, and Ickes. In the first meeting, Frank Knox spoke for the group, demanding that Roosevelt stop the 87-octane sleight of hand and punish Japan by lowering the approved octane number to 67. Hull retorted that if the U.S. pinched off Japan's aviation-fuel supply by lowering the octane level, the Japanese would be forced to go south for oil, and the United States might find itself involved in an unwanted war in Asia. U.S. Navy officers were focused on the Atlantic and did not want a war in the Pacific. Hull slapped Knox's suggestion down as Roosevelt listened without comment. Secretary Ickes summed up the Warriors' disgust:

> As usual, Hull did not want to do anything. He wouldn't consent to an embargo on scrap until Japan had actually invaded Indochina and, as Henry [Morgenthau] and I agreed after [the] Cabinet meeting, he won't agree to an embargo on gasoline until after Japan has taken the Dutch East Indies. How the President can put up with the State Department I do not understand. I do not doubt Hull's sincerity but the fellow just can't think straight and he is totally lacking in imagination. He makes no move until his hand is forced and then it is too late to

be effective. If we had embargoed scrap and petroleum products two or three years ago, Japan would not be in the position that it is, and our position, relative to Japan, as well as that of England, would be infinitely stronger.[29]

Stimson took the lead in pummeling Hull in the October 4 cabinet meeting. He began by distributing copies of an article from the August issue of *Amerasia* magazine entitled "A Bit of American History," by Henry Douglas. Stimson had previously sent copies to Frankfurter, Morgenthau, and Knox, but not to Hull or Roosevelt. The First Wise Man also did not inform the president and cabinet that *Amerasia*'s publisher was a founding member of the Stimson Committee and that the author of the article under discussion had been paid by the China Lobby to write articles in favor of embargoing Japan.

In the article, Douglas recalled an irrelevant 1918 incident in which the Japanese moved seventy-two thousand troops into Siberia and then withdrew them after the United States threatened to stop importing silk from Japan. As it happened, factors other than America's trade threat — mostly domestic Japanese concerns about the huge military expense — caused Japan to withdraw its troops, but the article claimed that when a tough American president warns the little Japanese, Tokyo listens. Douglas, not surprisingly, advocated an aggressive approach to Asian affairs, as summarized by the First Wise Man:

Japan has historically shown that she can misinterpret a pacifistic policy of the United States for weakness. She has also historically shown that when the United States indicates by clear language and bold actions that she intends to carry out a clear and affirmative policy in the Far East, Japan will yield to that policy even though it conflicts with her own Asiatic policy and conceived interests. For the United States now to indicate either by soft words or inconsistent actions that she has no such clear and definite policy toward the Far East will only encourage Japan to bolder action.[30]

For an hour and a half Roosevelt's cabinet had what Stimson called "a red hot debate on the Far East." As before, the Warriors wanted to cut Japan's oil supply, but Hull still held enough sway with Roosevelt and power in Congress to resist. Hull would agree only to small moves, like a vague tightening of the scrap embargo and Roosevelt's suggestion that the fleet at Pearl Harbor be brought to full strength, hoping that these actions would be enough to warn Japan.

Stimson had been checkmated by Hull again, but he had also succeeded in focusing an hour and a half of the president's time on demands for FDR to get tough with Japan. In his diary entry about the meeting, the First Wise Man wrote, "On the whole it was one of the best debates I have heard."[31]

Roosevelt was riding herd on an increasingly large number of Washington Warriors who—like the American public—were calling for him to cut off Japan's oil and steel. While many accused FDR and Hull of having no clear policy, they actually did: keeping the U.S. out of a Pacific war by appeasing Japan. Indeed, in spite of all the criticism, FDR was allowing Japan to buy more oil than ever.

Roosevelt intended to warn Japan about further advancement into Southeast Asia with small hints like the transfer of the fleet to Pearl Harbor, a partial aviation-fuel embargo, the loan to Chiang, a scrap embargo, and the reinforcement of Pearl Harbor. Why he believed that these moves would be interpreted in the manner he intended by a people he knew little about, he didn't explain. Instead of understanding FDR's line in the sand, Japanese leaders felt the fearful tightening of the ABCD encirclement, the American-British-Chinese-Dutch mob choking Japan.

On September 30, Japanese planes bombed the city of Kunming, China, for the first time, marking an expansion of the fighting. Japanese navy pilots flew out of their newly acquired airport near Hanoi that until recently had been controlled by the French. In the Japanese planes' bellies was U.S. gasoline. The bombs that fell on the Noble Chinese Peasants were made from U.S. steel.

*   *   *

Roosevelt's 1940 Republican challenger for the presidency was Wendell Willkie, a corporate attorney who had never been elected to public office. With the majority of the American electorate isolationist, Willkie had gained in the polls by repeatedly portraying FDR as a warmonger, going so far as to declare, "You may expect war by April, 1941, if [Roosevelt] is elected."[32] FDR's close personal aide Harry Hopkins fretted, "This fellow Willkie is about to beat the Boss."[33]

In October, as the president and his speechwriter Robert Sherwood rode north on the campaign train through New England, FDR received telegrams from Democratic leaders pleading with Roosevelt to assure the country he would keep America out of the war. Roosevelt exploded to Sherwood, "It's in the Democratic platform and I've repeated it a hundred times." Sherwood responded, "I know it, Mr. President, but they don't seem to have heard you the first time."[34] In a major speech in the Boston Garden, Roosevelt said, "And while I am talking to you mothers and fathers, I give you one more assurance. I have said before, but I shall say it again and again and again: Your sons are not going to be sent into any foreign wars."[35]

Roosevelt and Willkie did agree about China: the Middle Kingdom would be changed by outside forces, and if Americans helped him, Chiang would push back Japan, and China would emerge as America's best Asian friend. It was a feeling in Yankee hearts from the time of the merchants and missionaries. As Willkie put it, Chiang Kai-shek was a great man whose struggle against Japan was "one of the decisive battles in mankind's long fight for freedom and for a better life." There was no doubt in Willkie's mind that America's "best ends will be served by a free, strong, and democratically progressive China, and we should render China economic assistance to that end."[36]

On election night, November 5, 1940, Warren Delano's grandson was in Sara Delano Roosevelt's home when he learned that he had won an unprecedented third term by a large margin. The voter turnout was huge—62.5 percent of the electorate—and Roosevelt captured 55 percent of the popular vote and 449 votes in the Electoral College to Willkie's 82.

At a postelection November cabinet meeting. Roosevelt emphatically repeated his dictum that the best policy to keep peace in the Pacific was to continue to supply Japan with oil. A Treasury Department summary recalled that Roosevelt "announced definitely that if we went further in our embargo there was danger that Japan would go out on her own against the Far Eastern possessions of England and Holland, particularly the latter. Apparently this is to be our policy until the Japanese, by some overt act, cause us to change."[37]

Eleanor Roosevelt—honorary chairwoman of the China Emergency Relief Committee and a friend of Mr. and Mrs. T. V. Soong's—pestered her husband about why he didn't follow the China Lobby line and just cut off Japan's oil. FDR replied that it would be "an encouragement to the spread of war in the Far East...if we forbid oil shipments to Japan, Japan...may be driven by actual necessity to a descent on the Dutch East Indies."[38]

T. V. Soong had previously asked President Roosevelt for hundreds of millions of dollars only to get the quick twenty-five million promised in July over an Oval Office sandwich. Now, postelection, Roosevelt looked for a chance to up U.S. backing of T.V.'s brother-in-law. On November 28, Tokyo announced that it would recognize a puppet regime in Japanese-controlled Nanking as the legitimate government of China. After fleeing Nanking, Chiang ceded land for time and established a new inland capital over the mountains in Chungking, a city in Sichuan Province. Roosevelt ("in strictest confidence") instructed Secretary of the Treasury Morgenthau and Warren Lee Pierson, president of the Export-Import Bank, to give Chiang a one-hundred-million-dollar loan in two fifty-million-dollar chunks within twenty-four hours.[39] Roosevelt said the U.S. had to "do something fast" to save "free China." "It is a matter of life and death...if I don't do it...it may mean war in the Far East."[40]

Two poker-playing buddies of T. V. Soong's would dispense the money in two equal chunks: fifty million from Morgenthau and fifty million from Pierson. The U.S. would pay the money to the Bank of China—controlled by Ailing—with T. V. Soong "guaranteeing" the loan. The hundred million dollars in "aid to China" would flow through T. V. Soong's hands to Ailing and on to Chiang.

These massive loans, like the blowout credit in 1938 offered while Secretary Hull was at sea, were down payments on America's long future slog in Asia. Franklin Roosevelt engineered these commitments in Asia in the same style as Theodore Roosevelt had: in secret, with little knowledge of reality in Asia and at the direction of a buddy from Harvard whispering in his ear. A young administration official later summed up T.V.'s coup:

> Think of it! A Chinaman comes flying into Washington. He takes a room in a hotel, he talks to a couple of people, he tells a story and sticks to it. And, first thing you know, that Chinaman walks off with a hundred million dollars in his pocket. A hundred million dollars! Just think of it.[41]

Life magazine claimed that just the "announcement that the $100,000,000 loan had been approved by Congress on Dec. 2 1940, hit China like 100,000,000 volts of electricity." *Life* further reassured readers that "for $100,000,000 China promised to keep 1,125,000 Japanese troops pinned in the field; to keep Japan's formidable fleet from blockading the China shore; to retard the aggressors' march in the direction of immediate U.S. interests. The merchandise was fantastically cheap at the price."[42]

As usual, the mirage in Washington was the opposite of the reality in China. Chiang had no intention of escalating his battle against the Japanese. Eliminating Japan was to be the job of Chiang's new barbarian, Franklin Roosevelt, whom T.V. was now asking for airplanes. Americans believed that Southern Methodist Chiang was leading the Noble Peasants in a valiant war against the mad-dog Japanese, but the Four Hundred Million were becoming disgusted by Chiang's nonresistance to the Japanese barbarians and his policy of having Chinese kill Chinese.

Since the Shanghai fighting, Chiang had rested on his China Lobby propaganda laurels, and his rule became even more confused and decadent. He was a dismal administrator, an anal-retentive executive who could not delegate authority. Chiang held over eighty titles, from chief of the government to president of the Boy Scouts. Historian Michael Gibson did a detailed study of Chiang's forces and concluded that "by the end of 1938, the Central Army had all but ceased to exist as an effective fighting force."[43] Many of Chiang's officers couldn't read maps; only 25 percent of junior officers had received an education. Chiang's regional commanders were on-and-off allies, sometimes with him, sometimes not. The foot soldiers had little to fight for; they were Chiang's kidnapped victims. An indication of the scale of deaths and desertions among Chiang's armies is that he had ordered the conscription (kidnapping) of one and a half million men annually from 1938, yet overall strength remained steady at four million men. Chiang's surviving soldiers were serving time in a kind of hell, and they took it out on the peasants.

Theodore White — one of the few Americans fluent in Chinese — wrote of the time he was traveling on horseback with Chiang's forces. They stopped at a village and White was startled when one of Chiang's officers asked the locals for food and water and identified himself to them as one of Mao's men. White later wrote,

> I asked him why he said that; we were a Nationalist group. And he snapped at me, "Shut up! If we tell them we're Nationalist guerrillas, they won't feed our horses or water them." The episode, which I thought then to be unimportant, keeps coming back to haunt me. The message that the Communists bore, true or false, had penetrated into the hills; they held the "hearts and minds" of these people who could neither read nor write.[44]

While T. V. Soong was making the heart-tugging case to Roosevelt that without American dollars, China might be lost to the United States, Mao Zedong was in the midst of a titanic battle against the Japanese military. Yet Secretary of War Stimson had almost no information about Mao's one-hundred-million-person empire or how and why Mao was adding supporters while Chiang was losing them. No one in Stimson's War Department was studying Mao's groundbreaking military techniques or coming to terms with the fact that Mao—who had beaten Chiang every time the two men's armies fought—was the more potent military power in China. With T. V. Soong coaching him, the First Wise Man agreed that Mao was just a nuisance bandit.

On August 20, 1940, Mao had ordered one hundred of his regiments to attack Japanese positions in North China. In what would later be called the Hundred Regiments Offensive, Mao threw 430,000 of his warriors—backed by millions of supportive peasants—against 830,000 Japanese troops. To put that into perspective, the Battle of Gettysburg in the American Civil War involved 90,000 Union forces against 70,000 Confederate forces. In the later Battle of the Bulge, the U.S. and the Allies pitted 600,000 men against 500,000 Germans.

Mao's forces tore up Japanese-held railways and destroyed Japanese coal mines, bridges, and power stations. They launched lightning attacks on hundreds of isolated Japanese army outposts while separate units ambushed Japanese soldiers coming to the rescue.

Mao's achievements were truly stunning. While Chiang was kidnapping his recruits, Mao had the message and political savvy to attract and hold followers and mold them into warriors fighting enthusiastically for a cause. Mao got weapons from the fleeing Japanese, and food, clothing, shelter, and hospital services from the sea of peasants.

Mao's Hundred Regiments Offensive—which killed over twenty thousand Japanese soldiers and captured great quantities of arms— unnerved the Generalissimo. As he had for so many years, rather than applaud a fellow Chinese's success against Japan, Chiang thought only of how to destroy Mao's growing power. And when the Generalissimo learned from T. V. Soong of the $100 million coming from his newly recommitted American barbarians, he realized he could now move against Mao.

In January 1941, a unit of Mao's army—then supposedly Chiang's ally in the United Front—was camped south of the Yangtze River. The group was not a regular fighting force but rather a headquarters unit with a command staff, hospital personnel, and teachers, many of them women. Chiang ordered this unit to move immediately across the Yangtze to a specified location on the north bank. Mao's commanders protested that Chiang's order would force them directly into the guns of waiting Japanese troops. To accept the route set by Chiang would have been suicide for them, which was Chiang's intention.

Mao's commander decided to repudiate the instructions and take his headquarters unit—ten thousand troops, officers, nurses, and teachers—east downriver so they could cross the Yangtze at a point less well guarded by the Japanese.

General Ku Chu-t'ung—one of Chiang's warlord allies acting on his behalf—surprised Mao's unit with a vastly larger force and massacred many of Mao's men. The men and the unattractive women were butchered; the pretty women, some of them schoolgirls, were raped by the Nationalist soldiers. (Chiang later promoted General Ku to commander in chief of all his armies.)

Once again—as in 1927—Chiang had sundered the United Front. When Chairman Mao learned the details of the massacre, he cabled this message to the Generalissimo:

> Those who play with fire ought to be careful. We formally warn them. Fire is not a very good game. Be careful about your skull.... Our retreat has come to an end. We have been struck with a hatchet and our first wound is a serious one. If you care for the future, you ought to come to offer medical treatment. It is not too late. We have to give this warning for the last time. If things continue to develop this way, the whole people of the whole country will throw you into the gutter. And then if you feel sorry, it will be too late.[45]

Chapter 8

SECRET EXECUTIVE
AIR WAR IN ASIA

*Japan can be defeated in China. It can be defeated by an Air Force so small
that in other theaters it would be called ridiculous. I am confident that,
given real authority in command of such an Air Force, I can cause the
collapse of Japan.*
—*Claire Chennault, letter to President Franklin
Delano Roosevelt*[1]

T. V. Soong's lobbying efforts in the fall of 1940 were double-barreled. President Roosevelt had come through with more than one hundred million dollars. Now it was time to get Chiang planes and pilots.

Chiang believed that American airpower was the magic barbarian force that would oust the barbarian Japanese from China. An American-supplied and -operated air force held a number of attractions for Chiang, including the fact that it would be fully under his control; he wouldn't have to deal with managing a patchwork of alliances with local warlords, as he did in the ground war.

Chiang's idea was to install five hundred planes with pilots at airfields near China's coast. This armada would first bomb the Japanese military bases in China and their navy ships at sea, then move north to Japan's home islands to burn down its wooden cities.

Chiang's dream, however, would be impossible to realize. Effective air war depends first upon secure airfields. Chiang couldn't hold territory that the Japanese military coveted. If American barbarian planes attacked the Japanese from Chinese territory, the million-soldier-strong Japanese army would simply wipe out the air bases.

Still, dictators have the power and funds to hire sycophants who encourage them in their delusions. For the past three years, Chiang had had a former U.S. Army Air Corps pilot by his side who'd agreed that Japan could be beaten with five hundred airplanes. Chiang paid the American much more than he would have gotten had he stayed in the U.S. military. To avoid State Department complaints that the pilot was a mercenary in Chiang's employ, Chiang had T. V. Soong pay him as an adviser to the Soong family's Bank of China. The pilot's highest rank in the U.S. military had been captain. When he went to work for the Soong-Chiang syndicate, he started referring to himself as colonel. The Generalissimo had hired mercenaries from many countries, but this American was Chiang's favorite air strategist, a man who, like himself, ignored logistics and military reality. His name was Claire Chennault.

In 1937, forty-three-year-old Captain Claire Chennault realized that his U.S. Army Air Corps career would soon be over. Long at odds with the top USAAC brass, who criticized him for poor strategic and leadership skills, Chennault saw the writing on the wall. The Army wanted him out. This realization hit Chennault hard, and he was hospitalized for what might have been a nervous breakdown.

While still on active duty, Captain Chennault inquired if Chiang Kai-shek could use a mercenary for hire. Chiang viewed him as a U.S. military officer in good standing and had little idea that he was being squeezed out. Chiang made an offer. Chennault recalled: "Would I consider a three-month mission to make a confidential survey of the Chinese Air Force — terms: $1,000 a month plus expenses, a car, chauffeur, and interpreter, and the right to fly any plane in the Chinese

Air Force? I would!"[2] Having secured a juicy job with Chiang, Chennault resigned from the U.S. Army on April 30, 1937, and was off to China the very next day.

Claire Chennault met Madame Chiang on June 3, 1937, in the drawing room of the Soong mansion in Shanghai. Chennault's reminiscences give a hint of Mayling's winning ways with American men:

> It was the Generalissimo's wife, looking twenty years younger than I expected and speaking English in a rich Southern drawl. This was an encounter from which I never recovered. To this day I remain completely captivated.... She will always be a princess to me.... I believe she is one of the world's most accomplished, brilliant, and determined women.[3]

Mayling told Chennault that he was to study the Chinese air force and make recommendations pronto.

Mayling Soong and Claire Chennault. "She will always be a princess to me," Chennault wrote. (CPA Media / Pictures From History)

Chiang valued yes-men. *Yes* was Chennault's favorite word when dealing with his employer; he assured him that, yes, it was possible to vanquish Japan with five hundred barbarian warplanes.

In October of 1940, T. V. Soong advised Chiang that the time was ripe to make a pitch for the barbarians to provide an air force. Chiang called for Chennault and told him: "You must go to the United States immediately. Work out the plans for whatever you think you need. Do what you can to get American planes and pilots."[4] When Chennault landed in Washington the next month, he went directly to T.V.'s mansion.

The War Department was the place to take a foreign country's request for warplanes, but the generals would have looked askance at both the message and the messenger — a washed-out American military man making a killing as a high-priced foreign mercenary. To get around this, T.V. told Chennault they would target the two officials who might fall for Chiang's impossible dream: Franklin Delano Roosevelt and Henry Morgenthau.

T.V. wanted Roosevelt to meet Chennault personally, but that was politically impossible; the subject under discussion was the creation of a U.S.-funded and -staffed secret air force in Asia while the United States was not at war. Instead, Roosevelt asked Tommy the Cork to check out Chennault.

Corcoran had a hand in many of the New Deal revolutions. With his superb people skills and sharp intelligence, he had ingratiated himself with Roosevelt and become arguably the second most powerful man in the country. But by 1940, an administration official observed that Tommy was not the same man he had been earlier in the decade: "Then he had the appearance and the lingo of a campus leader — youthful, full of zest and fun, but essentially the sophomore. There is something hard and tough in his appearance now, and it all came back to me — the resemblance to the hard-bitten tough-guy cynical ward leaders in Chicago."[5] Another insider remembered, "The problem between Tom and the President was that Tom would stand in front of the President and insist on a course of action and pound on the desk. Now you know, no one pounded the desk with Roosevelt."[6]

Roosevelt began relying less on Tommy and more on Harry Hopkins, his alter ego, chief aide, closest confidant, and global gofer. FDR's wife, Eleanor, had brought Hopkins to Roosevelt's attention when he had been governor. Hopkins was from Iowa, and he was unconventional and got the job done. He had served FDR as a social worker, head of the Federal Emergency Relief Administration, chief of the Works Progress Administration, and secretary of commerce. In 1940, after an operation to cure his stomach cancer, he had moved into the White House. Hopkins once told Corcoran, "Remember, Tommy, anything you spend an entire day doing I can undo in ten minutes after supper."[7]

As the 1940 presidential campaign geared up, the Skipper wasn't calling Tommy. Corcoran knew Roosevelt well enough to realize what that meant, and after the election, Tommy informed FDR he was leaving to open a private law practice. Roosevelt gracefully asked Corcoran to stay. Tommy thanked him and politely fibbed that he wanted to get back into private life. FDR took Tommy's new telephone number and wished him luck.

Corcoran opened a law office at 1511 K Street, four blocks from the White House, a street that today is known as Lobbyists' Row. Tommy — recognizing that the coming war would make the New Deal yesterday's game — went on to become Washington's number-one lobbyist for what President Eisenhower would call the military-industrial complex. The Cork had a burning desire to remain in the middle of the game. One insider remarked, "It hurts to be dropped as Tommy was dropped, especially in Washington. And he can't prove he still has power except by fees."[8]

One of Tommy's first clients was T. V. Soong. Whether Roosevelt realized it is unclear, but when he asked Corcoran to size up Chennault, the president was requesting one China Lobby employee to evaluate another.

Corcoran had no military experience and he knew next to nothing about air-war strategy. In meeting with Chennault, Tommy was not evaluating the wisdom of a secret bombing campaign in Asia but the odds that FDR could launch such a questionable scheme and get away with it. And now that he was in business for himself, Tommy was influenced by another variable: if the decision went a certain way, Corcoran would make a lot of money.

Chennault's pitch was that if FDR provided Chiang with an air force, victory over Japan was a simple matter. He explained that "a small but well-equipped air force" operating from China would bomb "the airfields, ports, staging areas, and shipping lanes where the Japanese were accumulating their military strength," which would "force the postponement or cancellation of the Japanese offensive plans." Once Japan was on the ropes, Chennault would move to his second phase, "directed against the Japanese home islands, to burn out the industrial heart of the Empire with fire-bomb attacks." Chennault told Corcoran that the airfields were already available along the Chinese coast, "only three to five air hours from the biggest industrial cities in Japan."[9]

Remembered Corcoran, "If [Chennault] had left in the first ten minutes, I would have written him off as a fanatic."[10] But as Chennault described a country and strategies about which Tommy knew little, he, whether for reasons of patriotism or profit, became convinced that it was a good plan.

Tommy never asked some critical questions. For instance, what would happen once Japan responded to the assaults of FDR's secret air force and sent its enormous army to attack the Chinese airfields? Chennault had said his airfields were located "three to five air hours from the biggest industrial cities in Japan," but he'd said nothing about the powerful Japanese air force's likely retaliation. Nor did Tommy consider the American and international laws that Roosevelt would break by creating a U.S.-funded covert air force in Asia. And what was the United States going to do if Japan shot down a U.S. aircraft and then paraded the American aircrew through the streets of Tokyo? These were some of the questions left unasked.

Tommy reported to FDR that Chennault was a "most original fighting man."[11] Remembered Tommy, "Roosevelt sent back orders for me to take Chennault around town and introduce him to influential men who could keep their mouths shut."[12] The China Lobby had just struck gold.

As Tommy and Chennault made the rounds of Washington's power brokers, T. V. Soong brought Chiang's air-war plan to Henry Morgenthau. Morgenthau thought Chiang's scheme a winner and told T.V. that he would talk to Roosevelt about getting some of America's highest-tech weapons: long-range bombers.

Morgenthau discussed Chiang's proposal with Roosevelt over a White House luncheon that was also attended by Mrs. Morgenthau and T. V. Soong and his wife. FDR liked it and told Morgenthau that "overnight [Chiang's plan] would change the whole picture in the Far East." But five hundred planes and five hundred pilots was an impossible request for Roosevelt to fulfill. The Army Air Corps wanted every airplane that came off factory lines to train pilots for the European war. (Winston Churchill had successfully pried a few airplanes from the War Department's grasp, but only a few.) Roosevelt left the door open by telling Morgenthau, "It would be nice if the Chinese would bomb Japan."[13]

Morgenthau recorded what happened when he left Roosevelt:

> After lunch at the White House, T. V. Soong was with me going back in the car and I said, "Well, his asking for 500 planes is like asking for 500 stars." I then said that we might get him planes by 1942, but what did he think of the idea of some long-range bombers with the understanding that they were to be used to bomb Tokyo and other Japanese cities? Well, to say he was enthusiastic is putting it mildly.[14]

Of course Soong was excited. After ten years of trying to snare a barbarian to build Chiang an air force, T.V. had just heard the president's best friend suggest that the U.S. was ready to help. Morgenthau told Soong that their exchange should be kept hush-hush, that Soong should relay the president's thoughts "to General Chiang Kai-shek and to nobody else in Washington."[15]

The date of these giddy conversations was December 8, 1940, one year before Pearl Harbor.

Tommy the Cork advised people who wished to influence Roosevelt that the best way to get the Skipper's attention was to use colorful visual aids, the bigger and brighter, the better. T.V. took Corcoran's advice and personally delivered to Morgenthau's house a large map of China with brightly colored areas indicating proposed American airfields. (Mao Zedong's growing empire was not represented.)

When Morgenthau phoned FDR and told him that "Chiang Kai-shek's message was that he wanted to attack Japan," Roosevelt exclaimed, "That's what I have been talking about for four years."[16] Morgenthau presented Chiang's air-war plan in a morning cabinet meeting. Roosevelt, according to Morgenthau's notes, believed that such an operation might have a positive effect in both Asia and Europe. After the cabinet meeting, Roosevelt summoned Secretaries Hull, Stimson, Knox, and Morgenthau to further discuss T. V. Soong's colored map.

"The President was delighted," Morgenthau told T.V. the next day. "I said, and I hope you will back me up, that if they could get [pilots] who knew how to fly these four-engine bombers, that China would be glad to pay up to $1,000 a month in United States dollars. Was that too high?" T.V. replied, "No, not at all." Cost was no object to Soong because the bills would be paid with U.S. tax money that came out of Morgenthau's treasury. Excited, Morgenthau asked, "This Colonel Chennault, where is he?" Soong replied, "He is here now in Washington."[17]

The evening of Saturday, December 21, the treasury secretary hosted some China Lobbyists in his living room. Morgenthau discussed maps of China and lists of American airplanes with T. V. Soong, Claire Chennault, and General Mow, the head of the Chinese air force. It must have been exciting for the balding bureaucrat to be operating as America's secret air marshal, enthusiastically discussing various types of planes and flying tactics that he knew almost nothing about.[18]

The president's best friend and one of the nation's most powerful officials was having a conversation with three China Lobbyists about how American planes and pilots would terror-bomb Japanese cities, an act condemned by FDR when the Japanese bombed civilians in China.

While the operation was to be kept secret from the American public, General George Marshall, FDR's brilliant and starchy Army chief of staff, learned that administration civilians were planning for a secret air war in Asia. Marshall had little regard for Chennault, who, of course, had been drummed out of the U.S. Army Air Corps three years earlier. Now "Colonel" Chennault had come to Washington trying to sell a harebrained air-war scheme that the Army's number-one man knew couldn't work.

General George Marshall, U.S. Army chief of staff. Marshall had served in China and knew of Chiang Kai-shek's military incompetence, but he was a savvy bureaucratic player who saw the domestic political pressure on President Franklin Delano Roosevelt. (Courtesy Everett Collection)

Marshall had served in China and knew about Chiang's leadership and his locust armies. It must have been galling for a traditionalist like Marshall to discover that a Chinese financier and his American soldier of fortune had gone around established State and War Department channels to influence the president and the treasury secretary. Marshall invited Soong and Chennault to private meetings.

Marshall was a good soldier and an adroit bureaucratic survivor who understood that his commander in chief was a politician, that the majority of American voters wanted to help the Noble Chinese Peasants, that the president of the United States and his secretary of the treasury were on Chiang's side, that the two men had just given one hundred million dollars to the Generalissimo, and that Chiang wanted even more. On the afternoon of Sunday, December 22, Marshall tried to talk some sense into Secretary of the Treasury Morgenthau.

Two types of airplanes were on the table: long-range bombers and short-range fighters. Marshall's strategy with Morgenthau was to nix talk of bombing Japan while giving Chiang a few outdated fighter planes to satisfy FDR. The general explained to the treasury secretary that every bomber that came off the production line was needed to train thousands of new pilots in support of America's Europe-first policy. Marshall then adroitly offered Morgenthau half a loaf: he was willing to extend some form of air support to Chiang, but he believed it was in America's best interests to send only fighter planes. Morgenthau agreed.

Marshall had averted a potential disaster. Fighter planes had a limited range, so he wouldn't have to worry about U.S. bombers piloted by American mercenaries getting shot down over Japan while the U.S. was not officially at war with the country.

Hull hosted a meeting on Monday, December 23, at the State Department for Morgenthau, Knox, Stimson, and Marshall to formulate a policy that would please FDR and mollify Chiang. All agreed that the United States would transfer a hundred outmoded P-40 fighter planes to the Chinese. Roosevelt immediately approved the compromise.

FDR chose to control this secret air force from outside the War Department and within the White House, creating the historical precedent for the executive branch's use of air war with no Pentagon or congressional oversight. Roosevelt instructed T. V. Soong to establish a private company to purchase the airplanes, ship them to China, and clandestinely recruit U.S. Armed Services personnel as mercenaries. FDR even suggested the name of Soong's company: China Defense Supplies. FDR and T.V. agreed that Tommy Corcoran would run CDS under the title of adviser. Tommy hired his brother David Corcoran as president and staffed CDS with men from the administration, some of whom Roosevelt personally recommended. Roosevelt wanted a dignified figure to serve as CDS's honorary chairman and chose his uncle Franklin Delano. And now that the Stimson Committee was disbanded, Tommy hired former executive director Harry Price—the chief Manhattan missionary—to work in the CDS accounting department.

In less than six months, T. V. Soong had gotten Roosevelt to authorize what the U.S. State and War Departments had long opposed. And the expenses were paid by the U.S. Treasury, with money and supplies flowing through T. V. Soong and on to Asia, where Ailing and Chiang waited with open arms.

The first months of 1941 were ones of impressive creativity for Henry Luce. On February 17, he authored a lengthy *Life* magazine editorial called the "The American Century," his signature piece that would be cited in his obituary. Luce then defined Asia's place in his American Century with an April 1941 spread in *Fortune* entitled "The New China." To birth his New China, Luce created the biggest propaganda organization for a foreign country in U.S. history: United China Relief.

"The American Century" was a missionary call for U.S. global domination:

> America as the dynamic center of ever widening spheres of enterprise, America as the training center of skilled servants of mankind, America as the Good Samaritan, really believing again that it is more blessed to give than to receive and America as the powerhouse of the ideas of Freedom and Justice....

We are, for a fact, in the war.... We are not in a war to defend American territory. We are in a war to defend and even to promote, encourage and incite so-called democratic principles throughout the world.[19]

Luce called for the American military to push into Asia, with trade to follow, for which Asians should be thankful. America would be thankful too, as trade with Asia "will be worth to us four, five, ten billion dollars a year."

Like his hero Theodore Roosevelt, Luce saw the U.S. as the world's helpmate and guardian. America would give technical, economic, and military aid to nations felt to be friendly but would take a "very tough attitude toward all hostile governments."

Luce's *Fortune* article was a description of a place that existed only in the American imagination. Chiang was presented in the sort of hyperbolic terms that one would expect from a dictator's press office. This, however, was America's most popular and respected business magazine:

> China may someday be a democracy. Today her government is this man. Probably no chief of state in the world, whether temporary like Churchill or with a pretense of permanence like Hitler, has a hold on his country as does Generalissimo Chiang Kai-shek.... Among the people he has achieved the status of legend while still alive. The common farmers say and believe that he sits like a mountain, moves like a dragon, and walks with the sure step of a tiger.[20]

Luce hired one of the Stimson Committee's top Manhattan missionaries — Mr. Bettis Garside — to help him birth the organization Luce named United China Relief. Luce got the ball rolling with a donation of $60,000 from his own fortune, and together, he and Garside consolidated a number of the China aid organizations.

Luce used the UCR to further convince Americans that China was a land much like the United States and that it was full of people who

Pearl Buck's Noble Chinese Peasants as presented by Henry Luce's United China Relief (Sawyers, Martha, 1902–1988. China first to fight!: United China Relief participating in National War Fund. *U.S.A. UNT Digital Library, http://digital .library.unt.edu/ark:/67531/metadc367/)*

sought to replace their outmoded past with a future based on the American way. In publications with names like *China Fights for Democracy,* Luce's UCR minions wrote, "Despite geographical, racial and linguistic barriers [Chinese and Americans] think alike, react alike and hold much the same ideals."[21]

Despite apparent differences, these two nations [America and China] have many common characteristics. China, with all its changes in governmental forms, has for four thousand years been fundamentally democratic. The Chinese people have long looked to America with admiration and friendship, and have turned to us for leadership and example in every phase of the sweeping changes they have made during the last thirty years. Chinese, trained in American universities or in American-supported colleges and universities in China, occupy a majority of the places of importance throughout China today.[22]

United China Relief's board of directors had star power. Eleanor Roosevelt became honorary chairwoman of UCR's national advisory committee, Pearl Buck was chairwoman, and UCR board members included luminaries like John D. Rockefeller III, movie producer David O. Selznick, Theodore Roosevelt Jr., Wendell Willkie, and Luce himself. T. V. Soong chaired UCR's National Committee on Chinese Participation.

In fact, United China Relief was a propaganda machine that sent little money to China. *Relief* was in the name, but creating images of New China in the American mind was Luce's game. Luce installed almost thirty Time Inc. professionals to run UCR's publicity department, and they suggested various public relations ideas: pro-Chiang children's books; a Times Square Chinese pagoda; a Chinese library; pretty Chinese girls parading down towns' Main Streets; events like China Nights, China Weeks, and China Luncheons; a national Chinese chess tournament; a radio program to publicize the adoption of Chinese orphans; Chinese-clothing fashion shows. Luce mailed a personal appeal to all *Time* magazine subscribers soliciting donations for UCR. Donating money to UCR, he said, was "the most effective means of translating American sympathy and admiration for China into concrete measures of assistance."[23] Generous contributors became members of the China Legion, an honor that came with a certificate signed by Madame Chiang.

UCR employees flooded American airwaves and mailboxes with pro-China press reports, celebrity testimonials, booklets, flyers, and posters; they distributed pieces of imitation Chinese jewelry and thousands of buttons with cute Chinese mottos. The organization had Hollywood stars broadcast New China messages on the radio and established a UCR Children's Committee—headed by none other than Walt Disney—with branches in cities across the country where children could deposit the pennies, nickels, and dimes they'd collected in UCR coin boxes for the cause. Drivers on America's roads saw UCR billboards with suffering Noble Peasants and bold headlines:

3,000,000 CHINESE
HAVE GIVEN THEIR LIVES FOR DEMOCRACY
What have you given?

Frank Price—Mayling's favorite missionary—was UCR's coordinator in Chungking, from where he shoveled China Lobby propaganda. Luce asked Walt Disney and comic-strip writers to introduce Chinese

A billboard for United China Relief. (Courtesy of UCLA, Library Special Collections, Charles E. Young Research Library)

scenes and personalities into their work. UCR mailed China news items to major newspapers and radio stations, from whom Time Inc. also bought advertising. UCR boasted in an internal memo that "a comprehensive program of publicity and promotion was developed, including not only releases and other articles for the press but also departments for radio, motion pictures, speakers, merchandising, and special features."[24]

The UCR speakers' bureau got the word out. One of the organization's most popular speakers was UCR chairwoman Pearl Buck, who told audiences:

> The Chinese people deserve every honor that can be given them, every penny that can be sent to help them, every aid that can be found to preserve their democracy. It is for them that we Americans must work wholeheartedly through all the agencies in which we are working. I am one of a group of Americans who are trying at this moment to raise a million dollars to buy medical supplies to send to China for the millions of people who need them, and there are many other groups working for other Chinese causes.[25]

Another of UCR's popular speakers was William Bullitt, the man who had shuttled messages between FDR and Chiang. Bullitt told audiences, "The Chinese and Americans believe in the same moral code and speak the same moral language."[26] China was proclaimed "our Western front," and Chiang was fighting what was really "our battle."[27] The Generalissimo now stood "at China's Valley Forge."[28]

To further focus Americans on New China, Luce decided to orchestrate a national speaking tour for Mayling Soong. Mayling had been broadcasting to the U.S. for years; she regularly contributed to many American magazines and was often voted one of America's most admired women. Luce wrote Chinese ambassador Hu Shih:

> The central problem of the campaign is to lift the story of China out of the "old old story" category and to present it for what it truly is—the newest story in the world! This will

require at least one very dramatic symbol. We therefore very much hope that Madame Chiang will come to this country for a brief visit.[29]

For years, a small group of Harvard graduates in Washington had been swaying policy toward China: President Roosevelt, T. V. Soong, Felix Frankfurter, Lauchlin Currie, Henry Stimson, Tommy the Cork, and many Hotdogs spread throughout the administration. Realizing the rewards that could come from such networks, the Soong-Chiang syndicate hired a young Harvard graduate named Theodore White as an adviser to their propaganda arm, the Ministry of Information. White joined an America-friendly government led by the American-educated Ailing and Mayling and the Southern Methodist Generalissimo. The finance minister, H. H. Kung, and the minister of foreign affairs were Yale graduates; the minister of education had a degree from the University of Pittsburgh; Sun Yat-sen's son, with degrees from Columbia and the University of California, presided over the legislature. Hollington Tong, the minister of information and White's boss, was a graduate of the Missouri School of Journalism and Columbia University. T. V. Soong, currently head of the Bank of China and later China's prime minister, was a Harvard graduate, class of 1915. The list of American-educated Chinese ran from the national health administrator to the foreign trade commissioner. China's ambassadors were almost all Ivy League; there was a Cornell and Columbia graduate in Washington and a University of Pennsylvania graduate in London; the ambassador to Paris had three degrees from Columbia and a son who was on the *Crimson* staff at Harvard.

Teddy White was one of the very first Harvard graduates who spoke Chinese and who had studied Chinese culture. Professor John Fairbank had founded Harvard's China program only recently, in 1936, and White was one of his original students.

White's title was adviser to the Chinese Ministry of Information. Teddy later recalled, "In reality, I was employed to manipulate American public opinion."[30]

Since almost none of the American journalists in China read or spoke

Chinese, they were at the mercy of their minders, who kept them in a New China bubble. To house American reporters, the Soong-Chiang clan built new hotels in Chungking where there were beautiful Chinese girls to bond with these lonely travelers. At lavish and convivial banquets, visiting Americans heard about how, with just a little U.S. money and a few airplanes, Chiang would push the Japanese out and transform the Middle Kingdom into a democracy. Most exciting of all for the newsmen was a trip to the "front," where, from Chinese army trenches, the Americans could peer through binoculars and see a Japanese soldier in the distance (actually a Chinese soldier dressed in a Japanese uniform).

The American correspondents were not stupid; many were their generation's best and brightest. But they came from a country whose exclusion acts had kept Chinese people out for sixty years. The correspondents couldn't tell the difference between a Chinese, a Japanese, and a Korean.

On a postelection fishing trip, FDR dreamed up the concept that would later be passed into law and known as the Lend-Lease policy: the attractive fiction that after their wars were over, England, Russia, and China would return the materials the U.S. lent to them. Lend-Lease gave Roosevelt centralized power to decide which countries would get what supplies.

T. V. Soong heard about Lend-Lease from his employee Ludwik Rajchman—who was probably tipped off by Supreme Court justice Felix Frankfurter—before Roosevelt announced it to the public. Soong immediately recognized the potential and asked Roosevelt to send Lend-Lease administrator Harry Hopkins to China. Roosevelt wanted Hopkins to deal with Churchill, so to handle China he chose instead Lauchlin Currie.[31] Currie had never been to Asia and knew little about China—which was just how T.V. liked it.

Using American aid as a carrot, FDR thought he could convince Chiang to "call off the civil war." Once Chiang and Mao were working together, Roosevelt would "give China a budget." Chiang, with Mao's support, would then wage a New Deal–style "war for social justice." The benefits would be huge; Roosevelt foresaw "the industrialization of Asia" with China as "a new frontier for industrial expansion." Legions of Chinese would be "open to friendly American enterprise."[32]

Warren Delano's grandson believed that China had to regenerate itself, and what better example existed than his New Deal? Roosevelt adopted a respectful tone with Chiang, praising him as "a fellow leader of democracy," with the expectation that Chiang would "become a popular leader on the Roosevelt model."[33] Barbara Tuchman later wrote that Roosevelt's approach to China "was a policy of make-believe [that] grew out of genuine conviction."[34]

Although FDR officially delegated him, Currie traveled to China on a Soong-Chiang syndicate salary plus expenses. T. V. Soong gave Currie an advance of $2,500 before he left.[35] The investment in the Harvard Hotdog was worthwhile, T.V. assured Chiang, because Currie was "fully alive to [the] necessity of expediting decision on aircraft, particularly on bombers, in view of the general situation and the continuous bombing of Chungking."[36]

Mayling arranged two meetings between Chiang and Currie, both on weekends in February. The president's emissary did not bring his own interpreter; there were likely few, if any, people in the Roosevelt administration who were fluent enough in Chinese to interpret, so Currie relied on Mayling and chief propagandist Hollington Tong to translate. Chiang's responses could thus be sanitized and embellished by a smart Wellesley girl and a sharp Columbia journalism school graduate who knew how to handle Harvard men.

Currie wrote of their first encounter, "Chiang met me as I entered the room. He shook hands warmly and smiled, making a succession of little friendly noises (this went on throughout the conference). He placed me next to him. I gave him the President's letter, after thanking him for his greetings and reception." Physically, the Chinese leader was more than expected: "Chiang is a handsome and striking person. His photographs do not do him justice as they miss his coloring and

Lauchlin Currie and Mayling Soong. "We discussed the state of democracy in China," Currie told FDR. (Carl Mydans / Getty Images)

the sparkle of his wide-open eyes and the general impression of health and vitality. He appeared to be a little nervous during the interview and I was extremely nervous. We both kept our hands clasped."[37]

Chiang said that he had a great "sentimental attachment and admiration for America," that President Roosevelt was "the greatest man in the world," and that he'd read "every word" of FDR's speeches.[38] Currie quickly replied with the words that must have confirmed to Chiang and Mayling that, after a decade of trying, they had finally hooked their barbarian:

> In regard to America's supply of military equipment to China there is no question at all. One great assurance in this respect from America is the fact that besides the sentimental reasons America is helping China in her own interests. Your war is our war.[39]

240

Here was one of Frankfurter's more brilliant Harvard Hotdogs, the first economic adviser to a president in American history, FDR's point man on China, and yet he had no idea that Chiang's war was not against the Japanese but against Mao. The American misperception of "your war is our war" would embolden Chiang and enrich the Soongs as they sat back and waited for their American barbarians to perform their assigned function.

The Lend-Lease pipeline started in the Oval Office, and Mayling asked Currie to suggest to Roosevelt that he use her private code system to keep messages between Chungking and the White House outside of regular diplomatic channels. Currie agreed.

Currie gently explained that if Chiang made himself more politically popular by implementing FDR-style policies, he could win the battle against Mao for China's hearts and minds, just as FDR had cobbled his New Deal coalition together in the face of Republican opposition. He suggested that—like Roosevelt—Chiang should employ a "technique of making adjustments rather than repression."[40]

No British, Russian, French, or Japanese diplomat would have believed that Chiang could become a New Deal liberal—this, too, was part and parcel of the mirage. Currie had clearly laid out what Roosevelt expected Chiang to do in exchange for Lend-Lease aid: fight Japan, unite with Mao, cut military expenditures, raise land taxes, boot out the tradition-bound conservatives, and let a liberal progressive China bloom. But Chiang's number-one priority since he'd teamed with the Soongs had been to kill Mao and *all* Communists. Just two months earlier, Chiang's allies had ambushed thousands of Mao's staff. A United Front?

FDR's suggestion that Chiang balance his budget by cutting military expenditures and raising land taxes must have confirmed to Chiang how little Roosevelt understood reality in China. Chiang's power rested on his ability to funnel barbarian aid to warlord allies. Cutting military expenditures would destroy Chiang's power base. And raising taxes? One of Mao's main attractions for the peasants was that he was *reducing* their onerous taxes. Trying to squeeze more out of the beleaguered Chinese peasant would only increase animosity toward Chiang's regime; he'd be playing into Mao's hands.

Roosevelt's recommendation that Chiang move away from an army-dominated rule of repression to an accommodating populist New Deal liberalism must also have amazed the Generalissimo. Ailing Soong had allied China's richest family with Chiang precisely because he had a large club and would use it to beat out the liberal flames that Mao had lit in Chinese hearts.

Like Chiang's Anti-Opium Suppression Bureau that was actually Ailing's opium monopoly, the legislature and government bureaus that Professor Currie saw on his tour were like movie-lot fronts designed to fool Americans. So, too, were Chiang's replies to Currie's questions; they were curated distortions of what Currie knew FDR wanted to hear. So Currie concluded that Chiang was eager to follow in FDR's footsteps, that the Chinese would embrace the New Deal creed, and that Roosevelt was right to imagine China as America's good friend.

Mayling and Chiang hosted a gala banquet for their bought-and-paid-for barbarian. Currie sat next to Ailing's husband, the rotund, chuckling H. H. Kung, supposedly the seventy-fifth lineal descendant of Confucius. A 1916 Yale graduate, Kung was fluent in American English; he was also Standard Oil's man in China and one of the country's wealthiest citizens. Currie wrote that he and Kung talked about "the extent of democracy in China." Currie enjoyed himself, noting, "I was toasted three times."[41] Chiang wrote to T. V. Soong in Washington, "When [Currie] returns to the United States he will surely prove to be of the greatest assistance to our cause."[42]

Currie's confidential report to FDR was a jumble of mirage assumptions that would eventually lead the United States down a disastrous path in Asia. Furthering the New Deal fantasy, Currie wrote that Chiang "wished to avoid great inequality in incomes and wealth, and that he was determined to carry out land reforms so that those who tilled the soil would own it."[43] Currie assured FDR that Chiang would serve as an effective block to Japan's push into Southeast Asia: "The Indochina-

Chinese border is now very strongly defended and the General Staff is confident that the Japanese cannot penetrate there."[44] Currie was particularly impressed with Chiang's foresight:

> The Chinese are making great efforts to build a number of airfields that can carry the weight of our flying fortresses. I inspected one at Chengtu, which was being built by 75,000 peasants with no power-driven machinery of any kind. The man in charge was a Chinese civil engineer trained at the University of Illinois.[45]

As for troops, here too Currie saw only a sliver of the picture. "By all accounts the morale of the Chinese soldier is good," he wrote. "Certainly, in the Military Academy I visited, I could not hope to see a harder-working nor more serious-minded group of men."[46]

Currie was clearly not completely oblivious to Chiang's imperfection as a political leader, because he wrote, "In connection with the growing disaffection of the liberal elements...I argued as strongly as I dared for a policy of conciliation rather than suppression."[47]

Much of Currie's report read as if it had sprung from Roosevelt's mind; if FDR treated Chiang as a liberal democrat, Currie wrote, Chiang would grow into the role. Currie admitted that while Chiang was a dictator running a dictatorship, he *sincerely* wanted to be more like the leader of the free world. Currie urged FDR to obscure the distasteful aspects of Chiang's rule and promote the New China mirage:

> I think that Chiang can be held in line with a little care and attention from America. His attitude toward America is compounded partly of sentiment and partly of self-interest. He admires America, and particularly you, tremendously, and to be treated as an equal or ally would mean a great deal to him.... He is most anxious that China be regarded as a "democracy," taking part in the common world struggle of democracies....
>
> I think it is most important, in addition to giving material aid, to go out of your way to say nice things about China and to speak of her in the same terms now used toward England.[48]

A few days after receiving Currie's report, in a speech at the White House Correspondents' dinner, President Roosevelt proclaimed,

> China…expresses the magnificent will of millions of plain people to resist the dismemberment of their historic nation. China, through the Generalissimo, Chiang Kai-shek, asks our help. America has said that China shall have our help.[49]

After he briefed Roosevelt, Currie billed T. V. Soong $1,388.88 for his salary from January 25 to March 11, 1941, with expenses of $1,681.53.[50] Secretary Morgenthau complained to his staff, "The trouble with Mr. Currie is, I don't know half the time whether he is working for the President or T. V. Soong, because half the time he is on one payroll and the rest of the time he is on the other."[51]

Chapter 9

A WAR OVER OIL

*The support of America against the Japanese was the government's only
hope for survival; to sway the American press was critical. It was
considered necessary to lie to it, to deceive it, to do anything to persuade
America that the future of China and the United States ran together against
Japan. That was the only war strategy of the Chinese government.*
—*Theodore White, adviser to China's Ministry of Information*[1]

Dean Acheson was born on April 11, 1893, in the brick rectory of
Holy Trinity Church in Middletown, Connecticut, where his father,
Bishop Acheson, was rector. As a boy, Acheson listened to his father
lecture Middletown's citizens on right and wrong. Over time, he developed a self-righteousness that would inform his life and career.
Once, in a heated argument, Acheson called his father a fool, and
Bishop Acheson kicked Dean out of the house for one year. Eventually Bishop Acheson seemed to forgive his son, but Dean never apologized for the insult. When he later wrote his memoirs, the younger
man made no mention of the episode. Dean Acheson was not one to
admit mistakes.

Young Dean Acheson had many reasons to believe he existed above
most mere mortals. Acheson attended the elite Groton School in Groton, Massachusetts, where he studied Latin, mathematics, physics,

*Dean Acheson and Felix Frankfurter. Acheson was one of Frankfurter's
Harvard Hotdogs—both men admired the First Wise Man, Henry Stimson—
and Acheson would go on to become the leader of the Wise Men.
(Courtesy Everett Collection)*

chemistry, Greek, Roman, and European and U.S. history. Like fellow
Groton alumnus Franklin Delano Roosevelt, Acheson learned a tremendous amount about a tiny part of the earth—Europe—and virtually nothing about Asia.[2]

Felix Frankfurter recognized Acheson's brilliance at Harvard Law
School and recommended him to Roosevelt, who appointed Acheson
undersecretary of the treasury on May 19, 1933. Acheson agreed to
serve Roosevelt but was determined not to be servile:

> The President could relax over his poker parties and enjoy Tom
> Corcoran's accordion, he could and did call everyone from his
> valet to the Secretary of State by his first name and often made up

Damon Runyon nicknames for them, too — "Tommy the Cork,"
"Henry the Morgue," and similar names; he could charm an individual or a nation. But he condescended. Many reveled in apparent
admission to an inner circle. I did not...to me it was patronizing
and humiliating.[3]

When Secretary of the Treasury William Woodin fell ill, Acheson
found himself acting secretary. The strong-willed and overconfident
Acheson soon clashed with Roosevelt. ("My attitude toward the President," Acheson wrote, "was one of admiration without affection."[4]) He
resigned in a huff and returned to his legal practice. As with his father,
Acheson never apologized. And, like Bishop Acheson, Roosevelt
seemed to forgive the younger man. Frankfurter kept Acheson's name
in front of FDR, and from time to time Acheson lent his legal skills to
the Roosevelt administration. Acheson had a strong bond with Henry
Morgenthau, who had succeeded him as secretary of the treasury and
whom Acheson admired as a true Washington Warrior:

> Henry Morgenthau was the most dynamic character in Wash-
> ington; he had passion. His description of the kind of man he
> wanted hired was: "Does he want to lick this fellow Hitler...
> that is what I want to know....Does he hate Hitler's guts?"
> Henry did.[5]

Like Morgenthau, Acheson bought the First Wise Man's China
Lobby line that the U.S. could embargo Japan with no repercussions.
He also agreed that a few Wise Men should control U.S. foreign policy,
that transparent democracy was fine for domestic matters but secrecy
was vital in the conduct of foreign affairs.

On February 1, 1941, Frankfurter looked on as his fellow Supreme
Court justice Louis Brandeis swore Acheson in as undersecretary of
state for economic affairs. (Morgenthau had probably suggested to
FDR that he appoint Acheson under Hull to put some spine in the
State Department.) Morgenthau, Stimson, Knox, and Ickes now had a
kindred spirit within State. Wrote John Morton Blum, author of *From
the Morgenthau Diaries,* "There was no one at the State Department

with whom [Morgenthau] could talk candidly except for Dean Acheson."[6] It went both ways. Recalled Acheson, "There was no one at all with whom I could talk—sympathetically. From top to bottom our Department, except for our corner of it, was against Henry Morgenthau's campaign to apply freezing controls to axis countries and their victims."[7]

Acheson was a fighter who believed that "by the spring of 1941 the American people were ready for a stronger lead toward intervention." He chafed at Secretary Hull's deliberate pace, deciding, "What was most often needed was not compromise but decision." Acheson complained that Hull was "slow, circuitous, cautious—concentrated on a central political purpose, the freeing of international trade from tariff and other restrictions as the prerequisite to peace and economic development." He ridiculed in writing Hull's oft-repeated goal of "mutually beneficial reciprocal trade agreements" by making fun of Hull's speech impediment: "wecipwocal twade aqueements." And Acheson dismissed Roosevelt's decision-making ability: "Unfortunately, the capacity to decide does not descend in Pentecostal fashion upon every occupant of the White House."[8]

President Roosevelt thrived on intrigue and secrecy, and in 1941 he enjoyed plenty of both. FDR was enthusiastic about communicating with Chiang and Mayling through their secret code and was soon having confidential chats with them. Ambassador Clarence Gauss complained to Hull and pleaded for "normal diplomatic channels of communication," pointing out that "no Ambassador to China can function intelligently and efficiently under present conditions without some background on what is transpiring through other than the usual diplomatic channels."[9]

Hull asked Currie to have "messages which he sends to officials in Chungking pass through the hands of our own Ambassador."[10] Currie agreed to report regularly to the State Department. Finally Hull succeeded in stopping FDR's back-channel discussions. (Currie wrote Mayling that Roosevelt "would communicate more frequently directly with me if it were not for the very understandable resistance of the

State Department.")[11] History will never know how many secret conversations occurred or what Roosevelt promised.

Another of FDR's intrigues in the spring of 1941 was the clandestine air force he was arranging for Chiang. Purchasing and then shipping fighter planes from the U.S. to the receiving docks in Rangoon, Burma, was relatively easy to manage and keep secret. Roosevelt was much more concerned that he might be held responsible for creating a corps of American mercenaries. Remembered Corcoran, "Roosevelt was troubled by the soiled label that Chennault's irregulars might wear." Tommy showed FDR a British martial poem called "Epitaph on an Army of Mercenaries," about the first 160,000 English soldiers to die in World War I; they were called mercenaries because, unlike the draftees that followed them, they were a paid prewar army. Corcoran wrote that Roosevelt "was moved by the poem's wisdom. It bolstered his determination to act."[12] Tommy and the Skipper cooked up a scheme that utilized private front companies to recruit and pay American pilots outside of government channels (a process the CIA would later call sheep-dipping). U.S. Army pilots and airmen would "resign" from the service and then sign private contracts with CAMCO, Ailing Soong's company.

Roosevelt asked Lauchlin Currie to take Chennault to the War Department to pitch his plan to the head of the U.S. Army Air Corps, General Henry "Hap" Arnold. FDR might have assumed that the presence of Currie, a top presidential assistant, would influence Arnold, but in the 1930s the general had been in the forefront of those who ousted Chennault, and he wanted nothing to do with FDR's secret mercenary effort. Currie and Chennault next knocked at the Navy's Bureau of Aeronautics and spoke to Rear Admiral John Towers, who also turned his back on FDR's half-baked air-war scheme.

Having been rejected by his uniformed military, Roosevelt turned to Corcoran, who approached the military's two civilian bosses, Henry Stimson and Frank Knox. Tommy told them what the president wanted. In the end, Currie had to draw up a formal presidential directive ordering Stimson and Knox to release pilots from their military service:

I suggest...that beginning in January, you should accept the resignations of additional pilots and ground personnel as care to accept employment in China, up to a limit of 100 pilots and a proportional number of ground personnel.[13]

Chennault recalled that when his recruiters visited air bases across the U.S. offering "a one-year contract with CAMCO to 'manufacture, repair, and operate aircraft' at salaries ranging from $250 to $750 a month...several spluttering commanders called Washington long distance for confirmation of their orders."[14]

For additional cover, Ailing's CAMCO and FDR's CDS disguised the fighter squadrons as "advanced training units"; the airplanes were "advanced trainers," and Chennault was a "supervisor."[15] Sensing which way FDR's winds were blowing, Hull caved in. He informed the Chinese embassy that, though the U.S. would not accept an open military alliance, it was willing to issue passports to Americans to work in China as "aviation instructors."[16] Chennault later described his interaction with a State Department clerk in the passport division:

In applying for my passport, I listed my occupation as farmer. The clerk was skeptical. "I own land in Louisiana, and I make a living from it," I replied to him. "That makes me a farmer." He insisted I change my occupation. It took a call to the White House to convince him that I was a farmer.[17]

Roosevelt was now running an off-the-books secret executive air force through Ailing's front companies. Claire Chennault was a private contractor—a mercenary—being paid by the China Lobby. Roosevelt was sheep-dipping: taking U.S. personnel, cleansing them with the fiction of their resignations, and then sending them off as secret mercenaries. Today, many mistakenly believe that Chennault's mission was an American invention controlled by the U.S. military, but when he returned to Asia, Chennault reported back to Washington not through American military channels but privately, through his boss, T. V. Soong.

*   *   *

In March of 1941, T. V. Soong presented his Lend-Lease shopping list: a thousand planes, three hundred fifty technical assistants, two hundred flying instructors, enough arms and supplies to outfit thirty infantry divisions, and sufficient equipment for what would have been the world's largest construction project: a highway and a railway connecting China and India.[18] T.V. expected that his enormous requests would be filled as quickly as possible. When he went to Roosevelt, FDR was noncommittal. Soong complained to his China Lobby man on the Supreme Court, Justice Felix Frankfurter, that he had "begged [FDR] specifically to say that China's demands would be granted." Roosevelt had smiled and responded, "So long as the Battle of the Atlantic is won everything will be all right."[19]

T.V. was also frustrated with Henry Morgenthau, who was refusing to hand over the entire $100 million that FDR had promised. (Morgenthau wanted the loan released in installments of $5 million per month.) Soong asked Frankfurter to take time out from his duties and dicker with the president over terms. Soong also contacted China Lobbyist Thomas Corcoran, and together Tommy and Frankfurter argued T.V.'s case to FDR, who in turn pressured Morgenthau, who then complained to associates about T. V. Soong's "special representatives" and "special attorneys," wondering "who is on the U.S. payroll and who is on the Chinese payroll and who is working for what."[20]

The Currie-FDR plan to "say nice things" about Chiang surfaced in the form of an article about Currie's mission to China that appeared in *Life* magazine on May 5, 1941. The piece was crafted by China Lobbyist Eliot Janeway, who wrote that FDR believed Chiang was "Roosevelt's fellow-leader of democracy," a man through whom the president would promote the "democratic principles of the New Deal."[21]

That same month, Henry Luce ventured to the country of his birth with his wife, Clare Boothe Luce. By the time the couple arrived in Chungking, on May 8, 1941, Ailing and Mayling had already run hundreds of Americans through the Soong-Chiang drill. Ailing housed the Luces in her Western-style Chungking home, where she could almost literally watch their every move. The Soongs controlled the Luces' schedule; the publisher and his wife went where the Soong sisters wanted them to go, and they met the people who were put in front of them. The Soong sisters kept the Luces on a stimulating treadmill of daily meetings with graduates of U.S. universities and late-night banquets hosted by smiling American-trained Chinese who, in American-style English, toasted Henry's brilliance and Clare's beauty.

The Luces were accompanied on parts of their trip by their newly hired *Time* magazine correspondent Teddy White, lately of Chiang's Ministry of Information.

Luce was thrilled to witness a Japanese air raid on Chungking, which he observed from the safety of the American embassy, located across the river from the city. "There they come!" Luce wrote. "There

Henry Luce and Theodore "Teddy" White. Luce hired White from Chiang's Ministry of Information. (Time & Life Pictures / Getty Images)

they come! I could hear nothing nor see anything except the blazing sky. Then: Corrump, corrump, corrump, corrump. And again: Corrump, corrump, CORRUMP."[22] Luce admitted that he never actually saw any Japanese aircraft, but Minister of Information Hollington Tong told him there had been forty-two Japanese airplanes, which Luce reported as fact. After the bombing, Luce and company crossed the river and drove through Chungking's streets. He saw no injured people, but Tong said there had been casualties, which Luce also reported.

No barbarian's tour of the China Lobby's New China theme park would be complete without a visit to "the front," so Luce took a short airplane hop north to the city of Xian and was thrilled to find that it was becoming Americanized with "wide long straight streets with sidewalks...Western clothes...and above all, rubber tires—rubber tires even on oxcarts."[23]

Tong roused the Luces at 3:15 the next morning so they could witness the army's dawn rituals. Well-muscled troops in crisp uniforms paraded past the publisher, came to attention, saluted a flag, and listened to a band. After the men marched away, Tong told Luce there were twelve thousand such troops in the area fighting the Japanese, another unverifiable claim parroted by Luce in his dispatch home.

Escorted by General Chow, the Luces went to "the wall of the city nearest the river and the Japanese." In the city was a frontline headquarters. A colonel sat the Americans down to tea and showed them brightly colored maps. The colonel next took them to an observation post, and then Henry Luce—dressed in suit and tie with polished shoes—descended with the commander into the trenches.

> Luce wound through the trenches, encountering soldiers who were reading, not fighting, and finally made his way to the observation point: "On the cliffs beyond we could see the gun emplacements and then we spotted one Japanese sentry and through the glasses we could see the flag of Nippon. That was all."[24]

Did Luce see a real Japanese soldier or one of Hollington Tong's Chinese actors? Luce—and the American reader—never knew.

Henry Luce at the "front" in suit and tie
(Courtesy Henry Luce Foundation)

Based on his observation of a few hundred soldiers and his examination of war maps over tea, Luce reported that Chiang had an army of three million snappy, ready-to-fight soldiers:

> Let it be said right now that the Chinese Army of Chiang Kai-shek has a fine morale, as strict discipline, as earnest and as intent an expression as ever characterized any army in history.[25]

When the Luces met with the Generalissimo and Madame Chiang, Henry found it a transcendent experience. Mayling greeted them first and Luce wrote, "We were in almost no time at all talking 100% American faster than I have ever heard it talked." When Chiang arrived, the four of them had a simple lunch, and Luce presented the Generalissimo with a portfolio of photographs. Luce concluded, "An hour later we left knowing that we had made the acquaintance of two people, a man and a woman, who, out of all the millions now living, will be remembered for centuries and centuries."[26]

There were three Chinas at that point: Chiang's, Mao's, and Japan's. Henry Luce had fully examined none of them; he had obediently stayed within the China Lobby bubble. Perhaps if the publisher had not been a missionary's son, someone at Time Inc. might have reported on Mao's China and revealed the twentieth century's largest revolution as it developed from embryo to maturity.

Had Luce made his way to Yan'an, no lavish banquets in marble halls would have been awaiting him. But Luce would have found that Yan'an, which six years earlier most Chinese had never heard of, was now one of China's largest educational centers. Before Mao had marched to Yan'an, there had been few schools scattered across a vast area of North China, and what schools there were taught only the Confucian Four Books and Five Classics. Mao founded the University of Resistance, which graduated over ten thousand students a year. He built primary schools, middle schools, three colleges, the largest arts academy in China, and a vocational training school. A publishing house hidden deep in the loess hills printed books, magazines, and newspapers. A factory produced many types of medicines.

Before Mao's arrival, women in North China were hired out as labor by their husbands and fathers, who collected their wages. Mao created the Women's University, housed in a series of caves connected by internal walkways. The Women's University had students of all ages who were from all over China — astonishing, considering that Chiang had this area surrounded and that the aspiring scholars who ventured to Yan'an risked arrest.

Even if he had traveled to Yan'an, Luce might not have comprehended what he was seeing. Luce, like most Westerners, understood only positional warfare, maps with lines of troops facing each other. A map of Mao's empire would have resembled a net. The Japanese

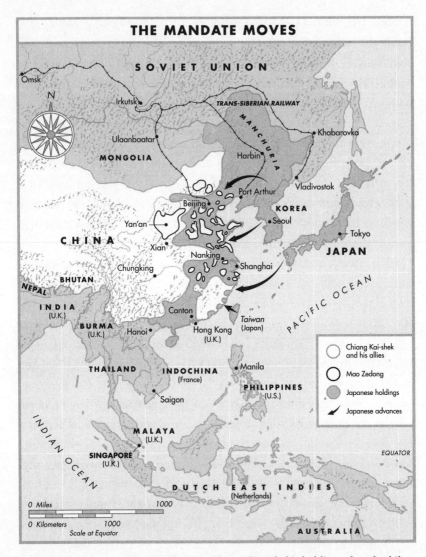

THE MANDATE MOVES

The late 1930s saw chaos in China as Chiang Kai-shek's holdings shrunk while Mao Zedong and the Japanese expanded.

lifelines—cities and connecting roads—were the cords. The open spaces—the majority of the net—were the areas under Mao's influence. When the Japanese advanced, Chiang retreated. Into the resulting vacuum Mao dispatched his acolytes to teach the villagers a new type of resistance warfare.

Mao—like Chiang—had a torture and detention center out of sight. After all, this was a Chinese civil war, and Mao was no saint. The difference was that Mao inspired the Four Hundred Million to reclaim their country.

In the ten months following FDR's July 1940 partial embargo, the Japanese purchased more oil than they had in 1939, and they obtained State-approved licenses for five million gallons more. Shipments from California to Japan in May of 1941 totaled over two million barrels, a record for the year. Newspaper photographs of Japanese ships loading oil in California ports infuriated many Americans, who were two to one in favor of "nonparticipation in Japanese aggression." It was "ghastly" how we were letting Japan "pile up" oil, complained Henry Morgenthau.[27]

Surprisingly, despite all the controversy, the Roosevelt administration's contacts with the Japanese were minimal and limited mostly to official exchanges. No individual Japanese had anything like the personal access to the Roosevelt administration that the China Lobby had. Indeed, the Japanese ambassador was an old navy admiral with minimal English skills. Kichisaburo Nomura was dispatched from Tokyo to Washington in November 1940 because he had served in Washington when Roosevelt was assistant secretary of the Navy. In Tokyo's eyes, Nomura's value in Washington was symbolic. He represented the Japanese navy, which, like the U.S. Navy, did not want war. Roosevelt respected Nomura, but the admiral had none of the public relations skills possessed by Baron Kaneko or T. V. Soong. Nomura's diplomatic experience was limited and he had never attended any overseas English-speaking school, let alone Harvard. Without the benefit of Ivy League ties, the communication between Tokyo, through its embassy in Washington, and the Roosevelt administration was stilted and formal.

In the spring of 1941 Roosevelt agreed to let members of his administration talk with the Japanese government, but, perhaps because of the public's sympathy for the Noble Chinese Peasants and China Lobby pressure, FDR green-lighted the negotiations only if Secretary of State Hull conducted them in secret. On April 14, 1941, Nomura quietly called on Hull at his apartment at the Wardman Park Hotel. Hull's speech impediment and pronounced Tennessee drawl exacerbated the challenges raised by Nomura's poor grasp of English and the complex, layered language of diplomacy.

The subject of their first talk was a draft understanding that Nomura had given to Hull days earlier. Written by a Japanese army colonel in the Japanese embassy in Washington, the draft understanding was a wish list that expressed the Japanese desire to maintain their presence in China. Tokyo officials were unaware of its existence, yet Nomura had submitted it to Hull.

Hull told Nomura up front that their meetings did not constitute formal negotiations, that before the U.S. and Japan could begin talks, Japan must agree to "the integrity and sovereignty of China and the principle of equality of opportunity in China."[28] Hull had just informed Nomura that Japan had to reopen the Open Door before the U.S. would even *begin* negotiations. Nomura—quickly lost in the twists and turns of Hull's legalistic language—never grasped that the secretary of state had drawn a line in the sand.

Two days later, at another meeting in the secretary's apartment, Hull educated Nomura on the four principles upon which any U.S. agreement with Japan must be based:

(1) Respect for the territorial integrity and the sovereignty of each and all nations.
(2) Support of the principle of noninterference in the internal affairs of other countries.
(3) Support of the principle of equality, including equality of commercial opportunity.
(4) Nondisturbance of the status quo in the Pacific except as the status quo may be altered by peaceful means.[29]

Hull was demanding that Japan get out of China, a momentous change in American policy that was expressed in secret by a man who couldn't speak Japanese to a man who barely understood English. Hull's goal was "regeneration," the theory that if the U.S. forced the Japanese military into a humiliating withdrawal from China, moderates in Tokyo would seize power from the militarists. Hull had no interpreter and recorded in his memoirs that Nomura "spoke a certain—sometimes an uncertain— amount of English," so Hull "took care to speak slowly and to repeat and reemphasize some of [his] sentences." Hull concluded that he "was not sure" whether Nomura understood him.

Nomura asked Hull a yes-or-no question: Did the U.S. agree with the draft understanding Japan had submitted? Nomura struggled to comprehend Hull's answer: "If your Government is in real earnest about changing its course, I can see no good reason why ways could not be found to reach a fairly satisfactory settlement of all the essential questions presented."[30]

Unsure if Hull had answered yes or no, Nomura optimistically guessed it was a yes.

None of what Hull had carefully laid out to Nomura was transmitted to Tokyo. Nomura simply cabled the draft understanding to Japan's Foreign Ministry, saying that Hull was willing to go ahead with it. Historian Robert Butow noted,

> Nomura's brief account gave not the slightest hint of the innumerable statements with which Hull had patiently built up his position like a mason carefully laying one stone upon another. The ambassador's few clipped words did not even report the sense of what he had been told by the American Secretary of State.[31]

The drawling Hull had asked Nomura to have Tokyo examine the draft understanding so Japanese leaders could decide whether they wished Japan to officially present it to the State Department *as a basis for starting negotiations*. Instead, Nomura implied to his superiors an American eagerness to go ahead *on the basis of the draft understanding*. Nomura's vague and stilted phrasing led Tokyo officials to conclude that the draft understanding was an *American* plan prepared as a response to the various inside moves initiated by Nomura and his staff. Nomura also failed to forward Hull's crucial four principles, which effectively demanded that Japan withdraw from China.

The draft understanding cabled by Nomura was received in Tokyo on April 18 "like welcome rain in the desert" and a "boon from Heaven." As army minister Hideki Tojo later said, "We regarded the Japanese-American negotiations as having begun from the moment we were asked to indicate our attitude with respect to this proposal."[32] Suddenly what was the draft understanding in Washington became the "American plan" in Tokyo.

Tokyo responded on May 12 with its answer to the American plan, which Hull accepted as Japan's initial offer. Thus, as a result of this tragicomedy of errors, from May 12, 1941, negotiations were doomed; when Hull suggested changes, leaders in Tokyo were outraged that he was backing down on the promises he had made in the American plan.

Arthur Schlesinger Jr. wrote in *The Age of Roosevelt* of FDR's management style:

> In many cases jurisdictions overlapped each other and even spilled into cabinet departments. This was sloppy and caused much trouble. Yet this very looseness around the joints, this sense of give and possibility which Henry Stimson once called the "inherently disorderly nature" of Roosevelt's administration, made public service attractive to men of a certain boldness and imagination. It also spurred them on to better achievement. Roosevelt liked the competitive approach to administration, not just because it reserved the big decisions for the President, but perhaps even more because it enabled him to test and develop the abilities of his subordinates. How to tell which man, which approach was better? One answer was to let them fight it out.[33]

By early May, the study groups established by the canny bureaucrat Henry Stimson had produced eighteen plans on how to cripple Japan with economic warfare.[34] The First Wise Man initiated no accompanying analysis of how Japan might react.

In May of 1941 Roosevelt established the Office of Petroleum Coordinator for National Defense, headed by Secretary of the Interior

Harold Ickes. Ickes was knowledgeable about domestic energy, but he had no foreign-policy experience. Like Morgenthau had, Ickes complained that the secretary of state was a softy:

> All that [Hull] ever tried to do in addition to his futile protests at continued encroachments by the dictators, was to negotiate reciprocal trade agreements. These were all right so far as they went; they might have led to something in ordinary times when peace was the principal preoccupation of the nations of the world, but as I remarked to the President on one occasion, with the world in a turmoil they were like hunting an elephant in the jungle with a fly swatter.[35]

Ickes searched for a way to cut Japan's oil, publicly (and incorrectly) blaming Japan's purchases of oil on the West Coast for a gas shortage on the East Coast. Hull complained to Roosevelt. FDR scolded Ickes, telling him that oil exportation to Japan was a sensitive issue, "so much a part of our current foreign policy that this policy must not be affected in any shape, manner or form by anyone except the Secretary of State or the President."[36]

Roosevelt and Hull wanted the Japanese to have all the California oil they desired. A growing team of Warriors was trying to shut off the oil spigot, but as long as the president and his secretary of state remained vigilant, the U.S. would not be drawn into an unwanted war in Asia.

June of 1941 saw secret turmoil in the lives of the president and the State Department's two top officials.

Undersecretary of State Sumner Welles was accused of making homosexual advances to black Pullman porters on the presidential train. While some warned FDR that Welles was a criminal who should be fired, Roosevelt stuck by Welles.

At 9:30 p.m. on June 21, a U.S. Navy ambulance arrived at the White House, and medics carried Missy LeHand out on a stretcher. Missy had been at FDR's side as his secretary and companion since the early 1920s; she had arranged the president's days and enlivened his nights. Her bedroom was above FDR's in the White House. Wrote historian Doris Kearns Goodwin, "Missy was in love with her boss and regarded herself as the other wife."[37] Presidential speechwriter Raymond Moley said about FDR's affection for her: "There's no doubt that Missy was as close to being a wife as he ever had—or could have."[38]

Missy had suffered a stroke, leaving the president for the first time in decades without her organizational skills and affection.

Hours after the person who had been closest to FDR left him, Germany invaded Communist Russia. Something momentous had just taken place on the world stage, but Secretary of State Hull was on his way to White Springs, West Virginia, for an extended vacation. Hull was sick, tired, and probably frustrated that the president hardly seemed to need him; FDR was outsourcing many of his diplomatic moves through Harry Hopkins. Hull would be gone for six weeks at a time when the president was recovering from a tragic personal and professional loss, and a besieged Sumner Welles ran the State Department.

While FDR and Tommy the Cork could keep their Asian air-war scheme a secret from the American public, the enemy was not fooled.

After the first contingent of FDR's mercenaries sailed to Rangoon, Burma, aboard the *President Pierce,* Japanese intelligence informed their offices in Nanking, Shanghai, Beijing, and Canton:

> The first party of 100 members of American aviators and technicians dispatched recently has arrived in Rangoon...it is expected that large numbers will be sent out from the United States...Chungking requested that the United States supply some 500 first-class airplanes, and as a result of the contacts made by T. V. Soong...for the time being, a mere 80 planes had been supplied.[39]

In early July, about ten "retired" U.S. Army Air Corps pilots and a hundred and fifty mechanics quietly checked into San Francisco's swanky Mark Hopkins Hotel. Their U.S. passports identified them as ordinary missionaries, clerks, bankers, teachers, and students. Farmer

Claire Chennault joined them on July 7 for a night of partying. The next day Chennault boarded a Pan American clipper, and two days later—escorted by American naval vessels—FDR's second contingent of mercenaries sailed out of San Francisco Bay aboard the Dutch freighter *Jagersfontein.*

Chennault later admitted that after the *Jagersfontein* pulled out of San Francisco Bay, his men heard a Japanese radio broadcast boast, "That ship will never reach China. It will be sunk."[40]

At a meeting in Emperor Hirohito's presence on July 2, Japanese leaders decided to go south beyond China toward the rich resources of Southeast Asia. Because U.S. code breakers had decrypted Japanese diplomatic communications, Roosevelt and a few others were aware that Japan intended to occupy the southern half of Indochina and use it as a staging area—a serious challenge to the ABCD powers because Japan could place bombers within range of their Philippines, Malaysian, and Dutch East Indies colonies.

Roosevelt had earlier frozen German and Italian funds deposited in the United States. The freeze process existed, and Japan could be added with a stroke of FDR's pen. Welles now suggested that FDR freeze Japanese assets. Roosevelt took no action.

Roosevelt continued to spend much more time focused on Europe than Asia. Working around his State Department, FDR sent Harry Hopkins to England to meet with Winston Churchill and arrange a secret meeting between the two leaders in Canada. Via Hopkins, Roosevelt briefed Churchill on his strategy of keeping peace in the Pacific. Roosevelt wanted the U.S. and Japan to agree to "neutralize" Indochina, turning the area into a neutral zone from which both Japan and the U.S. would acquire resources. But first Japan would have to withdraw from Indochina.

On July 18, Roosevelt informed his cabinet that a reliable source (his code breakers) thought that Japan would occupy southern Indochina within three or four days. Roosevelt said that the U.S. should do little, especially not embargo oil, since "to cut off oil altogether at this time would probably precipitate an outbreak of war in the Pacific and endanger British communications with Australia and New Zealand."[41]

Roosevelt instructed Welles to draft regulations for a freeze of Japanese assets, but he had not decided whether to implement it. Edward Miller wrote,

> Welles was an unusual choice because financial sanctions...
> were the province of Morgenthau's Treasury Department. Per-
> haps Roosevelt thought an official of the softer State Depart-
> ment would carry out his policy of a partial freeze more reliably
> than the pugnacious Morgenthau.[42]

Welles sketched out a freeze of Japanese assets in the U.S., giving Roosevelt a leash to control Japanese purchases. If FDR froze their holdings, the Japanese would have to ask his permission when they wanted to use their funds, and Roosevelt could veto their choices. Welles knew that FDR wanted Japan to continue to get U.S. oil and he designed a system that would release sufficient funds for Japan to purchase plenty of oil from California. Welles outlined the plan on Saturday, July 19, and asked Dean Acheson to draft the details.

Acheson thought it was insane and immoral for FDR to continue selling Japan oil. Like the First Wise Man, Acheson believed America had a share in Japan's war guilt. Acheson ignored Welles's orders and drafted a tough, sweeping embargo against Japan. Later Welles deleted Acheson's more aggressive wording and redrafted the document himself. (Acheson's attempt to radically alter Welles's draft was insubordinate, but in the loosey-goosey Roosevelt administration, Acheson kept his job, just as Morgenthau had remained after he had tried to cut Japan's oil by altering Welles's July 1940 draft.)

On July 23, Roosevelt approved the American Military Mission to China (AMMISCA), a grandly named but relatively small group of Army officers who were to study Chiang's Lend-Lease needs. Roosevelt also approved 269 additional fighters and 66 bombers for the Chiang-Chennault scheme. These moves were groundbreaking: for the first time, FDR established an official U.S. military connection with Chiang. And bombers were offensive weapons, which the Japanese spies watching the Rangoon docks would surely note to Tokyo.

FDR defended his oil sales to Japan in public for the first time in a speech he gave at Hyde Park to the Volunteer Participation Committee, a group dedicated to informing their fellow Americans of fast-changing world events. In a folksy manner, FDR explained,

> Here on the East Coast you have been reading that the Secretary of the Interior, as Oil Administrator, is faced with the problem of not enough gasoline to go around in the East Coast, and how he is asking everybody to curtail their consumption of gasoline. All right. Now I am — I might be called — an American citizen, living in Hyde Park, N.Y. And I say, "That's a funny thing. Why am I asked to curtail my consumption of gasoline when I read in the papers that thousands of tons of gasoline are going out from Los Angeles — the west coast — to Japan; and we are helping Japan in what looks like an act of aggression?"
>
> All right. Now the answer is a very simple one. There is a world war going on, and has been for some time — nearly two years. One of our efforts, from the very beginning, was to prevent the spread of that world war in certain areas where it hadn't started. One of those areas is a place called the Pacific Ocean — one of the largest areas of the earth. There happened to be a place in the South Pacific where we had to get a lot of things — rubber, tin, and so forth and so on — down in the Dutch Indies, the Straits Settlements, and Indochina. And we had to help get the Australian surplus of meat and wheat, and corn, for England.
>
> It was very essential, from our own selfish point of view of defense, to prevent a war from starting in the South Pacific. So our foreign policy was trying to stop a war from breaking out down there....

All right. And now here is a nation called Japan. Whether they had at that time aggressive purposes to enlarge their empire southward, they didn't have any oil of their own up in the north. Now, if we cut the oil off, they probably would have gone down to the Dutch East Indies a year ago, and you would have had war.

Therefore, there was — you might call — a method in letting this oil go to Japan, with the hope — and it has worked for two years — of keeping war out of the South Pacific for our own good, for the good of the defense of Great Britain, and the freedom of the seas.

You people can help to enlighten the average citizen who wouldn't hear of that, or doesn't read the papers carefully, or listen to the radio carefully, to understand what some of these apparent anomalies mean.[43]

Roosevelt had for the first time publicly revealed that he was appeasing Japan with oil in the hopes of garnering domestic support for his Pacific peace policy. He had clearly signaled that continuing oil sales to Japan was his way of keeping the U.S. out of an unwanted Pacific war. But his American audience had been so bamboozled by constant China Lobby propaganda that they couldn't fathom why FDR would be concerned about Japanese retribution. Liberal journalist I. F. Stone complained in the *Nation* magazine,

The President committed a historic blunder when he [admitted that] we had to sell oil to Japan to keep it from seizing the Dutch East Indies. This translates bitterly into Chinese, for it says that we were content to fuel the bombers that mangled China's children as long as Japan kept out of the rich imperialist preserves in the Indies.... We have been supplying two-thirds of Japan's oil.... There is no way of knowing what has happened to our exports to Japan since March. Neither State Department nor Export Control has ever given out the details... a nation-wide fight must be organized against this most vicious kind of secret diplomacy.[44]

On Saturday, July 26, FDR issued Executive Order No. 8832, which froze all assets owned 25 percent or more by Japanese interests.[45] Now all Japanese transactions in the U.S. were under FDR's control. While this action made him appear to be getting tough, Roosevelt intended to release plenty of frozen dollars so Japan could purchase the items it needed to fuel its military, especially oil. FDR hoped that the freeze would mollify the China Lobby, calm an aroused American public, and shock Tokyo but not lead to war. As Roosevelt told Harold Ickes, he planned to use the freeze order as a "noose around Japan's neck," and he would "give it a jerk now and then."[46]

Treasury agents now oversaw Japanese banks in the United States. The Japanese in the U.S. got busy filling out Treasury forms to release their frozen dollars.

Roosevelt's actions were understood by many on the inside. Admiral Harold Stark, chief of naval operations, assured his commanders that FDR's financial freeze didn't mean an oil embargo against Japan. He wrote, "Export licenses will be granted for certain grades of petroleum products."[47]

Thus, with his right hand, Roosevelt showed his domestic audience that he was cracking down on Japan. With his left, FDR intended to approve Japan's buying enough oil to keep peace in the Pacific. But at this moment, the president was focused on events across the Atlantic. And even Warren Delano's grandson had only two hands.

Late Friday, July 25, Roosevelt received a cable from Harry Hopkins in England:

> I am wondering whether you would think it important and useful for me to go to Moscow. Air transportation good and can reach there in twenty-four hours.... If Stalin could in any way be influenced at a critical time I think it would be worth doing by a direct communication from you through a personal envoy. I think the stakes are so great that it should be done. Stalin would then know in an unmistakable way that we mean business on a long-term supply job.[48]

FDR knew very little about what had happened in Russia since the German invasion; foreigners in Moscow were completely in the dark regarding Stalin's plans. Roosevelt, eager to supply Stalin with military equipment to slow Hitler, responded immediately, "Welles and I highly approve Moscow trip....I will send you tonight a message for Stalin."[49]

Roosevelt spent a long weekend at Hyde Park and then returned to Washington on Monday, July 28, prepared to focus on aid to Communist Russia. He was disappointed to find that most of the Soviet requests for military equipment that he'd thought were moving through the system were in fact stalled in Stimson's War Department. Morgenthau expressed FDR's sense of urgency that the Russians "have just got to get this stuff and get it fast...we will never have a better chance... somebody has been looking over this country and the good Lord has been with us, but we can't count on the good Lord and just plain dumb luck forever."[50]

To administer his freeze on Japanese assets, Roosevelt created a nuanced interdepartmental process. First, the State Department would decide how much oil Japan could purchase, continuing FDR and Hull's exclusive control of America's oil spigot. State's decision would move to Treasury, which would calculate how many Japanese-owned dollars had to be unfrozen to meet State's dictate. Then the Foreign Funds Control Committee (FFCC), a newly created three-man panel, would release the Treasury-approved dollars for the Japanese to use to purchase their State-approved oil. The FFCC wasn't involved in policymaking; it existed only as a mechanism to release to the Japanese the dollars State had authorized and Treasury had calculated. Little did Roosevelt imagine that an obscure committee deep within his bureaucracy would catapult America into World War II.

The FFCC was made up of three representatives, one each from the Departments of State, Treasury, and Justice. Since it was designed to have no important decision-making function, there was no need for the secretaries of each department to serve on the committee, so they appointed surrogates: Dean Acheson from State, Edward Foley from

Treasury, and Francis Shea from Justice. Acheson stood head and shoulders above Foley and Shea in prestige, education, experience, chutzpah, and age (forty-eight for him, versus thirty-five for Foley and thirty-six for Shea). Neither Foley nor Shea had much exposure to foreign affairs, whereas Acheson was an officer in the esteemed diplomatic branch.

After listening to FDR's Hyde Park speech about appeasing Japan with oil to prevent war, Acheson sniffed that "the Foreign Funds Committee was not enlightened on administering the President's policy of no policy."[51]

Harry Hopkins met Joseph Stalin on Wednesday, July 30, in Stalin's enormous Kremlin office. Hopkins told the sixty-two-year-old Communist leader, "The President considered Hitler the enemy of mankind and...he therefore wished to aid the Soviet Union in its fight against Germany" and consequently Roosevelt was determined "to extend all possible aid to the Soviet Union at the earliest possible time."[52]

On Thursday, July 31, 1941, Roosevelt met with a Soviet military delegation. Communists were in the White House.

American and Japanese newspapers were full of stories guessing what the U.S. freeze would mean to Japan. The British ambassador wrote that FDR's policy on oil shipments was to "keep the Japanese in a state of uncertainty."[53] FDR was confident that once the Japanese learned they would get all the oil they desired, just under new rules, there would be no war in the Pacific.

Roosevelt was focused on Europe. His closest adviser, Hopkins, was in Moscow, and FDR and Churchill were excited about their coming secret rendezvous. At an August 1 cabinet meeting, Roosevelt once more demanded that aid to Communist Russia get moving. Ickes recalled FDR giving Stimson "one of the most complete dressings down that I have witnessed for giving Russia the 'run-around.' "[54] Roosevelt said he was "sick and tired of promises" and ordered Stimson to "get the planes right off with a bang next week!"[55] A fuming Stimson, whom few had criticized so harshly, complained later to his diary that Roosevelt "was really in a hoity-toity humor and wouldn't listen to argument."[56]

That same day the State Department notified the FFCC that it had approved hundreds of thousands of dollars of oil for Japan. The still vacationing Hull spoke to Welles by phone the next day, August 2. Both men were relieved that Japan would get oil, thus keeping peace in the Pacific.

The White House told the press a cover story that Roosevelt was going on a ten-day fishing trip off the coast of Maine aboard the presidential yacht *Potomac*. On Sunday, August 3, FDR arrived by train at New London, Connecticut, where he transferred to his yacht. In Scotland, his counterpart Winston Churchill boarded the *Prince of Wales* for his five-day trip across the Atlantic.

On Monday, August 4, the *Potomac* sailed into Nonquitt, Massachusetts, where Roosevelt picked up a group of exiled Norwegian royals for a day of fishing. Hundreds of people ashore saw the president. That evening, many watched as the *Potomac* sailed away with the presidential flag flying and a small party visible on deck, including the figure of the president sitting in a chair. It wasn't Roosevelt, but a double. The Secret Service had covertly transferred Roosevelt to the battleship USS *Augusta,* which proceeded secretly to Canada.

Roosevelt had left Washington believing that his loose noose around Japan would on the one hand satisfy domestic American opinion and on the other allow Japan enough purchases to prevent a war in Asia. For a year, since July of 1940, FDR had gotten the better of Stimson, Morgenthau, Knox, and Ickes on the oil issue. Twice — once with Morgenthau in July 1940 and again just recently with Acheson — Welles had caught Warriors changing official language in order to cut Japan's oil. Now Roosevelt was incommunicado out at sea, Hull was worn down and in transit from his West Virginia vacation, and the embattled Welles was flying north to rendezvous with Roosevelt. The cats were distracted and away from Washington. The mice decided to play.

At the August 5 meeting of the FFCC, Acheson, Foley, and Shea reviewed the flow of oil to Japan and were aghast. As Jonathan Utley explains, "When they saw how much oil Japan would be able to buy under the freeze guidelines, they agreed not to release funds to Japan for the purchase of items for which [Japan had been] issued licenses."[57] Waldo Heinrichs noted, "The decision on an oil embargo was closely held and deviously managed. Action proceeded not in the formal realm of peacetime quotas and proclamations restricting export, for on paper Japan was supposed to receive some quantities of some kinds of oil, but in the shadowy world of inaction, circumvention, and red tape."[58]

To confront Japan's State-approved and Treasury-calculated requests with a definitive no would have attracted FDR's attention. As Acheson later explained to a British associate, he had "discovered by accident the technique of imposing a total embargo by way of its freezing order without having to take decisions about quotas for particular commodities."[59] Acheson and Morgenthau passed the buck back and forth to each other, running the Japanese through a bureaucratic maze. A Treasury official later wrote, "The Japanese tried every conceivable way of getting the precious crude oil, but to each proposal the [FFCC] had an evasive answer ready to camouflage its flat refusal."[60]

Acheson had just secretly changed Roosevelt's Asian policy and done the specific thing the president feared would lead to war. As Utley wrote, "Roosevelt intended the freeze…to bring Japan to its senses, not to its knees."[61] History well notes the insanity of Japan's attack on Pearl Harbor but little notes the inanity of the so-called Wise Men — focused on the China Lobby mirage — who provoked it.

In early August of 1941 two Japanese oil tankers docked at the port of San Pedro, California. Japanese officials had sought and received approval from the State Department for the oil months earlier, and the Treasury Department had determined the amount of dollars required. Japan expected that its tankers would be filled as soon as the FFCC released its funds.

Hull had returned to the State Department on August 4 but did not realize that Acheson, aided by Morgenthau, had essentially imposed a complete embargo by refusing to release funds to Japan. Hull was still exhausted; he had been absent for six weeks and had a backlog of work. Indeed, from Hull's vantage point, the system seemed to be functioning as planned. On August 11, an unaware Hull approved three more Japanese licenses to purchase California oil. Two Japanese embassy officials immediately applied to the FFCC for release of their frozen dollars.

For the past eight months Morgenthau had monitored Japanese transfers from American banks to Brazilian banks. Creating another bureaucratic tar pit, Acheson arbitrarily told the Japanese embassy that their State-approved oil should be paid for from their "free funds" in Brazil rather than from their frozen accounts in the United States. Japanese embassy officials complained that private companies were purchasing the oil while the cash in Brazil belonged to the Japanese navy. Acheson suggested that they try harder to bring the funds from Brazil.

Throughout August, the Japanese met repeatedly with U.S. officials to get their State Department–approved oil. Cleverly, Morgenthau and Acheson never outright refused the Japanese requests, but there was always some small nit to be picked, an unexpected twist or turn to be negotiated. If they did bring dollars up from their South American accounts, Japanese officials asked, would the U.S. promise to let them use those dollars to buy oil? Acheson responded that the question was hypothetical; Japan should transfer the dollars, and then Acheson would decide. The Japanese finally agreed to try Brazil. Acheson then told his Japanese counterparts that the U.S. would accept their "free funds" from Brazil only if Japan identified the sources and locations of *all* its South American accounts. Often, Japanese officials found their phone calls unreturned, and they were told that "many State Department high officials were absent in those hot summer days."[62]

For the entire month of August, Tokyo officials waited as tankers sat empty in San Pedro. They would have to either persuade FDR to reopen his California oil spigot or advance militarily south and seize oil in the Dutch East Indies. Utley noted, "The policy that was supposed to avoid provoking Japan was transformed into full-scale economic warfare that led to the attack four months later on Pearl Harbor."[63]

Japan was solvent and had plenty of liquid assets to pay for its oil — dollars as well as gold and silver bars in both the U.S. and Japan. Yet

Roosevelt had effectively made Japan illiquid. Now Japan was dependent on FDR's rules and regulations. As despair mounted in Tokyo, Hull was focused on the aftermath of his talks with the befuddled Nomura, continuing to question and criticize Japan's terms. Hull thought he was negotiating, but Tokyo believed he was backpedaling from his initial offer in the American plan. Like the Foreign Funds Control Committee, Hull kept asking Japanese diplomats for more information without signaling progress. Many Japanese leaders sensed in Washington's delay tactics the tightening of the ABCD encirclement.

Dean Acheson was not the first to attempt to cut Japan's oil supply. Morgenthau, Ickes, and a number of Washington Warriors within Roosevelt's helter-skelter administration had all given it a try. In each of those cases, however, Hull, Welles, or Roosevelt had become aware of what was going on and intervened before any serious damage could be done. The only thing that was different about Acheson's successful exploit was that—supported by Morgenthau, Stimson, and Ickes—he got away with it.

Acheson later defended his insubordination by writing that "no rational Japanese could believe that an attack on us could result in anything but disaster for his country."[64] Acheson—like most Americans—was saturated in China Lobby propaganda and he assumed that the Japanese would react just as the First Wise Man predicted. The legendary English military historian Sir Basil Henry Liddell Hart later explained what the Wise Men had missed: "No Government, least of all the Japanese, could be expected to swallow such humiliating conditions, and utter loss of face."[65] As Roland Worth asks in *No Choice but War,* "If the United States would have launched a preemptive war under such circumstances, why is it so surprising that the Japanese did so?"[66]

Chapter 10

ASLEEP AT THE WHEEL

The Pacific War was a war that need not have been fought.
—John Toland[1]

Roosevelt's flotilla arrived at Placentia Bay on the coast of New-foundland early on Thursday, August 7. Soon the bay was full of American warships and the sky crisscrossed with patrolling war-planes. Roosevelt was delighted that he would fool the press about his whereabouts for over one week, not realizing that back in Washington some Warriors were proud of another deception.

FDR had his friend Sumner Welles at his side when he met with Churchill. Roosevelt also brought along General George Marshall, Admiral Harold Stark, Major General Hap Arnold, and Admiral Ernest King. The commander in chief invited his military heads to work with him directly; his secretaries of state, war, and the Navy would be informed later.

Roosevelt, Churchill, and their military chiefs discussed war in Europe at the same moment Dean Acheson was starting one in Asia. In a foggy Atlantic bay, the Europe-first deliberations focused on Gibraltar, West Africa, Iceland, the Faroe Islands, North Atlantic escort operations, the bomber ferry route, Vladivostok, the Persian Gulf–Iranian route, the Arctic passage, stabilization of the front in the

Soviet Union, and the Iberian Peninsula. No one imagined that the American military's first assignment in World War II would be fighting the Japanese on Guadalcanal, a faraway Pacific island not discussed at the Atlantic Conference.

Since the dawn of the oil age, America had provided Japan with the lifeblood of its military-industrial society, and now Tokyo saw that pipeline abruptly going dry, leaving Japan an industrialized beached whale. Acheson's oil embargo set the war clock ticking in Tokyo. Distinguished historian Akira Iriye wrote,

> The oil embargo had a tremendous psychological impact upon the Japanese. The ambivalence and ambiguities in their perception of world events disappeared, replaced by a sense of clear-cut alternatives. Hitherto they had not confronted the stark choice between war and peace as an immediate prospect and had lived in a climate of uncertainty from day to day. Now, with the United States resorting to decisive measures, that phase passed. Any wishful thinking that America would tolerate the invasion of southern Indochina was dissipated; either Japan would stay in Southeast Asia at the risk of war with the Anglo-American countries or it would retreat to conciliate them. The military judged that it was too late for conciliation; Japan would now have to consider the likelihood of war, with the United States as its major adversary.[2]

Neither Tokyo nor Washington wanted to fight each other in August of 1941. No Japanese leader ever proposed an invasion of the United States. Admiral Isoroku Yamamoto lamented that to "fight the United States is like fighting the whole world...Tokyo will be burnt to the ground three times."[3]

On the American side, neither Roosevelt, Hull, Stimson, Morgenthau, the Hotdogs, the Washington Warriors, nor the U.S. military wanted war with Japan. The U.S. Navy at that point had no up-to-date military maps of the Solomon Islands, where the U.S. Marines would later fight America's first battle of World War II. Indeed, Stimson, Morgenthau, Ickes, and Acheson—all upholders of the China Lobby mirage—believed that their subversion of FDR's Asia policy could result only in peace; the mad-dog military in Japan would be humiliated, and democracy would bloom. In *Fateful Choices,* Ian Kershaw points out what the Wise Men missed:

> For no faction of the Japanese elites could there be a retreat from the goals of a victorious settlement in China and successful expansion to establish...Japanese domination of the Far East. These objectives had not just become an economic imperative. They reflected honor and national pride, the prestige and standing of a great power. The alternatives were seen as not just poverty, but defeat, humiliation, ignominy, and an end to great power status in permanent subordination to the United States.[4]

Emperor Hirohito was much more troubled about battling America than his grandfather Meiji had been about taking on the Russian bear. But it was a matter of life or death for the empire; with no oil, there would be no Japan. After the California oil pump was cut off, Japan felt forced to thrust south to the Dutch East Indies, as Roosevelt and Hull had predicted. Japan's leaders leaped off the war cliff, hoping that by disabling the American fleet at Pearl Harbor, they would keep the U.S. from interfering with its advance into Southeast Asia.

Roosevelt and Churchill enjoyed each other's company. Churchill would have been pleased if Roosevelt had committed the U.S. to fighting Hitler, but FDR was cautious, not wanting to get out in front of Congress and American public opinion. Roosevelt's aim was to establish a political rationale for any coming war. In what was later called the Atlantic Charter, Roosevelt and Churchill agreed that their own countries would not seek territorial gains, that changes in borders should not be made without the consent of the peoples concerned, and that all people had the right to self-determination.

In Japanese eyes, the document was blatantly hypocritical. At the moment that Churchill agreed that everyone had the right to self-determination, Britain held hundreds of millions of Asians and Africans in colonial bondage, from Hong Kong to India to Kenya.

As the Japanese tankers sat empty off San Pedro, Roosevelt— unaware that Morgenthau, his best friend, was helping Acheson cut Japan's oil—attended Sunday church services hosted by Churchill on the *Prince of Wales*. The leaders and their entourages sang "Onward, Christian Soldiers."

Over the next two days Churchill asked Roosevelt to warn Japan that if it made any more aggressive moves, it would mean war with the Anglo-Americans. Roosevelt was noncommittal.

Sunday church services aboard the HMS Prince of Wales, where Franklin Delano Roosevelt and Winston Churchill sang "Onward, Christian Soldiers," August 10, 1941. For one whole month Roosevelt would not know that his administration had cut Japan's oil supply. (CSU / Everett Collection)

*   *   *

Roosevelt left Placentia Bay on August 12, sailed into American waters, transferred back to the *Potomac* in Blue Hill Bay, Maine, and actually did some fishing. The *Potomac* docked at Rockland, Maine, the afternoon of August 16. Reporters came aboard and Roosevelt spoke eloquently about his agreements with Churchill and movingly about their joint church service. Later FDR and Hopkins were driven past large crowds to the train station, where they boarded the presidential train for Washington.

For years, the president of the United States had been clear and consistent in stating that the one action that would precipitate a war in the Pacific would be a U.S. embargo of Japan's oil. Dean Acheson had decided to cut off Japan's oil almost two weeks earlier, yet, incredibly, Roosevelt, Hull, and other top policy makers still had no idea what had happened. Returning to Washington, Sumner Welles asked Acheson to brief him on important events. Acheson reported that Hull had granted Japan oil-export licenses but neglected to mention that he and Morgenthau had thrown a wrench in the works.

Roosevelt met with Ambassador Nomura a few hours after his return to Washington on August 17. While Churchill had goaded FDR to get tough, the president's soft handling of Nomura shows that he wanted to avoid confrontation with Japan. Instead of giving Nomura a strong warning that continued Japanese aggression would mean war, as Churchill had requested, Roosevelt read him a State Department document that stated vaguely that the U.S. would take undefined steps if Japan advanced farther.

Roosevelt was still unaware that Tokyo believed he and his administration were squeezing Japan's oil supply. Indeed, most top officials were in the dark concerning Acheson's scheme. On August 20, Vice President Henry Wallace chaired a meeting of the Economic Defense Board with Acheson in attendance representing State. Wallace complained that the administration was still allowing oil shipments to Japan and suggested that they be cut off. It had been over two weeks since Acheson had decided to do just that, but he told Wallace that

FDR and Hull were "working on this question and...it would prove embarrassing if the Economic Defense Board went into the matter."[5]

On August 28—three weeks after his underlings' subversion— Roosevelt still assumed that oil was flowing, referring in a White House meeting to "the oil quota allowed Japan."[6] The State Department went on granting Japan licenses for oil, and Japan had plenty of funds, but Morgenthau and Acheson continued to ping-pong Japanese diplomats from one inconclusive meeting to the other.

By September 4, no oil had left the U.S. bound for Japan for a month. In a meeting that day, Nomura suggested to Hull that both the U.S. and Japan should "permit export to the other of commodities in amounts up to the figures of usual or pre-war trade."[7] Hull was confused, as he thought that was the formula already being applied. Curious, the next day Hull called in Acheson, who apparently convinced him that it was Treasury that was responsible for delaying Japan's shipments of oil, because Hull then had Acheson contact Treasury to find out what was going on.

Hull must have been alarmed to discover that lower-level officials had effectively cut off Japan's oil for a month, because following his conversation with Acheson, Hull promptly headed for the White House. No record of what Hull told FDR over their lunchtime meeting that day has been found, but Roosevelt was likely shocked to learn the news. He faced significant political hurdles in *restarting* oil sales to the Japanese. The China Lobby—T. V. Soong, Tommy the Cork, Lauchlin Currie, Felix Frankfurter, Henry Stimson, Henry Morgenthau, Dean Acheson, and many millions of others in Protestant congregations, the U.S. Congress, and the media—was a palpable political force. The Stimson Committee had convinced the great majority of Americans that the U.S. could embargo Japan with no risk to itself. If Warriors within his administration were to go public about FDR restarting oil sales, Roosevelt would have been in the untenable political position of having to explain to all the mirage-believing Americans exactly why Japan should get *more* U.S. oil to kill Noble Chinese Peasants.

Hull and Roosevelt elected to leave the situation as it was, so in effect—with neither internal debate nor public announcement—they ratified the unplanned embargo on Japan's oil. Roosevelt and Hull had lost the administrative control they had used so effectively for over a year in their battles with the Warriors. Acheson would later boast, "Whether or not we had a policy, we had a state of affairs; the conclusion, that until further notice it would continue."[8]

By the time FDR learned of the de facto oil embargo, it was already month-old news in Tokyo. The day after the FDR-Hull lunch, Emperor Hirohito sat solemnly with government leaders listening to planning board director Teiichi Suzuki:

> As a result of the present overall economic blockade imposed by Great Britain and the United States, our Empire's national power is declining day by day. Our liquid fuel stockpile, which is the most important, will reach bottom by June or July of next year, even if we impose strict wartime control on the civilian demand. Accordingly, I believe it is vitally important for the survival of our Empire that we make up our minds to establish and stabilize a firm economic base.[9]

Admiral Osami Nagano—the chief of staff of the imperial Japanese navy—told Hirohito and assembled leaders,

> Since Japan is unavoidably facing national ruin whether it decides to fight the United States or submit to its demands, it must by all means choose to fight. Japan would rather go down fighting than ignobly surrender without a struggle, because surrender would spell spiritual as well as physical ruin for the nation and its destiny.[10]

Dean Acheson had cut off Japan's economic lifeblood, but Roosevelt's government did not track how the freeze and oil embargo was affecting Japan. Edward Miller wrote,

> The oversight is astonishing. U.S. civilian and military officials had studied Japan's dependence on foreign trade for more than four years. They understood that a nation heavily dependent on overseas commerce, especially with the United States, would

suffer grievously when its international financial resources were immobilized.[11]

The First Wise Man and the China Lobby had promised that once the oil was cut, the mad dog's military machine would stall, the military class would be humiliated, and democrats would arise in Tokyo and Chungking as American friends. It didn't work out that way. In a cabinet meeting on October 14, the relatively moderate Prime Minister Fumimaro Konoe suggested that the mad dogs withdraw from China. War Minister General Hideki Tojo bellowed, "I make no concessions regarding withdrawal! It means defeat of Japan by the United States— a stain on the history of the Japanese Empire!"[12] Instead of empowering moderates in Tokyo, Washington's demands resulted in the *fall* of a moderate government and in the Japanese military taking full control. The chief of the mad dogs, General Hideki Tojo, now became prime minister.

The Tojo government refused to withdraw from China, and in early November the Japanese tankers in San Pedro weighed anchor with no oil and left the West Coast. Tojo warned his compatriots,

> Two years from now we will have no petroleum for military use. Ships will stop moving.... We can talk about austerity and suffering, but can our people endure such a life for a long time?...I fear that we would become a third-class nation after 2 or 3 years if we just sit tight.[13]

Yoshimichi Hara, president of the imperial privy council (composed of Japan's ex-premiers), lamented Japan's situation:

> If we were to give in, we would give up in one stroke not only our gains in the Sino-Japanese and Russo-Japanese wars, but also the benefits of the Manchurian Incident. This we cannot do. We are loath to compel our people to suffer even greater hardships, on top of what they have endured during the four years since the China Incident. But it is clear that the existence of our country is being threatened, that the great achievements

of the Emperor Meiji would all come to naught, and that there is nothing else we can do.[14]

The Tojo government secretly defined its goals:

To expel the influence of [the United States, Great Britain, and the Netherlands] from East Asia, to establish a sphere for the self-defense and self-preservation of our Empire, and to build a New Order in Greater East Asia. In other words, we aim to establish a close and inseparable relationship in military, political, and economic affairs between our Empire and the countries of the Southern Region, to achieve our Empire's self-defense and self-preservation.[15]

Meanwhile, Henry Luce and his wife crisscrossed the country enlightening Americans about New China. Luce said, "The imperial Japanese army has been stopped cold in its tracks.... China's army is the out-standing creation of a very great leader of men — Chiang Kai-shek."[16] His wife said the Chinese were "spiritual allies" of America and "fellow Christians" and that Mr. and Mrs. Chiang Kai-shek were "the greatest married team in the world," with the exception of the Roosevelts.[17] On November 8, 1941, Luce mailed all *Time* subscribers a letter asking them to help the Chinese who "have incorporated many of our own hopes and aspirations into their Republic, now battling for its life."[18]

Luce had Teddy White write a series of Chiang-positive articles in *Fortune* magazine hinting that the national security of the United States would be at stake if America lost China:

For the chronicle of history the matter is very clear: this is not aid to a country in need, charity on a cosmic scale. This is part of the search by the American people for their own well-being and security. Thus, although China's moral claims may be as great as China's bitter wants, the determinant of U.S. action is the needs of the U.S.; and any examination of the record of

"Aid to China" must be judged in the light of U.S. strategy in a troubled world.[19]

On November 26, 1941, six Japanese aircraft carriers sailed from Hitokappu Bay in the Kurile Islands in the direction of Pearl Harbor. For over a decade, American military experts like General Billy Mitchell had warned of a troubling division of command at Pearl Harbor. The commanding Army general and Navy admiral in Hawaii barely spoke to each other. A divided command meant no defense at all and made the U.S. fleet a juicy and inviting target. The two civilian officials responsible for uniting the Hawaiian command—Secretary of War Henry Stimson and Secretary of the Navy Frank Knox—gave little thought to the problem. For almost a decade the First Wise Man had preached that Japan would never attack the U.S.

With China Lobby funds, the Stimson Committee's Manhattan missionaries had conned the American public into believing that the U.S. could cut Japan's oil supply and suffer no blowback. The mirage that the Generalissimo had been bravely fighting the Japanese had in turn allowed American officials to imagine that by standing with Chiang, they were increasing U.S. security in Asia. Now millions of neighbors in the Pacific would pay a terrible price.

In his history of American foreign policy, George Herring concludes that America's position on China involved it in war:

> Had the [United States] abandoned, at least temporarily, its determination to drive the Japanese from China and restored some trade, it might have delayed a two-front war when it was not yet ready to fight one major enemy. Having already learned what seemed the hard lessons of appeasement [in Europe], U.S. officials rejected a course of expediency. Rather, they backed a proud nation into a position where its only choices were war or surrender.[20]

The historian John Toland, in his bestselling *The Rising Sun: The Decline and Fall of the Japanese Empire,* concurred about the U.S. going to war over China:

America made a grave diplomatic blunder by allowing an issue not vital to her basic interests—the welfare of China—to become, at the last moment, the keystone of her foreign policy. Until that summer [of 1941] America had two limited objectives in the Far East: to drive a wedge between Japan and Hitler, and to thwart Japan's southward thrust. She could easily have obtained both these objectives but instead...insisted on the liberation of China.... America could not throw the weight of her strength against Japan to liberate China, nor had she ever intended to. Her major enemy was Hitler. [The Pacific War was] a war that need not have been fought.

World War II in the Pacific would result in the deaths of about one hundred thousand Americans and over two million Japanese. In the fall of 1941, the Wise Men didn't contemplate such horror. But if war did come, *Time* magazine prayed for the New China dream:

China is today the only great non-Christian state with a Christian head. The conversion of Constantine is not the only case where through political events Christianity has come into sudden power after long years of struggling growth.... Something not far different might occur in China. If anything should happen to bring the U.S. and Britain into an active shooting war at China's side, enthusiasm for their allies might make millions of Chinese receptive converts to Christianity.[21]

On Sunday, December 7, 1941, Thomas Corcoran was at home and read in the *New York Times* that Senator Harry Truman was calling him to testify before his committee about lobbying for military contractors. Corcoran phoned his client T. V. Soong, probably so the two men could get their stories straight. T.V. greeted Tommy with shocking news: "Your fleet is at the bottom of Pearl Harbor."[22]

Americans would always "Remember Pearl Harbor," but the attack was not meant to be an invasion of the U.S.; rather, it was an attempt to cripple the U.S. Navy's ability to block Japan's all-important thrust south. The much more significant opening salvo of the Pacific war occurred one hour and twenty minutes prior to Pearl Harbor, when General Hirofumi Yamashita landed twenty thousand troops on the east coast of Malaysia and sent them south — as Franklin Delano Roosevelt had predicted — to Singapore and then on to the Dutch East Indies for oil.

In military parlance, the term *blowback* refers to the unintended consequences of a covert operation. Americans experiencing the blowback of their government's actions saw Japan's act of violence as a surprise attack; they were unable to put it into context because they were unaware of the United States' secret acts of violence against the other country. The American public did not know that Acheson had cut Japan's oil without FDR's knowledge or that Roosevelt had been building an air force for Chiang to burn down Japan or that Tokyo knew of T. V. Soong's lobbying of FDR and of the airplanes and pilots arriving at Rangoon. As lawyer and author Alan Armstrong wrote in *Preemptive Strike,* if the public had been aware that for one year FDR had been planning offensive air operations against Japan, "President Roosevelt may have risked impeachment."[23]

In the Tokyo war-crimes trials after Japan surrendered, the U.S.-run tribunal defined *aggression* as "a first or unprovoked attack or act of hostility." Koichi Kido, a close adviser to Emperor Hirohito, argued that "Japan was provoked into a war of self-defense." William Logan — Kido's American associate counsel — summed up the Japanese case:

> We know of no parallel case in history where an economic blockade...was enforced on such a vast scale with such deliberate, premeditated, and coordinated precision....Responsible leaders at that time sincerely and honestly believed that Japan's national existence was at stake. [Because sanctions] threatened Japan's very existence and if continued would have destroyed her, the first blow was not struck at Pearl Harbor. The Pacific

War was not a war of aggression by Japan. It was a war of self-defense and self-preservation.[24]

When he learned of the Japanese attack on Pearl Harbor, Henry Luce phoned his father, who told him, "We will now all see what we mean to China and China means to us." Luce's biographer Swanberg observed, "The Japanese attack was a providential aid to Luce's own grand plans for Christianizing and Americanizing China at a speed hitherto undreamed of." That evening, Reverend Luce died in his sleep at the age of seventy-three. The next day, when Teddy White expressed his condolences, Henry Luce replied calmly, "It was wonderful that he lived long enough to see America and China as allies."[25]

Two days after the shock of Pearl Harbor, the *New York Times* published an editorial entitled "United We Stand."

> We have as our loyal ally China, with its inexhaustible manpower—China, which we did not desert in her own hour of need—China, from whose patient and untiring and infinitely resourceful people there will now return to us tenfold payment upon such aid as we have given. In the presence of these allies we shall find the key to the strategy of the Pacific.[26]

In China, the reality was the opposite. China Hand John Service remembered that when news of the Japanese attack on Pearl Harbor reached Chungking, "the Chinese were beside themselves with excitement and pleasure. To them this meant assurance of victory . . . they sat back after that and didn't do much."[27] A Chinese writer later recalled the reaction of those around Chiang:

> Officials went about congratulating each other, as if a great victory had been won. From their standpoint, it was a great victory, what they had waited for: America was at war with Japan. At last, at last, America was at war with Japan! Now China's strategic importance would grow even more. American money and equipment would flow in; half a billion dollars,

Southern Methodist Chiang and Christian Miss Soong. Note the strategically placed Roosevelt photo; FDR's support was their key to holding on to power. (Carl Mydans / Getty Images)

one billion dollars....Now Lend-Lease would increase....Now America would have to support Chiang, and that meant U.S. dollars into the pockets of the officials, into the pockets of the army commanders...and guns...for the coming war against Mao.[28]

Chiang Kai-shek—who for a decade had predicted a war "in which the United States will figure as the champion and savior of China"—was so happy when he learned of the Japanese attack on Pearl Harbor that he pulled out his phonograph and played a recording of "Ave Maria" over and over.[29] At long last, Chiang had his barbarian.

*   *   *

General Marshall was well aware that his commander in chief was emotional rather than realistic about China. Marshall's envoy in China, General John Magruder, wrote Marshall that Chiang intended to hoard American aid "largely with the idea of post-war military action" and that Chiang regarded his armies as "static assets to be conserved for assistance in fighting against...fellow countrymen for economic and political supremacy." Magruder called FDR's expectation that Chiang would fight the Japanese an "alluring fiction" from the world of "make-believe."[30] One of Magruder's men reported,

> The general idea in the United States that China has fought Japan to a standstill, and has had many glorious victories, is a delusion. Japan has generally been able to push forward any place she wanted to. She has stopped mostly because of the fact that a certain number of troops can safely hold only a certain number of miles of front without allowing dangerous holes to exist in it.
>
> The will to fight an aggressive action does not yet exist in the Chinese Army. If the Government of the United States is counting on such intent it should be cautioned against being too sure of any large-scale offensive action at present....The desire of the Chinese for more modern materiel was not, before December 8th, for the purpose of pressing the war against Japan, but was to make the Central Government safe against insurrection after diplomatic pressure by other nations had forced Japan out of China.[31]

The U.S. naval attaché in Chungking also warned Marshall about the mirage prevalent in Washington that Chiang was eager to fight Japan: "If such conception is seriously held by those controlling high strategy, it is fatally defective."[32] Added Magruder's man, "There is very little activity along the front...no contact between Chinese and Japanese troops at front was observed...the interest of the Chinese toward any aggressive action appears to be quite negligible, regardless of their statements that all they need is airplanes, tanks, and artillery in order to drive the aggressor from their shores."[33]

General Marshall had done his best to slow down the flow of airplanes for FDR's secret air war in Asia. In the first week of December, Claire Chennault counted just sixty-two outdated fighter planes at his airfield in Burma.

After Pearl Harbor, Chiang Kai-shek proposed that the U.S., Britain, China, the Netherlands, and Russia establish a war council in Chungking. The way Chiang saw it, airplanes would attack Japanese supply lines, cutting off their forces on the Asiatic mainland, after which his armies would smash the invaders. Chiang's grand plan did not address supply, logistics, and command and did not acknowledge the inconvenient war raging in Europe. Chiang was clear on one point: the Chungking war council would control "priorities and supplies."[34] The barbarians would fight Japan while Ailing and Chiang handled the foreign loot.

When he heard the news of Pearl Harbor, Prime Minister Churchill sped to Liverpool, boarded a warship bound for the U.S., and arrived at the White House in time for Christmas. Roosevelt informed Churchill that the war would be won by the "United Nations," a new term at the time. The Big Four of this United Nations would consist of the United States, the United Kingdom, the Soviet Union, and China. Churchill thought Roosevelt mad. China? Churchill later recalled his startled reaction:

> At Washington I had found the extraordinary significance of China in American minds, even at the top, strangely out of proportion. I was conscious of a standard of values which accorded China almost equal fighting power with the British Empire, and rated the Chinese armies as a factor to be mentioned in the same breath as the armies of Russia. I told the president how much I felt American opinion overestimated the contribution

which China could make to the general war. He differed strongly. There were five hundred million people in China. What would happen if this enormous population developed in the same way Japan had done in the last century and got hold of modern weapons? I replied that I was speaking of the present war, which was quite enough to go on with for the time being. I said that I would of course always be helpful and polite to the Chinese, whom I admired and liked as a race and pitied for their endless misgovernment, but that he must not expect me to adopt what I felt was a wholly unreal standard of values.[35]

Churchill would have been even more shocked if he had known that when Roosevelt first wrote out a list of the United Nations' Big Four, he had placed China second, after the United States, followed by the Soviet Union and the United Kingdom. Only later did FDR revise the list, placing the UK second and China fourth. On New Year's Day 1942, a declaration by the United Nations to fight the Axis powers was officially announced; FDR signed for the U.S., Churchill for Great Britain, and T. V. Soong for China.

After Pearl Harbor, Ailing, Chiang, T.V., and Mayling strategized. As had long been their wont, they didn't discuss how to confront the Japanese but instead planned how to extract money from FDR with the *promise* of fighting Japan. On December 30 Chiang asked U.S. ambassador Clarence Gauss for a cool half a billion dollars, to be handed over with no strings attached. The ambassador scoffed at the idea, apparently not aware of the China Lobby's pull in Washington. On January 9, 1942, FDR wrote Morgenthau, "I am anxious to help Chiang Kai-Shek...I hope you can invent some way of doing this."[36]

Morgenthau thought of how he could ensure this huge sum was used effectively; he wanted to pay part of the money directly to Chiang's soldiers with a new currency called the D-E-M-O (short for *democracy*). Morgenthau told his staff, "I was trying to think of some way so that while the boys fight they get their money, and if they don't fight, no money."[37]

But Chiang didn't want to fight the Japanese, and Ailing wanted her big chunk of dough, pronto. Word leaked from Chungking that without American aid, Chiang wouldn't be able to continue his valiant resistance against the Japanese and would be forced to make a separate peace with them. On January 30, T. V. Soong met alone with Roosevelt in the White House. Following the meeting, the president summoned his secretaries of State, Treasury, and Commerce, "ordering immediate action be taken to grant China the $500 million loan with no strings attached."[38]

When Congress approved it, Roosevelt wrote Chiang that the loan "testified to the wholehearted respect and admiration which the government and people of this country have for China."[39]

On Saturday, December 20, 1941, a week and a half before the signing of the Declaration by the United Nations, which pledged the signatories to the war effort, ten Japanese twin-engine Kawasaki bombers took off from Hanoi to attack Kunming, China. The squadron brought along no fighter escorts as they expected no opposition, and so they were defenseless in the air. Near Kunming, they were surprised by Claire Chennault's fighters, who shot down four of the Japanese bombers and killed at least fifteen Japanese airmen at the cost of one of Chennault's planes, which crash-landed when it ran out of gas. To celebrate, Soong-Chiang propagandists released Chennault's name to United Press International.

At that moment, the United States was on its heels, reeling from the Japanese onslaught; the Japanese were hammering General MacArthur's besieged soldiers in the Philippines, and U.S. Navy warships were still being fished out of Pearl Harbor. Now, suddenly, from deep in the hinterlands of China, came news of an American fist striking Japan's chin. U.S. newspapers published the account on December 21, running it as a small-fry story about a militarily insignificant clash over a distant city no one had ever heard of; their front pages were dominated by stories of major cities in flames around the globe. The *New York Times* ran the story on page 27. Henry Luce read the *New York Times* daily; it was his major source for news. Thus alerted, Luce put Teddy White on the case, and on December 29, *Time* magazine published a breathless story subtitled "Blood for the Tigers":

> For three years the Japanese had been bombing China from the coast. Their bombs had crunched through the masonry of every major provincial capital in Free China. They had laughed at the ineffectual popping of Chungking's worn anti-aircraft guns, had shot down fledglings of the Chinese Air Force like wounded ducks.
>
> Last year lean, hard-bitten, taciturn Colonel Claire L. Chennault (U.S. Army, retired), adviser to Chiang Kai-shek's Air Force, left Chungking for the U.S. He rounded up U.S. volunteers to fly 100 new P-40s purchased from the U.S. If U.S. aid were to flow in over the Burma Road, U.S. flyers would have to protect it. All through the summer months Colonel Chennault whipped his volunteers (dubbed the "Flying Tigers") into shape. By the time he was ready to fight, he had an added incentive: the Japanese were now the enemies of his own country.
>
> Last week ten Japanese bombers came winging their carefree way up into Yunnan, heading directly for Kunming, the terminus of the Burma Road. Thirty miles south of Kunming, the Flying Tigers swooped, let the Japanese have it. Of the ten bombers, said Chungking reports, four plummeted to earth in flames. The rest turned tail and fled. Tiger casualties: none.[40]

Flying Tigers! Luce and White had taken an obscure and insignificant air battle deep in China's interior and turned it into a sensation. Claire Chennault and the other CAMCO employees didn't style themselves as tigers; they had decorated their airplanes with shark teeth painted on their noses. But realizing the value of a good brand, Tommy the Cork and China Defense Supplies asked Walt Disney to design a snappy logo, which he did, an insignia consisting of a winged tiger flying through a large victory *V.* The mythologizing of the Flying Tigers would reach Hollywood—a John Wayne movie was based on their daring adventures, and they became a part of American military myth from then on.[41]

When Charlie Soong, North Carolina's first Chinese Christian, had promoted the China mirage to the men of the Old Club in Durham, he had compared Abraham Lincoln's "Of the people, by the people, and for the people" to Sun Yat-sen's "Nationalism, Democracy, and People's Livelihood." Thirty-seven years later—in 1942—the most prominent Chinese Christian in the U.S. was Charlie's son T.V., who whispered his father's pitch into Warren Delano's grandson's ear. He, in turn, put the Lincoln/Sun Yat-sen comparison on a U.S. postage stamp. Meanwhile, across the Pacific, blood flowed.

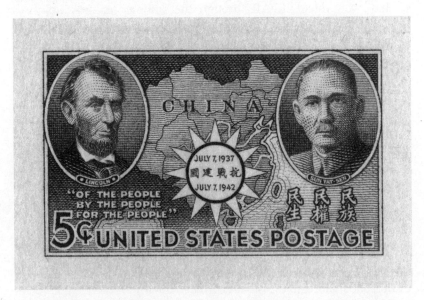

Five-cent U.S. stamp, 1942: Abraham Lincoln and Sun Yat-sen. "Of the people, by the people, for the people." With the politically powerful China Lobby influencing him, FDR equated China with the United States. (CPA Media / Pictures From History)

President Franklin Delano Roosevelt, U.S. Postmaster General Frank Walker, and T. V. Soong examining the new Lincoln/Sun stamp. (Courtesy of the Library of Congress)

Chapter 11

THE MANDATE OF HEAVEN

We are in the process of throwing away a nation of people who could and would save democracy with us.
—*Pearl Buck*[1]

What will the American people say when they finally learn the truth?
—*General Joseph Stilwell*[2]

On February 9, 1942, General Joseph Stilwell went to the White House to meet with the president. Secretary of War Stimson and General Marshall had recommended Stilwell as commander of the China theater because he had served there, spoke Chinese, and was a top-tier Army tactician and strategist. Today was the meeting in which Stilwell would receive FDR's orders, but once in the Oval Office, Stilwell learned that his commander in chief had nothing definite to say:

Call at White House. 12:00 to 12:20. F.D.R. very pleasant, and very unimpressive. As if I were a constituent in to see him. Rambled on about his idea of the war..."a 28,000 mile front is my conception," etc., etc. "The real strategy is to fight them all," etc., etc. Just a lot of wind. After I had enough, I broke in and asked him if he had a message for Chiang Kai-shek. He

Chiang Kai-shek, Mayling Soong, and General Joseph Stilwell (Getty Images)

very obviously had not and talked for five minutes hunting around for something world-shaking to say. Finally he had it — "Tell him we are in this thing for keeps, and we intend to keep at it until China gets back all her lost territory."... He was cordial and pleasant... and frothy.[3]

Once Stilwell arrived in China and met with Chiang, he told a reporter off the record, "The trouble in China is simple: We are allied to an ignorant, illiterate, superstitious, peasant son of a bitch."[4] In his diary, Stilwell referred to Chiang as "Peanut" and constantly criticized him: "Chiang Kai-shek has been boss so long and has so many yes-men around him that he has the idea he is infallible on any subject.... He is not mentally stable, and he will say many things to your face that he doesn't mean fully or exactly."[5] Stilwell understood that he was dealing with two realities:

We were fighting Germany to tear down the Nazi system—
one-party government, supported by the Gestapo and headed
by an unbalanced man with little education. We had plenty to
say against such a system. China, our ally, was being run by a
one-party government and supported by a Gestapo and headed
by an unbalanced man with little education. This government,
however, had the prestige of the possession of power—it was
opposing Japan, and its titular head had been built up by propaganda in America out of all proportion to his deserts and
accomplishments.[6]

The War Department required American correspondents reporting
from China to sign an agreement that they would submit their work to
War Department censors. In her Pulitzer Prize–winning book *Stilwell
and the American Experience in China, 1911–1945,* Barbara Tuchman
explained why the American press was unable to break through the
wall of China Lobby propaganda:

Owing partly to censorship but more to voluntary reticence, the
press up to 1943 published nothing realistic about the brave and
favorite ally. Probably never before had the people of one country viewed the government of another under misapprehension
so complete.[7]

A February 1942 Gallup poll showed that 62 percent of Americans
favored focusing the major military effort against Japan to save New
China; only 25 percent thought the priority was to defend England
against Germany.[8] For more than a year after Pearl Harbor, the Chinese were the Americans' favorite allies. Chungking's Ministry of
Information fed America fables about how U.S.-Chinese interests
were aligned in the fight against Japan and told brave tales about valiant soldiers and Noble Peasants who yearned to be like Americans.
Ministry of Information scribes—many with American educations—
wrote convincing press releases about Chinese victories over the Japanese in battles that had never occurred. In the U.S., these stories were

heralded as fact by China Lobbyists in Washington, in the press, and in the pulpits.

Many outside the U.S. cultural box understood that China was not destined to evolve into a Christianized and Americanized nation. Winston Churchill wrote to one of his generals, "I must enlighten you upon the American view. China bulks as large in the minds of many of them as Great Britain.... If I can epitomize in one word the lesson I learned in the United States, it was 'China.' "[9] Americans had long been sold on Chiang Kai-shek as a valiant warrior and Southern Methodist democrat, but in England the more realistic British enjoyed a radio comedy program that featured a Generalissimo character named General Cash My Cheque.

The China Lobby continued to surround Roosevelt. His cousin Joe Alsop, on T. V. Soong's payroll, wrote newspaper columns praising Chiang and Chennault and criticizing Stilwell. T. V. Soong and Tommy the Cork constantly complained to FDR about Stilwell and wanted him ousted in favor of Chennault, who had become a Flying Tiger folk hero in the U.S. but who now had to serve under Stilwell. In October of 1942 Chennault wrote a letter to Roosevelt that Barbara Tuchman called "one of the extraordinary documents of the war...the self-annunciation of a military messiah."[10] Chennault promised Roosevelt:

> Japan can be defeated in China. It can be defeated by an Air Force so small that in other theaters it would be called ridiculous...I am now confident that given full authority as the American military commander in China that I can not only bring about the downfall of Japan but that...I can create such good will that China will be a great and friendly trade market for generations.[11]

This was great news to Roosevelt. And the price was cheap— Chennault requested only one hundred and forty-seven airplanes, and in exchange, FDR would get everything he wanted: the China Lobby off his back, the defeat of Japan, and China's everlasting friendship.

In his letter, Chennault employed the word *simple* four times, as in "The military task is a simple one." FDR's eyes must have popped over Chennault lines like this: "I can accomplish the overthrow of Japan... within six months, within one year at the outside.... It will make China our lasting friend for years after the war."[12]

Roosevelt, Hopkins, Currie, and Corcoran loved Chennault's plan and were enthusiastic about getting rid of Stilwell and replacing him with Chennault. FDR forwarded the memo to the War Department, where both Chennault's bucking of the military chain of command and his ideas were met with icy derision. General Marshall judged Chennault's plan "just nonsense; not bad strategy, just nonsense."[13]

Chiang was frustrated with Stilwell, who constantly prodded the unwilling Generalissimo to confront the Japanese. Chiang much preferred his yes-man Chennault and their plan for a barbarian air force. Chiang wrote Roosevelt and asked him to call Chennault to Washington once again so he could pitch the dream. The War Department ordered Chennault and his superior Stilwell to Washington. Recalled Chennault about a meeting in the Oval Office,

> The President asked if a China-based air force could sink a million tons of Japanese shipping a year. I replied that if we received 10,000 tons of supplies monthly my planes would sink and severely damage more than a million tons of shipping. He banged his fist on the desk and chortled, "If you can sink a million tons, we'll break their back."[14]

Stilwell, who lived in the real world rather than in Chennault's world of mirage, had no chance with FDR. As Chennault wrote in his memoirs,

> At one Trident conference when Stilwell was expostulating on the poor quality of Chinese leadership, the President interrupted him.
>
> "What do you think of the Generalissimo?" he asked.

"He's a vacillating, tricky, undependable old scoundrel, who never keeps his word—" Stilwell growled.

"Chennault, what do you think?" the President interrupted, turning to me in the corner.

"Sir, I think the Generalissimo is one of the two or three greatest military and political leaders in the world today. He has never broken a commitment or promise made to me," I replied.[15]

In his notes, Stilwell says he tried to warn Roosevelt that the Chiang-Chennault air-war plan was a hoax, a military joke:

> Any increased air offensive that stung the Japs enough would bring a strong reaction that would wreck everything and put China out of the war.... The first essential step was to get a ground force capable of seizing and holding airbases, and opening communications to China from the outside world. Overruled.... But what's the use when the World's Greatest Strategist is against you.[16]

Sixty-two years after Julian Carr picked up Charlie Soong at the Durham train station, Franklin Delano Roosevelt greeted Mayling Soong at the Washington train station and took her to the White House, where she slept down the hall from FDR.

The U.S. House of Representatives was packed on February 18, 1943, to witness the China mirage incarnate. Speaker of the House Sam Rayburn introduced her as "Madame Chiang Kai-shek, one of the outstanding women of all the earth."[17]

Mayling was confident that she could make her case because, as a U.S.-educated Chinese, she grasped the hall-of-mirrors quality of America's China mirage. In his last book, David Halberstam described it:

> The China that existed in the minds of millions of Americans was the most illusory of countries, filled as it was with dutiful, obedient peasants who liked America and loved Americans, who longed for nothing so much as to be like them. It was a

Franklin Roosevelt and Mayling Soong, Washington, D.C., February 18, 1943.
Mayling brought her own silk sheets to sleep at the White House.
(Courtesy Everett Collection)

country where ordinary peasants allegedly hoped to be more Christian and were eager, despite the considerable obstacles in their way, to rise out of what Americans considered a heathen past. Millions of Americans believed not only that they loved (and understood) China and the Chinese, but also that it was their duty to Americanize the Chinese. "With God's help, we will lift Shanghai up and up, ever up until it is just like Kansas City," said Senator Kenneth Wherry of Nebraska....

There were two Chinas. There was the China in the American public mind, a China as Americans wanted it to be, and the other China, the real China.... The illusory China was a heroic ally, ruled by the brave, industrious, Christian, pro-American Chiang Kai-shek and his beautiful wife, Mayling, a member of one of China's wealthiest and best connected families, herself

Christian and American-educated, and who seemed to have been ordered up directly from Central Casting for a major public relations campaign. The goals of the Generalissimo and his lady, it always seemed, were exactly the same as America's goals, their values the same as ours as well.[18]

From the floor of the U.S. Congress, Mayling delivered the China Lobby's well-rehearsed myth:

> You, as representatives of the American people, have before you the glorious opportunity of carrying on the pioneer work of your ancestors [who] braved hardships to open up a new continent.... You have today:...the immeasurably greater opportunity to implement these same ideals and to help bring about the liberation of man's spirit in every part of the world.... If the Chinese people could speak to you in your own tongue, or if you could understand our tongue, they would tell you that... we are fighting for the same cause, that we have identity of ideals.... I assure you that our people are willing and eager to cooperate with you in the realization of these ideals.[19]

"Goddam it," one emotional congressman said. "I never saw anything like it. Madame Chiang had me on the verge of bursting into tears."[20] Clare Boothe Luce—now a Republican representative from Connecticut—said Madame Chiang was "too proud to beg us for what is China's right and too gracious to reproach us for what we have failed to do."[21] Eleanor Roosevelt wrote, "She was a person, a great person, receiving the recognition due her as an individual valiantly fighting in the forefront of the world's battle."[22] *Fortune* magazine called Mayling "the most effective ambassador ever to represent a foreign power in the U.S....She came to offer us a way—a way that would benefit us as much as the Chinese—a deal in which Chinese manpower would use American equipment."[23]

At a joint press conference with Madame Chiang, Roosevelt described what we can now recognize as his New China dream: "The people of

China well over a century have been, in thought and in objective, closer to us Americans than almost any other peoples in the world—the same great ideals. China, in the last—less than half a century has become one of the great democracies of the world."[24]

A reporter asked Mayling about rumors that her husband was less than aggressive in fighting the Japanese. Mayling replied primly, "We are using as much manpower as there are munitions to be used. We can't fight with bare hands." All eyes then focused on Roosevelt, who quickly promised that he would send China more munitions "as soon as the Lord will let us." Mayling flashed FDR a knowing smile and quickly added, "The Lord helps those who help themselves."[25]

Mayling then took her show on the road, wowing audiences from Madison Square Garden to the Hollywood Bowl. After Mayling returned to China, parishioners of St. John's Church in Massena, New York, installed a large stained-glass window depicting Madame Chiang alongside other Christian saints.

In 1943, while the mirage burned ever brighter in the United States, to many Americans in China it was clear that Chiang was losing and Mao gaining the Mandate. In his notes, Stilwell compared Chiang's government to Mao's:

> [On Chiang] Corruption, neglect, chaos, economy, taxes, words and deeds. Hoarding, black market, trading with enemy.
>
> [On Mao] Reduce taxes, rents, interest. Raise production, and standard of living. Participate in government. Practice what they preach.[26]

Stilwell described Chiang's military strategy:

> [He] hates the so-called Communists. He intends to crush them by keeping any munitions furnished him and by occupying their territory as the Japs retire. [He] will not make an effort to fight seriously. He wants to finish the war coasting, with a big supply of material, so as to perpetuate his regime.[27]

*　　*　　*

President Roosevelt handed the China Lobby a propaganda triumph when he agreed to sit for photos with Chiang at the Cairo conference in late 1943. Joseph Stalin, who was shouldering most of the burden of fighting Germany at this point, thought so little of Chiang as a war leader that he refused to attend the conference. Winston Churchill turned purple about acknowledging General Cash My Cheque as one of the Big Four but acceded to Roosevelt's request because he was dependent on the United States.

Photos showed Roosevelt, Churchill, Chiang, and Mayling smiling as if engaged in friendly banter, but the truth was that Chiang and FDR could not understand each other, and an irritated Churchill repeatedly ignored Mayling by speaking to photographers in front of him.

Stilwell asked Roosevelt to define American policy toward China. According to Stilwell's diary, FDR responded by reaching back into his family lore:

> You know I have a China history. My grandfather went out there, to Swatow and Canton, in 1829, and even went up to

Chiang, FDR, Churchill, and Mayling, Cairo, 1943. Roosevelt said Chiang was "the first real Oriental" he had met. (Courtesy Everett Collection)

Hankow. He did what was every American's ambition in those days—he made a million dollars, and when he came back he put it into western railroads. And in eight years he lost every dollar. Ha! Ha! Ha! Then in 1856 he went out again and stayed there all through the Civil War, and made another million. This time he put it into coalmines, and they didn't pay a dividend until two years after he died. Ha! Ha! Ha![28]

Roosevelt later admitted that Chiang was "the first real Oriental" he had ever met.[29]

General Hap Arnold, head of the U.S. Army Air Force, visited Chungking and met with Chiang and Chennault, who pitched him the same crazy dream that FDR and Tommy the Cork had bought in 1941. When Arnold brought up the challenges of building, maintaining, and protecting airfields, he found that Chiang and Chennault glossed over the issues with waves of their hands. "They could not or would not be bothered with logistics," Arnold observed. Chiang complained to Arnold, "Excuses, excuses...there are ways and means of doing things and they must be done....Tell your President that unless I get [my demands] I cannot fight this war and he cannot count on me to have our Army participate in the campaign."[30]

One of Roosevelt's shrewdest wartime moves was to arm Communist Russia, allowing Joseph Stalin's soldiers and civilians to bear the brunt of Germany's military juggernaut. For example, on June 6, 1944—D-day at Normandy—the Allies suffered about ten thousand casualties. But at Kursk a year earlier, the Russians and the Germans had waged the biggest tank battle in world history, a conflict that produced over a million casualties. The Battle of Stalingrad saw an incredible two million German and Russian dead and wounded. The vast majority of German soldiers who died in World War II were killed by Communists armed by Franklin Delano Roosevelt.

Roosevelt reached out to the Chinese Communists also with the idea of arming them in their fight against Japan. After all, every Japanese soldier killed in China meant one less for America to confront. Mao had invited U.S. observers to Yan'an in 1942. General Stilwell, John Service, John Davies, General Marshall, and President Roosevelt were all interested in learning more about Mao, his fighting potential, and his usefulness against the Japanese. Roosevelt sent polite memos to Chiang asking his permission to let the U.S. accept Mao's invitation. Stilwell, Service, and Davies presented FDR's requests, but an FDR-Mao alliance would be the worst possible development for Chiang, and he and his China Lobby network did all they could to throw up roadblocks.

At one point, John Davies was surprised to learn that T. V. Soong knew the details of a confidential meeting about China held just the day before in Washington. When Soong noticed Davies's consternation, he said, "There are no secrets in Washington. Rest assured, Mr. Davies, that no conference takes place regarding which I do not have accurate and complete information."[31]

It wasn't until the summer of 1943 that a few — very few — American journalists sounded the alarm about the New China dream. *Reader's Digest* and the *New York Times* hit the nail on the head with articles entitled, respectively, "Too Much Wishful Thinking About China" and "Our Distorted View of China." Readers were told that "the Chinese Army is a comic opera chorus," that China was ruled by "old war lords, in new clothing, for whom war is a means for personal aggrandizement and enrichment," and that the American public had been fed a mirage by "missionaries, war relief drives, able ambassadors and the movies."[32] But such snippets of reality could not compete with the century-old merchant-and-missionary mirage.

A conflicted Pearl Buck wrote an article for *Life* magazine called "A Warning About China." Its subtitle was "A Great Friend of the Chinese People Points to Dangers That May Lose Us a Valuable Ally." Buck reluctantly admitted, "Oppressive elements in the government are being more oppressive. Chungking is a place where free speech is less and less possible and those who want to be free are going to other places." But she also wrote, "Chiang Kai-shek is still the rallying point and the center of unity for China's war." Buck—who had not been back to Asia for years—proceeded to take Americans to task for not giving sufficient support to New China:

> The Chinese are brave and ready fighters and if they are not fighting it is because they have nothing to fight with except plenty of empty-handed men...nothing could please the Japanese better than the way we are now treating the Chinese people....We are in the process of throwing away a nation of people who could and would save democracy with us but who if we do not help them will be compelled to lose it because they are being lost themselves.[33]

In China, Stilwell told his diary a different story:

> The picture of this little rattlesnake being backed up by a great democracy, and showing his backside in everything he says and does, would convulse you if you could get rid of your gall bladder. But to have to sit there and be dignified, instead of bursting into guffaws, is too much to ask for the pay I get. What will the American people say when they finally learn the truth?[34]

FDR finally forced Chiang to allow U.S. officials to contact Mao. In July of 1944, one month after D-day in Europe, the U.S. Observer Group, including the OSS (the World War II precursor to the CIA), U.S. military personnel, and China Hands like John Service, flew into Yan'an. At that moment the interests of the Americans and Mao Zedong coincided; each sought an ally against the Japanese, and both sides were eager for China to unify against that common enemy.

The China Hands immediately noticed differences between Mao's China and Chiang's China. On the bumpy ride from the landing strip into Yan'an, one observed, "The people alongside the road were robust, so were the horses, so were the mules, so were the dogs. Our officers exclaimed over the contrast to Chungking."[35] The OSS agents were especially enthusiastic because they had the chance to interrogate Japanese prisoners, something Chiang—whose troops rarely engaged the

Zhou Enlai, Zhu De, John Service, Mao Zedong, unknown (Courtesy Service Family)

enemy—could not offer. John Service wrote in his diary, "We have come into a different country and we are meeting different people.... Morale is very high."[36]

After one month, Mao invited Service to his cave home, where the two men talked for eight hours, with a break for dinner cooked by Mao's wife, Jiang Qing. Service had more substantial conversations with Mao than any other American government official would have for the next quarter century.

Mao told Service, "The fact is clear...that China's political tendency is towards us.... Chiang holds the bayonets and the secret police" over the people and was "determined on Communist elimination...Chiang Kai-Shek was elected President by only ninety members of a single party...even Hitler has a better claim to democratic power." Mao suggested that Roosevelt face reality regarding Chiang:

Fundamentally he is a gangster.... The United States has handled Chiang very badly. They have let him get away with blackmail — for instance, talk of being unable to keep up resistance, of having to make peace, his tactics in getting the $500 million loan.... With Chiang you can be friendly only on your own terms. There is no longer any need or any reason to cultivate, baby or placate Chiang. The United States can tell Chiang what he should do.... American help to Chiang can be made conditional on his meeting American desires.[37]

Mao told Service that the U.S. could be "decisive" in "preventing civil war" in China. But Mao said that Americans too often uncritically accepted Chiang's false descriptions of reality, chiding Service, "How many American observers do you now have in the front lines?"

In the course of conversation, Service mentioned that the U.S. officially recognized Chiang, and any American recognition of Mao would be "interference in the domestic affairs of another country." Mao retorted,

America has intervened in every country where her troops and supplies have gone...for America to insist that arms be given to all forces who fight Japan, which will include the Communists, is not interference. For America to give arms only to Chiang will in its effect be interference.[38]

Mao described a relationship between the U.S. and China that today in the twenty-first century is a reality:

The Russians have suffered greatly in the war and will have their hands full with their own job of rebuilding. We do not expect Russian help.

China must industrialize. This can be done — in China — only by free enterprise and with the aid of foreign capital.... Chinese and American interests are correlated and similar. They fit together, economically and politically. We can and must work together...we will be interested in the most rapid possible development of the country on constructive and productive lines.... America does not need to fear that we will not be cooperative. We must cooperate and we must have American help...we cannot risk crossing you—cannot risk any conflict with you.[39]

Mao Zedong had just extended the hand of friendship to Roosevelt through the highest-ranking American official to whom he had access. The vision he described to Service was the one that eventually came true in the 1980s and beyond: the U.S. and China cooperating to industrialize China, with Russia a far distant partner. Mao was so pleased to be talking to Americans that he wrote an article entitled "On Diplomatic Work" about future cultural and political collaboration with the United States.

Historians argue that Mao was insincere, that he was sweet-talking Moscow at this same time. But Mao was much more a realist in search of power than a political ideologue. Support from the richest country on earth, the most industrialized World War II power with the world's deepest pools of capital—doesn't it make sense that practical and ambitious Mao would have deserted Joe Stalin for FDR any day?[40]

In the summer of 1944, the predictions of Generals Marshall and Stilwell came true: after Chennault stung them with his airpower, the Japanese wiped out his air bases. Suddenly Chennault and his men were fleeing for their lives. Henry Morgenthau, Franklin Roosevelt, Thomas Corcoran, and others had been wrong to believe the Chiang-Chennault dream against the better judgment of the War Department.

By the summer of 1944, many believed that Chiang had lost the contest for the Mandate of Heaven: Mao was attracting followers while Chiang was losing them. Chiang's locust soldiers were throwing their weapons down as they ran from the marauding Japanese, and even Chiang's wife—the Christian Miss Soong—had seemingly abandoned him. Mayling had tired of the Generalissimo after she'd found the high heels of one too many of Chiang's sexual conquests under his bed, and she'd moved in with Big Sister Ailing. Ailing then cashed in her Soong-Chiang chips, which probably cost Chiang 10 percent of his national treasury. In July, Ailing and Mayling left Chungking and flew to Rio de Janeiro with ten attendants. Ailing did some wheeling and dealing with the dictator of Brazil, President Getúlio Vargas, adding to her already substantial U.S.-funded investments in Brazilian companies and property.

Although the Soong-Chiang syndicate was collapsing in China, it still had presidential pull in Washington. In August, Mayling cabled little brother T.V. that she was tired of Brazil's humidity. T.V. made a phone call to his Harvard friend in the Oval Office, and on September 6, 1944, Roosevelt dispatched his private plane — the *Sacred Cow* — to Rio to pick up the Soong sisters.

Ailing and Mayling settled in River Oaks, a seventeen-room mansion in the tony Riverdale section of New York City. As the Mandate moved farther from Chiang in China, Ailing tended to her U.S. financial pipeline while Mayling minded the China Lobby propaganda front. As a break from her efforts, Mayling had a Secret Service agent teach her how to drive.

One of the private citizens Roosevelt used to circumvent the State Department was Patrick Hurley, a vain and pompous Oklahoma lawyer whose original claim to fame was that he had negotiated favorable leases in Mexico for the Sinclair Oil Company. When Hurley's friends learned that FDR was sending him to the Middle Kingdom as his personal representative, they asked him if China — a country he had never visited — wasn't a huge challenge. Hurley replied that the Chinese were just like Mexicans and that he could handle Mexicans. (At first, Hurley referred to Chiang Kai-shek as "Mr. Shek," not understanding that he was Mr. Chiang.)

Roosevelt's instructions to Hurley are unclear; as usual with China matters, the president held things close to his chest. Hurley would later write the State Department that his policy "is to prevent the collapse of the National Government" and "to sustain Chiang Kai-Shek as President of the Republic and Generalissimo of the armies."[41]

FDR initially sent Hurley to Chungking to referee the spat between

Stilwell and Chiang. Stilwell and the China Hands had become an enormous threat to Chiang. They were talking with Mao, and Chiang was afraid Washington might realize that Mao was the future and Chiang the past. When he arrived in China, Hurley announced what he interpreted as FDR's dictum: Chiang is China's future. Stilwell and the China Hands disagreed. Stilwell made it clear to Hurley that he planned to use Mao's forces to help battle the Japanese.

In retrospect, Stilwell's advice could well have resulted in a lasting friendship between China and the United States, saved millions of lives, and averted the Chinese civil war, the Korean War, and the Vietnam War. But Hurley was just the type of go-between that Chiang wanted: a man ignorant of China, an American already marinated in the myths and eager to toe the China Lobby line. Hurley cabled Washington complaining that his mission was encountering opposition directed toward himself by the "Un-American" elements in the State Department.[42]

Roosevelt was annoyed with Stilwell's views and wrote Marshall,

> Stilwell has exactly the wrong approach in dealing with Generalissimo Chiang who, after all, cannot be expected, as a Chinese, to use the same methods that we do.... All of us must remember that the Generalissimo came up the hard way to become the undisputed leader of four hundred million people — an enormously difficult job to attain any kind of unity from a diverse group of all kinds of leaders — military men, educators, scientists, public health people, engineers, all of them struggling for power and mastery, local or national, and to create in a very short time throughout China what it took us a couple of centuries to attain.... He is the Chief Executive as well as the Commander-in-Chief, and one cannot speak sternly to a man like that or exact commitments from him the way we might do from the Sultan of Morocco.[43]

General Marshall was at the crossroads of the China mirage. From China, his subordinates were calling Chiang a little Hitler, while in

Washington his commander in chief considered Chiang to be the undisputed leader of "one of the great democracies of the world."[44] After the war, U.S. Army historians asked Marshall, "What was the President's policy toward China? Did he ever explain it to you?" All Marshall could say was that Roosevelt wanted "to treat China as a great power."[45]

Tuchman wrote that Roosevelt's wartime policy toward China

> was not made in terms of current information but in terms of the accumulated notions of a lifetime by which minds had already been formed...information coming from the field had to battle against this accumulated weight.[46]

Chiang convinced Hurley that Stilwell had to go, and Hurley endorsed Chiang's request in a cable to FDR, who fired Stilwell. The news hit the China Hands like a bomb. John Service wrote, "Our dealings with Chiang Kai-shek apparently continue on the unrealistic assumption that he is China and he is necessary to our cause....We should end the hollow pretense that China is unified and that we can only talk to Chiang....This puts the trump card in Chiang's hands...more than ever, we hold all the aces in Chiang's poker game. It is time we started playing them."[47]

Instead, Roosevelt put the cards in Hurley's hands by naming him the new ambassador to China.

John Service traveled from Chungking to Washington in November of 1944. Washington officials were largely ignorant about Mao Zedong's successes and Service told them about Mao's rescues of downed American aircrews and his eagerness to cooperate with the United States in the war effort against Japan and in rebuilding China afterward. Service also reported Mao's concern that if the United States continued to arm only Chiang, the Generalissimo would launch another civil war when Japan was defeated, a contest that Chiang couldn't win. Service shared his observations with officials and journalists. He lunched with Henry Luce, who sat stone-faced. "I made no effect on Luce at all," Service remembered.[48]

Service also briefed Harry Hopkins, who had earlier read some of the China Hands' reports and passed them on to FDR. Hopkins's White House office was, Service recalled, "a plain small basement room not much larger than the cluttered desk." Before Service left Yan'an, Mao's men had given him a map showing their expanding empire and demonstrating how Mao could assist with a U.S. military landing on China's Pacific coast. Service spread out Mao's map on Hopkins's office floor and the two men got down on their knees to examine it. Service pointed out Mao-controlled areas, his guerrilla bases behind Japanese lines, sites of key Japanese troop concentrations, escape routes for downed American fliers, and potential landing areas for U.S. troops. For forty-five minutes, Service — the U.S. official who knew Mao best — tried to break through to Hopkins, saying that Mao's men were not Russian stooges and that they desired cooperation with the U.S. But Hopkins's laconic conclusion demonstrated that China Lobby messaging was stronger than Service's presentation of reality. Hopkins said, "Very interesting, I have no doubt that the picture you give is largely correct, but the only Chinese that most Americans have ever heard of is Chiang Kai-shek." As for Mao and his millions, "They call themselves Communists."[49] The discussion was over.

Perhaps Service — who had been born in China, was fluent in the language, and had spent most of his adult life there — did not understand the China mirage's hold on stateside Americans' minds. One U.S. official warned him that speaking the truth about China in Washington was dangerous: "Jesus, Service! I read that thing of yours, and I certainly agree with you but it is going to get you in a lot of trouble."[50]

Ambassador Hurley never came close to comprehending that Mao was China's future. Instead, he likened the Chiang-Mao fight to the tussles between Democrats and Republicans in his native Oklahoma. In Yan'an, Hurley had presented himself to Mao as a neutral negotiator, but it soon became apparent that Hurley was the Generalissimo's errand boy. Mao was surprised that FDR's top man in China was so deep in Chiang's pocket, but he continued to speak of his desire to

Mao Zedong, Ambassador Patrick Hurley, and Chiang Kai-shek. Hurley called
Mao "Moose Dung," Mao called Hurley "the Clown," and Chiang appreciated
Hurley's lack of knowledge about China. (Jack Wilkes / Getty Images)

cooperate with the United States and have Roosevelt arm him against
the Japanese.

In a report to the State Department, John Davies — who, like John
Service, was in and out of Yan'an during 1944 and 1945 — tried again
to awaken Washington to the opportunity slipping through its fingers:

> The United States is the greatest hope and the greatest fear of
> the Chinese Communists. They recognize that if they receive
> American aid, even if only on an equal basis with Chiang, they
> can quickly establish control over most if not all of China,

317

perhaps without civil war. For most of Chiang's troops and bureaucrats are opportunists who will desert the Generalissimo if the Communists appear to be stronger than the Central Government.

We are the greatest fear of the Communists because the more aid we give Chiang exclusively the greater the likelihood of his precipitating a civil war and the more protracted and costly will be the communist unification of China.

So the Chinese Communists watch us with mixed feelings. If we continue to reject them and support an unreconstructed Chiang, they see us becoming their enemy. But they would prefer to be friends...the Communists are in China to stay. And China's destiny is not Chiang's but theirs.[51]

On January 9, 1945, concerned that the truth was not getting through, Mao reached out from Yan'an to President Roosevelt in Washington. Major Ray Cromley—acting chief of the U.S. mission in Yan'an—forwarded this message to U.S. Army headquarters in Chungking: "Mao and Zhou will be immediately available either singly or together for exploratory conference at Washington should President Roosevelt express desire to receive them at White House as leaders of a primary Chinese party."[52]

Before Cromley sent it, Zhou Enlai had warned, "Hurley must not get this information, as I don't trust his discretion."[53] Unknown for decades was that U.S. Navy technicians led by Captain Michael Miles intercepted and decoded the message sent to Chungking and shared it with Dai Li, the head of Chiang's gestapo. Miles and Li rewrote the memo to make it appear that Mao was attempting to discredit Hurley in FDR's eyes.[54]

On January 14, Hurley buried Mao's invitation deep in a turgid thirteen-page cable to the White House, saying that he had been delayed by a plot hatched "within our own ranks" to undermine his efforts at a Chiang-Mao reconciliation. If Hurley had not heroically discovered this plot, "it would be futile for us to try to save the National Government of China." All would soon be well in China, Hurley assured FDR; he was fully in charge, and Chiang and T. V. Soong were "now favorable to unification... and agreement with the Communists," and after Hurley's negotiations succeeded, Roosevelt could meet with both Chiang and Mao. In the meantime Hurley urged FDR to get Churchill's and Stalin's approval for "your plan for... a post-war free, unified democratic China."[55]

Dai Li also gave Ambassador Hurley fabricated accounts of John Service's efforts to undermine him. When Service returned to Chungking from the U.S., Hurley warned him, as Service later remembered, "If I interfered with him he would break me."[56]

Here are some of the great what-ifs of American-Chinese relations. FDR met with Russian Communists in the White House. What if Mao's message had not been spiked by Chiang's secret police and Roosevelt had met with a Chinese Communist? What if Zhou Enlai had told Roosevelt that he was being blackmailed by Chiang? What if Mao had convinced the American commander in chief that his Chinese Communist forces armed by the U.S. could succeed against the Japanese, just like Soviet Communist forces were pounding Germany? What if Mao could have told FDR about his desire to cooperate with Wall Street to industrialize China?

Historians examine Mao's actions after he took over China in 1949 and conclude he did not want fruitful relations with the United States. But that was five years after the U.S. had refused his outstretched hand. Some still argue that he was not sincere, but the fact is that Mao made great efforts to reach out to Roosevelt, and it's easy to believe that with Europe and Russia bleeding men and money, he would have loved to be allied with Washington and Wall Street.

A visibly ailing Roosevelt made the arduous journey to the war-ravaged Crimea to meet with Joseph Stalin and Winston Churchill and discuss the reorganization of Europe and Asia after the war. At the Yalta Conference (February 4 to February 11, 1945), Roosevelt secretly promised Stalin that Russia could retake the Chinese territory that it had lost to Japan after the Russia-Japanese war if Stalin entered the war against Japan. Covertly doling out another country's territory didn't square with FDR's Atlantic Charter, but Roosevelt hoped the Russians would absorb much of Japan's punch, thus saving many American lives. FDR told himself that he would later straighten the whole thing out with Chiang. John Davies summed up FDR's management of the China theater as "the inevitable result of two illusions. One was an American romantic image of China. The second was an assumption that the United States could pretty much work its will on China."[57]

Mao now oversaw an empire of one hundred million, about twice the population of Britain, but FDR continued to see Chiang as China's postwar leader and Mao as just a disaffected party. By getting Stalin and Churchill to join with the U.S. in supporting Chiang, FDR imagined that Mao would be forced to compromise and accept Chiang's leadership. As John Service observed in 1976, "Roosevelt and Stalin strangely found that their mutually unrealistic views on China coincided.... That made inevitable a Chinese civil war in which the U.S. was hopelessly tied to the side of Chiang Kai-shek's Kuomintang. And thus was needlessly sealed the unhappy course of American-Chinese relations for the next 27 years."[58]

Mao commanded a million-man army of warriors, and John Service tried to educate the U.S. military brass in China about Mao's military might. In early February 1945, Service arranged a meeting between State Department officer Ray Ludden and General Albert Wedemeyer, who had replaced General Stilwell. Ludden had just spent four months marching with Mao's warriors behind Japanese lines on a grueling twelve-hundred-mile winter trek from Yan'an to the outskirts of Beijing and back to Yan'an. Ludden saw enthusiastic peasant support for Mao, something he insisted could not have been "a stage setting for the deception of foreign visitors."[59] Ludden told Wedemeyer, "Popular support of the Communist armies and civil administration is a reality which must be considered in future planning."[60] General Stilwell had entertained similar ideas and he'd been fired. General Wedemeyer wrote the Joint Chiefs in Washington that Mao's movement could be put down with relatively small assistance given to Chiang's government.

Many important Hotdogs and Warriors continued to misread reality in China. Joe Alsop, the distant relative of FDR who cashed China Lobby checks, wrote that Americans like John Service and John Davies were "childish to assume that the Chinese Communists are anything but an appendage of the Soviet Union," and that the idea of the U.S. using Mao's forces was "dangerous and idiotic." Alsop's solution was for the U.S. to give more aid to Chiang and work with the Generalissimo to "create a strong army, and then assisting (by our own forces if necessary) in unifying the country, liquidating the Communists, and establishing a strong government."[61]

At Ambassador Hurley's and Joseph Stalin's urging, in late January, Mao Zedong sent Zhou Enlai to Chungking to discuss terms with Chiang and Hurley. Chiang refused to share any power with Mao and threw sand in Hurley's gears by appointing several hard-line anti-Communists to official posts. Hurley reported optimistically to FDR that negotiations were right on track.

John Service wrote privately to John Carter Vincent, director of the State Department's Bureau of Far Eastern Affairs, complaining that Hurley was clueless, that he had no grasp of the bloody history and deep mistrust between Mao and Chiang: "It is essential that we get PH [Pat Hurley] out of the chair he now holds." Hurley was a "bull in a China shop...the antithesis in this delicate situation of what a good servant of the American government should be.... He is an idiot playing with fire. I may sound strong. But I'm not alone in thinking these things."[62]

Chiang Kai-shek told Ambassador Hurley that he was worried about what Roosevelt had promised Stalin at Yalta. On February 19, 1945, in Chungking, Hurley and General Wedemeyer boarded a plane bound for Washington. In their absence, chargé d'affaires George Atcheson would run the embassy and General Mervin Gross would be the top

U.S. Army officer. Atcheson and Gross agreed with Service that Hurley's optimistic reports to FDR were misleading, that U.S. support for only Chiang would plunge China into civil war, and that Mao's obvious popularity and strength must be acknowledged. Atcheson proposed an extraordinary manifesto to be signed by all the embassy's political officers. He asked Service to write it and on February 28 cabled the final version to the State Department with this unusual note: "This telegram has been drafted with the assistance and agreement of all the political officers of the staff of this embassy and has been shown to General Wedemeyer's Chief of Staff, General Gross."

The China Hands' cable warned that Washington was not achieving its goals against Japan, that Chiang had the U.S. over a barrel while Mao — who, in contrast, could help the U.S. defeat Japan — was becoming convinced that FDR was "committed to the support of Chiang alone." The cable noted that if American military forces landed on China's Pacific coast, they would need Mao's cooperation, and it argued that Mao should be "helped by us rather than seeking Russian aid or intervention." The China Hands suggested that FDR inform Chiang that "military necessity requires that we supply and cooperate with the Communists and other suitable groups who can assist the war against Japan."[63]

After the cable was dispatched, Service confided to his mother in a letter, "We may become heroes — or we may be hung."[64]

The China Hands' cable was embraced by many in the State Department as an act of courageous truth-telling. John Carter Vincent wrote, "There should be no question of an exercise of our prerogative, dictated by military necessity, to utilize all forces in China capable of cooperating with us in the fight against Japan. Chiang, having failed to effect military unity, should now be told that he has forfeited any claim to exclusive support."[65]

War Department planners were anticipating landing along the China coast preceding an invasion of Japan. Wedemeyer received secret orders to "arm any Chinese forces which they believe can be effective employed against the Japanese."[66]

The State and War Departments were adjusting to reality in China, but Hurley stood firm. When John Carter Vincent showed him the cable signed by his Chungking embassy staff, Hurley exploded in rage: "I know who drafted that telegram: *Service!*" Hurley shouted, "I'll get that son-of-a-bitch if it's the last thing I do!"[67]

On March 9, 1945, John Service returned to Yan'an. In the summer of 1944, Americans had been Mao's "greatest hope." Now there was a chill in the air, and Service was told that Ambassador Hurley "had gone back on his word and had become in effect a spokesman for [Chiang]"[68] and that Mao and his people would "seek friends wherever they can find them."[69] Despite having been rejected by the U.S., Mao's men remained confident, one even patting Service on the knee and chuckling as he said, "We don't really expect any arms from you. Ultimately we'll get them from [Chiang] anyway."[70]

Late one night Mao surprised Service by showing up for a chat that would last three hours. He had obviously thought deeply about his message, and Service's roommate remembered that Mao was particularly animated. Mao's message to Service was that FDR's support of only Chiang was "not the best way to fight the war" and that his, Mao's, policies had popular support; his warriors were aided by the masses like fish swimming in the sea. (Service noted in his report that, by contrast, for peasants in Chiang's China, "the war meant little except the constant fear of the death sentence of conscription, steadily higher tax demands and the unending impositions of a half-starved soldiery."[71])

Mao said that Chiang was "incapable of improving the condition of China's masses" and repeated that the United States was his choice to help rebuild China:

> Between the people of China and the people of the United States there are strong ties of sympathy, understanding and mutual interest.... China's greatest postwar need is economic development. She lacks the capitalistic foundation necessary to carry this out alone.... America and China complement each other economically; they will not compete.... America is

not only the most suitable country to assist this economic development of China, she is also the only country fully able to participate. For all these reasons there must not and cannot be any conflict, estrangement or misunderstanding between the Chinese people and America....[72]

When attacked, we will fight back. We are not afraid of the outcome because the people are with us. The Japanese haven't been able to wipe out the liberated areas; how can Chiang's conscripted un-indoctrinated army of unwilling peasants? Chiang could not whip us during the civil war when we were a hundred times weaker.[73]

Service concluded in his report that if the U.S. continued to exclude Mao and support only Chiang, "Disunity will be stimulated and the consequences will be disastrous."[74]

The State Department forwarded the China Hands' manifesto to the White House, but history doesn't reveal if FDR considered it. Roosevelt's health was failing. When he appeared before a joint session of Congress on March 1 to report the Yalta agreement, observers were surprised to see the diminished president seated in his wheelchair, the first time he had done so when addressing Congress. Roosevelt explained, "I have just completed a fourteen thousand mile trip."[75] When FDR met with Vice President Harry Truman, Roosevelt's hands shook so much that he could not drink a cup of coffee without spilling it. General Wedemeyer recorded his thoughts after a meeting in the White House: "I had not seen the President for several months and was shocked at his physical appearance. His color was ashen, his face drawn, and his jaw drooping. I had difficulty in conveying information to him because he seemed in a daze. Several times I repeated the same idea because his mind did not seem to retain or register."[76]

The exhausted and rapidly declining president met with Hurley several times to decide American policy toward China. Neither man took notes, and Hurley later gave contradictory descriptions of what transpired. Apparently the ever clueless and optimistic Hurley reassured the failing FDR that, yes, the president's long-held dream of a "unified, democratic China" was just around the corner, because with pressure from Washington, London, and Moscow, Mao would be forced to join Chiang's government. Years later, John Service observed:

> One may wonder...how thoroughly Roosevelt was briefed, and how clearly he understood the dispute over American policy in China as Hurley was representing it....Nonetheless, Roosevelt was astute enough as a politician to be keenly aware that China policy was a sensitive subject, that Chiang Kai-shek had a large and fervent band of American supporters and that "Communist" was a dirty word to important segments of American opinion.[77]

Thus in the warmth of the Oval Office, the decision that would ruin America's relationship with China for a generation was made: China would be changed by outside forces—the U.S., the USSR, and the UK—and Chiang would be their vehicle. The China Hands warned that no amount of money and equipment could save Chiang, but in America, *Time* magazine had not produced a single cover with Mao's face. Courtesy of the China Lobby, Southern Methodist Chiang and the Christian Miss Soong were the only Chinese most Americans knew. In China, the Mandate had already passed on to Mao, but the merchant-missionary dream was just too strong for Warren Delano's grandson to resist.

On March 29, 1945, Roosevelt went to the Little White House at Warm Springs, Georgia, where he played a secret right hand/left hand game in his personal life. Portrait artist Elizabeth Shoumatoff journeyed there with her friend Lucy Mercer Rutherfurd, Roosevelt's current mistress. On the afternoon of April 12, Roosevelt was sitting for Shoumatoff with Lucy by his side when he suddenly exclaimed, "I have a terrific pain in the back of my head."[78] He slumped forward in his chair, unconscious, and was carried into his bedroom. Shoumatoff and Rutherfurd rushed away. Roosevelt died at 3:35 p.m. Eleanor went to Warm Springs to claim his body, and she learned about Lucy and

The idea that the United States would nurture and change China has deep roots in America. (B. A. Garside, Box No. 11, Accession No. 80054-14.12. Courtesy of Hoover Institution Library & Archives, Stanford University)

that her daughter, Anna, had for some time been the communications link between FDR and his last mistress.

One of Roosevelt's final acts had been to follow the China Lobby and sanction Chiang as China's future, ignoring the China Hands' plea that he recognize Mao's growing influence. If Roosevelt hadn't propped up the faltering Soong-Chiang syndicate, a Chinese civil war might have been avoided and Mao Zedong might have claimed the

Mandate earlier than 1949. Instead, the American belief that China would change according to the U.S. plan would flourish for a few more years, resulting in the deaths of millions of people. But the tide of Chinese history would soon overwhelm barbarian dreams. When Ambassador Hurley later briefed Winston Churchill on Roosevelt's plan for a united, democratic China under Chiang, the prime minister referred to FDR's thinking as "the Great American illusion."[79]

Chapter 12

WHO LOST CHINA?

Who lost China?
—Senator Joseph McCarthy[1]

I am not going to lose Vietnam. I am not going to be the President
who saw Southeast Asia go the way China went.
—President Lyndon Baines Johnson[2]

J. Edgar Hoover's FBI career was rooted in the Red Scare of the 1920s. Since then he had kept an eagle eye out for isms to exploit, especially the evil of Communism. Hoover was a big fan of Chiang Kai-shek as well as a China Lobby insider and a friend of Patrick Hurley.

When *Amerasia* magazine editor Philip Jaffe, whom Hoover suspected of Communist leanings, came to DC, Hoover illegally bugged his hotel room. John Service was in Washington, and at the direction of Lauchlin Currie, he was giving background briefings to journalists, a common practice for U.S. government officials. At six o'clock at night on April 19, 1945, Service walked into Jaffe's hotel room, and the FBI listened as Service told Jaffe he would give him some relatively innocuous documents about Chiang and Mao. Hoover swung into action. FBI agents searched Service's State Department office and decided that there was something suspicious about his writings about

Chinese Communists—even though these were the people he was paid to keep tabs on. They knocked on Service's door at 5:03 on a June night: "We're from the F.B.I. You're under arrest."[3] Ambassador Hurley had his first son of a bitch. The China Lobby went into overdrive. Service was dragged into court and eventually subjected to seven State Department investigations, but each inquiry concluded that Service was innocent and had caused no harm.[4]

Mao was upset over Service's arrest. He dashed off an editorial to his followers accusing Ambassador Hurley of not being an honest broker and warned that if the U.S. continued to support only Chiang Kai-shek, America would cause a Chinese civil war after the Japanese were defeated.

The U.S. military brought Japan to its knees by burning out its cities with napalm. General Curtis LeMay was one of the great pilots of the European front. Assigned to bomb Japan, LeMay traveled to China and saw that, contrary to Chiang and Chennault's preachings, China wasn't a secure site from which to launch air attacks on Japan. LeMay instead based his B-52s on the Pacific islands of Tinian, Saipan, and Guam. Indeed, the battle of Iwo Jima was fought to clear the middle airspace between these southern airfields and Japan, far to the north. On March 11, 1945, American B-52s with bellies full of napalm flew over Iwo Jima, headed north. LeMay launched the biggest air attack in history against Tokyo, killing around one hundred thousand civilians in about three hours. More Tokyo civilians died in a shorter time than in any previous military operation in any war. As LeMay later wrote, "We scorched and boiled and baked to death more people in Tokyo on that night of March 9–10 than went up in vapor at Hiroshima and Nagasaki combined."[5] LeMay exaggerated a bit, but his point was that the two atomic bombs dropped on Hiroshima and Nagasaki later overshadowed the powerful role of his groundbreaking napalm bombings, which reduced the majority of Japan's cities to ash and made an astonishing fifteen million urban Japanese homeless.[6]

At 7:00 p.m. on August 14, 1945, President Truman announced the

Japanese surrender. Three hours later, Mayling Soong came on the air, broadcasting from Ailing's Riverdale mansion: "Now that complete victory has come to us, our thoughts should turn first to the rendering of thanks to our creator and the sobering task of formulating a truly Christian peace."[7]

At the time of Tokyo's surrender, the majority of Japanese troops in China were stationed in the north. This was Chairman Mao's territory.

In Europe, General Dwight Eisenhower negotiated with Russian Communists over who would accept which German prisoners. While military reality in Asia dictated that Mao had the quickest, cheapest, and most effective way to disarm the Japanese soldiers, General MacArthur ordered the Japanese to surrender only to Chiang. Since many of Chiang's troops were far away in southern China, Mao watched, astonished, as the U.S. mounted a massive cross-country air-lift of the Generalissimo's soldiers. Equally astonishing to Mao, Truman inserted American troops into North China to protect railways and other strategic resources for Chiang and ordered them to treat as enemies Mao's warriors, men who had previously risked their lives to rescue downed U.S. fliers. Now there were no American observers in Yan'an, and having had his outreached hand swatted away a number of times, Mao concluded the obvious, that the United States had rejected his attempts at friendship.

Earlier in the year, John Service had tried to inform Washington about Mao Zedong. Now another young American attempted to awaken Harry Truman's Wise Men to the rise of Ho Chi Minh, the leader of the anti-French Vietminh freedom fighters. In the spring of 1945, thirty-one-year-old Captain Archimedes Patti of the OSS parachuted into Ho Chi Minh's base north of Hanoi. Patti spoke French fluently, and Ho liked to smoke Patti's Chesterfields. Patti was an intelligent and canny operative, and he interviewed the French colonizers and many French-speaking Vietnamese. Indeed, over several months, Patti spent hours in conversation with Ho Chi Minh.

On September 2, 1945, General MacArthur took the Japanese surrender in Tokyo Bay. To an international radio audience, MacArthur promised that the defeat of Japan had liberated Asia.

On that same day, four hundred thousand joyful Vietnamese gathered in Hanoi's central square. The vast crowd strained to see the diminutive fifty-five-year-old Ho Chi Minh as he walked across the enormous stage, stepped up to the microphone, and proclaimed,

> All men are created equal; they are endowed by their Creator
> with certain inalienable Rights; among these are Life, Liberty,
> and the pursuit of Happiness. This immortal statement was
> made in the Declaration of Independence of the United States
> of America in 1776. In a broader sense, this means: All the
> peoples on the earth are equal from birth, all the peoples have a
> right to live, to be happy and free.[8]

Quoting Thomas Jefferson in Vietnam's declaration of independence was a pretty broad hint that Ho Chi Minh desired friendship with the United States. Captain Patti and other American OSS officers stood nearby as Ho told the world that Vietnamese, and not foreigners, would now control Vietnam. Americans on the spot admired Ho and could see that the future was his. Patti wrote reports to Washington concluding that Ho Chi Minh had both widespread popular support and a potent plan to repel invaders. Julia Child—later America's TV chef—was the young OSS secretary who wrapped Patti's reports in burlap for their long journey to Washington.

As Mao Zedong had, Ho Chi Minh extended his hand in friendship to the United States, sending a number of entreaties to President Truman and Secretary of State Acheson along the lines of this one: "I therefore most earnestly appeal to you personally and to the American people to interfere urgently in support of our independence."[9] Neither Truman nor Acheson responded.

This was not an oversight. The Wise Men disagreed about whether Asians should be free. America's defeat of Japan did not result in liberty for Asians. On President Truman's orders, the U.S. Navy ferried British,

Dutch, and French government officials and military men back to Southeast Asia to reassert control of their colonies. The merchant-missionary dream that foreigners would control events in Asia was still alive.

After the failure of the Chiang-Chennault air-war dream, Generals Marshall and Arnold had given Chennault the boot. Chennault left China on August 8, 1945. (Since he had contributed so little to Japan's defeat, no one in the War Department asked him to attend the victory celebration in Tokyo Bay.) Nevertheless, Chennault—who had now been drummed out of the U.S. military twice—would continue to spin the mirage in Washington, and with Tommy the Cork and the Soong family, he would make his postwar fortune in Asia through the private airline they founded, China Air Transport (CAT).

China Air Transport was an airline with few customers; most Chinese couldn't afford a plane ticket. No matter—Corcoran solved CAT's cash-flow problem. Tommy's old friend Fiorello La Guardia, former mayor of New York, was in 1945 the director general of the United Nations Relief and Rehabilitation Administration. Tommy presented La Guardia with a plan to have CAT deliver UNRRA supplies within China. UNRRA officials turned down this costly proposal. China Air Transport was an upstart airline fronted by the discredited Chennault with shadowy China Lobby ties. Tommy pressured La Guardia, who told him there was nothing he could do. Tommy kept the heat on. Just before he resigned as director general, La Guardia reversed his officials' ruling and awarded CAT a nearly four-million-dollar UNRRA contract.

To accept UNRRA aid, Ailing and T. V. Soong created the Chinese National Relief and Rehabilitation Administration (CNRRA). With skids greased by the China Lobby, UNRRA gave Chiang more aid—$518 million—than it awarded any other country. This UNRRA aid passed through the hands of the Soong family, who also, through CAT, were charging the United Nations big delivery fees and splitting the take with their American friends, the same ones who in 1940 had sold Franklin Delano Roosevelt on a secret air war in Asia.

*   *   *

President Truman continued FDR's policy of supporting only Chiang, and as the China Hands had predicted, civil war broke out. Many Americans were surprised because the China Lobby line held that once the Japanese left, Chiang's America-loving New China would arise. During four years of war, FDR had promoted the Soong-Chiang myth, and Mao's mastery was hidden under a pile of *Time, Life,* and *Fortune* magazines.

In September of 1945 an increasingly frustrated Ambassador Hurley left Chungking and returned to the comfortable mirage back home. On November 26, Hurley was in Washington and learned that six congressmen had criticized "the rotten Hurley policy" that had "now committed us to armed intervention" in China's internal affairs.[10] An infuriated Hurley responded with a letter of resignation to Truman:

> It is not secret that the American policy in China did not have the support of all the career men in the State Department. The professional foreign service men sided with the Chinese Communist armed party....Our professional diplomats continuously advised the Communists that my efforts in preventing the collapse of the National Government did not represent the policy of the United States...the chief opposition to the accomplishment of our mission came from the American career diplomats in the Embassy at Chungking and in the Chinese and Far Eastern Divisions of the State Department.[11]

This was the first blast of the who-lost-China fears that would later fuel McCarthyism, the witch hunt for the enemy within. Truman dispatched General Marshall to China to referee the spat between Chiang and Mao, but Marshall failed to bring peace between the two men. The China Lobby raised new suspicions about officials who were losing China: they even attacked the great General Marshall—the man who had won World War II for FDR—by accusing him of having been duped by traitors.

The U.S. military and media remained virtually clueless regarding Mao Zedong's military strategies. In 1947, American newspapers reported as militarily significant Chiang's capture of Yan'an and the fact that Mao was supposedly on the run. Sidney Rittenberg—an American who spent time with Mao in those years—explained:

> Mao deliberately used Yan'an as bait. Then after Yan'an was occupied, he used himself as bait, personally, to lead this huge, well-trained, well-equipped—with American military equipment—this army of Chiang Kai-shek's deep into the wilderness of Shansi province, where the population was sparse and heavily supportive of the Communists. Then he used his person to lead them on a merry chase every day until he got them into the ambush spot he wanted them in.[12]

By June of 1948, Mao and Chiang had roughly equal numbers of men and armaments. In October 1948, an astonishing three hundred thousand of Chiang's soldiers defected to Mao's side. The final showdown was near.

The China Hands had predicted that U.S. policy supporting the Generalissimo only would force Mao to turn to the Soviet Union. When Mao did exactly that, Americans believed he was a Soviet pawn, because the first assumption of the mirage was that China could not be reformed from within, only by outside Western forces. Not realizing that Mao's first choice of an ally had been the United States, Americans saw Mao's success as part of a worldwide Communist conspiracy emanating from Moscow.

In November of 1948 Chiang sent a "direct and urgent appeal" to Truman, warning that Mao's warriors were "within striking distance" of Shanghai and Nanking and asking for "speedy and increased military assistance" and "a firm statement of American policy in support of the cause for which my Government is fighting." Chiang contended that such a statement from Truman "would serve to bolster up the morale of the armed forces and the civilian population and would strengthen the Government's position."[13] But a memorandum prepared by the Joint Chiefs of Staff told Truman there was "now obviously grave doubt as to whether the arrival in China of any further military equipment for the Chinese National Government will buy any time at all. It might, in fact, have the opposite result in that such equipment might pass into the hands of victorious Communist forces."[14]

Mayling arrived in Washington at the end of 1948 with a demand for three billion dollars in aid. Truman had Mayling cool her heels for nine days before seeing her. (Like the British, Truman referred privately to Chiang as "Generalissimo Cash My-check.")[15] Truman later remembered,

> She came to the United States for some more handouts, I wouldn't let her stay at the White House like Roosevelt did. I don't think she liked it very much, but I didn't care one way or the other about what she liked and what she didn't like....
>
> I discovered after some time, that Chiang Kai-shek and the Madame and their families, the Soong family and the Kungs, were all thieves, every last one of them, the Madame and him included. And they stole seven hundred and fifty million dollars out of the 3.5 billion that we sent to Chiang. They stole it, and it's invested in real estate down in Sao Paolo and some right here in New York. And that's the money that was used and is still being used for the so-called China Lobby. I don't like that. I don't like that at all. And I don't want anything to do with people like that....[16]
>
> They wanted me to send in about five million Americans to rescue him [Chiang], but I wouldn't do it....He was as corrupt as they come. I wasn't going to waste one single American life to save him....They hooted and hollered and carried on and said I was soft on Communism...[but] I never changed my mind about Chiang and his gang. Every damn one of them ought to be in jail, and I'd like to live to see the day they are.[17]

In *The Last Empress*, Hannah Pakula wrote, "Most people assumed that Madame Chiang, having failed to get U.S. support, would turn around and go home, but she had another plan, involving settling down in the United States and strengthening the China Lobby, which she apparently believed to be at least partially responsible for the abrupt end to the country's generosity."[18] Mayling held meetings to pressure the U.S. government into reviving its support for Chiang. Wrote Pakula, "The Republicans took on the fight against the Communists as a moral cause; the military men were concerned about a future conflict with the USSR; and the churchmen embraced it as a struggle against the Antichrist in Asia."[19]

In 1948 Henry Stimson published his autobiography, *On Active Service in Peace and War,* coauthored by McGeorge Bundy, a young Harvard Wise Man. Unlike a mere mortal, who refers to him- or herself with the first-person pronoun *I,* the First Wise Man employed the third-person: "Stimson said...Stimson felt." Curiously, he did not mention his years of service as honorary chairman of the American Committee for Non-Participation in Japanese Aggression, through which position he so successfully convinced the majority of Americans that the U.S. could embargo Japan's oil and suffer no blowback. He also didn't mention the creation of a secret air force for Chiang Kai-shek or Dean Acheson's cutting off Japan's oil when Roosevelt was out of town. And while he devoted four pages to Army/Navy football games, the First Wise Man made no mention of the twentieth century's most successful revolutionary, Mao Zedong.

After its defeat, Japan was forced to return Taiwan (then commonly called Formosa) to China, and with American help, Chiang Kai-shek dispatched troops there to take over. Locals recently freed from Japan's yoke were quickly disillusioned: Chiang's officials took the best houses and over 90 percent of the important industries, and they replaced Taiwanese workers with mainlanders. Soon, Chiang's Taiwanese economy was in the same sorry shape as his Chinese one.

Beginning in 1947, local Taiwanese began to rebel against the heavy-handedness of Chiang's carpetbagging officials. Chiang's troops—mainland Chinese—flooded the streets. Bodies showing signs of gruesome torture soon lined the roadsides; many men had been castrated and had had their noses and ears sliced off.

In January of 1949, Chiang realized the game was up in mainland China, and he prepared to flee. But first he made a stop in Shanghai to transfer the government's gold reserves to Taiwan, an operation that took place late one February night after Chiang's soldiers had cordoned off the Bund, Shanghai's Wall Street. A file of coolies with bamboo poles across their backs balanced wrapped packages of gold bullion as Chiang absconded with the small portion of China's gold wealth that Ailing Soong had not yet extracted.

In her book *Shanghai*, Stella Dong wrote, "Chiang Kai-shek's henchmen made Shanghai's last weeks under Nationalist rule a nightmare of disorder and brutality." One American witnessed "the street execution of half a dozen captive students. Bound and kneeling, they had their brains blown out by Chiang's warriors before a great crowd of people."[20]

The ultimate incarnation of the China mirage was the American fantasy that Chiang's island of Taiwan was now the Republic of China. No one would ever recognize Bermuda as the seat of the British Empire, but with hardly the blink of an eye, Americans accepted that a tiny rock in the Pacific was now the rightful inheritor of a five-thousand-year-old legacy and that a few tens of millions on an island were the real Chinese, while the Five Hundred Million on the mainland were not.

Millions of American believers in the coming of a Christianized New China were shocked when the godless Mao Zedong stood triumphantly overlooking Tiananmen Square on October 1, 1949, and announced his rule from the Son of Heaven's traditional home. Standing near him was Chingling Soong, whose presence as Sun Yat-sen's widow added luster to Mao's claim on the Mandate of Heaven. After a century of his country's humiliation by foreign powers, Mao proclaimed that China would "never again be an insulted nation" now that the Chinese people had "stood up."[21]

For generations Americans had funneled a river of money from their collection plates across the Pacific to China as *Time, Life,* and *Fortune* magazines assured readers that China was about to come America's way. The United States had invested more money in backing Chiang than it had in developing the atom bomb. Then, just like

Mao Zedong, Tiananmen Square, 1949 (Everett Collection / Mondadori Portfolio)

that, China had been taken over by a pagan Communist who had recently been living in a cave.

Americans felt they had lost China, but they hadn't felt they'd lost anything when Russia had gone Communist. Then again, the Russian Orthodox Church did not have a direct connection to millions of American hearts the way the Protestant missionaries writing their fictions from China had, and there had been no Russia Lobby sloshing money into Washington's trough. Through the China Lobby's constant efforts, Chiang and Mayling had become the ultimate Noble Chinese Peasants. In contrast, few Americans knew of the Romanov family or cared when they were shot. Russia had never been considered America's, so it couldn't be lost. But the mirage held that China was destined to follow the American way, so America had now lost China.

When Mao Zedong claimed the Mandate, the chief Wise Man — Secretary of State Acheson — saw him as not a "real" Chinese, but as Moscow's puppet, writing, "The Communist leaders have foresworn their Chinese heritage and have publicly announced their subservience to a foreign power, Russia."[22]

Who lost China? Hell, *someone* must have; perhaps a Benedict Arnold — or a bunch of them. The Republicans taunted the Truman administration: "Stupidity at the top. Treason just below."[23]

Joseph McCarthy of Wisconsin was sworn in as a United States senator on January 3, 1947. In Washington, he was a bachelor far from home. Sometimes on Friday afternoons, McCarthy would take a taxi from his office to the airport, where a Kennedy family private plane would whisk him and Congressman John F. Kennedy to Hyannis Port for the weekend. As a frequent guest, McCarthy played touch football with Jack, Bobby, and Teddy, and he fancied Eunice. (His wedding present to Eunice Kennedy and R. Sargent Shriver was a silver cigarette box on which he had had inscribed, *To Eunice and Bob. From the one who lost. Joe McCarthy.*)[24] Catholic and conservative, Joe McCarthy, a young man on the make, listened attentively as the rich, Catholic, and conservative Joe Kennedy explained his strategy of accusing the Truman administration of losing China.

On January 30, 1949, thirty-one-year-old Representative Jack Kennedy foreshadowed McCarthyism in a speech in Salem, Massachusetts. In a city known for past witch hunts, Kennedy said,

> We almost knowingly entered into combat with Japan to preserve the independence of China.... Contrast this policy ... to the confused and vacillating policy which we have followed since that day.... This is the tragic story of China, whose freedom we once fought to preserve. What our young men had saved, our diplomats and our President have frittered away....

Our relationship with China since the end of the Second World War has been a tragic one, and it is of the utmost importance that we search out those who must bear the responsibility for our present predicament....The chief opposition to the accomplishment of our mission came from the American career diplomats, the embassy at Chungking, and the Chinese and Far Eastern divisions of the State Department.[25]

One year later, on February 9, 1950, Senator Joe McCarthy addressed a Republican Women's Club in Wheeling, West Virginia.

Today we are engaged in a final, all-out battle between communistic atheism and Christianity....As one of our outstanding historical figures once said, "When a great democracy is destroyed, it will not be because of enemies from without, but rather because of enemies from within...."

It has not been the less fortunate or members of minority groups who have been selling this Nation out, but rather those who have had all the benefits that the wealthiest nation on earth has had to offer—the finest homes, the finest college education, and the finest jobs in Government we can give.

This is glaringly true in the State Department. There the bright young men who are born with silver spoons in their mouths are the ones who have been the worst....

When Chiang Kai-shek was fighting our war, the State Department had in China a young man named John S. Service. His task, obviously, was not to work for the communization of China. Strangely, however, he sent official reports back to the State Department urging that we torpedo our ally Chiang Kai-shek—and stating, in effect, that communism was the best hope of China.

Later, this man—John Service...was picked up by the Federal Bureau of Investigation for turning over to the Communists secret State Department information. Strangely, however, he was never prosecuted....This man...was not only reinstated in the State Department but promoted....

This, ladies and gentlemen, gives you somewhat of a picture of the type of individuals who have been helping to shape our foreign policy. In my opinion, the State Department, which is one of the most important government departments, is thoroughly infested with Communists.

I have here in my hand 57 cases of individuals who would appear to be either card-carrying members or certainly loyal to the Communist Party, but who nevertheless are still helping to shape our foreign policy.[26]

Two weeks later, on April 30, the *New York Times* asked, "Who's feeding McCarthy his stuff?" The paper concluded, "That such a thing as a 'China Lobby' exists is indisputable in the minds of most observers... [it is] a loose conglomeration of persons and organizations which for various reasons are interested in China." The China Lobby drew its strength from people "who passionately believe American policy to be wrong; who think that American withdrawal from China has caused a needless and dangerous break in the dike against the spread of communism."[27] At the time, no one reflected that the China Lobby first took root during the flowering of the T. V. Soong–Franklin Roosevelt relationship in the early 1930s, and few were aware of how the lobby had manipulated FDR's blunder into the Pacific war and Truman's nonrecognition of Mao.

Senator McCarthy defended his sensational accusations for the first time in a speech before the American Society of Newspaper Editors. McCarthy's fearmongering focused on who lost China: "Communists and queers have sold 400 million Asiatic people into atheistic slavery and they now have the American people in a hypnotic trance, headed blindly toward the same precipice."[28]

John Service, John Davies, and John Carter Vincent had accurately predicted that Mao Zedong would rise and Chiang Kai-shek would fall, in direct contradiction to Americans' long-held belief in the coming of an Americanized and Christianized New China. After McCarthy's blasts, the State Department fired Service, Davies, and Vincent.

David Halberstam recounted how Henry Luce also served the China Lobby's interests during the McCarthy period:

> Luce allowed McCarthyism to take place, he created a vacuum in which the misinterpretation of events led to conspiracy theories. He had no sympathy for those men who had been right and were about to be sacrificed to the witch-hunters.... His publications formed a major obstacle to anyone trying to restore any reality to American Asian policy. He never really recognized Communist China and never accepted the verdict of history. At a personal level this might have been admirable — Harry Luce had not betrayed old friends, he had honored his father's memory — but at a journalistic level it was intensely dangerous. He was unbending. In the pages of *Time* Chiang had never slipped from power and never slipped from grace.[29]

In 1986 Walter Isaacson and Evan Thomas coauthored a book entitled *The Wise Men: Six Friends and the World They Made,* about Henry Stimson's ideological descendants, the officials most responsible for the creation of the post–World War II national security state. The six Wise Men were Dean Acheson, Charles Bohlen, Averell Harriman, George Kennan, Robert Lovett, and John McCloy, all of whom had served one or more U.S. presidents from Franklin Roosevelt to Lyndon Johnson and who first coalesced as a group under Harry Truman. Truman relied upon the Wise Men for foreign policy advice, and they became the architects of the Truman Doctrine, the Marshall Plan, and Cold War containment policy.

Isaacson and Thomas's book deals mostly with how the Wise Men contained the Soviet Union in Europe. Left out of their tale is the disastrous course the Wise Men pursued in Asia.

It began in what some refer to as the Age of Acheson, when, as undersecretary and then later secretary of state, Acheson influenced decision-making. "I had a constituency of one," Acheson said of his close relationship with President Harry Truman.[30] In his living room

Acheson displayed a photo of Henry Stimson.[31] Acheson's age would see the official who had thrust the U.S. into World War II lead the country into unnecessary wars in Korea and Vietnam.

Korea—due to its location—was the crucial keystone in North Asia. It was Japan's occupation of Korea that had allowed it to invade China. On August 10, 1945—the day after the second atomic bomb exploded over Nagasaki—Wise Man John McCloy divided Korea for the purposes of accepting the surrender of Japanese troops. He drew an imaginary line at the thirty-eighth parallel. Above the parallel would be a new country called North Korea dominated by Russia; below it would be the U.S. ally South Korea. No Wise Man thought to consult the Korean people about this division of their ancient land.

Koreans were even more outraged to learn that U.S. officials would govern South Korea with help from the Koreans' former Japanese colonial masters. North Koreans watched uneasily as South Koreans who had cooperated with the Japanese occupation now helped the United States gain influence on the Korean Peninsula. Koreans had just suffered forty years of Nazi-like domination by the Japanese. North Korean leader Kim Il Sung had begun his military career fighting the Japanese in the spring of 1932, and his government was first of all, and above all else, anti-Japanese.

A major concern of Dean Acheson's was reinvigorating the world economy after the devastation of World War II. In Europe, the U.S. would adopt a program of economic aid called the Marshall Plan; in Asia, it was known as the Policy for Asia, National Security Council document 48/2. According to NSC-48/2, Japan would become Asia's industrial economy, fired by U.S. companies. Washington would "connect up" other Asian economies to Japan's and keep them in subservient roles as suppliers to Japan's industrial machine and as markets for Japanese goods (thus isolating and containing China).[32] The Wise Men opposed the industrialization of the rest of Asia, the former and current colonies of Japan, the UK, Holland, the U.S., and France.

Instead, their plan called for Korea, Vietnam, and other Asian countries to be the supply/consumption machines within the U.S.-Japanese orbit. The American military would provide an umbrella of security for Japan and keep the other Asian countries in line.

The Wise Men didn't understand that their Policy for Asia looked to many Asians alarmingly like imperial Japan's recent attempts at empire. To them, it was as if the U.S. was green-lighting another era of Japanese dominance with American backing. When North Korean leaders realized that Washington wanted Japan to once again dominate Korea, they perceived a mortal threat.

The Wise Men's Policy for Asia was a blueprint for American disaster in post–World War II Asia, as it called for the U.S. military to enforce the Japan-centric model, a "for us or against us" policy designed to contain Mao Zedong. Bruce Cumings, one of the leading historians on Korea, wrote about the Policy for Asia, "The United States would now do something utterly unimagined at the end of World War II: it would prepare to intervene militarily against anti-colonial movements in East Asia — first Korea, then Vietnam, with the Chinese revolution as the towering backdrop."[33]

In Korea, the two sides skirmished, each repeatedly violating the other's borders. Acheson testified in secret to the Senate that the U.S. had drawn a line of containment in Korea and asked for funding to turn back Communism there. However, Congress and the Pentagon balked at spending Acheson's requested $600 million for Korea, which seemed too high compared to the $225 million for containment in Greece and Turkey that Congress had approved.

Dean Acheson published his memoir *Present at the Creation* in 1969. The title referred to the birth of the modern U.S. state, which he had done so much to midwife. Acheson recounts the founding of the CIA, the Defense Department, the NSA, the World Bank, and other organizations. But in his Pulitzer Prize–winning tome, the aging Wise Man didn't mention perhaps his biggest contribution to modern America: the secret policy that he as secretary of state had inspired and that reoriented the United States, changing it from a robust democracy with a small professional military into the militarized national security state it had become by the time he published his book. Acheson's fateful 1950 policy document was still classified top secret in 1969.

In 1950, despite the Marshall Plan and the Policy for Asia attempts at stimulating the global economy, the Wise Men saw that Germany and Japan were still not performing adequately, thus threatening to slow growth in the United States. Acheson analyzed the U.S. economy during World War II, when massive production of armaments for use around the world had provided a powerful stimulus. A good friend of English economist John Maynard Keynes, Acheson wondered if a huge Keynesian expansion of U.S. military spending could prime the worldwide pump.

Acheson's top secret policy was laid out in National Security Council document 68, or NSC-68, which called for something new in American history: an enormous U.S. military encircling the globe to protect the "war-making capabilities" of its allies, a euphemism referring to countries with resources that American industry needed to manufacture arms to contain Communism worldwide. The Constitution was written by men who feared the corrosive effects of a large standing army under a powerful executive, but with NSC-68, Acheson was tilting government funds away from domestic programs and toward a military stimulus.

President Truman signed NSC-68, but at that point it was only a Wise Men's wish list and had no congressional funding. Following U.S. tradition, Truman had drastically reduced the military's size after World War II. In 1945 the U.S. military had more than eleven million members and a sixty-billion-dollar budget. By 1948, Truman had trimmed this to fewer than a million members and a budget of thirteen billion.

North Korea crossed the thirty-eighth parallel in force on June 25, 1950. Cumings wrote, "The North Koreans attacked the South because of fears that Japan's industrial economy and its former position in Korea were being revived by recent changes in American policy."[34] For many North Korean soldiers, this fighting was the continuation of their recent war against the Japanese.

The Wise Men misinterpreted an incident in a small Asian civil war as a challenge to their global containment policy, incorrectly concluding that Moscow — working through Beijing and Pyongyang — had ordered the crossing, when it was only a North Korean action.

By this time the China Lobby had been assailing the Truman administration for months over losing China. The day after the North Korean crossing, Senator Styles Bridges, a China Lobby stalwart, said on the floor of the Senate, "Will we continue appeasement?... Now is the time to draw the line."[35] Senator George Malone said, "It is fairly clear that what happened in China and what is now happening in Korea were brought about deliberately by the advisers of the president [Roosevelt]... and by the advisers of the State Department since then."[36] Senator William Knowland (known as the Senator from Formosa) said, "If this nation is allowed to succumb to an overt invasion of this kind, there is little chance of stopping communism anywhere on the continent of Asia."[37]

In *The Wise Men,* Isaacson and Thomas wrote that Acheson "considered Asia to be a nuisance and a distraction."[38] Acheson had made eleven trips to Europe but couldn't be bothered to make one trip to Asia, and his decision-making showed his continuing tone-deafness about peoples across the Pacific. Isaacson and Thomas noted that "Acheson's great fear was that Korea was a fake, a diversionary move from a true Soviet onslaught in Western Europe."[39] When he heard the news of North Korea's move, Acheson withdrew to a room alone with a yellow legal pad and, according to Isaacson and Thomas, "scrawled little notes: What were the Soviets up to? Where else would they probe? Berlin? Greece? Turkey? Iran?"[40]

Acheson advised Truman to move quickly and commit troops to Korea without consulting Congress. "[Truman] did not want to slow down the process, and his constant struggles with the Congress over the issue of China and Chiang made him wary of dealing with his enemies in the Senate,"[41] David Halberstam wrote in *The Coldest Winter.* "The issue of China itself hovered over every decision."[42]

Acheson urged Truman not only to go to war in Korea with no congressional consultation,[43] but also to send covert military aid to the French in Indochina for their war against Ho Chi Minh. With no debate—and none was sought—a Wise Man, rattled by events in Asia he little understood, committed the U.S. to current and future wars. A few days later, on June 29, 1950, eight U.S. Air Force cargo planes flew to Asia with war matériel for the French, the beginning of America's long nightmare in Vietnam. (Truman secretly gave the French military more money to fight Ho Chi Minh in Asia than he publicly gave Paris under the Marshall Plan to promote democracy in Europe.)

Kim Il Sung had crossed the five-year-old thirty-eighth parallel—not an international boundary like that between Canada and U.S., but the Wise Men's imaginary line bisecting an ancient nation. Acheson did not comprehend the local antagonisms; he saw only advantage for his NSC-68 Keynesian military stimulus. He later observed, "June 25 removed many things from the realm of theory. Korea seemed to— and did—confirm NSC-68."[44] Martin Walker wrote in *The Cold War: A History,* "Without the war, the costly plans of NSC-68 would have faced an arduous uphill campaign."[45] Cumings wrote, "[Kim Il Sung's] invasion solved a number of critical problems for the Truman administration, and did wonders in building the American Cold War position on a world scale."[46] Acheson later told a class at Princeton University that Korea "came along and saved us."[47]

In bitter fighting, the North Korean army almost pushed the South Korean and American armies off the Korean Peninsula and into the sea, but the latter two regrouped and fought their way north, back to the thirty-eighth parallel.

Having forced the North Koreans to retreat to their original border, the Wise Men could have declared victory. But they wondered if a bold move against Communism was needed and would atone—at least symbolically—for the loss of China. The Wise Men decided to go beyond containing Communism and proceed to a rollback strategy, with U.S. troops crossing the border and marching into North Korea.

The possibility that the American army might cross the thirty-eighth parallel and invade a country on China's border got Mao Zedong's attention. The Wise Men assumed that Mao would *never* risk confronting the atomic-armed U.S. military, just as the First Wise Man had preached that Japan would not respond to an oil embargo. Though Mao's China was exhausted by decades of civil war, the U.S. military advancing to China's borders was an intolerable barbarian threat.

Korea was General Douglas MacArthur's responsibility. MacArthur was seventy years old now and a China Lobby favorite. (He shared the record of most appearances on *Time*'s cover—seven—with Chiang.) He had presided over Japan's surrender and had ruled the country as its temporary father-emperor. The old general had not stepped foot on the Asian mainland since 1905 and was sometimes delusional as he fanta-sized about New China.

MacArthur boasted that if Mao confronted the U.S. military, "[I will] deliver such a crushing defeat that it would be one of the decisive battles of the world—a disaster so great it would rock Asia and perhaps turn back Communism."[48] MacArthur, like the rest of the U.S. military establishment, completely missed the effectiveness of Mao's war strategies, continuing to believe that modern airpower could defeat Mao any day. MacArthur made bellicose threats about ways the United States might invade China, even suggesting attacking it with atomic bombs.

Returning to Washington after an August vacation in the Adirondacks, Acheson told Truman that MacArthur should be allowed to push north over the thirty-eighth parallel. Truman agreed with his Wise Man.

Just as he had with President Roosevelt in 1945, Mao reached out to President Truman. As his messenger, Mao chose K. M. Panikkar, the Indian ambassador in Beijing. A top Chinese military official informed Panikkar that Mao would act if American troops threatened China's border. Alarmed, Panikkar asked if Mao had fully evaluated the risks of confronting the mighty U.S. military. Reflecting Mao's thinking, the Chinese official told Panikkar: "We all know what we are in for, but at all costs American aggression has to be stopped. The Americans can bomb us, they can destroy our industries, but they cannot defeat us on land.... They may even drop atomic bombs on us. What then? They may kill a few million people. Without sacrifice a nation's independence cannot be upheld."[49]

On October 2, Chinese premier and foreign minister Zhou Enlai summoned Ambassador Panikkar to the foreign ministry. Zhou was somber and his message was simple. If the Americans crossed the thirty-eighth parallel, Mao would intervene. At 5:35 a.m. on October 3, a State Department official awakened Dean Acheson with Panikkar's message conveying Mao's warning. Acheson ridiculed the idea of Mao entering the conflict as the "mere vaporings of a panicky Panikkar."[50]

When MacArthur's troops crossed the thirty-eighth parallel, on October 9, 1950, the Wise Men assumed Mao would not be riled, yet when the North Koreans had violated that same border just months earlier, they themselves had judged it intolerable. As the U.S. — allied with Japan — marched toward China's border, Mao ordered hundreds of thousands of troops to confront them.

Though the Chinese had no airpower, they pounded the Americans on the ground in their first clashes. Mao's troops pushed MacArthur's forces out of North Korea within two weeks.

The irrational fear of worldwide Communism as a result of the Wise Men's misunderstanding of a small Asian civil war persuaded Congress to dramatically increase funding for the military. Martin Walker wrote,

> The first defense budget presented by President Truman after the war began was for $50 billion, the precise figure Acheson had hoped for. The US Army doubled, to over three million men. The number of Air Groups doubled to ninety-five, and were deployed to new bases in Britain, Libya, Morocco and

Saudi Arabia. Everything changed with Korea. American diplomacy, defense budgets and military reach exploded across the globe.[51]

Bruce Cumings concludes,

> The Korean War was the crisis that finally got the Japanese and West German economies growing strongly, and vastly stimulated the U.S. economy. American defense industries hardly knew that Kim Il Sung would come along and save them either, but he inadvertently rescued a bunch of big-ticket projects....[52]
>
> The Korean conflict [would transform] the United States into a very different country than it had ever been before: one with hundreds of permanent military bases abroad, a large standing army and a permanent national security state at home.[53]

If the Wise Men had not so bungled the U.S. relationship with China, John Service might have been able to telephone his friends in Beijing to sort things out before trouble erupted. But the mirage lived on. When Truman fired the Mao-beaten MacArthur, the China Lobby shouted that the American anti-Communist crusade in Asia had been undermined. Senator McCarthy snarled about the president, "The son of a bitch should be impeached."[54] In a speech to the Senate, McCarthy asked,

> How can we account for our present situation unless we believe that men high in this Government are concerting to deliver us to disaster? This must be the product of a great conspiracy, a conspiracy on a scale so immense as to dwarf any previous such venture in the history of man. A conspiracy of infamy so black that, when it is finally exposed, its principals shall be forever deserving of the maledictions of all honest men.[55]

In 1952, Democratic incumbent President Truman, having come from behind to win the 1948 election but now tarred by the powerful China Lobby with losing China and almost losing Korea, decided not to run again for president. The 1952 Republican Party's national convention featured a conga line of China Lobbyists, including Senator McCarthy, Ambassador Hurley, and General MacArthur.[56]

In a 1954 press conference, President Eisenhower spoke of the domino theory in terms of Vietnam—an idea that had initially entered Washington's collective consciousness during the Roosevelt administration:

> You have broader considerations that might follow what you would call the "falling domino" principle. You have a row of dominoes set up, you knock over the first one, and what will happen to the last one is the certainty that it will go over very quickly. So you could have a beginning of a disintegration that would have the most profound influences.[57]

Many know that Eisenhower handed his covert war against Fidel Castro to John Kennedy, whose CIA-led invasion of Cuba ran aground at the Bay of Pigs. Fewer link the 1960s killing of millions in Asia with the baton of misperceptions relayed from Roosevelt to Truman to Eisenhower and then onward to Presidents Kennedy, Johnson, and Nixon.

Ho Chi Minh was a brilliant political and military strategist committed to ending foreign domination of Vietnam, but Eisenhower saw him as a tool of international Communism. To contain Ho, Eisenhower created a Potemkin country—South Vietnam—that had never existed in history and, despite billions of dollars in U.S. aid, would fall after just two decades.

To lead his new Asian state, South Vietnam, Eisenhower anointed Ngo Dinh Diem president. Like Chiang, Diem was allied with the wealthy, who kept the peasants in near servitude. Like Chiang, Diem lacked popular support and ruled brutally through his military. And like Chiang, Diem enjoyed excellent press in the U.S., mostly because he was a Christian. (Eisenhower had chosen a Catholic to lead an overwhelmingly Buddhist country.)

The 1954 Geneva Accords ending the French-Vietnamese War called for free elections in Vietnam in 1956. Eisenhower-era Americans were told that the U.S. encouraged democratic elections in other countries, but the president secretly scuttled the Vietnamese vote because, as Ike later admitted, "It was generally conceded that had an election been held, Ho Chi Minh would have been elected Premier."[58] In the 1930s and 1940s Henry Luce had supported an Asian dictator whom he'd nicknamed Southern Methodist Chiang. In the 1950s Luce was for another Christian loser, this man dubbed the Tough Miracle Man of Vietnam. The American press, still mostly unaware of Asian affairs, followed Luce's line. *Newsweek* magazine: "Ngo Dinh Diem is living proof of what is often called a miracle...proof of what an authentic patriot...can accomplish." The *New York Herald Tribune:* "The Miracle-Maker from Asia—Diem of South Vietnam." The *New York Journal-American:* "How did the miracle of South Viet Nam happen?...The story is largely written in the ascetic personality of Ngo Dinh Diem." Edward R. Murrow: Diem "has made so much progress in the past six months that some people use the overworked word 'miracle' in describing improvements in South Vietnam."[59]

Many believed that the Chinese Mandate of Heaven had moved to Mao Zedong by 1943, the year FDR hosted Mayling in the White House and posed for photographs with Chiang in Cairo. Likewise, by 1957 the Vietnamese Mandate was clearly Ho Chi Minh's, and President Diem's only base of support was Dwight Eisenhower.

On the hot and muggy day of May 8, 1957, television viewers witnessed a historic event: President Eisenhower at Washington National Airport, squinting into the sun, looking up as his personal plane, the *Columbine III,* brought President Diem of South Vietnam for a visit.

Eisenhower greeted Diem, escorted him down the ranks of his honor guard, and said into a microphone, "Mr. President, it is indeed an honor for any American to invite you to this country. You have exemplified in your part of the world patriotism of the highest order."[60] Eisenhower and Diem rode into Washington smiling at each other in an open limousine as crowds cheered.

Eisenhower lavished attention on his miracle man: a private White House meeting and a state dinner, and he attended a dinner in the South Vietnamese embassy hosted by Diem. Diem also addressed a joint session of Congress and the National Press Club.

Just as the Protestant China Lobby had propagandized for Chiang, a

*President Eisenhower greeting President Diem, Washington National Airport,
May 8, 1957 (Courtesy Everett Collection)*

Catholic Vietnam lobby—called the American Friends of Vietnam—
beat the drums for Diem. When he addressed Congress, his script,
authored by the Vietnam lobby, made complicated matters easy to understand. He compared the CIA-instigated exodus of Christians from North
to South Vietnam to the pilgrims on the *Mayflower*. Republican senator
Jacob Javits dubbed Diem "one of the real heroes of the free world."[61]

In New York, an estimated 250,000 people cheered Diem in a
parade from lower Broadway to City Hall. That evening the American
Friends of Vietnam threw a glittering banquet to honor him; it was
hosted by Henry Luce and attended by Senator John F. Kennedy and
Eleanor Roosevelt, among other luminaries. Luce said, "President Ngo
Dinh Diem is one of the greatest statesmen of Asia and of the world....
In honoring him we pay tribute to the eternal values which all free
men everywhere are prepared to defend with their lives."[62]

Diem's eleven-day visit continued, and he traveled on to Michigan, Tennessee, California, and Hawaii. Just as with Chiang, Diem became the only Vietnamese Americans knew: a Christian miracle man who would plant the American flag in Asia.

John Service, John Davies, and other China Hands had been hounded out of the State Department, so they couldn't warn President Eisenhower that history was repeating itself. Instead of offering Ike advice on avoiding Roosevelt's missteps in Asia, John Service was selling steam equipment in New York, and John Davies was manufacturing furniture in Lima, Peru.

The 1950s saw Americans knowing less about the Middle Kingdom than ever. Henry Luce and his Time-Life empire didn't dispatch anyone to China for a firsthand view. Most of what Americans learned about China in this period were slanted stories disseminated from Taiwan by the CIA. In 1957, *Time* reported that journalist William Worthy, a reporter for the *Baltimore Afro-American,* "became the first American reporter to enter China in seven years."[63] When Worthy returned to the U.S., President Eisenhower's administration took his passport away.[64]

In 1958, author Edgar Snow observed that there was not one Chinese-speaking officer remaining in the State Department.

The China Lobby, first seeded by Charlie Soong in 1905 and planted in the Oval Office by T. V. Soong in 1933, had great staying power. In 1960, author Ross Koen was getting ready to publish his book *The China Lobby* when shadowy yet powerful China Lobbyists forced Koen's publisher, Macmillan, to withdraw the exposé. It was allowed to emerge only fourteen long years later, as a paperback.

All of the 1960s presidential candidates had witnessed the who-lost-China political knife fights in the Truman administration earlier in their careers. John Kennedy, Richard Nixon, Lyndon Johnson, Barry Goldwater, and Hubert Humphrey had been young senators then, and all understood the political peril in losing an Asian nation. In his book *The Best and the Brightest,* David Halberstam wrote that when Kennedy and Johnson considered their options in Asia, there were no experienced China Hands available to guide them:

> That was the terrible shadow of the McCarthy period.... All of the China experts, the Asia hands...had had their careers destroyed with the fall of China. The men who gave advice on Asia were either Europeanists or men transferred from the Pentagon....[65]
>
> Had there been some high Washington officials who had gone through the China experience and survived the aftermath, they would immediately have recognized [the problems in Vietnam].... But people in the administration either did not know what had happened in China, or in a few cases, they knew but desperately wanted to avoid a repetition of it.[66]

A few months into the Kennedy administration, Edgar Snow came calling on Dean Rusk, who had become secretary of state. Snow had just returned from China, where he'd discerned that Mao Zedong — whom he had known for over twenty years — was interested in relations with the United States. Here was Mao once again extending his hand in friendship, but Rusk met with Snow for only ten unreceptive minutes. So it would be.

By the 1960s, Henry Luce had been wrong, wrong, and wrong about Asia for four decades. Now Luce sat knee to knee with JFK and LBJ to push his father's missionary dream. Luce's sister later recalled, "Henry was always looking for the opportunity to overthrow the Communist regime in China. He knew that the United States could not simply declare war on the Communists, but he thought that the wars that the Communists started could give us the opportunity to go to China. Part of him really wanted the Korean War to become an American war with China, and he talked about Vietnam the same way."[67]

Two Catholic presidents had opposed the insertion of American combat troops into Vietnam's civil conflict — John F. Kennedy and Ngo Dinh Diem. They were both assassinated within weeks of each other in November of 1963. Two days after JFK's murder, the new U.S. president, Lyndon Baines Johnson, met in the White House with the U.S. ambassador to South Vietnam, Henry Cabot Lodge, a rock-ribbed Republican and a China Lobby man. When Ambassador Lodge walked into his office, Johnson blurted out, "I am not going to lose Vietnam. I am not going to be the President who saw Southeast Asia go the way China went."

Johnson called his friend newspaper publisher John Knight:

JOHNSON: What do you think we ought to do in Vietnam?
KNIGHT: I never thought we belonged there. Now that's a real tough one now, and I think President Kennedy thought at one time we should never, that we were overcommitted in that area.
JOHNSON: Well, I opposed it in '54. But we're there now, and there's only one of three things you can do. One is run and let the dominoes start falling over. And God Almighty, what they said about us leaving China would just be warming up, compared to what they'd say now.[68]

Johnson telephoned his longtime political ally Senator Mike Mansfield, a fellow Democrat and the current holder of LBJ's former post as Senate majority leader. Mansfield was away from his office when the president called, so Johnson left a message saying, "We do not want another China in Vietnam." Mansfield responded to the president's fear of "another China" in a memo:

I would respectfully add to this observation: Neither do we want another Korea. It would seem that a key (but often overlooked) factor in both situations was a tendency to bite off more than we were prepared in the end to chew. We tended to talk ourselves out on a limb with overstatements of our purpose and commitment only to discover in the end that there were not sufficient American interests to support with blood and treasure a desperate final plunge. Then, the questions followed invariably: "Who got us into this mess?" "Who lost China?" etc.[69]

Johnson's national security adviser was McGeorge Bundy, a well-connected and highly credentialed Wise Man. McGeorge's father had worked for Henry Stimson, who later honored the Bundy family by choosing McGeorge to cowrite his autobiography. In the early 1950s, Bundy had worked clandestinely with the CIA, and in 1953, at the age of thirty-four, he was appointed dean of the faculty of arts and sciences at Harvard, the youngest in Harvard's history. To top it off, Bundy's wife, Mary, was the daughter of the leading Wise Man, Dean Acheson, upon whom McGeorge relied for advice.

National security adviser Bundy—who kept a framed photo of Henry Stimson on his desk—disagreed with Senator Mansfield's memo. Acheson's son-in-law warned LBJ "as an ex-historian" that "the political damage to Truman and Acheson from the fall of China arose because most Americans came to believe that we could and should have done more than we did to prevent it. This is exactly what would happen now if we should seem to be the first to quit in Saigon."[70]

Henry Stimson had been almost clueless regarding Mao Zedong's long rise, and Dean Acheson, McGeorge Bundy, Henry Kissinger, and

McGeorge Bundy and Lyndon Johnson. Bundy kept a framed photo of the First Wise Man on his desk. (LBJ Library photo by Yoichi Okamoto)

many other Wise Men never understood Ho Chi Minh's strategy to beat them, which was based on Vietnam's two-thousand-year history of expelling invaders, a well-documented chronicle of military triumphs against foreigners. The Wise Men worried about Mao Zedong toppling Asian dominoes instead.

In 1963, in a televised interview, President Kennedy was asked about the domino theory. Kennedy responded, "I believe it. I believe it…China is so large, looms so high just beyond the frontiers, that if South Vietnam went, it would not only give them an improved geographic position for a guerrilla assault on Malaya, but would also give the impression that the wave of the future in southeast Asia was China and the Communists. So I believe it."[71]

Secretary of Defense Robert McNamara was typical of the men who ran national security: a Harvard graduate (in his case, Harvard Business School) and a Europe-focused Wise Man. In 1964 the domino theory became formalized as U.S. policy when McNamara wrote National Security Action Memorandum 288:

> We seek an independent non-Communist South Vietnam… unless we can achieve this objective…almost all of Southeast Asia will probably fall under Communist dominance.[72]

While Johnson told the public that the object of the fighting was an "independent, non-Communist South Vietnam," the president was reading secret memos from McNamara, who wrote that U.S. objectives in Vietnam were in "support of a long-run United States policy to contain China":

> China — like Germany in 1917, like Germany in the West and Japan in the East in the late 30s, and like the USSR in 1947 — looms as a major power threatening to undercut our importance and effectiveness in the world and, more remotely but more menacingly, to organize all of Asia against us.[73]

Johnson again expressed his who-lost-China fears:

> If I don't go in now and they show later I should have gone, then they'll be all over me in Congress. They won't be talking

about my civil rights bill, or education and beautification. No, sir, they'll push Vietnam up my ass every time. Vietnam. Vietnam. Vietnam. Right up my ass.[74]

In 1968, Lyndon Johnson became the second incumbent Democratic president to not run for reelection because of an Asian domino.

In 1973, as America withdrew from Vietnam in defeat, sixty-year-old Archimedes Patti asked the CIA if he could see the reports he had written from Hanoi about Ho Chi Minh in 1945 as an OSS officer. They were still tightly wrapped in Julia Child's burlap, unread by the Wise Men. Patti observed,

> In my opinion the Vietnam War was a great waste. There was no need for it to happen in the first place. At all. None whatsoever....During all the years of the Vietnam War no one ever approached me to find out what had happened in 1945....In all the years that I spent in the Pentagon, in the Department of State and in the White House, never was I approached by anyone in authority.[75]

Many years later, former secretary of defense McNamara explained why the Wise Men had so little understanding of events in Asia:

> Our government lacked experts for us to consult to compensate for our ignorance. When the Berlin crisis occurred in 1961 and during the Cuban Missile Crisis in 1962, President Kennedy was able to turn to senior people...who knew the Soviets intimately. There were no senior officials in the Pentagon or State Department with comparable knowledge of Southeast Asia.... The irony of this gap was that it existed largely because the top East Asian and China experts in the State Department—John Paton Davies, John Stewart Service, and John Carter Vincent— had been purged during the McCarthy hysteria of the 1950s. Without men like these to provide sophisticated, nuanced insights we, certainly I, badly misread China's objectives and mistook its bellicose rhetoric to imply a drive for regional hege-

mony. We also totally underestimated the nationalist aspect of
Ho Chi Minh's movement. We saw him first as a Communist
and only second as a Vietnamese nationalist.[76]

The Chiang-Chennault illusion that American airpower could have
dramatic effects on the Asian mainland had long legs. Harvard Wise
Men McGeorge Bundy, Robert McNamara, and Henry Kissinger
dropped more bombs on Asia than the U.S. military had worldwide in
all of World War II, yet they lost.

American airpower in Asia was defeated by the same simple and
relatively cheap defense that Mao Zedong had employed: the people
went underground. The most heavily bombed country in the world is
Laos, which was attacked hour after hour for a decade by U.S. bombing raids. In 2011 I toured the northern mountain strongholds where
Laotian Communists had waited out the American air assault. Many
thousands of people had been comfortably housed in enormous cav-
erns, and trucks had rumbled along internal roads connecting massive
supply areas. The underground theater had a huge stone stage and up
to two thousand audience members could sit on polished slabs of stone.
Theatergoers remembered enjoying elaborate stage performances as
American bombs exploded against the rocks outside. When the Americans eventually stopped bombing, the Communists emerged from
their mountain haven and took control of Laos.

The United States dropped 2 million tons of bombs on the combined European and Pacific theaters in World War II, but more than
three times as much — 6.7 million tons — on Southeast Asia.[77] McNamara later estimated that the U.S. had killed 1.2 million Vietnamese
civilians.[78] The U.S. bombing killed, maimed, or made homeless tens
of millions of Vietnamese, Laotians, and Cambodians.

In 2004, a much older Robert McNamara admitted to the *Harvard
Business School Alumni Magazine* that the validity of the domino theory "was never debated at the government's highest levels."[79]

Chapter 13

THE CHINA MIRAGE

If the United States in 1945 had been able to... shed some of its illusions
about China, to understand what was happening in that country, and to
adopt a realistic policy in America's own interests, Korea and Vietnam
would probably never have happened.... We would not still be confronted
with an unsolvable Taiwan problem.... And Mao's China, having come to
power in a different way and not thrust into isolation by a hostile West,
might be quite a different place.
—John Service[1]

Harvard's Theodore Roosevelt told Harvard's Baron Kaneko that he should use the bully pulpit of the Harvard Club to convince the American public that Japan deserved to colonize Korea. Harvard's T. V. Soong — recommended by Harvard's Felix Frankfurter — sold a secret air war in Asia to Harvard's Franklin Delano Roosevelt, who tasked Harvard's Thomas Corcoran to run the covert operation. Theodore White later recalled that his Harvard degree carried him further in Chungking than it would have in Boston and that the Harvard Club of China had a larger proportion of high government officials than the Harvard Club in Washington.

In the 1960s, McGeorge Bundy and Henry Kissinger of Harvard

served as national security advisers to three presidents and recommended massive bombing in Vietnam. (Bundy was such an all-knowing Wise Man that he authored the initial plans that called for bombing Ho Chi Minh into submission without even visiting Vietnam.)

Within the national security apparatus was a brilliant Harvard graduate named Daniel Ellsberg. By 1971 Ellsberg decided that the United States' bombing of Vietnam was not effective and was wrong. He then risked his freedom by using his top secret clearance to make unauthorized photocopies of a secret Defense Department study documenting presidential deceptions from Presidents Truman through Johnson. If Ellsberg made these Pentagon papers public, he would be in legal jeopardy, so he traveled back to Cambridge to seek assistance from Harvard Law School professor Jim Vorenberg. The two men sat in Vorenberg's living room and, after pleasantries, Ellsberg revealed his evidence of executive war crimes and his belief that in a democracy, the public had a right to know.

> [Vorenberg] suddenly held up a hand and said, "I have to stop you right now. I'm afraid I can't take part in this discussion any further."
>
> "Pardon me?"
>
> "You seem to be describing plans to commit a crime. I don't want to hear any more about it. As a lawyer I can't be a party to it."

Ellsberg then leaped out of his chair and said, "I've been talking to you about seven thousand pages of documentation of crimes: war crimes, crimes against the peace, mass murder. Twenty years of crimes under four presidents. And every one of those presidents had a Harvard professor at his side, telling him how to do it and how to get away with it."[2]

In the 1940s Mao Zedong declared it was important for America and China to be friends, that the United States and China were a much better fit than Russia and China, and that both sides would benefit from the combination of U.S. technological know-how and skilled Chinese manpower. A generation later, President Richard Nixon—motivated by the American quagmire in Vietnam and competition with Russia—came to a similar conclusion.

In 1971 Nixon announced his upcoming journey to the Middle Kingdom, and many turned to the banished China Hands, the last American officials who had had talks with Mao Zedong, back in the caves of Yan'an. One week after Nixon's announcement, John Service and John Davies appeared before the Senate Foreign Relations Committee. Service joked, "This is the first Senate meeting where I have appeared without need of counsel."[3] Senator William Fulbright recalled that the China Hands had paid a heavy price for bucking the mirage: "It is a very strange turn of fate that you gentlemen who reported honestly about the conditions in China were so persecuted because you were honest about it."[4] After their Senate hearings, the China Hands went from the doghouse to the spotlight. Service observed, "Even *Time* magazine just fell over itself to be friendly."[5]

Service traveled to China at the invitation of Zhou Enlai, the premier of the People's Republic. In Beijing, Service met secretly with Henry Kissinger. Kissinger was excited by Service's insights and hinted about a meeting between Service and Nixon. But the invitation never came. As Lynne Joiner wrote in *Honorable Survivor,* her insightful book about John Service, "Years later a former aide explained... they had to be extremely careful not to inflame the China Lobby."[6]

After he returned from China, where he saw Zhou Enlai and other friends from their days in Yan'an, Service testified to the Senate again:

> My recent visit to China convinces me that the root of the current Chinese reality may be found in what we reported from Yan'an in 1944.... I think that our involvement in Vietnam, our insistence on the need to contain China and to prevent what we thought was the spread of Communist influence in Southeast Asia, was based very largely on our misunderstanding and our lack of knowledge of the Chinese, the nature of the Chinese Communist movement, and the intention of their leaders. We assumed that they were an aggressive country, and I don't

John Service and Zhou Enlai (Courtesy Service Family)

believe that they really have been, and, therefore, I think that we got into Vietnam largely, as I say, through the misinterpretation and misfounded fear of China.[7]

For centuries, foreign devils had journeyed to Beijing to pay homage to the man who possessed the Mandate of Heaven. On February 21, 1972, Mao Zedong welcomed President Nixon to his library, where they sat in overstuffed chairs with spittoons at their feet. Now the symbiotic economic cooperation between the U.S. and China would begin, just as Mao had suggested to John Service twenty-seven years earlier.[8]

Richard Nixon and Mao Zedong. A generation after Mao had suggested it, the two countries would now combine U.S. technological know-how with China's motivated workers. (Courtesy Everett Collection)

In 1973, the American Foreign Service Association (a professional association of the United States Foreign Service) invited John Service and John Davies to the State Department for a luncheon in their honor. The AFSA president recalled, "The luncheon was needed to convince people in the department that McCarthyism was really dead."[9] Two hundred fifty people filled the auditorium and, in another room, three hundred watched on a closed-circuit television feed as speakers, including the historian Barbara Tuchman, praised Service and Davies. The tall, white-haired Service recalled the lesson he had learned about basing American foreign policy on a manufactured domestic mirage:

> There are still countries . . . where the situation is not unlike that
> in China during the 1940s. If we keep ourselves in ignorance

and out of touch with new popular movements and potentially revolutionary situations, we may find ourselves again missing the boat.... The measure of the need for such reporting is not popular sentiment in the United States as reflected in some segments of the press, or by some Congressional committees not charged with foreign relations...the legacy of Senator Joe McCarthy still needs, in some respects, to be shed.[10]

The luncheon was not an official State Department affair, however. Secretary of State William Rogers and national security adviser Henry Kissinger did not attend. It was 1973—forty years since T. V. Soong had used Felix Frankfurter to penetrate the Roosevelt administration— and the China Lobby still had political punch.

On April 30, 1975, I was a twenty-one-year-old sometime college student back home visiting my parents in Antigo, Wisconsin. A now-famous news photograph appeared for the first time that day; I'm sure that John Bradley, my fifty-three-year-old father, noticed it. All adult Americans probably did.

The photo depicted, according to its UPI caption, "A U.S. helicopter evacuating employees of the U.S. Embassy." I left Antigo a few days later for an Asian journey that would take me to Japan, Hong Kong, Taiwan, Thailand, Nepal, India, Pakistan, Afghanistan, Iran, and Turkey. I never discussed this photo with my father, who passed in 1994.

I wonder what John Bradley—whose iconic 1945 Iwo Jima image symbolized U.S. military victory—thought when just a generation later he saw this photo of American defeat. And what would he say now if he learned that the reality in Saigon that day was very different from what he was allowed to know back in Wisconsin?

In the Paris Peace Accords of 1973, the United States had agreed to withdraw its troops from Vietnam, so a U.S. military helicopter evacuating the U.S. embassy two years later appeared to be a legitimate, passive operation, rescuing embassy dependents from the embassy's roof.

This historic image was shot by news photographer Hubert Van Es, who later recounted that when he sent it from Saigon's post office to

April 29, 1975, Saigon, South Vietnam: symbol of American defeat in Asia. This photo shows a CIA Air America helicopter atop a CIA apartment building. Air America was the outgrowth of the secret executive air arm started by Franklin Delano Roosevelt in the winter of 1940–41 to save New China. (© Bettmann/CORBIS)

UPI's Tokyo headquarters, "for the caption, I wrote very clearly that the helicopter was taking evacuees off the roof of a downtown Saigon building." But in Tokyo—then as now a key node in the CIA's Asian operations—someone, no one knows who, changed the caption to: "A U.S. helicopter evacuating employees of the U.S. Embassy." Van Es observed thirty years later: "My efforts to correct the misunderstanding were futile, and eventually I gave up. Thus one of the best-known images of the Vietnam War shows something other than what almost everyone thinks it does."[11]

The apartment building at 22 Gia Long Street in today's Ho Chi Minh City still stands.[12] Senior CIA managers had lived there in 1975, and it was they and their families who were fleeing. The helicopter was also intentionally misidentified; it did not belong to the U.S. military but rather to the executive branch's secret air force, Air America.

Air America is another legacy of Franklin Roosevelt's secret executive air war in Asia run by Claire Chennault and Thomas Corcoran. In 1947 Chennault and Corcoran talked the CIA into purchasing China Air Transport. (Unknown is the extent of the Soong family's continuing financial involvement.) In early October of 1948, CAT flew its first mission, a CIA effort to support the crumbling Soong-Chiang regime.

Later, the CIA rebranded CAT as the airline Air America, based out of Chiang's New China on Taiwan.

Today, the president of the United States commands a private CIA air force. It all began when FDR went around General George Marshall, listened to the Chiang-Chennault siren song, and created a secret executive air force in Asia.

There are remarkable parallels regarding events in Asia during the presidencies of Theodore Roosevelt and Franklin Delano Roosevelt. Both presidents saw Japan launch surprise naval attacks. Theodore Roosevelt had considered the Japanese to be good Asians in 1904, but when Japan repeated its strategy thirty-seven years later, Franklin said it was a day of infamy.

Both Roosevelts would shape America's relations with Asia, believing that China was destined to be changed by Christian and American influences. Both made their Asian policies in secret, consulting neither their State Departments nor those few men around them knowledgeable about Asia. A Harvard-educated Japanese baron guided Teddy's approach. A Harvard-educated Chinese financier shared sandwiches with Franklin in the Oval Office and convinced him that an Americanized New China was near.

The Roosevelt cousins' attitudes toward Asia continued to ripple throughout the twentieth century and into the twenty-first. Today the executive branch dispatches troops overseas without congressional declarations of war. In 1900, Teddy cheered from the sidelines as the first U.S. troops ever dispatched to Asia without consulting Congress landed on the shores of China. Today the executive branch uses deadly drones with almost no congressional oversight and no judicial complaint.

Some may resist the uncomfortable historical connections between Teddy and Pearl Harbor; they may not think that FDR has anything to do with the later domestic political pressure on presidents not to lose an Asian country. After all, Theodore tossed Korea to the Japanese over a century ago, and it has been seventy years since Franklin chose Chiang over Mao. And while American historians do their best to whitewash the Roosevelts' disasters, memories are long in Asia.[13]

American misunderstanding of China caused the nation to support Southern Methodist Chiang, bring on a world war that didn't have to be, oppose the bandit Mao, and go on to fight two bloody Asian wars. About one hundred thousand Americans died in World War II in the Pacific. About fifty-six thousand Americans died in Korea, and another fifty-eight thousand in Vietnam. The total cost of America's wars in Asia is staggering. Millions of lives terminated, trillions of dollars devoted to rifles, airplanes, and napalm rather than to roads, schools, and hospitals. America's social fabric was stretched and then torn by the latter two Asian wars, which challenged its citizens' belief that their country was a beacon of freedom.

Perhaps America's most costly diplomatic mistake was the Chinese Exclusion Act.[14] If Americans had accepted Chinese people into their mosaic then, the United States would have had many more Americanized Chinese as citizens, ensuring a strong bridge of understanding across the Pacific. If the bridge had not been weakened in 1882, perhaps John Bradley would not have had to listen to his buddies scream to death on Iwo Jima in 1945. Perhaps one of his sons—my eldest brother, Steve Bradley—would not have been almost killed in Vietnam in 1968. Perhaps two hundred thousand Americans would not have died in Asian wars. Perhaps a wider and sturdier Pacific bridge is now a good idea.

Theodore Roosevelt and Franklin Delano Roosevelt were neither the first nor the last to imagine New China. There are still among us many Americans who, like Warren Delano, Henry Stimson, Pearl Buck, Henry Luce, Claire Chennault, and Joseph McCarthy, feel the urge to Americanize Asia. After all, the dream is as old as the Republic, a myth that took root when the United States was newly born. From those early days until now, America has dispatched its hopeful sons and daughters to faraway Asia in search of a mirage that never was. And never will be.

COPYRIGHT
ACKNOWLEDGMENTS

ACKNOWLEDGMENTS

Writing a book is an adventure. To begin with, it is a toy and an amusement; then it becomes a mistress, and then it becomes a master, and then a tyrant. The last phase is that just as you are about to be reconciled to your servitude, you kill the monster, and fling him out to the public.
— *Winston Churchill*[1]

Thank you to Reagan Arthur, Kate Barry, Don Belanger, Alison Bradley, Mark Bradley, Fred Branfman, Chris Cannon, Kangyan Chen, Shirley Chen, Victoria Chow, Frederick Courtright, Catherine Cullen, Nicole Dewey, Will Di Novi, Zoë Eager, Max and Sarah Eisikovic, Lisa Erickson, Heather Fain, Dr. Tina Miao Hall, Owen Laster, Kenneth Leong, Gary McManis, Ying Ni, Miriam Parker, Michael Pietsch, Liz Seramur, Robert Service, Michael Sieberg, Geoff Shandler, Allie Sommer, and Ashlee Wu.

Asya Muchnick, Tracy Roe, and Betsy Uhrig edited this book with consummate skill. The reader will not recognize their critical contributions, but I will always remember.

Eric Simonoff was instrumental in shaping the concept, and he provided invaluable guidance throughout.

ACKNOWLEDGMENTS

I honor my father for giving me my focus on America's relationship with Asia. I thank my children—Michelle, Alison, Ava, and Jack—for their love and support.

James Bradley
December 2014

NOTES

EPIGRAPH

1. John Service, *Lost Chance in China: The World War II Dispatches of John S. Service,* ed. Joseph W. Esherick (New York: Random House, 1974), 372–73.

INTRODUCTION

1. Kentaro Kaneko, "A 'Japanese Monroe Doctrine' and Manchuria," *Contemporary Japan* 1 (June 1932).
2. Excerpts from the joint press conference with Madame Chiang Kai-shek, February 19, 1943, American Presidency Project; available at http://www.presidency.ucsb.edu/ws/?pid=16366.
3. Sumner Welles, *Seven Decisions That Shaped History* (New York: Harper and Brothers, 1951), 68.
4. Raymond Moley, *After Seven Years* (New York: Harper and Brothers, 1939), 93–95.
5. Christine M. Totten, "Remembering Sara Delano Roosevelt on Her 150th Anniversary," *Rendezvous* (Winter 2005): 2.
6. China statement of Hon. John F. Kennedy of Massachusetts, extension of remarks of Hon. George J. Bates of Massachusetts in the House of Representatives, Monday, February 21, 1949, *Congressional Record.*

CHAPTER 1: OLD CHINA, NEW CHINA

1. Arthur Henderson Smith, *Chinese Characteristics* (New York: Fleming H. Revell, 1894), 325, 330.
2. Geoffrey C. Ward, *Before the Trumpet: Young Franklin Roosevelt 1882–1905* (New York: Harper and Row, 1985), 352.
3. J. Mason Gentzler, *Changing China: Readings in the History of China from the Opium War to the Present* (New York: Praeger, 1977), 25.
4. These buildings were called factories, but to avoid confusion I refer to them as warehouses.

5. Frederic Wakeman Jr., "The Canton Trade in the Opium War," in *The Cambridge History of China,* vol. 10, *Late Ch'ing, 1800–1911,* ed. John K. Fairbank (New York: Cambridge University Press, 1978), 172.

6. Carl A. Trocki, *Opium, Empire, and the Global Political Economy: A Study of the Asian Opium Trade, 1750–1950* (New York: Routledge, 1999), 52.

7. Jacques M. Downs, *The Golden Ghetto: The American Commercial Community at Canton and the Shaping of American China Policy, 1784–1844* (Cranbury, NJ: Associated University Presses, 1997), 335.

8. In 1834, Howqua estimated his fortune at $26 million. (I've spelled Howqua's name with a *w,* as most of the American traders at the time favored that spelling.)

9. Ward, *Before the Trumpet,* 71.

10. The government official with a New York City Chinatown statue who was mentioned in the introduction is Commissioner Lin.

11. Fordham University, *Modern History Sourcebook,* Commissioner Lin, Letter to Queen Victoria, 1839; available at http://www.fordham.edu/halsall/mod/1839lin2.asp.

12. Timothy Brook and Bob Tadashi Wakabayashi, eds., *Opium Regimes: China, Britain, and Japan, 1839–1952* (Berkeley: University of California Press, 2000), 6.

13. John Quincy Adams, "Lecture on the War with China, Delivered Before the Massachusetts Historical Society, December 1841," *Chinese Repository* 11 (1842): 281.

14. Martin Booth, *Opium: A History* (New York: St. Martin's Press, 1996), 141.

15. Downs, *The Golden Ghetto,* 265.

16. Ibid., 81.

17. Rita Halle Kleeman, *Gracious Lady: The Life of Sara Delano Roosevelt* (New York: D. Appleton-Century, 1935), 60.

18. R. J. C. Butow, "A Notable Passage to China—Myth and Memory in FDR's Family History, Part 2," *Prologue* 31, no. 3 (Fall 1999).

CHAPTER 2: WIN THE LEADERS; WIN CHINA

1. Pearl S. Buck, "The Secret of China's Victory," in *China As I See It,* ed. Theodore F. Harris (New York: John Day, 1970), 146.

2. Smith, *Chinese Characteristics,* 325.

3. Ibid., 329–30.

4. John Barrow, "American Institutions of Higher Learning in China, 1945–1925," *Higher Education* 4 (February 1, 1948): 121–24.

5. Charles Denby, written in 1895, *Papers Relating to the Foreign Relations of the United States, Japan: 1931–1941* (Washington, DC: Government Printing Office, 1943), 2: 198. Hereafter cited as *FRUS.*

6. Marilyn Blatt Young, *The Rhetoric of Empire: American China Policy, 1895–1901* (Cambridge, MA: Harvard University Press, 1968), 221.

7. S. Wells Williams, *The Middle Kingdom* (New York: Charles Scribner's Sons, 1904), 2: 359.

8. Sherwood Eddy, *Pathfinders of the World Missionary Crusade* (Freeport, NY: Books for Libraries Press, 1969), 50.

9. Denby, *FRUS,* 197.
10. The exact quote is "Win the leaders and we win the Empire"; quoted in Jerry Israel, *Progressivism and the Open Door: America and China, 1905–1921* (Pittsburgh: University of Pittsburgh Press, 1971), 19.
11. Ibid., 122.
12. Paul A. Varg, *Missionaries, Chinese, and Diplomats: The American Protestant Missionary Movement in China, 1890–1952* (Princeton, NJ: Princeton University Press, 1958), 68.
13. B. A. Garside, *One Increasing Purpose: The Life of Henry Winters Luce* (New York: Revell, 1948), 36.
14. Theodore Harris, *Pearl S. Buck: A Biography* (New York: John Day, 1969), 309.
15. Nathaniel Peffer, *The Far East: A Modern History* (Ann Arbor: University of Michigan Press, 1958), 117–18.
16. Hilary Spurling, *Pearl Buck in China: Journey to "The Good Earth"* (New York: Simon and Schuster, 2010), 66.
17. Pearl S. Buck, *My Several Worlds: A Personal Record* (New York: John Day, 1954), 5.
18. Henry Luce speech at the Waldorf-Astoria Hotel, New York, to senior group of Time Inc. employees, quoted in John K. Jessup, ed., *The Ideas of Henry Luce* (New York: Atheneum, 1969), 380.
19. Pearl Buck, letter to Mrs. Coffin, December 12, 1918, Nora Stirling Collection, Lipscomb Library, Randolph College Archives, as cited in Spurling, *Pearl Buck in China,* 111–12.
20. Absalom Sydenstricker, "The Importance of the Direct Phase of Mission Work," *Chinese Recorder* 41 (June 1910): 389.
21. Jack Chen, *The Chinese of America* (San Francisco: Harper and Row, 1980), 153.
22. Stephen E. Ambrose, *Nothing Like It in the World: The Men Who Built the Transcontinental Railroad, 1863–1869* (New York: Simon and Schuster, 2000), 164.
23. Eric T. L. Love, *Race Over Empire: Racism and U.S. Imperialism, 1865–1900* (Chapel Hill: University of North Carolina Press, 2004), 95.
24. Wong Sin Kiong, *China's Anti-American Boycott Movement in 1905: A Study in Urban Protest* (New York: Peter Lang, 2002), 19.
25. Roger Daniels, *Coming to America: A History of Immigration and Ethnicity in American Life* (New York: HarperCollins, 2002), 271.
26. Thomas G. Dyer, *Theodore Roosevelt and the Idea of Race* (Baton Rouge: Louisiana State University, 1992), 140.
27. Department of the Interior Annual Report, 1885.
28. Ibid.
29. Ibid., 37, 38.
30. Craig Storti, *Incident at Bitter Creek: The Story of the Rock Springs Chinese Massacre* (Ames: Iowa State University Press, 1991), 166.
31. Butow, "A Notable Passage to China."
32. Elliott Roosevelt and James Brough, *A Rendezvous with Destiny: The Roosevelts of the White House* (New York: G. P. Putnam's Sons, 1975), 29.
33. Ward, *Before the Trumpet,* 77.
34. Ibid.

35. Ibid., 66.
36. John Morton Blum, *From the Morgenthau Diaries,* vol. 1, *Years of Crisis, 1928–1938* (Boston: Houghton Mifflin, 1959), 206.

CHAPTER 3: THE JAPANESE MONROE DOCTRINE FOR ASIA

1. Theodore Roosevelt to Theodore Roosevelt Jr., February 10, 1904, in Elting Morison and John Blum, eds., *The Letters of Theodore Roosevelt,* 8 vols. (Cambridge, MA: Harvard University Press, 1951–1954), 4: 724.
2. Prime Minister Yasuhiro Nakasone, in William E. Smith, "Diplomacy: Beef and Bitter Lemons," *Time,* January 31, 1983; http://www.time.com/time/magazine/article/0,9171,951916,00.html.
3. Peter Booth Wiley, *Yankees in the Land of the Gods: Commodore Perry and the Opening of Japan* (New York: Viking, 1990), 321.
4. John W. Dower, *Japan in War and Peace: Selected Essays* (New York: New Press, 1993), 1.
5. Walter A. McDougall, *Let the Sea Make a Noise: A History of the North Pacific from Magellan to MacArthur* (New York: HarperCollins, 1993), 354.
6. Ito had many titles, including marquis. I use his eventual title, prince, throughout to simplify.
7. Donald Keene, *Emperor of Japan: Meiji and His World, 1852–1912* (New York: Columbia University Press, 2002), 594.
8. Isaac Don Levine, *The Kaiser's Letters to the Tsar* (London: Hodder and Stoughton, 1920), 105.
9. James L. McClain, *Japan: A Modern History* (New York: W. W. Norton, 2002), 296.
10. "Extract from Japanese Foreign Office Records," cited in Masayoshi Matsumura, *Baron Kaneko and the Russo-Japanese War,* trans. Ian Ruxton (Morrisville, NC: Lulu Press, 2009), 48.
11. Ibid., 8.
12. Prince Ito dined with President Roosevelt and Secretary of State John Hay in the White House on October 21, 1901.
13. Raymond A. Esthus, *Theodore Roosevelt and the International Rivalries* (Waltham, MA: Ginn-Blaisdell, 1970), 23.
14. Frank A. Vanderlip, *Century* (August 1898), cited in Sen. Doc. 62, pt. 1, 55th Cong., 3rd sess., 564.
15. Thomas F. Gossett, *Race: The History of an Idea in America* (New York: Schocken, 1970), 312.
16. Keene, *Emperor of Japan,* 580.
17. For a complete discussion of Roosevelt's racial beliefs and how they affected his policies in Asia, see James Bradley, *The Imperial Cruise* (Boston: Little, Brown, 2009).
18. Richard Hofstadter, *Social Darwinism in American Thought* (New York: George Braziller, 1959), 175.
19. Gossett, *Race,* 329.
20. Terence V. Powderly, "Exclude Anarchist and Chinaman!," *Collier's Weekly* 28 (December 14, 1901).

21. Keene, *Emperor of Japan*, 611.
22. Theodore Roosevelt to William Woodville Rockhill, August 29, 1905, in Morison and Blum, *The Letters of Theodore Roosevelt*, 4: 1327.
23. Theodore Roosevelt to David Bowman Schneder, June 19, 1905, in ibid., 4: 1240–41.
24. Address of Theodore Roosevelt to the Naval War College, Newport, Rhode Island, June 2, 1897, in Dyer, *Theodore Roosevelt and the Idea of Race*, 42.
25. Ibid., 136.
26. Theodore Roosevelt, annual message to Congress, December 6, 1904, in *FRUS*, 41.
27. Theodore Roosevelt, *Theodore Roosevelt: An Autobiography* (New York: Macmillan, 1913), 545.
28. Also known as King Kojong, King Gojong, and Emperor Kojong, he ruled from 1863 to 1907. Before 1897 he was King Gojong and after 1897 he was Emperor Gojong. Although he was King Gojong in 1882, I use Emperor Gojong for continuity.
29. Yur-Bok Lee and Wayne Patterson, eds., *One Hundred Years of Korean-American Relations, 1882–1982* (Tuscaloosa: University of Alabama Press, 1986), 20.
30. Frederick A. McKenzie, *Korea's Fight for Freedom* (New York: Fleming H. Revell, 1920), 77–78.
31. Theodore Roosevelt to Hermann Speck von Sternburg, August 28, 1900, in Morison and Blum, *The Letters of Theodore Roosevelt*, 2: 1394.
32. Theodore Roosevelt to Sternburg, February 6, 1904, in Howard K. Beale, *Theodore Roosevelt and the Rise of America to World Power* (Baltimore: Johns Hopkins University Press, 1956), 291.
33. Theodore Roosevelt to Theodore Roosevelt Jr., February 10, 1904, in Morison and Blum, *The Letters of Theodore Roosevelt*, 4: 724.
34. *San Francisco Call*, Sunday, March 13, 1904, cited in Matsumura, *Baron Kaneko and the Russo-Japanese War*, 23.
35. Raymond A. Esthus, *Theodore Roosevelt and Japan* (Seattle: University of Washington Press, 1966), 40.
36. Matsumura, *Baron Kaneko and the Russo-Japanese War*, 52.
37. Esthus, *Theodore Roosevelt and Japan*, 41.
38. Matsumura, *Baron Kaneko and the Russo-Japanese War*, 53.
39. Julian Street, "A Japanese Statesman's Recollections of Roosevelt," *New York Times*, July 31, 1921.
40. Matsumura, *Baron Kaneko and the Russo-Japanese War*, 54.
41. Ibid., 132.
42. Ibid., 91–92. Since 1871, when Meiji first allowed Christians to proselytize in Japan, American missionaries had worked in that country, but Japan's population was a fraction of China's, and it is estimated that there was never more than 1 percent of the Japanese population converted to Christianity.
43. The Harvard Club of Japan reprinted the *Boston Herald*'s version of Kaneko's words; see Matsumura, *Baron Kaneko and the Russo-Japanese War*, 92.
44. Matsumura, *Baron Kaneko and the Russo-Japanese War*, 55.
45. Theodore Roosevelt to Hay, July 26, 1904, in Morison and Blum, *The Letters of Theodore Roosevelt*, 4: 865.

46. Theodore Roosevelt to Theodore Roosevelt Jr., March 5, 1904, cited in Beale, *Theodore Roosevelt and the Rise of America to World Power,* 269.

47. Matsumura, *Baron Kaneko and the Russo-Japanese War,* 286.

48. Keene, *Emperor of Japan,* 612.

49. Theodore Roosevelt to Taft, April 20, 1905, in Morison and Blum, *The Letters of Theodore Roosevelt,* 4: 1162.

50. Shumpei Okamoto, *The Japanese Oligarchy and the Russo-Japanese War* (New York: Columbia University Press, 1970), 119.

51. Theodore Roosevelt to Henry Cabot Lodge, June 16, 1905, in Morison and Blum, *The Letters of Theodore Roosevelt,* 4: 1229, 1232.

52. Beale, *Theodore Roosevelt and the Rise of America to World Power,* 334.

53. Street, "A Japanese Statesman's Recollection of Roosevelt."

54. Matsumura, *Baron Kaneko and the Russo-Japanese War,* 382.

55. Ibid., 383.

56. Kaneko, "A 'Japanese Monroe Doctrine' and Manchuria."

57. Ibid.

58. For more information, see Bradley, *The Imperial Cruise.*

59. Tyler Dennett, "President Roosevelt's Secret Pact with Japan," *Current History* 21, no. 1 (October 1924); http://www.icasinc.org/history/katsura.html.

60. Ibid.

61. It wasn't until nineteen years later—after Roosevelt's death—that a researcher came across Taft's top secret summary of his meeting with Katsura. For protection, Taft had composed his memo with no direct quotes.

62. Theodore Roosevelt to Taft, telegram, July 31, 1905, in Morison and Blum, *The Letters of Theodore Roosevelt,* 4: 1293.

63. "Japan's Policy Abroad," *New York Times,* July 30, 1905.

64. McKenzie, *Korea's Fight for Freedom,* 77–78.

65. He was given the Nobel Peace Prize for bringing Russia and Japan together, not for actually negotiating the treaty.

66. Matsumura, *Baron Kaneko and the Russo-Japanese War,* 450.

67. Kaneko said, "I intend to report this very important and valuable piece of advice to our government's leaders on my return to Japan. And after the war I hope that our policy in Asia will be executed and managed along these lines, and that Your Excellency will consent to this," in ibid., 451.

68. Ibid., 450–51.

69. Homer B. Hulbert, *The Passing of Korea* (New York: Doubleday, Page, 1906), 223–24.

70. Ibid., 221.

71. Homer Hulbert, letter to the editor of the *New York Times,* reprinted in *The Fatherland,* January 19, 1916; http://www.homerhulbert.com/Fatherland _Roosevelt_1916.pdf.

72. Woonsang Choi, *The Fall of the Hermit Kingdom* (Dobbs Ferry, NY: Oceana, 1967), 47.

73. Un-yon Kim, *Nikkan Heigo* (Tokyo: Dodo Shuppan, 1996), 195, as cited in Keene, *Emperor of Japan,* 641.

74. Hulbert, *The Passing of Korea,* 9.

75. Jongsuk Chay, *Diplomacy of Asymmetry: Korean-American Relations to 1910* (Honolulu: University of Hawaii Press, 1990), 146.

76. Hulbert, letter to the editor of the *New York Times.*

77. Tyler Dennett, *Roosevelt and the Russo-Japanese War* (New York: Doubleday, Page, 1925), 304.

78. Ibid., 307.

79. Herbert Croly, *Willard Straight* (New York: Macmillan, 1924), 188.

80. Theodore Roosevelt, *America and the World War* (New York: Charles Scribner's Sons, 1915), 29.

81. Roosevelt, *Theodore Roosevelt,* 545.

82. Hulbert, letter to the editor of the *New York Times.* The statue in downtown Seoul mentioned in the introduction honors Homer Hulbert.

83. Beale, *Theodore Roosevelt and the Rise of America to World Power,* 322.

84. Esthus, *Theodore Roosevelt and Japan,* 299.

CHAPTER 4: THE NOBLE CHINESE PEASANT

1. Address given by Luce at United Nations service in tribute to China, December 13, 1942, in box 48, United China Relief, United Service to China Records, Seeley G. Mudd Manuscript Library, Princeton University (hereafter referred to as UCR-USC Records), as cited in T. Christopher Jespersen, *American Images of China, 1931–1949* (Stanford, CA: Stanford University Press, 1999), 37.

2. Soong was "the first [Chinese] that has ever submitted to the ordinance of Christian baptism in North Carolina," according to the *Wilmington Star,* November 7, 1880.

3. Charlie had two other sons born slightly later: T. L. Soong and T. A. Soong. Both became bankers and were not central to the Soong-Chiang penetration of the United States.

4. Edgar Snow, *Journey to the Beginning* (New York: Random House, 1958), 88–89.

5. Ibid.

6. Laura Tyson Li, *Madame Chiang Kai-shek* (New York: Atlantic Monthly Press, 2006), 39.

7. Warren I. Cohen, *America's Response to China: An Interpretative History of Sino-American Relations* (New York: John Wiley and Sons, 1971), 101.

8. Chiang speech at Omei College, September 1935, as cited in Jonathan Fenby, *Chiang Kai-shek: China's Generalissimo and the Nation He Lost* (New York: Carroll and Graf, 2003), 225.

9. *Proceedings of Conference on Chiang Kai-shek and Modern China,* vol. 3, *Chiang Kai-shek and China's Modernization* (Taipei: China Cultural Service, 1987), 151.

10. Jonathan Fenby, *The Penguin History of Modern China: The Fall and Rise of a Great Power, 1850–2008* (New York: Penguin, 2008), 295.

11. Fenby, *Chiang Kai-shek,* 226.

12. Chieh-ju Ch'en, *Chiang Kai-shek's Secret Past,* ed. Lloyd E. Eastman (Boulder, CO: Westview Press, 1993), 155.

13. My discussion of Chiang Kai-shek and Mao Zedong is relatively narrow, focused on how and why the Chinese people granted Mao Zedong the Mandate of Heaven. Both men had many faults, both men caused and then covered up massive famines that killed millions, both used terror and torture to discipline the populace, and each was single-minded in his belief that he was right while others were wrong. But one of them captured the Mandate, and I try to explain why.

14. Edgar Snow, *Red Star Over China* (New York: Random House, 1938), 133.

15. Ibid., 138.

16. Ibid., 119.

17. Maurice Meisner, *Mao Zedong: A Political and Intellectual Portrait* (Malden, MA: Polity Press, 2007), 32.

18. R. H. Tawney, *Land and Labour in China* (London: George Allen and Unwin, 1932), 77.

19. Meisner, *Mao Zedong,* 45.

20. Philip Short, *Mao: A Life* (New York: Henry Holt, 2000), 301–2.

21. Edgar Ansel Mowrer, *Mowrer in China* (Harmondsworth, UK: Penguin, 1938), 80–81.

22. Sterling Seagrave, *The Soong Dynasty* (New York: Harper and Row), 261.

23. Service, *Lost Chance in China,* 79.

24. FBI memorandum to the director, January 9, 1943, quoted in Fenby, *Chiang Kai-shek,* 164.

25. Chiang Kai-shek, *China's Destiny and Chinese Economic Theory* (New York: Roy Publishers, 1947), 118.

26. Seagrave, *The Soong Dynasty,* 284.

27. Ibid., 411.

28. Fenby, *Chiang Kai-shek,* 166.

29. Jung Chang, *Madame Sun Yat-sen* (London: Penguin, 1986), 66.

30. Snow, *Journey to the Beginning,* 85.

31. Lancelot Foster, "The Generalissimo and Madame Chiang Kai-shek," *Hibbert Journal* (October 1937): 100, as cited in Jespersen, *American Images of China,* 35.

32. Jespersen, *American Images of China,* 85.

33. Snow, *Journey to the Beginning,* 89–90.

34. Guangqiu Xu, *War Wings: The United States and Chinese Military Aviation, 1929–1949* (Westport, CT: Greenwood Press, 2001), 89.

35. *Milwaukee Sentinel,* October 24, 1930.

36. Ibid.

37. Li, *Madame Chiang Kai-shek,* 97.

38. Ibid.

39. Jessup, *The Ideas of Henry Luce,* 380.

40. W. A. Swanberg, *Luce and His Empire* (New York: Charles Scribner's Sons, 1972), 142.

41. Ibid., 96.

42. Jespersen, *American Images of China,* 35.

43. Theodore White, *In Search of History* (New York: Harper and Row, 1978), 207.

44. "The New China," *Fortune,* April 1941, 94.

45. David Halberstam, *The Powers That Be* (New York: Knopf, 1975), 49.

46. Swanberg, *Luce and His Empire,* 258.

47. Address given by Luce at United Nations service in tribute to China.
48. Raymond Fielding, *The March of Time, 1935–1951* (New York: Oxford University Press, 1977), 134.
49. "Foreign News: Progress," *Time,* October 4, 1937, 19.
50. "Man and Wife of the Year," *Time,* January 3, 1938.
51. "The Army Nobody Knows," *Time,* June 16, 1941, 23–24.
52. "China: Chiang Dares," *Time,* November 9, 1936; "The Finance Minister of the Republic of China," *Fortune,* June 1933.
53. Pearl Buck, *The Good Earth* (New York: John Day, 1931). The novel was published on March 2, 1931.
54. Paul Hutchinson, "Breeder of Life," *Christian Century* 48 (May 20, 1931): 683.
55. "Japan: Fissiparous Tendencies," *Time,* September 5, 1932.
56. George H. Blakeslee, "The Japanese Monroe Doctrine," *Foreign Affairs* 11, no. 4 (July 1933): 671–81.
57. Lieutenant General Sadao Araki, quoted in "Japan: Fissiparous Tendencies," *Time.*
58. Robert J. C. Butow, *Tojo and the Coming of the War* (Princeton, NJ: Princeton University Press, 1961), 106–7.
59. Fenby, *Chiang Kai-shek,* 201.
60. Kaneko, "A 'Japanese Monroe Doctrine' and Manchuria."
61. Kai Bird, *The Color of Truth* (New York: Simon and Schuster, 1998), 23.
62. David F. Schmitz, *Henry L. Stimson: The First Wise Man* (Lanham, MD: Rowman and Littlefield, 2000).
63. Johnson to Hornbeck, June 1, 1933, quoted in Dorothy Borg, *The United States and the Far Eastern Crisis of 1933–1938* (Cambridge, MA: Harvard University Press, 1964), 44. Johnson was a minister at this point and later became ambassador, but because he held a number of titles, I've simplified here.
64. Stimson diary, November 7 and November 19, 1931, Henry L. Stimson diaries, Sterling Library, Yale University, as cited in Schmitz, *Henry L. Stimson,* 106–7.
65. Schmitz, *Henry L. Stimson,* 2–3.
66. Stimson to Ford, April 3, 1931, cited in ibid., 19.
67. Stimson diary, December 6, 1931, as cited in ibid., 107.
68. Harvey Bundy, oral history, Columbia University Oral History Project, as cited in ibid.
69. Cohen, *America's Response to China,* 134.
70. Quoted in the *North China Herald,* November 3, 1931.
71. Fenby, *Chiang Kai-shek,* 203.
72. Greg Grandin, *Empire's Workshop: Latin America, the United States, and the Rise of the New Imperialism* (New York: Henry Holt, 2006), 3.
73. Henry L. Stimson and McGeorge Bundy, *On Active Service in Peace and War* (New York: Harper and Brothers, 1948), 182.
74. Stimson diary, January 26, 1932, as cited in Schmitz, *Henry L. Stimson,* 110.
75. Memo of conversation, May 24, 1932, Papers of Nelson T. Johnson, Library of Congress, as cited in Cohen, *America's Response to China,* 134.
76. Acting secretary of state telegram to the consul general at Shanghai (Cunningham), March 29, 1932, *FRUS,* 3: 643.
77. Castle to Consul General Cunningham, April 19, 1932, ibid., 3: 702.

78. Memorandum prepared by Hamilton, "American Aviation Training Mission in China," June 1, 1932, as cited in William Matthew Leary, *The Dragon's Wings: The China National Aviation Corporation and the Development of Commercial Aviation in China* (Athens: University of Georgia Press, 1976), 62.

79. Grew to the secretary of state, January 16, 1933, *FRUS,* 3: 94–95.

80. Buck, *China As I See It,* 77, 78, 80, 83.

81. Ibid., 17.

CHAPTER 5: THE CHINA LOBBY

1. Merle Miller, *Plain Speaking: An Oral Biography of Harry S. Truman* (New York: Berkley, 1974), 288–89.

2. One child, Franklin, born between James and Elliott, had died in infancy.

3. Jan Pottker, *Sara and Eleanor* (New York: St. Martin's, 2004), 83.

4. Stimson diary, November 9, 1932, as cited in Stimson and Bundy, *On Active Service,* 288–89.

5. Stimson diary, December 22, 23, and 24, 1932, as cited in Schmitz, *Henry L. Stimson,* 113.

6. Stimson diary, January 9, 1933; Stimson, "Memorandum of Conversation with Franklin D. Roosevelt," January 9, 1933, as cited in ibid.

7. Moley, *After Seven Years,* 95.

8. Stimson's memorandum of his conversation with Roosevelt, January 9, 1933, box 170, folder 20, Stimson Papers, Yale University Library, as cited in Robert Smith Thompson, *A Time for War: Franklin D. Roosevelt and the Path to Pearl Harbor* (New York: Prentice Hall, 1991), 26.

9. Mao Zedong, "Report on an Investigation of the Peasant Movement in Hunan" (March 1927); https://www.marxists.org/reference/archive/mao/selected-works/volume-1/mswv1_2.htm.

10. Ibid.

11. Ibid.

12. Edgar Snow, "China's Fighting Generalissimo," *Foreign Affairs* 16, no. 4 (July 1938): 616.

13. Hung-mao Tien, *Government and Politics in Kuomintang China, 1927–1937,* vol. 53 (Palo Alto, CA: Stanford University Press, 1972), 84.

14. John King Fairbank, *The United States and China* (Cambridge, MA: Harvard University Press, 1976), 246.

15. Snow, "China's Fighting Generalissimo," 624–25.

16. Mao Zedong, *Mao's Road to Power: Revolutionary Writings, 1912–1949,* ed. Stuart Schram (Armonk, NY: M. E. Sharpe, 1992), 1: 552.

17. Fairbank, *The United States and China,* 292.

18. Zedong, *Mao's Road to Power,* 1: 552.

19. Mao Zedong, *On Guerrilla Warfare,* trans. Samuel B. Griffith II (Champaign: University of Illinois Press, 2000), 92.

20. Sun Tzu, *The Art of War;* http://www.marxists.org/reference/archive/sun-tzu/works/art-of-war/ch01.htm.

21. Alexander V. Pantsov with Steven I. Levine, *Mao: The Real Story* (New York: Simon and Schuster, 2012), 222.

22. Snow, *Red Star Over China,* 174.
23. Louise Chipley Slavicek, *Mao Zedong* (New York: Infobase, 2009), 62.
24. Jerome Ch'en, *Mao and the Chinese Revolution* (New York: Oxford University Press, 1965), 156.
25. Peter Fleming, *One's Company* (London: Jonathan Cape, 1950), 176.
26. Barbara W. Tuchman, *Stilwell and the American Experience in China, 1911–1945* (New York: Macmillan, 1970), 109.
27. Snow, *Red Star Over China,* 109.
28. Michael Schaller, *The U.S. Crusade in China, 1938–1945* (New York: Columbia University Press, 1979), 9.
29. Ibid.
30. White, *In Search of History,* 116.
31. The speech was reprinted in "Dr. Soong Stresses Our Link with China," *New York Times,* May 18, 1933.
32. "The Finance Minister of the Republic of China," *Fortune.*
33. Cohen, *America's Response to China,* 135.
34. Arthur M. Schlesinger Jr., *The Age of Roosevelt* (Boston: Houghton Mifflin, 1959), 2: 527–28.
35. Ibid., 528.
36. John Paton Davies Jr., *Dragon by the Tail: American, British, Japanese, and Russian Encounters with China and One Another* (New York: W. W. Norton, 1972), 142.
37. Rexford G. Tugwell, "Roosevelt and Frankfurter: An Essay Review," *Political Science Quarterly* 85, no. 1 (March 1970): 99–114.
38. "Letters to President Franklin Roosevelt," Soong Archives, Hoover Institution, as cited in Seagrave, *The Soong Dynasty,* 18.
39. Missy LeHand, FDR's companion and secretary for over twenty years, was his best female friend.
40. John Morton Blum, *Roosevelt and Morgenthau* (Boston: Houghton Mifflin, 1970), xvi, 249.
41. Arthur Krock, "Quoddy Project Charges Kindles Republican Hopes," *New York Times,* July 3, 1935.
42. Delbert Clark, "The President's Advisors Come and Go," *New York Times Magazine,* August 4, 1935.
43. David McKean, *Peddling Influence* (Hanover, NH: Steerforth, 2004), 60.
44. Ibid., 70.
45. "Corcoran 'Deaf and Dumb' When Queried on Tydings," *New York Times,* September 15, 1938.
46. Michael Janeway, *The Fall of the House of Roosevelt: Brokers of Ideas and Power from FDR to LBJ* (New York: Columbia University Press, 2004), 15.
47. McKean, *Peddling Influence,* 71.
48. Noah Feldman, *Scorpions: The Battles and Triumphs of FDR's Great Supreme Court Justices* (New York: Twelve, 2010), 84.
49. Corcoran's power was also seen as a harbinger of the coming wave of Catholic influence in Washington.
50. McKean, *Peddling Influence,* 121.
51. Ibid., 72.

52. Ibid., 72–73.
53. Cordell Hull, *The Memoirs of Cordell Hull* (New York: Macmillan, 1948), 1: 207.
54. Robert Dallek, *Franklin D. Roosevelt and American Foreign Policy* (Oxford, UK: Oxford University Press, 1995), 29.
55. Snow, *Red Star Over China,* 179.
56. Short, *Mao: A Life,* 298.
57. Snow, *Red Star Over China,* 180.
58. Ibid., 205–6.
59. Kunming was then called Yunnan Fu.
60. John Service oral history, quoted in Lynne Joiner, *Honorable Survivor: Mao's China, McCarthy's America, and the Persecution of John S. Service* (Annapolis, MD: Naval Institute Press, 2009), 16.
61. Meisner, *Mao Zedong,* 73.
62. Borg, *The United States and the Far Eastern Crisis,* 75.
63. Arnold J. Toynbee, *Survey of International Affairs, 1934* (London: Oxford University Press, 1938), 193. See also "Unofficial Statement by the Japanese Foreign Office," *FRUS,* 1: 225.
64. Keiji Furuya, *Chiang Kai-shek: His Life and Times,* abridged by Chun-ming Chang (New York: St. John's University Press, 1981), 439.
65. Yosuke Matsuoka, "Matsuoka Challenges the Critics of the Japanese Policy on China," *New York Times,* April 29, 1934.
66. Hull to Clarence Gauss, January 26, 1935, *FRUS,* 3: 21.
67. Short, *Mao: A Life,* 353–56.
68. Snow, *Red Star Over China,* 109, 113.
69. Short, *Mao: A Life,* 364.
70. Tuchman, *Stilwell and the American Experience in China,* 153.
71. Ibid., 158.
72. "China: Chiang Dares," *Time.*
73. Ibid.

CHAPTER 6: THE FIRST WISE MAN'S NEW CHINA

1. John Service, interview with Mao Zedong, August 23, 1944, in *Lost Chance in China,* 302.
2. Madame Chiang, letter to Elizabeth Moore, November 2, 1939, box 4, United Board for Christian Higher Education in Asia (UBCHEA) Papers, as cited in Jespersen, *American Images of China,* 85.
3. Seagrave, *The Soong Dynasty,* 290.
4. Ibid., 291.
5. Li, *Madame Chiang Kai-shek,* 104.
6. Ibid., 102.
7. "Man and Wife of the Year," *Time.*
8. Li, *Madame Chiang Kai-shek,* 109.
9. Chiang Kai-shek, "What the Sufferings of Jesus Mean to Me," *Christian Century,* May 12, 1937, 612.
10. Jespersen, *American Images of China,* 35.
11. Quoted in Varg, *Missionaries, Chinese, and Diplomats,* 255.

12. Zedong, *Mao's Road to Power,* 5: 334.
13. Pantsov, *Mao: The Real Story,* 298.
14. John Service oral history, quoted in Joiner, *Honorable Survivor,* 18.
15. Chiang never forgave Marshal Zhang for siding with Mao. Chiang jailed Zhang in China from 1937 to 1949 and dragged him to a Taiwan jail when Mao gained the Mandate. Chiang died in 1975. Marshal Zhang was released from Chiang's jail in 1990, at the age of eighty-nine.
16. Buck, *China As I See It,* 135.
17. China Records Project, box 201, as cited in Jespersen, *American Images of China,* 34.
18. Snow, *Red Star Over China,* 390.
19. Elmer T. Clark, *The Chiangs of China* (New York: Abingdon-Cokesbury, 1943), 102.
20. Quoted in Ch'en, *Mao and the Chinese Revolution,* 230.
21. Borg, *The United States and the Far Eastern Crisis,* 315.
22. Steven W. Mosher, *China Misperceived: American Illusions and Chinese Reality* (New York: HarperCollins, 1990), 46.
23. Johnson to Hornbeck, March 22, 1938, file "Johnson 1938," Hornbeck Papers, as cited in Tuchman, *Stilwell and the American Experience in China,* 184.
24. Blum, *Roosevelt and Morgenthau,* 105.
25. Ibid., 244.
26. *The Sino-Japanese Conflict and the League of Nations, 1937: Speeches, Documents, Press Comments* (Geneva: Press Bureau of the Chinese Delegation, 1937), 127.
27. Dallek, *Franklin D. Roosevelt and American Foreign Policy, 1932–1945,* 148.
28. "Man and Wife of the Year," *Time.*
29. Ibid.
30. Ibid.
31. Akio Tsuchida, "China's 'Public Diplomacy' Toward the United States Before Pearl Harbor," *Journal of American–East Asian Relations* 17 (2010): 40.
32. Ibid.
33. Eliot Janeway, "Japan's Partner: Japanese Dependence Upon the United States," *Harper's* 177 (June 1938): 1–8.
34. In a July 1938 *Fortune* poll, Americans were asked what they thought the most disturbing global event of the year was; 29.4 percent said it was Japan's invasion of China, while 22.8 percent thought it was Germany's seizure of Austria; cited in Tae Jin Park, "In Support of 'New China': Origins of the China Lobby, 1937–1941" (PhD dissertation, West Virginia University, 2003), 114.

    Many thanks to Tae Jin Park and his PhD dissertation, "In Support of 'New China,'" which I encountered midway through my research for this book. Some of it confirmed the research I had already done, and other parts were new to me and were confirmed by other sources. Given the narrow subject — the creation of the China Lobby — and the few characters involved, there is inevitable overlap in our work. I cite "In Support of 'New China'" where Dr. Park provided unique guidance. Park's dissertation can be viewed in its entirety here:

http://wvuscholar.wvu.edu:8881//exlibris/dtl/d3_1/apache_media/
L2V4bGlicmlzL2R0bC9kM18xL2FwYWWNoZV9tZWRpYS82NzE3.pdf.

35. Carl Crow, "We Have Our Orders," *Reader's Digest* 37 (August 1940): 83–86.

36. American Committee for Non-Participation in Japanese Aggression, "America's Share in Japan's War Guilt" (New York: Academy Press, 1938), 2–3.

37. Ibid., 18.

38. Ibid., 16–17.

39. Donald J. Friedman, *The Road from Isolation: The Campaign of the American Committee for Non-Participation in Japanese Aggression, 1938–1941* (Cambridge, MA: East Asian Research Center, 1970), 13.

40. Ibid., 24–25.

41. Ibid., 22.

42. Ludwig Lore, "Behind the Cables," *New York Post,* reprinted in American Committee for Non-Participation in Japanese Aggression, "America's Share in Japan's War Guilt."

43. Owen Lattimore, "Rising Sun, Falling Profits," *Atlantic Monthly,* July 1938.

44. Division of Far Eastern Affairs memorandum, December 5, 1938, as cited in Irvine H. Anderson Jr., "The 1941 de Facto Embargo on Oil to Japan: A Bureaucratic Reflex," *Pacific Historical Review* 44 (May 1975): 203; http://www.jstor.org/stable/3638003.

45. Grew to secretary of state, January 7, 1939, in *FRUS,* 3: 478–81.

46. Hamilton memo, June 7, 1940, in ibid., 4: 576.

47. Bullitt to FDR, August 8, 1938, quoted in William C. Bullitt, *For the President, Personal and Secret: Correspondence Between Franklin D. Roosevelt and William C. Bullitt,* ed. Orville Bullitt (Boston: Houghton Mifflin, 1972), 278–79.

48. Interdepartmental meeting, September 6, 1938, box 138, Henry Morgenthau Papers, Manuscript Division, Library of Congress, as cited in Park, "In Support of 'New China,'" 176.

49. Harry Dexter White memo, October 10, 1938, folder 3, "China," White Papers, as cited in Jonathan Utley, *Going to War with Japan, 1937–1941* (Knoxville: University of Tennessee Press, 1985), 45.

50. Hamilton memo, November 13, 1938, *FRUS,* 3: 569.

51. Treasury meeting, September 22, 1938, Morgenthau Papers, box 142, 184–91, as cited in Park, "In Support of 'New China,'" 179.

52. Morgenthau to Kung, October 8, 1938, Morgenthau Papers, box 145, 69, as cited in ibid., 183.

53. Schaller, *The U.S. Crusade in China,* 29.

CHAPTER 7: WASHINGTON WARRIORS

1. Henry L. Stimson, letter to the *New York Times,* October 7, 1937.

2. Henry L. Stimson, letter to the *New York Times,* January 11, 1940.

3. "Shall America Stop Arming Japan?" (New York: American Committee for Non-Participation in Japanese Aggression, 1940), 37.

4. Quoted in Friedman, *The Road from Isolation,* 95.

5. Ibid., 49.

6. Ibid.

7. "China Fights Back!," *March of Time;* http://www.britishpathe.com/video/march-of-time-china-fights-back.

8. Friedman, *The Road from Isolation,* 66.

9. Jonathan Marshall, *To Have and Have Not* (Berkeley: University of California Press, 1995), xi.

10. Elliott Roosevelt, *As He Saw It* (New York: Duell, Sloan, and Pearce, 1946), 53.

11. Marshall, *To Have and Have Not,* 134.

12. Utley, *Going to War with Japan,* 116.

13. Gordon W. Prange, *At Dawn We Slept: The Untold Story of Pearl Harbor* (New York: McGraw-Hill, 1981), 38, 39.

14. Quoted in Hiroyuki Agawa, *The Reluctant Admiral: Yamamoto and the Imperial Navy,* trans. John Bester (Tokyo: Kodansha International, 1979), 227–28; emphasis in original.

15. Ernest O. Hauser, "China's Soong," *Life,* March 24, 1941.

16. Ibid.

17. Hornbeck to Welles, June 28, 1940, Hornbeck Papers, box 103, as cited in Park, "In Support of 'New China,'" 222.

18. Ibid.

19. Tuchman, *Stilwell and the American Experience in China,* 239.

20. Davies, *Dragon by the Tail,* 223–24.

21. Hauser, "China's Soong."

22. Davies, *Dragon by the Tail,* 215.

23. Hart to Stark, August 20, 1940, folder 14, Hart Papers, as cited in Utley, *Going to War with Japan,* 103.

24. Anderson, "The 1941 de Facto Embargo on Oil to Japan," 206–7.

25. John Morton Blum, *From the Morgenthau Diaries,* vol. 2, *Years of Urgency, 1938–1941* (Boston: Houghton Mifflin, 1965), 349–50.

26. Fred L. Israel, ed., *The War Diary of Breckinridge Long* (Lincoln: University of Nebraska Press, 1966). 140. See also diary entry for October 4, 1940, Stimson Papers, and memorandum of meeting, October 2, 1940, Morgenthau diary, vol. 318, 121–27.

27. Anderson, "The 1941 de Facto Embargo on Oil to Japan," 208.

28. Morgenthau memo, September 23, 1940, box 307, 294, Morgenthau Papers, as cited in Park, "In Support of 'New China,'" 233.

29. Harold LeClair Ickes, *The Secret Diary of Harold L. Ickes* (New York: Simon and Schuster, 1954), 3: 339.

30. Stimson and Bundy, *On Active Service,* 384–85.

31. Stimson diary, October 1, 2, 3, 1940, box 371, as cited in Utley, *Going to War with Japan,* 108.

32. Joseph Barnes, *Willkie: The Events He Was a Part Of, the Ideas He Fought For* (New York: Simon and Schuster, 1952), 254.

33. Joseph P. Lash, *Roosevelt and Churchill, 1939–1941: The Partnership That Saved the West* (New York: W. W. Norton, 1976), 235.

34. Robert E. Sherwood, *Roosevelt and Hopkins: An Intimate History* (New York: Harper, 1950), 191.

35. Address at Boston Garden, October 30, 1940, as cited in ibid.

36. "Text of the Address by Willkie," *New York Times,* March 27, 1941.

37. Charles Yost memo, November 15, 1940, cited in Utley, *Going to War with Japan,* 206.

38. Elliott Roosevelt, ed., *FDR, His Personal Letters, 1928–1945* (New York: Duell, Sloan, and Pearce, 1948), 2: 1077.

39. Treasury meeting, November 29, 1940, box 333, 31, in Blum, *From the Morgenthau Diaries,* 2: 363.

40. Dallek, *Franklin D. Roosevelt and American Foreign Policy,* 270.

41. Hauser, "China's Soong," 91.

42. Ibid.

43. Quoted in Fenby, *Chiang Kai-shek,* 344.

44. Thomas Griffith, *Harry and Teddy: The Turbulent Friendship of Press Lord Henry R. Luce and His Favorite Reporter, Theodore H. White* (New York: Random House, 1995), 8.

45. White, *In Search of History,* 115.

CHAPTER 8: SECRET EXECUTIVE AIR WAR IN ASIA

1. Chennault Papers, Hoover Institution, Stanford University.

2. Claire Chennault, *Way of a Fighter: The Memoirs of Claire Lee Chennault,* ed. Robert Hotz (New York: G. P. Putnam's Sons, 1949), 31.

3. Ibid., 34–35.

4. Ibid., 90.

5. David Eli Lilienthal, *The Journals of David E. Lilienthal: The TVA Years, 1939–1945* (New York: Harper and Row, 1964), 135.

6. McKean, *Peddling Influence,* 119.

7. Ibid., 121.

8. Jonathan Daniels, *Frontier on the Potomac* (New York: Da Capo Press, 1972), 135.

9. Chennault, *Way of a Fighter,* 97.

10. Daniel Ford, *Flying Tigers: Claire Chennault and His American Volunteers* (Washington, DC: Smithsonian Institution Press, 1991), 44.

11. McKean, *Peddling Influence,* 143.

12. Ford, *Flying Tigers,* 44.

13. Blum, *From the Morgenthau Diaries,* 2: 365.

14. Ibid.

15. Ibid.

16. Morgenthau memo of phone conversation with President Roosevelt, December 18, 1940, in Blum, *From the Morgenthau Diaries,* 2: 357.

17. Morgenthau conversation with Soong, December 20, 1940, in ibid., 2: 342, as cited in Ford, *Flying Tigers,* 47.

18. Morgenthau's aide Philip Young also attended. Notes on conference at home of the secretary, Saturday, December 21, 1940, in Blum, *From the Morgenthau Diaries,* 2: 368.

19. Jessup, *The Ideas of Henry Luce,* 108–9, 120.

20. "The New China," *Fortune,* April 1941.

21. *China Fights for Democracy* 1, ND, box 65, as cited in Jespersen, *American Images of China,* 73.

22. UCR statement, ND [1941], USC Papers, box 54, as cited in Park, "In Support of 'New China,'" 286.
23. "The Purposes and Program of United China Relief," box 418, Hornbeck Papers, as cited in ibid.
24. "Report to the Annual Meeting of UCR," box 5, UCR-USC Records, as cited in Park, "In Support of 'New China,'" 283–84.
25. Buck, *China As I See It,* 123.
26. William Bullitt, "China on the March," CBS radio, March 20, 1941, Soong Papers, box 20, folder 13, as cited in Jespersen, *American Images of China,* 156.
27. "Bullitt Declares 'China Guards Us,'" *New York Times,* April 28, 1941.
28. Bullitt, "China on the March."
29. Luce to Hu, February 14, 1941, box 281, Hornbeck Papers.
30. White, *In Search of History,* 76, 77.
31. Lauchlin Currie was later accused of espionage in the Silvermaster case, a topic that is well covered elsewhere and is not related to Currie's delusionary report to FDR about China.
32. Eliot Janeway, "Roosevelt vs. Hitler," *Life,* May 5, 1941, 100–103.
33. Ibid.
34. Tuchman, *Stilwell and the American Experience in China,* 239.
35. Currie to Soong, March 17, 1941, Currie Papers, Hoover Institution, Stanford University.
36. Joiner, *Honorable Survivor,* 25.
37. Interview with Chiang Kai-shek, February 7, 1941, Currie Papers.
38. Currie's confidential report to FDR, March 15, 1941, ibid.
39. Interview with Chiang Kai-shek, February 7, 1941, ibid.
40. Currie's notes, February 15, 16, and 22, 1941, Currie Papers.
41. Currie interview with Chiang, February 8, 1941, Currie Papers.
42. Chiang to Soong, February 27, 1941, Currie Papers.
43. Ibid.
44. *FRUS,* 4: 89.
45. Ibid., 90.
46. Ibid.
47. Ibid., 85.
48. Ibid., 95.
49. *Time,* March 24, 1941.
50. Currie to Soong, March 17, 1941, Currie Papers.
51. Transcript of Treasury Department group meeting, May 12, 1941, in Blum, *From the Morgenthau Diaries,* 1: 408–18.

Chapter 9: A War Over Oil

1. White, *In Search of History,* 76.
2. Young Dean Acheson did travel to Japan, but with uncomprehending eyes.
3. Dean Acheson, *Morning and Noon* (Boston: Houghton Mifflin, 1965), 165.
4. Dean Acheson, *Present at the Creation: My Years in the State Department* (New York: W. W. Norton, 1969), 3.
5. Ibid., 22.

6. Blum, *From the Morgenthau Diaries,* 2: 332.
7. Acheson, *Present at the Creation,* 23.
8. Ibid., 21, 17, 9, 10.
9. Gauss to Hull, July 24, 1941, *FRUS,* 5: 684.
10. Welles to Roosevelt, July 25, 1941, ibid., 685.
11. Currie to Madame Chiang, September 18, 1941, box 1, Currie Papers.
12. Ford, *Flying Tigers,* 54.
13. Secret memo from Franklin D. Roosevelt to Navy secretary Frank Knox, September 30, 1941, as cited in Alan Armstrong, *Preemptive Strike: The Secret Plan That Would Have Prevented the Attack on Pearl Harbor* (Guilford, CT: Lyons Press, 2006), 103.
14. Chennault, *Way of a Fighter,* 103.
15. Ibid., 102.
16. State Department to the Chinese embassy (oral statement), December 4, 1940, *FRUS,* 4: 706.
17. Chennault, *Way of a Fighter,* 103.
18. Soong's report on China's estimated requirements, March 27, 1941, box 31, Soong Papers, as cited in Park, "In Support of 'New China,' " 310.
19. Soong to Frankfurter, April 7, 1941, box 29, in ibid., 265.
20. Morgenthau's China diary, 377, 378, 388; http://ow.ly/A1PDP.
21. Janeway, "Roosevelt vs. Hitler."
22. Henry R. Luce, "China to the Mountains," *Life,* June 30, 1941.
23. Ibid.
24. Ibid.
25. Ibid.
26. Ibid.
27. Waldo Heinrichs, *Threshold of War: Franklin D. Roosevelt and American Entry into World War II* (New York: Oxford University Press, 1988), 133.
28. Hull, *Memoirs,* 2: 994.
29. Ibid., 2: 995.
30. From Hull's memorandum of the conversation between Hull and Nomura, May 16–June 16, 1941, in ibid., 994, 987, 996.
31. Robert J. C. Butow, "The Hull-Nomura Conversations: A Fundamental Misconception," *American Historical Review* 65, no. 4 (July 1960): 830.
32. Ibid., 832.
33. Schlesinger, *The Age of Roosevelt,* 2: 535–36.
34. Anderson, "The 1941 de Facto Embargo on Oil to Japan," 216.
35. Ickes, *The Secret Diary of Harold L. Ickes,* 3: 218–19.
36. Ibid., 3: 553–59.
37. Doris Kearns Goodwin, *No Ordinary Time: Franklin and Eleanor Roosevelt: The Home Front in World War II* (New York: Simon and Schuster, 1994), 20.
38. Ibid.
39. Tokyo Circular No. 1139, May 29, 1941, to Japanese offices in Nanking, Shanghai, Peking, and Canton concerning message number 267 from Hong Kong on May 28, 1941, as cited in Armstrong, *Preemptive Strike,* 125–26.
40. Chennault, *Way of a Fighter,* 104.

41. Robert P. Patterson memo to Stimson, July 18, 1941, correspondence box 387, Stimson Papers.

42. Edward S. Miller, *Bankrupting the Enemy: The U.S. Financial Siege of Japan Before Pearl Harbor* (Annapolis, MD: Naval Institute Press, 2007), 174.

43. U.S. Department of State, *Peace and War: United States Foreign Policy, 1931–1941* (Washington, DC: U.S. Government Printing Office, 1943), 702–4.

44. I. F. Stone, "Oil on the Pacific," *Nation* 153 (August 9, 1941): 109–10.

45. Press release, July 26, 1941, box 424, Morgenthau Papers. FDR's press release stated he had "extended the freezing control to Chinese assets in the United States . . . in accordance with the wishes of the Chinese Government." This was to stop Japan from using captured Chinese funds. What Roosevelt did not mention was that he was exempting from the freezing order all Soong-Chiang private holdings: the Bank of China, the Central Bank of China, and China Defense Supplies, as cited in Park, "In Support of 'New China,'" 302.

46. Ickes, *The Secret Diary of Harold L. Ickes,* 3: 588.

47. Testimony of Admiral Stark, Pearl Harbor Hearings, part 5, 2115, as cited in Anderson, "The 1941 de Facto Embargo on Oil to Japan," 220.

48. Sherwood, *Roosevelt and Hopkins,* 388.

49. Ibid.

50. Blum, *From the Morgenthau Diaries,* 2: 265.

51. Acheson, *Present at the Creation,* 25.

52. Michael Fullilove, *Rendezvous with Destiny* (New York: Penguin Press, 2013), 296–97.

53. Halifax to Foreign Office, August 2, 1941, as cited in Heinrichs, *Threshold of War,* 141.

54. Ickes, *Secret Diary of Harold L. Ickes,* 3: 592.

55. Stimson MS diary, August 1, 1941, 35: 1–2, as cited in *Rendezvous with Destiny,* 310–11.

56. Ibid.

57. Utley, *Going to War with Japan,* 155.

58. Heinrichs, *Threshold of War,* 177.

59. Sir R. Campbell to Foreign Office, September 27, 1941, as cited in ibid.

60. "Japan: Oil Shipments To" folder, FFCC, as cited in Utley, *Going to War with Japan,* 155.

61. Jonathan Utley, "Upstairs, Downstairs at Foggy Bottom: Oil Exports and Japan, 1940–41," *Prologue* (Spring 1976): 17–28.

62. Miller, *Bankrupting the Enemy,* 200.

63. Utley, *Going to War with Japan,* 154.

64. Acheson, *Present at the Creation,* 19.

65. B. H. Liddell Hart, *Strategy* (New York: Frederick A. Praeger, 1967), 269.

66. Roland Worth, *No Choice but War* (Jefferson, NC: McFarland, 1995), 129.

Chapter 10: Asleep at the Wheel

1. John Toland, *The Rising Sun: The Decline and Fall of the Japanese Empire, 1936–1945* (New York: Random House, 1970), 186–87.

2. Akira Iriye, *Power and Culture: The Japanese-American War 1941–1945* (Cambridge, MA: Harvard University Press, 1981), 28.

3. Sadao Asada, *From Mahan to Pearl Harbor: The Imperial Japanese Navy and the United States* (Annapolis, MD: Naval Institute Press, 2006), 276.

4. Ian Kershaw, *Fateful Choices: The Decisions That Changed the World, 1940–1941* (New York: Penguin, 2008), 380.

5. Minutes of the Economic Defense Board meeting, August 20, 1941, as cited in Anderson, "The 1941 de Facto Embargo on Oil to Japan," 229.

6. Memorandum of conversation, Roosevelt and Hull with Nomura, August 28, 1941, in *FRUS*, 2: 571–72.

7. Japanese proposal, September 4, 1941, in ibid., 600.

8. Acheson, *Present at the Creation*, 26.

9. Nobutaka Ike, ed. and trans., *Japan's Decision for War: Records of the 1941 Policy Conferences* (Palo Alto, CA: Stanford University Press, 1967), 147–48.

10. Asada, *From Mahan to Pearl Harbor*, 267.

11. Miller, *Bankrupting the Enemy*, 220.

12. Utley, *Going to War with Japan*, 161.

13. Ike, *Japan's Decision for War*, 286.

14. Ibid., 282.

15. Ibid., 152.

16. Swanberg, *Luce and His Empire*, 188.

17. Jespersen, *American Images of China*, 53–54.

18. Luce to *Time* subscribers, November 8, 1941, box 7, UCR-USC Records, as cited in Park, "In Support of 'New China,'" 292.

19. Theodore White, "Aid to China—When?," *Fortune*, September 1941, 142.

20. George C. Herring, *From Colony to Superpower: U.S. Foreign Relations Since 1776* (New York: Oxford University Press, 2008), 536.

21. "Christianity in China," *Time*, April 28, 1941, 54–56, as cited in Park, "In Support of 'New China,'" 290.

22. McKean, *Peddling Influence*, 163.

23. Armstrong, *Preemptive Strike*, 201.

24. R. John Pritchard, *The Tokyo Major War Crimes Trial: The Records of the International Military Tribunal for the Far East* (Lewiston, NY: Edwin Mellen Press, 1998), as cited in Miller, *Bankrupting the Enemy*, 243.

25. Swanberg, *Luce and His Empire*, 189.

26. *New York Times*, December 9, 1941.

27. Joiner, *Honorable Survivor*, 26.

28. Schaller, *The U.S. Crusade in China*, 88.

29. Memo, May 24, 1932, Nelson T. Johnson Papers, Library of Congress, as cited in Cohen, *America's Response to China*, 122.

30. Report of AMMISCA to War Department, December 10, 1941; Magruder to War Department, January 5, 1942, *FRUS*, 4: 796–71; Magruder to War Department, February 10, 1942, cited in Schaller, *The U.S. Crusade in China*, 89.

31. Memo, Sliney for Magruder, December 10, 1941, AMMISCA, folder 1, as cited in Charles F. Romanus and Riley Sunderland, *United States Army in World*

War II: China-Burma-India Theater (Washington, DC: Office of the Chief of Military History, 1952–1958), 44–45.

32. Tuchman, *Stilwell and the American Experience in China,* 222.
33. George W. Sliney and Edwin M. Sutherland, item 87, AMMISCA, folder 4, as cited in Romanus and Sunderland, *United States Army in World War II,* 36.
34. Hannah Pakula, *The Last Empress* (New York: Simon and Schuster), 370.
35. Winston Churchill, *The Second World War,* vol. 4, *The Hinge of Fate* (Boston: Houghton Mifflin, 1950), 119.
36. Maochun Yu, *The Dragon's War: Allied Operations and the Fate of China, 1937–1947* (Annapolis, MD: Naval Institute Press, 2006), 91.
37. Dallek, *Franklin D. Roosevelt and American Foreign Policy,* 330.
38. Yu, *The Dragon's War,* 91.
39. Dallek, *Franklin D. Roosevelt and American Foreign Policy,* 330.
40. "Battle of China: Blood for the Tigers," *Time,* December 29, 1941.
41. Chennault's many defenders point to his tactical brilliance and courage, the undoubted bravery and skill of his men, and the many Japanese planes and ships destroyed. But Chennault initiated a troubling pattern for the U.S. military on the Asian mainland: tactical excellence but strategic failure. The Chiang-Chennault plan to bomb Japan from China didn't work, and while Mao had no air force, he — not the U.S. Air Force's client — won the Chinese civil war. The U.S. Air Force — in thousands of successful tactical operations during the 1960s and 1970s — dropped more bomb tonnage on Vietnam than was dropped on all contestants in World War II and still lost to a foe with paltry airpower. In 1990, the U.S. Postal Service issued a Claire Chennault stamp, allowing him at long last to be associated with effective air operations.

CHAPTER 11: THE MANDATE OF HEAVEN

1. Pearl S. Buck, "A Warning About China," *Life,* May 10, 1943, 53.
2. Joseph Stilwell, *The Stilwell Papers,* ed. Theodore White (New York: Schocken, 1972), 332.
3. Ibid., 36.
4. White, *In Search of History,* 134.
5. Stilwell, *The Stilwell Papers,* 80.
6. Ibid., 320.
7. Tuchman, *Stilwell and the American Experience in China,* 355.
8. Dallek, *Franklin D. Roosevelt and American Foreign Policy,* 331.
9. Churchill, *The Second World War,* 4: 119.
10. Tuchman, *Stilwell and the American Experience in China,* 338.
11. Chennault Papers.
12. Ibid.
13. Tuchman, *Stilwell and the American Experience in China,* 338.
14. Chennault, *Way of a Fighter,* 225.
15. Ibid., 226.
16. Stilwell, *The Stilwell Papers,* 204–6.
17. "Madame Chiang Asks Defeat of Japan, and House Cheers," *New York Times,* February 19, 1943, as cited in Li, *Madame Chiang Kai-shek,* 201.

18. David Halberstam, *The Coldest Winter: America and the Korean War* (New York: Hyperion, 2007), 223.

19. Mayling Soong, "Addresses to the House of Representatives and to the Senate," February 18, 1943; transcript available at U.S.-China Institute, University of Southern California, http://china.usc.edu/ShowArticle.aspx?articleID=1297.

20. "China: Madame," *Time,* March 1, 1943, 23, as cited in Pakula, *The Last Empress,* 421.

21. Pakula, *The Last Empress,* 422.

22. Roosevelt, *My Day,* 77.

23. "Trials and Errors," *Fortune,* March 2, 1943, 62, as cited in Pakula, *The Last Empress,* 427–28.

24. Joint press conference with Madame Chiang Kai-shek; http://www.presidency.ucsb.edu/ws/?pid=16366.

25. Ibid.

26. Stilwell, *The Stilwell Papers*, 316.

27. Ibid., 340.

28. Ibid., 250.

29. Tuchman, *Stilwell and the American Experience in China,* 401.

30. Ibid., 357.

31. John Paton Davies Jr., *China Hand* (Philadelphia: University of Pennsylvania Press, 2012), 108.

32. Hanson Baldwin, "Too Much Wishful Thinking About China," *Reader's Digest* (August 1943), and Nathaniel Peffer, "Our Distorted View of China," *New York Times Magazine,* November 7, 1943, as cited in Pakula, *The Last Empress,* 460.

33. Buck, "A Warning About China," 56.

34. Stilwell, *The Stilwell Papers,* 332.

35. Joiner, *Honorable Survivor,* 67.

36. Service, *Lost Chance in China,* 179–80.

37. Interview with Mao Zedong, August 23, 1944, in ibid., 302–7.

38. Ibid.

39. Ibid.

40. Many China Lobbyists point out that the China Hands were naive to believe Mao's presentation of himself, that at the same time Mao was smiling at them in Yan'an, he was torturing people over the hills. But Mao's critics don't mention that the U.S. Navy helped Chiang's Himmler — Dai Li — with his Happy Valley torture camp, just over the mountains from Chungking. Also, for supporters of Chiang to complain about others being duped is questionable. Again, I examine Chiang and Mao not in search of perfection but to discover why one of them won the Mandate of Heaven.

41. Barbara Tuchman, *Notes from China* (New York: Macmillan, 1972), 94.

42. Christopher R. Lew and Edwin Pak-wah Leung, *Historical Dictionary of the Chinese Civil War* (Lanham, MD: Scarecrow Press, 2013), 95.

43. Romanus and Sunderland, *United States Army in World War II,* 279.

44. Joint press conference with Madame Chiang Kai-shek; http://www.presidency.ucsb.edu/ws/?pid=16366.

45. Tuchman, *Stilwell and the American Experience in China,* 239.

46. Ibid., 354–55.

47. Service, *Lost Chance in China,* 161–66.
48. John S. Service, "State Department Duty in China, the McCarthy Era and After: 1932–1977," an oral history interview conducted by Rosemary Levenson (Berkeley: Regional Oral History Office, Bancroft Library, University of California, 1978), as cited in Joiner, *Honorable Survivor,* 97.
49. Joiner, *Honorable Survivor,* 98.
50. Service, *Lost Chance in China,* 160.
51. John Davies memo, "The Chinese Communists and the Great Powers," *FRUS,* 6: 667–69.
52. Tuchman, *Notes from China,* 78.
53. Ibid., 96.
54. Schaller, *The U.S. Crusade in China,* 204–5.
55. Ambassador Hurley cable to President Roosevelt, January 14, 1945, *FRUS,* 7: 172–77; http://images.library.wisc.edu/FRUS/EFacs/1945v07/reference/frus .frus1945v07.i0006.pdf.
56. Joiner, *Honorable Survivor,* 113.
57. Roger J. Sandilands, *The Life and Political Economy of Lauchlin Currie* (Durham, NC: Duke University Press, 1990), 132.
58. John Service, "Chou En-Lai as Seen by an Old China Hand," *Los Angeles Times,* January 14, 1976; http://www.trumanlibrary.org/oralhist/service5.htm.
59. Joiner, *Honorable Survivor,* 117.
60. Ibid.
61. Service, *The Amerasia Papers,* 185, as cited in Joiner, *Honorable Survivor,* 119.
62. John Service, letter to John Carter Vincent, February 1945, as cited in Joiner, *Honorable Survivor,* 119.
63. Service, *Lost Chance in China,* 358–63.
64. Joiner, *Honorable Survivor,* 121.
65. Service, *The Amerasia Papers,* 108.
66. Ibid., 105.
67. Service, *Lost Chance in China,* 358.
68. Service, "State Department Duty in China," 308, as cited in Joiner, *Honorable Survivor,* 122.
69. Service, *Lost Chance in China,* 370.
70. Ibid., 378.
71. Service, *The Amerasia Papers,* 150, as cited in Joiner, *Honorable Survivor,* 124.
72. Service interview with Mao, March 13, 1945, as cited in Service, *Lost Chance in China,* 372–73.
73. Ibid., 384.
74. Ibid., 372.
75. Goodwin, *No Ordinary Time,* 586, as cited in Joiner, *Honorable Survivor,* 126.
76. Ibid., 571, as cited in Joiner, *Honorable Survivor.*
77. Service, *The Amerasia Papers,* 124–27, as cited in Joiner, *Honorable Survivor,* 128.
78. Geoffrey C. Ward, *Closest Companion: The Unknown Story of the Intimate Friendship Between Franklin Roosevelt and Margaret Suckley* (New York: Simon and Schuster, 2012), 418.
79. Jay Taylor, *The Generalissimo: Chiang Kai-shek and the Struggle for Modern China* (Cambridge, MA: Harvard University Press, 2009), 304.

CHAPTER 12: WHO LOST CHINA?

1. Richard Madsen, *China and the American Dream: A Moral Inquiry* (Berkeley: University of California Press, 1995), 31.
2. Tom Wicker, *JFK and LBJ: The Influence of Personality upon Politics* (New York: William Morrow, 1968), 205, and Robert Caro, *The Years of Lyndon Johnson: The Passage of Power* (New York: Knopf, 2012), 402.
3. Joiner, *Honorable Survivor,* 1.
4. John Service and Thomas Corcoran crossed paths in what is called "the *Amerasia* affair," which is well documented in a number of studies. There is still today tremendous China Lobby smoke around Service's actions, but no fire occurred.
5. Curtis E. LeMay with MacKinlay Kantor, *Mission with LeMay* (New York: Doubleday, 1965), 387.
6. For further discussion, see James Bradley, *Flyboys* (New York: Little, Brown, 2003).
7. Nancy MacLennan, "Mme. Chiang Opens Peace Campaign," *New York Times,* August 15, 1945.
8. "Declaration of Independence of the Democratic Republic of Vietnam," http://historymatters.gmu.edu/d/5139/.
9. Letter from Ho Chi Minh to President Harry S. Truman, February 28, 1946, National Archives; http://www.archives.gov/global-pages/larger-image .html?i=/historical-docs/doc-content/images/ho-chi-minh-telegram-truman-l .jpg&c=/historical-docs/doc-content/images/ho-chi-minh-telegram-truman .caption.html.
10. Felix Belair Jr., "Hurley Demands Hearing in Public," *New York Times,* December 1, 1945; "Five Representatives Ask U.S. to Quit China," *New York Times,* November 27, 1945.
11. Hurley's letter of resignation to Truman, November 26, 1945, *FRUS,* 7: 722–26.
12. *Mao's Bloody Revolution Revealed,* directed by Philip Short, documentary broadcast on UK Terrestrial Station Five in May 2007.
13. Chiang Kai-shek to Truman, November 9, 1948, as cited in Pakula, *The Last Empress,* 562.
14. Memo from Joint Chiefs of Staff to Secretary of State, December 16, 1948, as cited in Pakula, *The Last Empress,* 562.
15. Pakula, *The Last Empress,* 564.
16. Miller, *Plain Speaking,* 288–89.
17. Ibid., 283.
18. Pakula, *The Last Empress,* 567.
19. Ibid., 577.
20. Stella Dong, *Shanghai: The Rise and Fall of a Decadent City, 1842–1949* (New York: William Morrow, 2000), 291.
21. Stuart Schram, *Mao Tse-tung* (Harmondsworth, UK: Penguin, 1966), 251.
22. U.S. Department of State, *The China White Paper, August 1949* (Stanford, CA: Stanford University Press, 1967), 1: xvi.
23. Norman A. Graber et al., *America and the Cold War, 1941–1991: A Realist Interpretation* (Santa Barbara, CA: Praeger, 2010), 1: 167.

24. Thomas C. Reeves, *The Life and Times of Joe McCarthy* (Lanham, MD: Madison Books, 1997), 203.

25. William F. Buckley et al., *The China Lobby Man: The Story of Alfred Kohlberg* (New Rochelle, NY: Arlington House, 1969), 406.

26. James A. Henretta, *Documents for America's History,* vol. 2, *Since 1865* (New York: Macmillan, 2011), 307. (Note: There are tiny variations in different versions of McCarthy's unrecorded and later reconstructed speech.)

27. Cabell Phillips, "Is There a China Lobby? Inquiry Raises Questions," *New York Times,* April 30, 1950.

28. James Cross Giblin, *The Rise and Fall of Senator Joe McCarthy* (Boston: Houghton Mifflin, 2009), 104.

29. Halberstam, *The Powers That Be,* 87.

30. Halberstam, *The Coldest Winter,* 185.

31. Walter Isaacson and Evan Thomas, *The Wise Men: Six Friends and the World They Made* (New York: Simon and Schuster, 1986), 543.

32. In January 1947, Secretary of State George Marshall scribbled a note to Dean Acheson: "Please have plan drafted of policy to organize a definite government of So. Korea and *connect up* its economy with that of Japan "; quoted in Bruce Cumings, *Korea's Place in the Sun: A Modern History* (New York: W. W. Norton, 1997), 210.

33. Bruce Cumings, *The Korean War* (New York: Modern Library, 2010), 402.

34. Ibid., 208.

35. Robert J. Donovan, *Tumultuous Years: The Presidency of Harry S. Truman, 1949–1953* (Columbia: University of Missouri Press, 1996), 205.

36. Ibid.

37. Ibid.

38. Isaacson and Thomas, *The Wise Men,* 506.

39. Ibid., 512.

40. Ibid., 506.

41. Halberstam, *The Coldest Winter,* 99.

42. Ibid., 98.

43. Much of the military action was ordered by the UN; technically, the U.S. only supported the action, but at that point, the UN was a small entity controlled by the U.S.

44. Cumings, *The Korean War,* 205.

45. Martin Walker, *The Cold War: A History* (New York: Macmillan, 1995), 77.

46. Cumings, *The Korean War,* 208.

47. Ibid., 210.

48. Matthew Ridgway, *The Korean War* (New York: Doubleday, 1967), 37.

49. Halberstam, *The Coldest Winter,* 335–36.

50. Isaacson and Thomas, *The Wise Men,* 533.

51. Walker, *The Cold War,* 77.

52. Cumings, *The Korean War,* 216–17.

53. Ibid., 207.

54. Isaacson and Thomas, *The Wise Men,* 550.

55. Speech delivered by Senator Joseph McCarthy before the Senate on June 14, 1951; http://www.fordham.edu/halsall/mod/1951mccarthy-marshall.html.

56. On July 27, 1953, an armistice called for a 2.5-mile-wide buffer zone across the middle of Korea. Today this heavily fortified "demilitarized zone" still holds the peace in Korea.

57. Transcript of Dwight D. Eisenhower press conference, April 7, 1954, American Presidency Project, http://www.presidency.ucsb.edu/ws/index.php?pid=10202.

58. Dwight D. Eisenhower, *Mandate for Change 1953–56: The White House Years* (Garden City, NY: Doubleday, 1963), 337–38.

59. Seth Jacobs, *America's Miracle Man in Vietnam: Ngo Dinh Diem, Religion, Race, and U.S. Intervention in Southeast Asia* (Durham, NC: Duke University Press, 2005), 221.

60. Public Papers of the Presidents of the United States, Dwight D. Eisenhower, 1957, General Services Administration, National Archives and Records Service, Office of the Federal Register, United States Government Printing Office, June 1, 1999; available at the American Presidency Project, http://www.presidency.ucsb.edu/ws/?pid=11031.

61. Mark Moyar, *Triumph Forsaken: The Vietnam War, 1954–1965* (New York: Cambridge University Press, 2006), 77.

62. Ibid.

63. "The Press: Ban Broken," *Time,* January 7, 1957; http://content.time.com/time/magazine/article/0,9171,808926,00.html.

64. A citizen without a passport, Worthy was then incautious enough to travel to Cuba. When he returned home, President Kennedy's administration arrested him for entering the U.S. without proper documents.

65. David Halberstam, *The Best and the Brightest* (New York: Random House, 2002), xviii.

66. Ibid., 202.

67. Halberstam, *The Coldest Winter,* 243.

68. Transcript is available on the Bill Moyers website: http://www.pbs.org/moyers/journal/11202009/transcript1.html.

69. Memorandum from Senator Mike Mansfield to the president, January 6, 1964, *FRUS,* 1: document 2; http://history.state.gov/historicaldocuments/frus1964-68v01/d2.

70. Memorandum from the president's special assistant for National Security Affairs (Bundy) to the president, January 9, 1964, *FRUS,* 1: document 8; https://history.state.gov/historicaldocuments/frus1964-68v01/d8.

71. Marvin Kalb, *The Road to War: Presidential Commitments Honored and Betrayed* (Washington, DC: Brookings Institution Press, 2013), 53.

72. John Hollitz, *Contending Voices* (Boston: Wadsworth, 2010), 2: 232.

73. Robert McNamara, "Draft Memorandum from Secretary of Defense McNamara to President Johnson," November 3, 1965, State Department Office of the Historian; http://history.state.gov/historicaldocuments/frus1964-68v03/d189.

74. Halberstam, *The Best and the Brightest,* 530.

75. Interview with Archimedes L. A. Patti, 1981, http://openvault.wgbh.org/catalog/vietnam-bf3262-interview-with-archimedes-l-a-patti-1981.

76. Robert S. McNamara with Brian VanDeMark, *In Retrospect: The Tragedy and Lessons of Vietnam* (New York: Crown, 1995), 32–33.

77. John Morton Blum, *The National Experience: A History of the United States Since 1865* (Fort Worth, TX: Harcourt Brace Jovanovich, 1989), 777.

78. Robert McNamara, "The Post-Cold War World: Implications for Military Expenditures in Developing Countries," in *Proceedings of the World Bank Annual Conference on Development Economics 1991* (Washington, DC: International Bank of Reconstruction and Development, 1991), 111.

79. Garry Emmons, "One-on-One with Robert McNamara," *Harvard Business School Alumni Magazine* (September 2004); https://www.alumni.hbs.edu/stories/Pages/story-bulletin.aspx?num=2355.

CHAPTER 13: THE CHINA MIRAGE

1. Service, *The Amerasia Papers,* 191–92.

2. Daniel Ellsberg, *Secrets: A Memoir of Vietnam and the Pentagon Papers* (New York: Viking, 2002), 383. And the beat goes on. The man who wrote the legal opinion for President Obama to justify the first drone killing of an American citizen in 2012 was Harvard Law School professor David J. Barron. In 2014 Obama rewarded Professor Barron by appointing him to the United States Court of Appeals for the First Circuit in Boston.

3. Joiner, *Honorable Survivor,* 332.

4. Ibid.

5. Ibid.

6. Ibid., 333.

7. Ibid., 334–35.

8. Mao's imperial overreach in the Great Famine of the 1950s and the Cultural Revolution in the 1960s are well documented elsewhere and had no bearing on FDR's decision to support Chiang, on Truman's decision to anoint Taiwan as China, or on Nixon's rapprochement with Mao.

9. Joiner, *Honorable Survivor,* xvi.

10. John Service Papers, January 23, 1973, as cited in Joiner, *Honorable Survivor,* xvi–xvii.

11. Hubert Van Es, "Thirty Years at 300 Millimeters," *New York Times,* April 29, 2005; http://www.nytimes.com/2005/04/29/opinion/29van_es.html.

12. I stood on its roof in 2011.

13. In *Theodore Rex,* by Pulitzer Prize winner Edmund Morris, Homer Hulbert's name is absent and Prince Ito gets one passing mention. You finish the book with no understanding that Emperor Meiji and Prince Ito rolled Teddy regarding Korea during the secret, nineteen-month Roosevelt-Kaneko discussions.

    Likewise, if you read all 858 pages of *FDR,* by Jean Edward Smith (winner of the Francis Parkman Prize), you won't find T. V. Soong mentioned once, and you won't see any hint that China Lobbyists covertly cut Japan's supply of oil in August 1941 and that FDR was unaware of their action for one long month.

14. Slightly loosened in 1943 and then ended in 1965.

ACKNOWLEDGMENTS

1. From a Winston Churchill speech about authorship, National Book Exhibition at Grosvenor House, London, November 2, 1949.

INDEX

ABOUT THE AUTHOR

JAMES BRADLEY is the author of the *New York Times* bestsellers *The Imperial Cruise, Flyboys,* and *Flags of Our Fathers* and is a son of John Bradley, one of the men who raised the American flag on Iwo Jima.